Ireland, 1815–70

Emancipation, Famine and Religion

Donnchadh Ó Corráin & Tomás O'Riordan

EDITORS

FOUR COURTS PRESS

Set in 10.5 on 13 point AGaramond for
FOUR COURTS PRESS LTD
7 Malpas Street, Dublin 8, Ireland
http://www.fourcourtspress.ie
and in North America by
FOUR COURTS PRESS
c/o ISBS, 920 N.E. 58th Avenue, Suite 300, Portland, OR 97213.

ISBN 978-1-84682-232-2

Printed in England
by MPG Books, Bodmin, Cornwall.

Contents

11. Key concepts
Margaret Fitzpatrick, Eoin Hartnett, Donnchadh Ó Corráin & Tomás O'Riordan

12. Key personalities
Margaret Fitzpatrick, Eoin Hartnett, Donnchadh Ó Corráin & Tomás O'Riordan

Illustrations and tables

appear betwen pages 128 and 129

TABLES

Foreword

A society without a history is a society without an identity, and one without a future. That is why the teaching and study of history is so significant for society as a whole, and for the individual within it. However, not any kind of history will do, and there is no such thing as history without values. Only history that is the dispassionate search for truth and understanding (as far as this is possible) will answer society's needs. One must confront, calmly and honestly, the good and the bad in the past: fine literature, high culture, the pursuit of justice and human rights side by side with war, massacre, and inhumanity (and too often there is more of the latter). One must contemplate, with critical detachment, absolutism, militarism, imperialism, colonialism, racism, sectarianism and religious intolerance, nationalism, communism, rampant capitalism and other ideologies that have brought – and continue to bring – endless misery and death to countless human beings.

One must see Irish history as part of this larger canvas. History cannot, however, be a nursery of grievances, grounds for hostility towards one's neighbours and others, the motive for revenge. Rather, one must confront the past in the full knowledge that humanity is the same everywhere and at all times, and that what makes the difference between societies and nations is culture and opportunity. The object of history is understanding, compassion and, one hopes, some wisdom. This is the first of a series of textbooks on Irish history formed by these convictions.

The Act of Union, passed in 1800, deprived Ireland of its parliament and made Dublin a provincial city. The Union was the framework of government in Ireland and the context of all subsequent political activity in the nineteenth century, and the early twentieth. But Union did not mean integration: there was a subordinate executive in Dublin and what applied in the United Kingdom did not necessarily apply in Ireland. Benjamin Disraeli (British prime minister, 1866–8, 1874–80) put Ireland's problems thus in 1844:

> A dense population in extreme distress inhabits an island where there is an Established Church which is not their Church, and a territorial aristocracy – the richest of whom live in distant capitals. Thus you have a starving population, an absentee aristocracy, and an alien Church, and in addition the weakest executive in the world. That is the Irish question.

English attitudes to Ireland were deeply ambivalent. Lord Fitzwilliam speaking in the House of Lords, in March 1846, said:

> Ireland was a country of which Englishmen were exceedingly ignorant. It was a mirror in which England did not very well wish to look; but from which she

ought not to shrink, although she might see in that mirror much cause of regret, and much cause of shame.

This book covers the period from 1815 to 1870 when much of what is late modern Ireland came into being. Three great issues are central to this period and to this book: Catholic Emancipation, the Great Famine, and the emergence of the Catholic Church as a major religious, political and social force in Irish life – to some, an overbearing one.

Catholic Emancipation is one of the great civil-rights movements of modern history. A democratic and wholly legal movement, it was led by a remarkably gifted and charismatic lawyer-politician, Daniel O'Connell, and his able lieutenants, Thomas Wyse, Richard Lalor Shiel and others. By means of a superior organisation that involved every parish in the country, by petitions, peaceful demonstrations, and 'moral force' (as Wyse put it) the movement advanced its libertarian agenda, and forced the Duke of Wellington's government to remove the ban on Catholics as members of parliament in the whole of the United Kingdom (1829). In return for this concession, O'Connell had to accept a serious limitation of the franchise, a disability later gradually removed. The movement laid the foundations of Irish popular democracy on which Isaac Butt, Parnell and later leaders built though, for many, its reliance on the clergy gave the Catholic Church in Ireland too large and too strident a role in Irish political life.

The Famine was the greatest demographic catastrophe in modern Irish history and it had a profound impact on every aspect of Irish life: population, social structure, culture, emigration, and Ireland's relationship with Britain, the United States and Australia. It shaped all subsequent Irish political life. For example, every later Irish nationalist movement – cultural, political, and military – was funded by the large Irish-American community that owed its existence (and its attitudes) to Famine emigration. British reactions to the Famine are complex and contradictory. Government attempts at Famine relief (especially those of Lord John Russell's Liberal government) were tardy, inadequate, and ineptly organised. Some of this came from ideology, some from incompetence. Convinced (at least when it suited them) of *laissez faire*, government ministers refused to intervene to regulate the food market as prices rose beyond the pockets of the starving poor or bring order into the chaos and abject standards in shipping people (and food) in and out of Ireland. The British government's chief Famine administrator, Charles Edward Trevelyan, saw the Famine as an act of God: 'The judgement of God sent the calamity to teach the Irish a lesson … The real evil … is not the physical evil of the Famine, but the moral evil of the selfish, perverse and turbulent character of the people'. Racism (directed against the Irish, the Jews, fellow Europeans and Africans) was common in the British élite, as in other European élites – here one can name Acton, Arnold, Carlyle, Disraeli, Engels, Freeman, Froude, Kingsley, Round, Lord Salisbury and Stubbs – and racist views were openly expressed during the Famine. In 1847 *The Times*, the organ of the establishment, wrote with scant respect for history:

Before our intervention the Irish nation were a wretched, indolent, half-starved tribe of savages … notwithstanding a gradual improvement upon the naked savagery, they have never approached the standard of the civilized age.

In the same year, the same paper wrote of the Famine Irish:

They are going. They are going with a vengeance. Soon a Celt will be as rare in Ireland as a Red Indian on the streets of Manhattan.

Chilling words, indeed, written just when the white American genocide of native Americans was in full swing, especially in Texas and California.

These were the views of some British people. Others laboured long and hard from the beginning of the hunger, and gave generously to relieve famine in Ireland. The British Relief Association, formed in London on 1 January 1847 by Lionel de Rothschild, a Jewish banker and philanthropist (and, later, the first Jewish MP), was one of the most successful private relief bodies. Queen Victoria donated £2,000 to it in January 1847. Though not over-generous for the monarch, this made her the largest individual donor to Famine relief, and one of the most prompt. Her 'Queen's Letters', in March and October 1847, asked the people of Britain to donate money to relieve Irish distress. The response was swift and generous. One could sum up the British reaction as public parsimony and private generosity.

The third major theme is the rise of the Irish Catholic Church as a dominant institution in Irish life, a position it retained for over a century and a half. In European terms, Ireland was an oddity, an overwhelmingly Catholic kingdom – less than 150,000 Protestants in a population of about a million in the early seventeenth century – with a Protestant sovereign (cf. *cuius regio, eius religio* 'in the ruler's land, the ruler's religion', Peace of Augsburg 1555; Peace of Westphalia 1648). The Catholic Church lost all its property in the course of Henry VIII's suppression of the monasteries and the subsequent Protestant Reformation. It emerged from the penal laws as an institution officially without lands and churches, and one barely tolerated by government. Its situation changed dramatically in the late eighteenth and early nineteenth centuries, because of growing tolerance and the delicate diplomacy of the Catholic bishops. The Synod of Thurles (1850) marked an important stage in that change. The Synod dealt with two major issues: the re-organisation of the Church and the question of Catholic education. The romanisation, empowerment, and enrichment of the Catholic Church and a notable revolution in devotional practice were carried through with remarkable success. In third-level education the bishops overreached themselves, their Catholic University remained chronically underfunded, and the problems of Irish third-level education, many of their making, were not resolved until the early twentieth century.

JOSEPH CAREY
Chairman of the Multi Text Project in History

Introduction

This work offers a fresh approach to Irish history, 1815–70. In place of a general narrative, it focuses on three major aspects: Catholic Emancipation, the Famine, and the radical re-organisation and politicisation of the Catholic Church that began with the Synod of Thurles in 1850. All three events, in varying ways, changed the face of nineteenth-century Ireland. To get depth, we have narrowed the focus. However, three short survey essays at the beginning – on politics and administration, society and economy, and culture and religion – place these themes in their broader context. Two chapters are devoted to each major theme: the first is an analytical historical essay; the second is a broad selection of original historical documents, each with an introduction, an exact citation of source, and a concise presentation of its paraphrasable content. Lastly, there are short essays on historical concepts important in the period and brief biographies of major figures (each with a select bibliography). This book will answer to the needs of secondary and university students, the general reader, and all those interested in Irish history.

Readers will soon see that topics are touched on by the different authors in varying contexts, and there appears to be repetition and, on occasion, contradiction. This is deliberate. We preserve the integrity of our authors' essays and this will show, we hope, that professional historians may arrive honestly at disparate interpretations of historical evidence. Such genuine differences of opinion are vital to the discipline of history, and can bring about original and valuable insights that deepen and enrich historical understanding by asking new questions, prompting new arguments, and starting new lines of inquiry. This is part of the historian's experience, and it should be part of the student's education to know that things are so. Here there are manifold points of view: those of various modern historians, from quite different backgrounds and diverse in attitudes and interpretations, and those of the actors themselves, equally different in background, class, and convictions, expressed in a broad and generous selection of contemporary sources bearing on the great issues of the day. Readers must form their own opinions.

This is the first book on Irish history dynamically linked to a dedicated Internet site that extends its range and greatly supplements it, the MultiText Project (http://www.multitext.ie), established by Donnchadh Ó Corráin in 2000 and now managed by Tomás O'Riordan. The website has over a million words of modern Irish history and over 3,500 graphics – photographs, maps, cartoons and drawings – and serves the needs of those interested in Irish history worldwide. Available on the website is a full text of this work (and of several other works in preparation, soon to be published in this series), updates, additional historical materials, an archive of relevant graphics (far more than the samples in this book), and an extensive bibliography of Irish history and Irish studies, compiled by Donnchadh Ó Corráin, that will shortly be half a million words in size. MultiText's sister project CELT (http://celt.ucc.ie) (Corpus of Electronic Texts) is the largest full-text scholarly database of Irish history and literature on the Internet – a digital library of twelve million words of historical sources, original texts and translations, and bibliography. All texts on both sites are fully browsable and searchable, and may be freely downloaded by the readers of this book.

To help readers to find what they need quickly and easily, this book may be searched in three ways: by using the analytical table of contents, the detailed index, and the search utility on the MultiText website. References in the index are to chapter number and section number (for example, 5.14 refers to chapter 5, section 14), except where otherwise specified (for example table and figure numbers). We have tried to keep the spelling and punctuation of original documents. However, minor changes have sometimes been made to make them more readable, but these do not alter the sense.

We are indebted to many people and to many institutions, and we record with pleasure their contributions, their help, their co-operation, and their patience. First we thank our authors who, in the middle of busy academic lives where duties multiply, have given generously of their scholarship and their time and who have had to wait so long to see their work in print. Readers will observe a noteworthy north-south collaboration in this book, and this is something we are very glad about. Dr Gillian M. Doherty, project manager of MultiText (2000–2), brought dedication and professionalism to the undertaking and gave it a solid scholarly foundation from the start. To Tiarnán Ó Corráin we owe the architecture of the web site, the software that lies behind its user friendly interface (much praised by its users), and the day-to-day maintenance of the site itself. On the teaching side, we have had generous support. We thank John Dredge of the Second Level Support Service (SLSS) as well as the History Teachers' Association of Ireland (HTAI) for valuable feedback and help in publicising the project. Fidelma Maguire, former regional development officer with the History In-Service Team (HIST), read the whole work in draft and made important criticisms and suggestions. We are also grateful to Gerard O'Sullivan and Dr Pat Callan (both formerly of HIST) for comment and publicity. We owe much to Dr Dáithí Ó Corráin (St Patrick's College, DCU) who read the whole text and gave us valuable corrections. We thank present and former staff of the CELT Project, especially Beatrix Färber, Emer Purcell, Dr Benjamin Hazard, and Dr Julianne Nyhan, for their willing co-operation.

We are most grateful to the libraries, repositories, and organisations, and their supportive staff, who readily shared their valuable resources with us, especially historical documents and images: the British Museum, London, Kilmainham Gaol, the National Library of Ireland, the National Archives, the National Gallery of Ireland, the National Museum of Ireland, the Royal Irish Academy (RIA), Radio Telefís Éireann (RTÉ), the Public Record Office of Northern Ireland, the National Portrait Gallery, London, the Office of Public Works (OPW), the Ulster Museum, Cork City and County Libraries, and the Boole Library at University College Cork.

Nowadays, projects of this kind have to be funded outside the ordinary University budget. We are grateful to Professor Gerry Wrixon, for a seed-capital grant from the President's Fund that made it possible to begin. We are even more indebted to Mr

Joseph Carey, chairman of MultiText, whose financial support and constant encouragement has alone made this project and this publication possible. His practical patriotism and public-spirited generosity is a model for all who are concerned about culture and the arts in Ireland.

Lastly, we thank our publishers, Four Courts Press and the late Michael Adams (1937–2009), who were willing to publish a new type of historical text linked to the Internet and suffer in patience an old type of academic tardiness.

DONNCHADH Ó CORRÁIN AND TOMÁS O'RIORDAN

CHAPTER I

Politics and administration, 1815–70

1. The Act of Union

1.1. The Act of Union of 1 August 1800 marked the end of the Irish parliament. It also created a new political unit, the United Kingdom of Great Britain and Ireland. The idea of a legislative union was not new: political unions had taken place with Wales in 1536 and with Scotland in 1707. The Union with Ireland completed this process of political unification and meant that England, Ireland, Scotland and Wales were now governed by a parliament at Westminster, in London. As a consequence, Ireland lost its own parliament in Dublin. Henceforth, it sent 100 MPs (members of Parliament) to Westminster. The British parliament was exclusively Anglican (as the Irish parliament had been): neither Catholics nor members of dissenting Christian faiths nor Jews could be MPs. Parliament did not represent large sections of society: only wealthy people had the right to vote; and women could neither vote nor be elected MPs.

1.2. The immediate stimulus for the passing of the Act of Union had been a violent uprising in parts of Ireland in 1798. A political group known as the United Irishmen had led the rebellion. Many of its supporters had been inspired by the example of the American colonies which won political independence from Britain in the 1770s, and by the French Revolution of 1789. The leaders, who included Theobald Wolfe Tone, a Dublin Protestant, argued for a non-sectarian, inclusive approach to Irish politics. In order to achieve an independent Irish Republic, the United Irishmen were willing to use physical force, and requested military assistance from the French revolutionary government. The uprising in 1798 was short-lived but brutal. As many as 30,000 Irish people were killed in the conflict. Sectarian clashes heightened tensions between Catholics and Protestants, and sectarianism was fostered by the anti-Catholic sentiments of the newly founded Orange Order (1795).

1.3. The violence of the uprising alarmed Protestants and Catholics. Many Protestants felt vulnerable in the wake of the Rising, and the Union meant that they became part of a religious majority within the United Kingdom. This was important because the removal of many of the penal laws in the 1790s meant that Catholics were seen as a threat to Protestant supremacy. Protestants therefore saw the Union as a safeguard against revolution and radical politics. William Pitt, the British Prime Minister, suggested to Irish politicians that the Union would safeguard the Protestant ascendancy in Ireland, not overthrow it. Threats and bribery were used to persuade Irish MPs to agree to the Union. Although Pitt had considered making Catholic Emancipation (the right of Catholics to become MPs) a condition of the Union as a way of appeasing Catholics,

19

this scheme was abandoned. Consequently, the Union was the association of Great Britain with Protestant Ireland rather than with the Irish as a whole. For the majority of the Irish people, the Union was an irrelevance. For the Catholic middle classes, the refusal to grant full political rights left a legacy of distrust and resentment against the Union.

2. Daniel O'Connell and Emancipation

2.1. The question of Catholic Emancipation dominated Irish political life from 1801 to 1829. In the years following the Union, the main supporters of Catholic Emancipation were Protestant members of parliament who tried to secure it by constitutional means. However, conservative Irish Protestants, British public opinion, and the British monarchy continued to oppose the granting of full political rights to Roman Catholics within the United Kingdom. They argued that Catholics, whose first allegiance was to the Pope, would never be loyal British subjects.

2.2. Daniel O'Connell's greatest achievement was that he made the demand for Catholic Emancipation a popular movement that could not be ignored. In 1823, O'Connell founded a new Catholic Association with the dual aim of winning Emancipation and promoting the general interests of Catholics. The decision to reduce the fee for associate membership to one penny a month, the following year, increased membership and popular interest in the Association. The payment, referred to as the 'Catholic Rent', was greatly helped by the involvement of the Catholic clergy, who were automatically members of the Association. More importantly, the great mass of the Catholic peasantry felt engaged with the political process. But Catholic Emancipation would have little direct impact on their lives. Only a few upper-class Catholics would be admitted to parliament.

2.3. The rapid growth of the Catholic Association and O'Connell's fiery language (although he disliked and repudiated violence) alarmed the British government. O'Connell adopted a tactic of convening large public meetings that gave Catholic demands an unprecedented visibility and unity. Emancipation was helped by disarray within British politics after 1827 (there were seven different Prime Ministers between 1827 and 1834). O'Connell was able to take advantage of the situation by standing in a by-election in Co. Clare in 1828, even though he would be unable, under the law as it stood, to sit in parliament if elected. O'Connell's success in the election alarmed the government. The Prime Minister, Arthur Wellesley, 1st Duke of Wellington, supported by the Home Secretary, Robert Peel, dropped their previous opposition to Emancipation. When introducing the Bill in parliament, Wellington stated that if Emancipation was not granted the alternative was civil war.

2.4. The granting of Catholic Emancipation in 1829 was seen as a victory for O'Connell and his tactic of mass political organisation. At the same time, it was regarded as a defeat for the British government which had been forced to concede a measure that it did not support. As a consequence of the new Act, Catholics of the United Kingdom were eligible for most offices of state, with the exception of Regent, Lord Lieutenant, and Lord Chancellor. The Act had serious limitations: the Catholic Association was suppressed, and the property qualification for the franchise (the right to vote), was increased from forty shillings (£2) to £10 (approx. €840 at 2009 values). Consequently, many of O'Connell's supporters won the battle for Emancipation but lost the vote. O'Connell, however, emerged as the victor in the struggle with the British government. Moreover, Emancipation marked the beginning, not the end, of Catholic inroads on the Protestant establishment.

3. Electoral reform

3.1. The disfranchisement of the forty-shilling freeholders that came with Catholic Emancipation greatly reduced the number of voters. Electoral reform in 1832 increased their number somewhat, but property continued to influence electoral results. O'Connell's hope that the 1832 reform would restore the forty-shilling freeholders was not realised. However, the number of Irish MPs was raised from 100 to 105 (the boroughs of Belfast, Galway, Limerick, and Waterford, and the University of Dublin each gained an additional member). This increase did not reflect the large rise in the Irish population since 1800. Irish MPs remained a minority in parliament and Irish demands, notably Repeal of the Union, continued to lack majority support in Westminster.

3.2. Reform of local government took longer in Ireland and showed how differently voters in Britain and in Ireland were treated. The British municipal corporations had been reformed in 1834. Reform of the Irish system was not introduced until 1840. Although the 1840 legislation increased the number of voters, it was far more limited than in Britain where the franchise had been granted to all ratepayers. In Ireland, the franchise had been limited to £10 householders and thus only a small number had the vote in local elections. The corporations (with the exception of one) were controlled by Protestants. The restricted franchise disappointed O'Connell who had hoped to use the corporations to promote Repeal. Nonetheless, he was an immediate beneficiary of municipal reform. In the local elections at the end of 1841 he was elected Lord Mayor of Dublin, the first Catholic to hold this office since the 1680s. However, municipal reform, like much of the legislation passed in the decades following the Act of Union, showed that Ireland was not an equal partner within the Union.

4. The Orange Order and sectarian politics

4.1. The Orange Order was founded in Co. Armagh in 1795, after a sectarian clash between local Catholic and Protestant secret societies, known as the Battle of the

Diamond. The Order was an exclusively Protestant organisation (initially Anglican but later also Presbyterian) dedicated to the memory of William III, the victor at the battle of the Boyne (Co. Meath) in 1690. To commemorate the date of the William's victory it was decided to hold a parade on each 12 July. The first parades were held in parts of Co. Armagh in 1796 and were followed by sectarian attacks on local Catholics. During the 1798 Rising, the number of Orange lodges grew rapidly and, by the end of 1798, there were almost 400 in the country, including 38 in Co. Dublin and 78 in Co. Armagh. The government armed Orangemen during the uprising, using them as a counter-revolutionary force. From this time, the Order viewed itself as the defender of the British interest in Ireland, especially against the threat of disloyal Catholics.

4.2. The granting of Catholic Emancipation alarmed many Irish Protestants, not least because it coincided with a wave of evangelical Protestantism, led by Henry Cooke, an outspoken Presbyterian minister in Belfast. He appealed for a united Protestant front to oppose Emancipation and, later, Repeal. Consequently, in the 1830s and 1840s, conservative Protestant theology and conservative Protestant politics moved closer together. They saw Catholicism as their common enemy. Significantly, the Orange Order, which organised protests against Catholic Emancipation, increased in size, and many of its new recruits were Presbyterians. It attracted support from Protestant ministers, gentry, and members of the Irish constabulary and yeomanry. In 1835, a parliamentary report on the activities of the Orange Order found that it existed at all levels of society (the brother of the British monarch was a Grand Master of the Orange lodges). The report was generally critical of the activities of the Orange Order, especially because the routes chosen for the annual 12 July parades ran through Catholic areas, thereby increasing the likelihood of sectarian clashes.

4.3. Some British politicians demonstrated a concern to reduce religious tensions in Ireland. Robert Peel, despite his opposition to the Repeal movement and his willingness to use force to maintain order, introduced measures to appease Catholic opinion. He was particularly anxious to get middle- and upper-class Catholics to support the Union, especially following his conflict with O'Connell when he banned a Repeal meeting in Clontarf in 1843. In 1844, Peel established a new Board of Charitable Bequests, which had some Roman Catholic commissioners, including Archbishop Daniel Murray of Dublin. In 1845, Peel increased the annual grant to Maynooth College from £9,000 (approx. €810,000 at 2009 values) to £26,000 (approx. €2.35 million), and provided a capital grant of £30,000 (approx. €2.7 million) for buildings. In the same year, he introduced a Bill for the establishment of Queen's Colleges (in Belfast, Cork and Galway). Rather than winning Catholic support, each of these caused division and controversy and divided Catholic opinion. Archbishop John MacHale of Tuam and Daniel O'Connell saw these actions as a way of increasing the state's control over Catholics. Peel also angered Protestant opinion in Ireland and Britain. The onset of the Great Famine in 1845 and other factors led to the fall of Peel's government in the summer of 1846. This

€marked an end to this phase of conciliatory policies, but also placed relief measures at the centre of Irish policies. By 1850, both Peel and O'Connell were dead, and the death or emigration of over two million people had changed the social and political profile of Ireland.

4.4. In 1845, as a gesture of goodwill to Protestants in Ireland, especially the Orange Order, Peel legalised political parades. The government had banned parades in 1832 because the annual 12 July march in particular had became an occasion of sectarian fighting. Despite the onset of the Famine throughout Ireland, Orangemen were determined to march. Large 12 July parades took place, especially in the north of Ireland, in 1846, 1847, and 1848. The 1848 parade was regarded by the leaders of the Orange Order as significant because of the activities of Young Ireland in that year, and the prospect of a nationalist uprising. Some Orange Lodges offered to act as a 'native garrison' if there was a revolt.

4.5. Although a small uprising did take place at the end of July 1848, the Constabulary easily put it down. The Orange Order, however, saw it as a further example of Catholic disloyalty. They did not take into account that many of the leading Young Irelanders were themselves Protestant and that they advocated non-sectarian politics. The Orange Order saw the 12 July marches in 1849 as an occasion to celebrate the defeat of the Rising. The British government ordered additional troops to areas where disturbances were anticipated. Troops were sent to a small Catholic village called Dolly's Brae, near Castlewellan, Co. Down. A local Orange lodge decided to parade through it. The fighting was swift and brutal, but the military and constabulary initially did not get involved in the conflict or attempt to stop it. By the time they intervened, ten houses and the Catholic church had been burnt to the ground. Five Catholics had been killed and nine others badly wounded. The dead included Hugh King, a 10-year-old boy, who died of gunshot wounds and Anne Taylor, an 85-year-old woman, whose death was caused by a blow of a blunt instrument to the skull. Thirty-five Catholics were arrested, but no Orangemen. The conflict at Dolly's Brae angered public opinion in Ireland and Britain and the leaders of the local Orange lodges were condemned. The military were also criticised for failing to intervene more quickly to prevent the deaths.

4.6. In 1850, legislation (the Party Processions Act) was introduced to ban political parades. Nonetheless, the Orange Order survived the disgrace of Dolly's Brae and was revived in the 1860s under a new populist leader, William Johnston. He defied the ban on marches and, although imprisoned briefly, he emerged from jail an Orange hero and was shortly thereafter elected an MP for Belfast. Johnston was instrumental in having the Party Processions Act removed in 1872. The Orange Order also benefited from opposition to the Home Rule movement in the 1880s. Fear of a Home Rule parliament united Protestant opinion in Ireland and resulted in the formation of the Irish Unionist Party in 1885. In the final decades of the nineteenth century, therefore, a new form of militant

Unionism had emerged. This development ended the aspiration of Protestant national-ists, such as Wolfe Tone, William Smith O'Brien and John Mitchel who wished to keep sectarian differences out of politics.

5. Land politics: agrarian conflicts, secret societies, and the Tithe War

5.1. Secret societies were an important feature of agrarian life in the nineteenth century. There were many: Whiteboys, Rockites, Molly Maguires, Threshers, Defenders, Orange Boys, but the term Ribbonmen was increasingly used to for any Catholic secret society. Though the extent of agrarian crime may have been exaggerated, especially in British newspapers, it did make landlords feel threatened and less likely to carry out evictions. Irish landlords used the actions of secret societies to persuade the government to take repressive coercive measures. Popular opinion in Britain, however, tended to blame the landlords for the perceived economic backwardness of the country and the poverty of the population.

5.2. Catholic Emancipation gave many Catholics a new sense of political power and some of this was directed into a new campaign known as the Tithe War. Tithes (a tax of 10 per cent paid on crops and animals by all denominations for the upkeep of the Anglican Church of Ireland) were regarded as an unjust burden, especially by impover-ished Catholic tenants. Since the middle of the eighteenth century, various secret soci-eties protested against tithes. In the 1830s the resistance became more organised, and many refused to pay. The government responded by introducing the Tithe Rent Charge Act in 1838 by which tithes became payable by landlords rather than by occupiers of land. The fact that tithes were no longer directly a charge on the tenants reduced the sense of grievance.

5.3. Despite professing support for nationalist politics, the Ribbon societies and O'Connell had an uneasy relationship. O'Connell disliked the violent tactics of the secret societies, and saw them as competitors for the support of the peasantry. By the end of the nineteenth century the secret societies had largely been absorbed by bigger polit-ical movements such as the Land League. In parts of Ulster, however, some underground societies carried on intermittent sectarian feuding.

6. The Poor Law

6.1. The issue of poverty and how it should be relieved was a major concern of the British government in the early decades of the nineteenth century. This was evident after the end of the Napoleonic Wars in 1815 when unemployment increased. England, Wales, and Scotland had a state system of poor relief since the sixteenth century: Ireland had no national system of poor relief. The introduction of a 'new' Poor Law in England and Wales in 1834 reflected a belief that poverty was the fault of the individual, who should therefore be treated harshly. Politicians were concerned with introducing a system of poor relief in Ireland. Ireland's poverty was different from that in industrial regions in England. It was seasonal and depended more on the agricultural harvests. In England unemployment or low wages were linked to industrial cycles.

6.2. In 1838, a Poor Law was introduced in Ireland based on the revised English Poor Law of 1834. The conditions of relief provision in Ireland were deliberately made harsher than in England and relief could be provided only in workhouses. The country was divided into 130 new administrative units known as 'unions', each of which had its own workhouse, administered by an elected board of guardians. The upkeep of the work-houses came from taxes levied locally on the ratepayers. Workhouses were central to the new system of relief: only inmates got assistance. The workhouse buildings were to be a physical embodiment of the harsh regime of the relief system. They were built to a stan-dard basic design with no comforts. The mark of a successful workhouse was that it deterred people from applying for relief. Those who did come in were classed as paupers, and were expected to work, usually stone-breaking for men and housework or oakum picking for women. Children had to attend the workhouse school. The government feared that the Irish workhouses would be overwhelmed with applicants. In fact, during the first years of the workhouse system, few applied.

6.3. The workhouses had been built to accommodate 100,000 people. By 1845, 118 of the 130 workhouses were open and admitting paupers. Most were under half full. The fail-ure of the potato crop in 1845 initially had little impact on the numbers seeking work-house relief because Peel's government had introduced temporary relief measures. After the second failure of the potato crop in 1846, the impact on the workhouses was imme-diate and by the end of the year, over 100 were full. Because outdoor relief was not per-mitted, the guardians could not help those they could not accommodate.

6.4. In 1847, a major change was made in the Irish Poor Law and the system was made responsible for both permanent and temporary relief. Outdoor relief was permitted but the provisions governing it were strictly controlled. The responsibility for providing relief for such a large number of people (over one million in 1848) placed a great burden on ratepayers, and it fell heaviest on some of the poorest unions in the west of the country. To deal with the increased demands an additional 133 unions were created. Although the number of paupers in the workhouses fell dramatically after 1850, they remained higher than before the Famine. Increasingly, in the post-Famine decades, the workhouses became infirmaries for the poor.

7. Repeal

7.1. Catholic Emancipation marked a significant victory for Daniel O'Connell. His next objective, Repeal of the Union was more difficult: it did not have the support of either

Irish Protestants or British politicians. Although thirty Repealers had been returned to parliament in the general election of 1830, they were unlikely to win majority support within parliament.

7.2. The precise meaning of Repeal was unclear, and remained so. Although it generally meant the Repeal of the Act of Union, the future relationship of an independent Irish parliament with the British parliament and the British Empire was more ambiguous. In so far as Repeal meant a dismemberment of the United Kingdom (and of the British Empire), it was wholly unacceptable to British politicians and the British public. For its Irish supporters, however, Repeal could be offered as a remedy for every ill. Though Repeal candidates won thirty-seven parliamentary seats in the 1832 general election, the movement had not won support amongst British MPs. The majority of Irish MPs were opposed to it. In 1835, O'Connell changed his tactics. He reached an informal agreement with the Whig government, known as the Lichfield House Compact. The Whigs were assured of Irish votes in the Commons in return for promising to consider reforming legislation for Ireland. Peel's government was defeated over the question of Irish Church revenues and he subsequently resigned.

7.3. By 1840, O'Connell was disillusioned with the Whigs who, it seemed, would not win the next election. Moreover, his personal popularity had declined in Ireland: the number of Repeal candidates had fallen; and their income (known as 'the O'Connell tribute') had gone down. To revive his campaign, he decided to make Repeal a popular crusade like Catholic Emancipation. In April he launched the Repeal Association and issued a number of public 'addresses' in which he criticised government policy, in general, and the Union in particular. The re-election of Sir Robert Peel as Prime Minister (1841), helped Repeal because the Conservatives were regarded as being defenders of Protestantism and the Union, and consequently unsympathetic to Irish demands. The support of some Catholic clergy and bishops, including Archbishop MacHale of Tuam, was crucial for O'Connell in building a base of popular support, especially among the peasantry. Income, which was referred to as 'Repeal Rent', again flowed. O'Connell began organising what *The Times* (London) called 'monster meetings' throughout the country. The first was at Trim, Co. Meath, on 9 March 1843, and it attracted a crowd of over 100,000. Despite O'Connell's fiery rhetoric, such meetings were always peaceably conducted. His peaceful tactics won support for him outside Ireland, particularly in France and the United States. In America, however, O'Connell's principled condemnation of slavery lost him support, especially in the southern states.

7.4. Despite declaring 1843 a 'Repeal Year', O'Connell lacked the support of key groups. By linking the new Repeal campaign closely to the Catholic Church, he alienated moderate Protestant support in Ireland. He also failed to win any significant backing in the north of the country: in fact, he visited Belfast only once. O'Connell also had an uneasy relationship with secret societies and his violent language (which appeared to belie his support for moderation) lost him some middle-class support. For example, at a meeting in Mallow in June 1843 he told his audience: 'The time is coming when we must be doing. You may have the alternative to live as slaves or die as freemen.' It is estimated that three-quarters of a million people assembled on the Hill of Tara on 15 August 1843 to hear O'Connell speak. Whilst opinion in Ireland was divided on Repeal, public opinion in Britain was firmly against it. This sentiment was pointedly expressed by Sir Robert Peel who told the House of Commons in 1843: 'Deprecating as I do all war, but above all, civil war, yet there is no alternative which I do not think preferable to the dismemberment of this Empire.'

7.5. Peel got a chance to show his determination when O'Connell announced he was convening a 'Monster' Repeal meeting at Clontarf near Dublin on 8 October 1843. The day before, the government issued a proclamation prohibiting the meeting. O'Connell acquiesced and cancelled it. His readiness in doing so cost him much popular support, although it was in keeping with his promise that he would not break the law. Public support for O'Connell might have declined further but for the follow-up action of the government in prosecuting O'Connell and some of his associates. In May 1844, they were found guilty of conspiracy and imprisoned. O'Connell was sentenced to a year's imprisonment, a fine of £2,000 (approx. €150,000 at 2009 values), and ordered to give securities of £5,000 for seven years' good behaviour. He was released in September on appeal to the House of Lords. However, this was a turning point. It showed that unlike the Catholic Emancipation crisis in 1829, Peel was willing to face violent confrontation in Ireland rather than allow a break-up of the United Kingdom. It also showed that O'Connell, when challenged by the British government, would draw back. After 1843, his reputation was irreparably damaged, and the Repeal movement lost its vigour and direction.

8. Young Ireland

8.1. The Repeal movement was re-invigorated by a group of young thinkers and writers, men and women, known collectively as Young Ireland. The nationalist movement in Italy, under Mazzini, inspired these romantic nationalists. In October 1842 they began publishing a weekly newspaper called *The Nation*. It became an important means of promoting their view of Irish history and culture. The leaders of the Young Ireland group included Protestants, who were worried that the Repeal movement under O'Connell's leadership appeared to ally Irish nationalism with Roman Catholicism. They argued that if Ireland gained independence this should not result in a Protestant ascendancy being replaced by a Catholic one.

8.2. Various differences in approach and outlook between O'Connell and the Young Irelanders were evident from 1842. These came to a head in 1845 over the University question. O'Connell and Archbishop MacHale opposed Peel's plan to establish secular universities in Ireland, what O'Connell called 'godless colleges'. Young Irelanders, on the other hand, stood for non-sectarian education and supported the new universities. The split with O'Connell finally occurred in 1846, ostensibly over the question of using physical force. The Repeal movement was committed to peaceful constitutional methods and, although the Young Irelanders complied with this policy, they believed that at some stage it might be necessary to use physical force to achieve their ends. O'Connell used this difference to bring about a formal breach with the Young Irelanders. Because they refused to adopt a resolution that they would never use force, some were expelled from the Repeal movement and others soon left. The timing was significant. Following the fall of Peel's government, O'Connell hoped to renew his alliance with the Whigs and he realised that the Young Irelanders would not agree to this. The expulsion of Young Ireland weakened the nationalist movement just as the potato crop failed for the second time, triggering a period of abject hunger and distress.

8.3. Despite the national catastrophe facing Ireland, the Repeal movement remained divided. The split was formalised in January 1847 when the Young Irelanders established the Irish Confederation, under the leadership of William Smith O'Brien, a Protestant landlord of Gaelic stock. The condition of the country was so bad that for most people survival was more important than politics. At first, O'Connell welcomed the incoming Whig government under Lord John Russell and, despite his reservations about their relief policies, he generally supported the government until his death in May 1847. The Young Irelanders, however, were critical of Whig relief policies and O'Brien, the only member of the Confederation who was an MP, withdrew from Westminster in protest.

8.4. Events outside Ireland, rather than the Famine, prompted the Confederation to take a more aggressive approach to the government. In February 1848 there was a revolution in Paris, which overthrew the monarchy. This inspired nationalists and liberals throughout Europe to seek political changes in their own countries. The February revolution had been carried through with little violence and this encouraged some leaders of the Confederation to hope that Irish independence could be got without bloodshed. Some radical Young Irelanders, including John Mitchel, believed that the Irish people should organise a violent uprising. As summer came, an uprising appeared to be inevitable, although the Young Ireland leaders argued that it should not take place until the harvest had been gathered in, to avoid any worse hunger. The government, nervous at the revolutionary fervour throughout the United Kingdom, particularly in Ireland, took steps to counter an uprising. The Young Ireland leaders were arrested, and in May 1848 Mitchel was convicted of treason felony and transported to Van Diemen's Land (Tasmania). Over the summer, the government introduced various repressive measures – suspension of *habeas corpus*, the outlawing of radical newspapers, and increased troop presence, especially in Dublin. The actions of the government precipitated a very minor nationalist uprising at the end of July in Ballingarry in Co. Tipperary. It was small, uncoordinated, and undertaken reluctantly by its leader, William Smith O'Brien. There was little bloodshed – only two of the insurgents were killed. The leaders were convicted of treason and sentenced to be hanged – a sentence later commuted to transportation for life to Van Diemen's Land. The significance of the Young Ireland movement lay not in their failed and inglorious uprising but in their radical politics and use of physical force (which provided an important link with the 1798 rebellion and future movements) and their non-sectarian approach to Irish politics.

9. Government responses to the Famine

9.1. When the potato blight first appeared in Ireland in the autumn of 1845 it was impossible to foresee that it would reappear at varying levels of destructiveness over the following six years and cause a crisis that would change the subsequent economic and political state of Ireland. Sir Robert Peel, the Prime Minister, unlike many British politicians, had direct experience of Ireland and of dealing with its food shortages. His response to the first failure of the potato was the usual one: government grants were made available to local relief committees to provide food or paid employment and the government imported Indian corn to stabilise food prices. These measures were successful and few died in the first year. However, Peel also linked the potato failure in Ireland with his longer-term aim of repealing the Corn Laws, and as a result of this action, his government fell in June 1846.

9.2. The blight came back in 1846, on a much wider scale. Now the most pressing problem facing Peel's successor, Lord John Russell, was the food shortage in Ireland. The main thrust of Russell's relief policies, following the second crop failure, was public works. The relief works aimed to give the poor a minimal wage that would enable them to buy food. At the same time the government was anxious to ensure that only genuine applicants got its relief. The importation of food was to be left to private enterprise: the government promised merchants that it would interfere as little as possible with the market. However, it failed to take proper account of the level of hunger and disease in Ireland in the winter of 1846–7, made much worse by exceptionally cold weather. There was snow as late as April 1847 in parts of the country. Moreover, despite the assurances of the merchants, they brought little food into the country, while large amounts of foodstuffs continued to be exported. As food prices rose over the winter months, the wages paid on the public works were too low to keep people alive.

9.3. The failure of the public works as a relief measure prompted a change of policy at the beginning of 1847. The government set up a network of soup kitchens in where the destitute could get free rations. At the height of the scheme, in July 1847, over three million people a day, approximately 40 per cent of the population, availed of relief. From the outset, however, the measure was to be temporary until the Poor Law could be extended to cope with both ordinary and famine distress. Following the harvest of 1847, the government announced that the Famine was over and that any future relief would be provided by the Poor Law. For the government, a key advantage of this shift was that relief was now funded by locally raised taxation in Ireland. Russell hoped that by altering responsibility for relief the government could transfer the financial responsibility to Irish taxpayers. The demands on the Poor Law were immense: in 1848 over one million people were getting poor relief. The Famine was far from over and high levels of excess mortality, disease, eviction, misery, and emigration continued into the 1850s. Relief measures were inadequate: within a period of six years, over one million people died of famine or famine-related disease and even more emigrated. Moreover, the various relief policies that increasingly placed the burden on Irish taxpayers, proved that even at a period of crisis, Ireland was left to her own resources, though it was an integral part of the United Kingdom.

10. Fenianism

10.1. The failed uprising of 1848 seemed to mark the end of the radical politics of Young Ireland, but some had escaped to France and America. In America, anti-British feeling was kept alive by the flow of Irish immigrants who saw themselves as people forced into exile, victims of bad government and hunger. Moreover, deep-rooted political discontent had not disappeared; rather, it had been deepened by the experience of the Famine years. In 1858, James Stephens returned from Paris to Ireland where he established a new revolutionary organisation, known as the Fenian Brotherhood (or IRB). A parallel branch was formed in America by John O'Mahony. From the outset, the Fenians were opposed to constitutional tactics, believing that British rule could only be ended by armed insurrection. The Catholic bishops, led by Archbishop Paul Cullen, were implacably opposed to the Fenians.

10.2. The Fenian leaders believed that if an uprising was to succeed it should take place as soon as possible. However, the Civil War in America, the source of much of the financial support of the Fenians, delayed plans for an uprising. Stephens saw an advantage in the Civil War: it would (he thought) eventually provide the Fenians with a force of well-trained soldiers. In fact, the delay worked to the advantage of the government, which was well prepared for the insurrection when it came in 1867. It collapsed within twenty-four hours, as did some unsuccessful Fenian attacks in Britain. However, despite the failure of the Fenians, they had won a propaganda victory. While British public opinion was opposed to their violent tactics, it was acknowledged increasingly that Ireland's political problems could not be solved by ignoring them. In the final decades of the nineteenth century, therefore, British politicians made a renewed attempt to solve the Irish problem.

11. Liberal reforms

11.1. The Fenian uprising in 1867 was a reminder to British politicians and the British public that Irish grievances had not gone away. Moreover, the ability of the Fenians to organise in Britain and America demonstrated that Irish nationalism was no longer confined to Ireland itself. The political relationship between Ireland and Britain in the decades following the Fenian uprising was to a large degree shaped by the interest and actions of William Gladstone, the Liberal politician and four-time Prime Minister. His interest in Irish nationalism came late in his political career: by 1870 Gladstone had served parliament for almost thirty years. He was a devout and learned Anglican, and it was fitting that his first major Irish reform had to do with the Church. The Church of Ireland was the Established Church, that is, the richly endowed state church, even though the majority of the Irish people were Roman Catholic – a long-running grievance in Ireland. The Disestablishment Act of 1869 separated church and state, and made the Church of Ireland a voluntary body. More importantly, most of the very extensive property of the Church of Ireland was confiscated, and a portion of it was used for the relief of poverty.

11.2. For Gladstone, Disestablishment was only the first step. In his 1868 election campaign he promised to introduce land reform. The passing of the Landlord and Tenant Act (Ireland) in 1870 was the first in a series of measures that changed the balance of power between tenant and landlord. Although the terms of the 1870 act were limited, significantly the act underlined that land lay at the root of much Irish discontent. The 'John Bright Clauses' (which Gladstone accepted reluctantly) allowed tenants to borrow from the government two-thirds of the cost of buying their holding, at 5 per cent interest repayable over thirty-five years, provided the landlord was willing to sell (there were no compulsory powers). Fewer than 1,000 tenants took up the 'Bright Clauses' since the terms were beyond most tenants and many landlords did not wish to sell. Besides, many substantial leasehold farmers, who had led the campaign for land reform, were excluded from the Act because their leases were longer than thirty-one years. The beginning of the Land War in 1879, coinciding with an agricultural depression, demonstrated the ongoing tensions between landlords and tenants. Gladstone's Second Land Act, passed in 1881, granted the 'Three Fs' (that is, fixity of tenure, fair rent, and freedom of sale) which were supposedly the custom in Ulster; and it established the Irish Land Commission. By this stage, however, the piecemeal land reforms were insufficient to satisfy some of the more militant members of the Land League. Moreover, Charles Stewart Parnell had tied land reform with the demand for Home Rule. From the 1880s Irish political demands returned to constitutional tactics, under the guidance of Parnell, supported, in turn, by Gladstone.

11.3. The demand for Home Rule dominated Irish politics from the 1870s to 1914. Its strength was that the movement had the support of both radicals and moderates in Ireland while in Britain it had the support of many Liberals, led by Gladstone. However, Home Rule also proved to be divisive: in Britain it split the Liberal Party; and in Ireland it gave birth to a new brand of militant Unionism. The British Conservative Party, in turn, allied with the Unionist cause, most notably in the person of the flamboyant politician, Lord Randolph Churchill. During this period, too, Irish politics became increasingly polarised along denominational lines. This was summed up in Churchill's slogan 'Home Rule is Rome Rule'. Gladstone's Home Rule Bills of 1886 and 1893 were both defeated in the British parliament, but they sowed the seeds of a militant Unionism that was increasingly willing to use force to remain within the United Kingdom. The passing of the Third Home Rule Bill in 1912, which was due to be put on the statute books in 1914, caused a crisis in Irish politics and the outbreak of a civil war was averted by the beginning of the First World War. The 1912 Home Rule Bill was never implemented; instead, the British Prime Minister, David Lloyd George, introduced the government of Ireland Act in 1920. This created two new states in Ireland, largely divided along religious lines. As a result of the Act, the political boundaries of the United Kingdom and of Ireland were redrawn: twenty-six counties became the Irish Free State, while the six north-eastern counties became Northern Ireland and remained within the United Kingdom. The Act of Union, introduced in 1800, had survived intact for only 120 years.

CHRISTINE KINEALY

CHAPTER 2

Society and economy, 1815–70

1. Ireland in 1815

1.1. Ireland at the beginning of the nineteenth century was coming to the end of a long period of economic expansion. Rising demand for food – first from the British and French colonies in the West Indies and from the steadily increasing volume of shipping crossing the Atlantic, later from the new industrial centres of Great Britain – had encouraged a dramatic expansion of agriculture. There was also a growing industrial sector: an export-based linen manufacture; a woollen industry meeting most domestic needs; food processing enterprises such as brewing, distilling and flour milling; and luxury trades such as silk weaving, glass-making and coach-building. When, in the 1770s, English cotton manufacturers developed steam- and water-powered machinery for the spinning of cotton thread, Irish manufacturers responded with impressive speed, setting up factories using the new technology in a wide range of locations.

1.2. By the end of the eighteenth century, the effects of agricultural, industrial, and commercial expansion were everywhere to be seen. Dublin, Cork and other centres had expanded rapidly. Narrow crooked streets and timbered houses gave way to broad avenues lined with substantial town houses and public buildings. In the countryside, likewise, land was drained or reclaimed, fields were enclosed by ditches and hedges, and landlords invested their growing wealth in new mansions set in carefully laid out demesnes. The population had risen from less than 2.5 million in the early eighteenth century to perhaps 5 million by 1800.

2. Agriculture and living standards

2.1. With the benefit of hindsight it is possible to see that this facade of prosperity concealed dangerous weaknesses. Irish agriculture had responded to widening opportunities, but the average Irish farm was small, with little opportunity for capital investment. Instead, agricultural production relied on abundant supplies of very cheap labour. Wool, cotton, and other manufacturing enterprises, likewise, were in general smaller and less technologically advanced than their English and Scottish counterparts. Already by the 1780s the wool and silk industries showed signs of decline, as businesses failed and workers became unemployed.

2.2. Living standards were also low by comparison with most parts of Great Britain. The rise in population, which more than doubled in half a century, testified to the extent to which the prosperity of the eighteenth century had reached even the very poor, lifting the threat of famine and reducing child and adult mortality. But the expansion had greatly increased the relative size of the most vulnerable sections of the population: landless labourers, competing for work on the holdings of the relatively few larger occupiers, or seeking to support a family on small plots of land located on the margins of settlement, on mountain sides or reclaimed bog. In 1800, most people were still optimistic about Ireland's prospects, but it would not take much to expose the underlying fragility of its recent economic success.

3. Agricultural crisis and industrial decline

3.1. By the end of the eighteenth century Irish farmers had largely lost their transatlantic markets to the developing agriculture of the new United States. Instead, they had found a new and expanding market in the growing non-agricultural population of industrialising Britain. For the greater part of the period 1793–1815 war between Britain and France had pushed up demand, while at the same time restricting imports from continental Europe. By 1810–14, the price paid for Irish cereals was almost twice what it had been in the early 1780s; the price of meat and dairy products had more than doubled. The defeat of France in 1813, however, led to a slump in demand, while it reopened the British market to continental suppliers. Between 1812 and 1816 grain prices on the Dublin market fell by between 40 and 50 per cent, meat prices by more than half, and the price of butter by about one-third. Prices recovered somewhat in the years that followed, but throughout the period 1815–45 they remained well below their wartime peak, and there were further slumps in the early 1820s and again in the early 1830s.

3.2. The results, for all classes of rural society, were disastrous. Landlords, burdened by debts and other commitments, dating from the years of prosperity, struggled with falling payments from tenants. Farmers found rents that had been reasonable in the years of high prices now impossible to pay. Most of all, the rural poor discovered that plots of land that had barely supported a family in former years could not now provide even a minimum subsistence. Work on other men's land also became harder to get, as price trends favoured livestock farming over more labour-intensive tillage. Meanwhile, population, though growing less quickly than in the boom years, continued to creep upwards, from 6.8 million in 1821 to 7.8 million by 1831 and 8.2 million in 1841. By 1845, perhaps 1¼ million families were dependent for their support on holdings of less than five acres. A detailed enquiry into rural poverty reported in 1836 that an agricultural labourer could, on average, count on 134 days of paid employment in a year.

4. The collapse of the wool and cotton industries

4.1. The second major blow to the Irish economy came in the mid-1820s: the catastrophic collapse of two major industries, wool and cotton. Irish manufacturing in the late eighteenth century had flourished behind a wall of import duties. The Act of Union provided for the phasing out of all duties by 1824, creating a free trade area within the new United Kingdom. Modern studies suggest that already before 1800 Irish producers had fallen behind their English and Scottish rivals in technological sophistication, to the point where no feasible system of protection could have allowed them to hold out indefinitely against competition from across the Irish Sea. But the sudden withdrawal of protection meant that what might have been a gradual decline was instead brutally swift. The Currency Act (1825) assimilated the Irish pound to the British as from 5 January 1826. Over 60 English banks were forced to suspend payments in December 1826, causing severe recession and business failures in all parts of the British Isles. By the late 1830s most of the mills that had once held out the promise of an Irish industrial revolution, had closed or were operating at a much reduced level. Ireland now depended on English and Scottish imports for the great bulk of its cotton and woollen cloth.

4.2. The failure of the woollen and cotton industries must be seen in perspective. The crisis, in the first place, was confined to these two branches of manufacturing. There was no general collapse of Irish industry. Secondly, the decline of cotton and woollen textile manufacture must be set against the very different story of linen. The first quarter of the nineteenth century had been difficult. Flax fibre was too fine to be machine spun, and linen had lost ground to the cheaper cotton cloth woven from factory-spun thread. By the mid-1820s, however, the invention of a wet spinning process had made possible the machine spinning of linen yarn. In north-east Ulster, the traditional home of the linen industry, industrialists transferred resources from a declining cotton trade to newly profitable linen. Belfast, the centre of the new factory-based industry, grew rapidly, sucking in population from the surrounding countryside. Between 1831 and 1841 its population grew by almost half, from 53,000 to 75,000. By the early 1840s it could be described as Ireland's Manchester.

4.3. The spectacular success of linen in the north-east makes it impossible to claim that Ireland did not share in the industrial revolution. Indeed there is a case for saying that what happened in Ireland differed only in scale from what happened elsewhere in the British Isles, where a few regions (the Clyde valley, south Wales, the English north and midlands) developed as centres of factory-based industry, while elsewhere agriculture and small-scale handicrafts remained dominant. But the problem remained that the industrialisation of the north-east, though impressive, was not by itself sufficient to offset the rise in population in the island as a whole, now that it was no longer accompanied by exceptionally rapid agricultural growth.

5. Pre-Famine crisis?

5.1. At first sight, then, the story of the Irish economy between 1815 and 1845 was one of deepening crisis. Population had risen sharply during the exceptionally favourable conditions of the second half of the eighteenth century. Prolonged agrarian depression after

1815 created inevitable problems. The failure of manufacturing industry outside the north-east meant that there was no prospect of a surplus rural population being absorbed, as in England and Scotland, by expanding industrial centres. Instead growing numbers clung to inadequate holdings of land, or to precarious earnings as labourers in an overcrowded market, pitiably vulnerable to every fluctuation in prices or crop yields. Against this background the disastrous Famine of 1845–50 is often seen as the culmination of a classic crisis of subsistence, with rising population pressing against the ceiling of limited resources.

5.2. More recent assessments, however, have warned against assuming that pre-Famine Ireland was a society doomed to catastrophe. Despite its evident problems, the economy was not stagnant. Agricultural output, of both livestock and tillage products, rose steadily. One estimate puts overall growth between 1800 and 1845 at between 80 per cent and 100 per cent. Some of this increase was due to the gradual spread of improved techniques of cultivation, new livestock breeds, or more effective crop rotations. Much was the result of increasingly intensive land use, and the desperate pursuit of the marginal gains from the reclamation of bog and mountainous areas. The techniques used were often primitive. From another point of view, this can be seen as an effective use of Ireland's main resource – abundant supplies of cheap labour. Manufacturing also had its successes as well as its failures. Brewing, distilling, and flour milling – all solidly based on Ireland's agricultural resources – expanded during the first half of the nineteenth century, making increasing use of the new technology of steam power. The advent of steam shipping from the mid-1820s helped to destroy the cotton and wool manufactures, but opened up the British market to Irish flour, beer, spirits, meat, and dairy produce. Internal transport also improved, with a growing fleet of coaches and horse-drawn cars carrying passengers and goods along Irish roads. The 1830s and 1840s were also the heyday of Ireland's canals. Meanwhile, new legislation in 1821 encouraged the development, during the 1820s and 1830s, of a more extensive, and at the same time more stable, network of banks.

5.3. Alongside this evidence of economic progress must be set indicators of social and cultural change. Imports of tea, sugar, and tobacco stagnated in the years immediately after 1815, but rose significantly during 1830–45. The number of children attending school rose from 200,000 in 1806 to more than 560,000 by 1824. In 1841 it was found that almost two-thirds of all men and boys born between 1821 and 1830 were able to read and write. Meanwhile, the proportion of children growing up with knowledge of Irish had fallen from 45 per cent of those born in the late eighteenth century to only 28 per cent of those born in 1831–41. Language change and the rise of literacy were in turn crucial to another striking development of the 1820s and after: the spectacular growth of a sophisticated new style of popular politics, manifested first in the campaign for Catholic Emancipation and later in the Repeal movement. None of this is compatible with a society locked in uniform poverty and economic stagnation.

6. Social and economic indicators

6.1. Any discussion of economic and social change must take account of social and regional distinctions. Precise figures on the size of the different social groups in early nineteenth-century Ireland are impossible to obtain. But one recent analysis suggests that the farming population can be roughly divided into about 50,000 wealthy farmers, with an average of 80 acres per family, 100,000 'strong farmers', with an average of 100 acres, and 200,000 'family farmers', with an average of 20 acres. Below them came 250,000 smallholders, with an average of 5 acres per household, and one million labourers, who worked on other men's land either for a cash wage or as 'cottiers' in exchange for a plot of ground on which to grow food for themselves and their families. There were also important regional differences. The poor lands of the western counties supported a population mainly of smallholders, with few large occupiers or landless labourers. In the more fertile south and midlands reasonably comfortable medium and large farmers coexisted with a desperately poor population of smallholders, cottiers, and labourers. In the east, where conditions favoured tillage farming and towns offered alternative employment, farmers were in general comfortable and landless labourers somewhat better off than elsewhere. It seems safe to assume that rising literacy and higher levels of material consumption were felt more strongly among the medium and large farmers, and little if at all among the rural poor.

6.2. Even where the least advantaged sections of Irish rural society are concerned, however, it is necessary to be precise about the nature of their poverty. The potato provided a highly nutritious, if monotonous diet. The mud-walled huts of the rural poor, however crude, gave adequate shelter in the temperate Irish climate, while widespread peat bogs provided plentiful fuel. Levels of material consumption – furniture, clothing, and household utensils – were undoubtedly low by comparison with Great Britain, but levels of physical well-being were remarkably good. Evidence from registers of convicts, and from records of men recruited into the armed forces, indicates that the average Irishman of the poorer classes was, in fact, somewhat taller than his English counterpart. Life expectancy for adults was roughly the same as in Great Britain, although infant mortality was up to 50 per cent higher.

6.3. Against this background it becomes necessary to reconsider the image of an economic system on the brink of inevitable collapse. After 1815 the Irish economy passed through a difficult period. By the early 1840s, however, there were clear signs of adjustment to changing circumstances. Evidence from landed estates suggests that the repeated subdivision of holdings had been brought under control and that there had instead been a degree of consolidation of small plots into more substantial farms. In some regions livestock had expanded at the expense of less profitable tillage. Emigration had also increased – between 1815 and 1845 an estimated 1.5 million people left – and the age at marriage had also risen as it became more difficult to form new households. Population, therefore, was still rising, but at a much reduced rate: the extra 400,000 added between 1831 and 1841 was less than half the increase of the previous decade. Meanwhile, agricultural productivity was increasing, and manufacturing was slowly, but steadily, expanding. The rural population was for the most part poor, but well housed, well fed, and generally healthy. The sudden and unforeseeable failure of the potato was thus a violent external shock administered to a society which had passed through a difficult period of transition, but had begun to put its worst problems behind it. Without the potato blight it is easy to see how population could have stabilised at around seven to eight million, with cheap labour sustaining a large, and still profitable, tillage sector until the steady expansion of a range of mainly agriculturally-based industries gradually raised living standards.

7. The Great Famine

7.1. In 1844, the last year before the Famine, a total of 2.4 million acres sown with potatoes produced a crop of approximately 15 million tons. In 1845, blight cut the total produced to approximately 10 million tons. In 1846, yields fell catastrophically, so that 2 million acres produced less than 3 million tons of edible potatoes. In 1847, blight was less acute, but after two bad seasons only a little over a quarter of a million acres had been sown, so that the total crop was only 2 million tons. Blight returned in the years that followed, so that even with a somewhat larger acreage only 3 million tons were produced in 1848 and only 4 million in 1849.

7.2. This drastic fall in potato yields created an appalling crisis. The potato had been the ideal food for a relatively poor rural population. No other crop could be grown in such quantity on poor or reclaimed land; its low status and relative bulk limited commercial demand; and it was also highly nutritious. Its loss thus left millions facing imminent starvation. As the crisis continued, the rapidly rising price of all other produce brought hardship even to those who, in other circumstances, might have been able to provide themselves with alternative food. Widespread malnutrition also led to the rapid spread of a range of diseases, notably typhus and relapsing fever, which, in fact, killed far more than died of actual starvation. By 1850, an estimated one million people had died of hunger or disease, and another million had fled the country, emigrating to Great Britain or North America.

7.3. In the first year of the Famine, 1845–6, Sir Robert Peel's Tory government responded reasonably effectively to the partial failure of the crop by instituting public works and selling off imported grain at controlled prices. The Whig government that took office in June 1846, with its policy of *laissez-faire*, rejected any interference in the market, relying instead on an expanded public works programme. In February 1847, faced with evidence of large-scale suffering and death, the government reluctantly authorised the provision of free food. Over the next eight months soup kitchens provided emergency rations to an estimated three million people. From September 1847, however, the government insisted that the soup kitchens be phased out, leaving those still in need to be cared for entirely within the already overburdened workhouse system, a decision widely regarded as contributing to the heavy death toll that continued over the next three years.

8. Did the British government do enough?

8.1. Any assessment of the British government's handling of the Famine must take into account the limited resources available to a mid nineteenth-century administration. But most modern accounts agree that its response, nevertheless, amounted to far less than could have been done. The earlier introduction and continuation over a longer period of the soup kitchens, in particular, would undoubtedly have saved many lives. In all, British government spending on Famine relief amounted to £8.3 million (approx. €710 million at 2009 values), less than half of one per cent of the gross national product of the United Kingdom for a single year. Much of this money, moreover, was initially given in the form of loans rather than grants. Although the debts thus incurred were later written off, the effect at the time was to inhibit relief committees from spending money that they expected would later have to be repaid from local taxes.

8.2. The failure of the most economically advanced society in the world to intervene more effectively to prevent its citizens starving to death can be explained in various ways. In some cases, government initiatives were stifled or blunted due to the vested interests of landowners with Irish interests reluctant to see their estates burdened by the necessary taxation. But there were also two more general considerations at work. The first was a desire to ensure that local authorities would turn to central government only when their own resources were genuinely exhausted. Ministers were particularly committed to this stance because of their belief that Irish landlords were largely responsible, by their long-term indifference to the development of their estates and the welfare of their tenantry, for the disaster now unfolding in the Irish countryside. Irish property, they insisted, should pay for Irish poverty. Secondly, there was the belief that the potato blight, however terrible its consequences, provided an opportunity to reform Irish agriculture, by clearing away surplus population to leave a smaller class of more prosperous farmers and a shrunken, but securely employed, agricultural labour force. From this point of view over-generous relief, encouraging the destitute to remain where they were, would only prolong the agony.

8.3. Neither of these concerns – that local property owners should not evade their share of the responsibility, and that adjustment to changed conditions should not be impeded – were in themselves unreasonable. The problem arose because they were given such primacy in the shaping of overall policy. Here it is hard to deny that the response of the British politicians and public to the Famine reflected the psychological distance that existed between Ireland and other parts of what was theoretically a united kingdom.

There was a degree of sympathy for Irish suffering. But exposure to harrowing accounts of Irish poverty during earlier partial failures of the potato crop had helped to create a degree of what has been called compassion fatigue. Sympathy was further eroded when Great Britain itself was hit by recession in 1847, and when the return of a large Repeal contingent to parliament, followed by the Young Ireland insurrection of 1848, seemed to demonstrate the ingratitude of the Irish for what had been done for them. Some studies have also stressed the influence on key policy makers of a particular strain of Protestant evangelicalism, in which the undeniable horrors of the Famine could be interpreted as an example of the terrible but unquestionable workings of God's providence, operating to root out social and moral evils.

9. Post-Famine adjustment

9.1. To understand the long-term effects of the Famine on Irish agriculture, it is important to recognise that the potato was not just the staple food of a large section of the population. It was also, in many cases, a medium of exchange: farmers who would have found it difficult to pay cash wages for the labour necessary to pursue intensive tillage were able instead to hire cottiers who would give so many days' work in exchange for a small plot of otherwise fallow ground on which they could grow potatoes for themselves and their families. The collapse of potato yields, year after year, thus meant not only an immediate food shortage but also the collapse of a whole agrarian system. Even after 1850, when potato yields were still lower and less reliable than in the past, there was no going back. Instead, Irish agriculture was reorganised around the raising of livestock, in particular cattle. Between 1851 and 1871, the acreage devoted to grain fell by 30 per cent, while the area devoted to pasture for grazing and fodder rose by almost 20 per cent.

9.2. This transfer from tillage to stock-rearing was made possible by, and at the same time helped to bring about, a sharp decline in population. By 1851, Famine mortality and emigration had already reduced total numbers to 6.5 million, as compared to 8.2 million ten years earlier. By 1861, numbers had fallen still further, to 5.8 million, and by 1871 to 5.4 million. With subdivision of holdings now largely eliminated, and opportunities for paid employment sharply curtailed by the decline of tillage, it had become increasingly difficult to form new households, while growing numbers found that they no longer had a place within rural society. The second half of the nineteenth century thus saw a further rise in the average age at marriage for both men and women, as well as in the proportion of both who never married. Meanwhile, emigration in the years after 1850 continued at a level almost as high as during the Famine years. Between 1851 and 1871, a further 1.9 million people emigrated, mainly to Great Britain and North America. Not all emigrants should necessarily be seen as unwilling victims of social change. The heavy emigration of the Famine years had broken down previous barriers to mobility, creating an awareness of emigration as an option and establishing networks of friends and family abroad which made the path of future emigrants less daunting. Some at least of those who availed of the opportunities opened up probably thought more in terms of improving their lives than of being forced out by impossible pressures. But their decision to leave must still be seen in the context of the unappealing options that rural Ireland now offered, not only to the landless, but to those sons of farming households unfortunate enough not to inherit the family holding, and those daughters who did not get a dowry that would allow them to marry into a household broadly similar to their own.

9.3. Along with the decline in population went a marked change in social structure. All classes suffered during the Famine; disease, in particular, spared no social group. But it was inevitably the rural poor who were worst hit. By contrast, the number of farms over fifteen acres actually increased slightly between 1841 and 1851. Labourers and smallholders also contributed the largest share of the continued outflow after 1850. Before 1845, farmers had been outnumbered more than two-to-one by the rural poor. By the late nineteenth century, on the other hand, the landless labourer was part of a depressed minority in a society now dominated by the family farm.

9.4. This post-Famine re-adjustment took place against the background of a world-wide economic boom that continued into the early 1870s. Irish agriculture, reorganised around an export-based livestock sector and with a much-reduced labour force, benefited from a quarter-century of high food prices, interrupted only by a series of bad seasons, due to bad weather, in 1859–64. Between 1854 and 1874, the income of Irish farmers rose by almost two-thirds, that of agricultural labourers by around one quarter. (Irish landlords, contrary to their reputation as ruthless exploiters, settled for a mere 12 per cent increase in their rent rolls.) For Irish industry, too, this was an age of general prosperity. The east Ulster linen manufacture, now mechanised in both its spinning and weaving sectors, continued to expand. With the establishment in 1861 of Harland and Wolff, Belfast also began its development as a major centre of shipbuilding. In Dublin, Guinness's brewery, already a century old, enjoyed a period of rapid growth, tripling its output between 1855 and 1870. Other breweries and distilleries also flourished, as did flour milling and a range of other manufactures, including even a modest recovery in the woollen industry. Most Irish industrial ventures outside the north-east were local; in the more depressed conditions of the 1880s and after, they were to prove highly vulnerable to the dumping of cut-price goods by much larger English and Scottish producers. But for the moment they continued to benefit from buoyant home markets for their produce.

9.5. Overall, then, the 1850s and 1860s were a period in which a declining Irish population enjoyed the fruits of substantially increasing national wealth. With greater prosperity came accelerated social change. The proportion of persons able to read and write rose from 47 per cent in 1841 to 75 per cent by 1881. The proportion able to speak Irish, already only 23 per cent in 1851, fell further to 18 per cent thirty years later. The number of newspapers published in Ireland rose from less than 100 in 1852 to more than 140 by

1871. The great symbol of the modern age, the railway, had made small beginnings before 1850, with just over 400 miles of track. By 1870, there were almost 2,000 miles, and the number of passengers carried annually had risen to over 14 million. By this time, equally, over 400 Irish towns had telegraph offices linking them to the outside world: the intensely local, inward-looking society of the past was disappearing rapidly. Folklorists and antiquarians commented disapprovingly on the disappearance of a whole range of popular traditions and beliefs. But the political history of the 1870s and 1880s was to demonstrate the extent to which rising prosperity, education, and awareness of the world beyond one's immediate vicinity had combined to produce a new capacity for organisation and self-assertion.

S.J. CONNOLLY

CHAPTER 3

Culture and religion, 1815–70

1. Introduction

1.1. This was an important period for religious life in Ireland, when all churches faced challenges to their spiritual authority, or their status. Against a background of social and economic change, religious leaders tried to introduce reform, improve administration, and discipline their flocks. The churches were under increasing pressure from the secular world – from its ideas, its education, and its cultural activities. Nonetheless, there was an increase in religious fervour. In Protestant churches much of this can be explained by evangelicalism and its emphasis on a more 'enthusiastic' style of religious expression.

1.2. After the Famine, following a period of reform and the loss of its poorest members, Catholicism was marked by religious renewal and a more public display of faith. Practice differed from person to person and from place to place. Religious faith itself is difficult to measure; for some it was an intensely private matter; for many it was a mixture of ritual and tradition, the social and spiritual behaviour of a community. In fact, it is almost impossible to separate religion and culture. However, there were many cultural activities that were entirely secular. Religious leaders increasingly found they had to compete for the leisure time of their flocks.

2. Religion in pre-Famine Ireland

2.1. The first statistics for religion in Ireland are in the 1831 Census, and these give us some idea of the relative strengths of the major denominations before the Famine. The great majority of the population, around 80.3 per cent, were Catholic; 10.7 per cent were Anglican (Church of Ireland); and 8.1 per cent were Presbyterian. Denominational membership was not, however, evenly distributed in the island. The north-east was distinctive. The counties of Antrim, Down, Armagh, and Londonderry had Catholic minorities, while Fermanagh and Tyrone had almost equal numbers of Catholics and Protestants. Every other Irish county had a substantial Catholic majority. Moreover, because of earlier migrations from Scotland and England, 96 per cent of all Irish Presbyterians were located in Ulster. Most Anglicans (56 per cent) were also in the north-east, and the remainder were more generally dispersed throughout the island. The population of Ireland was, of course, dramatically affected by the Famine, and Catholics suffered greater losses than Protestants. The 1861 Census reflected the change: it recorded the population as 77.7 per cent Catholic, 12 per cent Anglican and 9 per cent Presbyterian. Class and geography were important. Catholics were largely concentrated in the west and south of the country, and they made up the majority of the lower classes in society.

2.2. There were other small religious groupings such as Baptists, Congregationalists, Plymouth Brethren, Quakers, and Methodists. Their numbers rose and fell over the century. However, even taken together, these made up only a small per centage of the population. The Methodists were probably the most significant in numbers and influence (see §6). None of the denominations operated in isolation. Apart from their interaction with each other, they were also affected by wider social and political events in Ireland itself, and were influenced, too, by international theological trends.

3. The Catholic Church

3.1. The nineteenth century was a time of progress and reform for the Catholic Church following the removal of almost all the legal obstacles imposed on it during the previous centuries. Significantly, Catholic Emancipation – and particularly the right to sit in parliament – remained to be achieved until 1829. Only then would full political participation be open to Irish Catholics. But the years of legal discrimination had inevitably weakened the overall structure of the Church and its ability to function effectively.

3.2. The most visible areas of concern were the shortage and inadequacy of churches and the scarcity of priests to minister to large and scattered congregations. It was estimated that in 1800 the ratio of priests to parishioners was about 1:2,100. At the beginning of the century bishops felt the need to standardise religious practices and to exert their authority in matters of discipline.

3.3. Progress was slow in the pre-Famine era. However, some important building work was begun and a new generation of reforming bishops brought their influence to bear on the lower clergy through regular conferences, retreats, and visitations. While priests were encouraged to improve their preaching and pastoral work, regulations were introduced to address personal standards of behaviour. Whilst discipline was tightened as a result of these measures, the rapid rate of population increase made any improvement in the ratio of priests to people impossible.

3.4. Great efforts were also made to regulate the behaviour of the wider Catholic community, particularly in regard to the rituals of faith. The difficulties of the previous century had led to a wide variation in religious practice and the merging of popular folk customs with Christian events. The 'merry wake' is probably the best example. While the priest delivered the last rites, the main activities surrounding the newly deceased were very much social and communal, from the keening women (*mná caointe*) following the funeral to the drinking, dancing, games, tricks, and general horseplay enjoyed by family, friends and neighbours. In country areas the funeral mass was often celebrated in the home, as were marriages and baptisms, though the priest's house was sometimes used. The Dublin diocesan statutes of 1831 ordered that the funeral mass be held in the church and, under Archbishop Cullen, the administration of the sacraments was transferred from home to church. The secular traditions surrounding the wake, however, proved more resistant to reform, though the elements most offensive to the priests – mimicry of the sacraments, especially marriage, and satirical attacks on the clergy – had largely disappeared by the second half of the century. Boisterous behaviour at 'patterns', the feast day of a parish's patron saint, also aroused the criticism of the hierarchy, who were particularly concerned about the opinions of their Protestant counterparts and how they viewed the apparent superstitious and immoral traditions that surrounded them. These pre-modern aspects of popular Catholicism presented the Church with significant challenges to its authority over social as well as religious life.

4. The Church of Ireland

4.1. As part of the constitutional establishment, the Church of Ireland operated within a particularly difficult framework and its pastoral relationship with its parishioners was complicated by tasks of civil administration. The parish, operating as a kind of unofficial local parliament, was responsible for the upkeep of church buildings, schools, and roads; for the burial of the destitute; for the welfare of deserted children; and for looking after the poor. Such responsibilities ensured that Anglican clergy had considerable influence in the community, a situation reinforced by their strong social ties with local gentry. And while the Church attracted a wide social range of followers among landlords, the professional and business classes and labouring families, the clergy themselves were most likely to come from the gentry or the professionals. Both the local and national power of the Established Church placed it in a position of privilege in relation to other religious denominations. This provoked considerable hostility from Catholics and Dissenters who greatly resented paying for the upkeep of a religious institution to which they did not belong.

4.2. The Established Church represented only a small minority of the people, and it is not surprising that it was the target of much hostile criticism in this period. However, complaints also focused on the pastoral role of the Church and its ministers. Pluralism (clerical double jobbing) and non-residence were cited as obvious examples of apathy and neglect. The Church's material and administrative inadequacies most clearly affected the services offered to the community, and the frequency of divine service, communion, and confirmation, was regarded as insufficient in many areas. Under pressure from an increasingly unsympathetic legislature, and under the critical scrutiny of the Presbyterian community, the Church of Ireland could not afford to be complacent.

4.3. During the first decades of the nineteenth century the Church of Ireland engaged in administrative improvements, redeploying its assets and reasserting its authority. By 1830, the province of Armagh could boast of 79 new benefices since 1782, while the number of glebe houses had increased to 93 per cent of all parishes. Such improvements meant an increase in the number of resident clergy, church services, and communicants. Its success, while limited, was due to different causes. These included the committed churchmanship of an increasing number in the upper and lower ranks of the Church, increased pressure from clergy and laity involved in evangelical societies, and the contribution of evangelicals striving to revitalise the Church from within. However, it was clear by the early 1830s that internal reform was not enough to satisfy the critics of the Church in an age of increasing accountability. Among a series of legislative measures imposed by the Whig government was the Church Temporalities Act which reduced the number of bishoprics from 22 to 12 and established a new body to deal with church administration and finance – the Ecclesiastical Commissioners of Ireland. The ancient and inefficient structure of the Church of Ireland was thoroughly overhauled, and more attention was given to efficiency than to tradition. The controversial issue of tithes was resolved by government intervention in 1838. The Church hierarchy, unsurprisingly, responded with alarm to what was believed to be an attack on property; but the vulnerability of the Protestant establishment in a mainly Catholic country would continue to increase in the course of the century.

4.4. The activities of evangelicals posed a different challenge for Church leaders. Characterised by an emphasis on personal salvation, the centrality of the Cross, and the authority of the Bible, Evangelicalism had been an important, though minor, undercurrent in Irish religious life since the late eighteenth century. It was most visible as an organised movement within Methodism, but individual members of the clergy and laity of other denominations were also influenced by its challenge to contemporary religious lethargy. In the early decades of the nineteenth century a small number of Anglican clergy showed their evangelical tendencies by forming religious societies, engaging in outdoor preaching, and co-operating with members of other denominations to spread the gospel. Church leaders regarded this kind of activity as a threat both to the hierarchical structure and to the wider authority of the establishment. They also feared the possibility of religious division, even schism. But while extempore prayer and popular hymn-singing were at first seen as worrying developments by a Church rooted in liturgical tradition, these tensions eased as the century progressed. Indeed, the gradual development of evangelical churchmanship within the Church of Ireland proved that co-operation between orthodoxy and Evangelicalism was not only possible but desirable. By the second half of the 1830s, church extension work and the formation of diocesan societies showed the extent to which they could co-exist, and by the middle of the century the Anglican Church in Ireland could be described as an evangelical institution.

5. The Presbyterian Church

5.1. The Presbyterian Church in Ulster has been described as virtually 'a state within a state', a self-regulating community organised according to its own principles and virtually independent of the wider structures of church and state. While Catholics and Anglicans came under the authority of Rome and Westminster respectively, the Presbyterian community selected its own ministers, built its own churches, and administered its own discipline. Though technically a dissenting church in Ireland, it did receive an annual government grant, the *regium donum*.

5.2. At the head of the numerically strong and geographically concentrated Presbyterian community was the Synod of Ulster, the provincial church government which had the loyalty of the vast majority of Ulster Presbyterians throughout the eighteenth and nineteenth centuries. There were, however, other significant minority groups such as the Covenanting or Reformed Presbyterian Church which had originated in the Second Scottish Reformation, and had put down somewhat delicate roots in Ulster during the troubled years of the mid-seventeenth century. The Associate Synod, or the 'Seceders', a Scottish breakaway sect which began to make an impact in Ulster in the 1740s, was numerically stronger than the Covenanters, and particularly successful in competing with mainstream Presbyterianism. Combining conversionist zeal and a strong emphasis on fighting sin with rigid orthodoxy and strict discipline, the Seceders had organised a total of sixteen congregations in Co. Down by 1818.

5.3. There were numerous doctrinal disputes and divisions within the Synod of Ulster itself. These were largely due to what has been described as 'the inherent tension of Presbyterianism, between traditional ecclesiastical orthodoxy and the right of private judgment'. In the early nineteenth century the major disputes were connected with the ideas of Arianism and subscription to the Westminster Confession of Faith. Arianism was a Christian heresy first proposed early in the fourth century by the Alexandrian presbyter Arius. It affirmed that Christ is not truly divine but a created being. Arius' basic premise was the uniqueness of God who is alone self-existent; the Son, who is not self-existent, cannot be God. It was a view offensive to more orthodox laity, and capable of creating bitter divisions. The frequency with which congregations took issue with each other, their ministers, or the Synod, over such matters, and the consequent forming of breakaway groups, suggests a degree of disharmony at grassroots level. This could divide communities, and significantly affect the cause of Presbyterianism in a locality. Matters came to a head in 1829, with the setting up of a separate Remonstrant Synod by the Arian Party, and the passing of a resolution that required full subscription to the Westminster Confession of Faith by all ministers in 1835. It is widely accepted in Presbyterian history that the split of 1829, begun by the Revd Henry Cooke, was both recognition of the growth of Evangelicalism within the church and a powerful stimulant to the evangelical cause. This was reflected in 1840 in the union of the Synod of Ulster and the Secession Synod into the new General Assembly and the beginning of a new era of missionary enterprise.

6. Methodism

6.1. Although it accounts for only about 1.5 per cent of the overall population, it is worth looking briefly at Methodism. It originated as a reforming society within the Church of

England and was, by the nineteenth century, a distinct religious body. Methodist preachers travelled extensively throughout Ireland, preaching outdoors, forming local societies, and spreading the message of justification by faith and Christian perfection. With its emotional class meetings, spiritual discipline and practical support, Methodism reached out to many of those neglected by the more established religions. The importance it attached to thrift and temperance perhaps appealed particularly to women, while the early use of women preachers introduced a dimension of novelty into popular religious life. It was particularly strong within traditional Anglican areas and in the 'linen triangle' of south Ulster.

6.2. The province of Ulster was Methodism's most successful recruiting ground: 68 per cent of Irish Methodists lived north of a line drawn from Sligo to Dundalk in 1815. Although very anti-Catholic, and specifically targeting the peasantry through Irish-speaking preachers, Methodism's most important contribution to Irish society was the stimulus it gave to a much-wider Evangelicalism. During the course of the nineteenth century many Methodist characteristics, particularly itinerant preaching and the establishment of voluntary religious societies, were taken up by individuals, missionary organisations, and eventually the main churches themselves.

7. Religious divisions

7.1. Each denomination was separated from the other by social, cultural, and political as well as by theological distinctions. Despite internal divisions, Ulster Presbyterians, with their strong Scottish links and sense of religious and political identity, formed a close-knit community. Most Presbyterian ministers were local men, serving the middle-class, mainly farming, communities, from which they came.

7.2. On the other hand, while Anglican ministers were likely to come from the educated middle classes, their adherents were more broadly representative of society in general. There is no doubt that evangelical outreach strategies introduced an element of rivalry into inter-church relations, but the most contentious area of competition was between Catholicism and the different branches of Protestantism.

8. Religious competition

8.1. Protestant Evangelicalism, vibrant and enthusiastic, was also assertively anti-Catholic, and hostility between the two major branches of Christianity became a marked feature of nineteenth-century Irish life. Many voluntary British religious agencies had made Ireland one of the chief targets for their conversionist zeal from around 1800. These established schools and distributed religious tracts and bibles. Their use of the Irish language to win over the peasantry was particularly irritating to the Catholic hierarchy. Against this background – and in the broader context of poor harvests, tithe wars, and the growth of Orangeism – the 1820s witnessed a version of rural millenarianism. This was based on the prophecies of Pastorini, a pseudonym of Charles Walmsley, a Catholic bishop and mathematician (1722–97). His millennial text, *A general history of the Christian Church* ..., written in 1790, predicted the downfall of Protestantism in 1821–5 and the triumphant emergence of the Catholic Church. A source of considerable embarrassment to the Catholic hierarchy, Pastorini was reported to be a household name in the South in 1822–3, especially in the Limerick area. His prophecy was widely believed in Ireland and the sixth edition of his book was published in Cork in 1820. Within a few years, however, the Catholic Emancipation campaign absorbed many of the feelings that had earlier found expression in agrarian violence and in the mood of millenarian expectation that had made Pastorini so popular.

8.2. The years 1826–7 saw the beginning of a more concerted evangelical challenge to Catholicism. The so-called 'Second Reformation' began in Co. Cavan with reports of the conversion of several tenants of the evangelical landlord, Lord Farnham. Accusations of proselytism quickly followed and were angrily refuted. However, the vulnerability of the tenantry (the linen industry in the area had virtually collapsed) and the extensive influence of the Farnhams were obviously significant factors. A challenge to the popularity of Daniel O'Connell's Catholic Association, the Second Reformation movement also testified to the evangelical belief in religious solutions to political problems. As with the teaching and Bible societies, the underlying motivation was the view that the only way to solve Ireland's problems was conversion to Protestantism, not concession to political demands. By October 1827 it was reported that there were 783 converts in Co. Cavan, but the 'Reformation' had little direct impact on other areas. Protestant evangelicals again came under attack in 1831, when famine on Achill Island inspired the Irish-speaker, the Revd Edward Nangle, to establish a Protestant settlement there, to teach and convert the Catholic population. He had a school that attracted 420 children within a year and a printing press dedicated to publishing attacks on 'the idolatry of the Roman Mass'. This made Nangle's settlement a focal point for evangelical visitors and, during the Famine of the 1840s, a target for accusations of 'souperism', the use of food as bribery to win converts.

8.3. The Reformation movement was also concerned to draw attention to the distinctions between Catholic and Protestant doctrine, and to this end organised a series of great public meetings. Reports of attendance at these meetings, where Catholic and Protestant clergy hotly debated theological questions, are varied. They usually continued for several days and stirred up considerable religious tension. While the number of converts to Protestantism was probably insignificant, these public confrontations both fed upon, and contributed to, the sectarian disturbances of the period. It has also been said that the necessity of defending Catholic doctrine united all classes in defence of the ancient faith, and in fact probably served to entrench Catholicism in the minds of the ordinary people.

8.4. For many members of the ascendancy class, the election of Daniel O'Connell and the granting of Catholic Emancipation, provoked fears for the future of Protestantism. Their anxiety was increased by the government's educational policies, which had been designed to put an end to the religious competition in schools. The National System of Education, introduced in 1831, aimed to bring all children together for general instruction while separating them for religious doctrine. However, the idea of providing inter-denominational education served mainly to increase denominational rivalry, and the hostility of both Catholic and Protestant clergy forced the government to compromise on its principles. Control of schooling by the Churches was not easily given up. Religious conflict also marked developments in higher education. Trinity College Dublin, though attended by some middle- and upper-class Catholics, was largely a stronghold of the Anglo-Irish, and the Catholic hierarchy banned attendance there. The government's plans to establish provincial non-sectarian colleges in Cork, Galway and Belfast in 1848 also failed to meet religious demands. The Queen's Colleges, linked two years after their formation as constituent colleges of Queen's University, were dubbed 'godless' by the Catholic hierarchy. The Catholic bishops founded an alternative Catholic University in Dublin in 1854, with Cardinal Newman as its head, but it struggled to survive. The 'University Question' (as it was called) remained largely unresolved until the early twentieth century.

9. Popular culture in pre-Famine Ireland

9.1. In the early nineteenth century education was also available in Sunday Schools attached to the various Churches. While there were schools throughout the country, they were particularly important in Ulster where the proportion of Sunday scholars to population was 1:14 in 1831. In addition to their specifically religious objectives, Sunday Schools were expected to instil good manners, sound morals, and respectable appearance. However, for the children who attended, they also offered educational and recreational facilities, and made a distinctive contribution to working-class culture through their anniversary celebrations, street parades, Whitsun outings, book prizes, and benefit societies.

9.2. Apart from education, another recurring theme in the evangelical crusade for moral reformation was temperance. Drunkenness was regarded as the prime cause of sexual immorality, gambling, broken homes, poverty, and social strife. The impetus for temperance societies originated in America, it was taken up by local clergy of various denominations, and with the support of influential laymen it spread rapidly throughout the province. By 1833, only four years after the first plans were published, there were 15,000 members of temperance societies in Ulster. The emphasis of these societies was on moderation rather than total abstention. The teetotal movement which was led by Fr Theobald Mathew (1790–1856), began in 1838 and was a popular Roman Catholic crusade against 'all intoxicating liquors', and its medals, speeches, bands, and banners provided a lively alternative to pub-based culture. Not only priests and evangelicals, but employers, landlords, radicals, and reformers in general supported the 'improving' movement, each viewing the advantages of a sober working class in a different light. The interest of employers in promoting the sobriety of their work force is self-evident, but Catholic nationalists were also convinced that the self-respect and self-esteem arising from sobriety could advance not only moral but political aspirations. Around five million people were estimated to have taken the pledge in the first five years of Father Mathew's movement.

9.3. A decline in the popularity of whiskey drinking and general drunkenness was noted by many visitors and commissioners in this period, but the problem of drunkenness in Ireland was by no means solved. Many thousands remained unmoved by the crusade while the resolutions of others were all too short-lived. Nor should all the responsibility for the reported decline in alcoholic consumption be attributed to the work of temperance campaigners. The introduction of revenue police and the reduction of duty on whiskey were undoubtedly significant factors in reducing the numbers of 'shebeens' and the local customs and festivities which surrounded them, while the increased supervision of 'improving' landlords and their agents was a further effective deterrent.

9.4. Secret societies and faction fights, an important part of rural Irish society in the late eighteenth and early nineteenth century, did not die out completely. However, they were declining in significance, aided by the condemnations of the clergy and of Daniel O'Connell and, from 1836, the presence of the Royal Irish Constabulary. The Famine greatly accelerated social changes already under way. The portrayal of pre-Famine Ireland in literature is very significant for social history. The work of William Carleton (1794–1869) is an important source. Carleton's own hedge-school education and carefree youth provided him with abundant materials for the lively tales of Irish peasant life which are an important part of our cultural heritage. Close familiarity and direct experience give life and vigour to his portrayals of local events and characters. *Traits and stories of the Irish peasantry*, first published in 1830–3, went though several editions. While writers such as Charles Lever (1806–72) and Samuel Lover (1797–1868) contributed to the popular image of the stage Irishman as a drunken buffoon, Carleton's vivid portrayals reflected a wider experience. His stories of wakes and weddings, faction fights, country dances, drinking dens, and sporting rivalries – events at the very core of community life – prompted J.M. Synge (1871–1909), the playwright, to call Carleton the 'father of Irish literature'.

9.5. There was, however, at least at intellectual levels, growing opposition both to the stereotypical view of Irish life, and the gradual encroachment of England evidenced in sports, literature, music-hall entertainment and, importantly, in the decline of the Irish language. The Royal Irish Academy, founded in 1785, had become the centre for scholarly study of Ireland's ancient civilisation. Editions and translations of Gaelic poetry, legends, and sagas were published by poets and scholars such as James Clarence Mangan,

John O'Donovan, Eugene O'Curry and others. O'Donovan published his monumental edition of the *Annals of the Four Masters* in 1848–51, revealing the rich sources in Irish for the medieval history of the Irish church and of society; O'Curry edited and translated medieval sagas and tales; and Bishop William Reeves and Dr J.H. Todd studied the early centuries of Irish Christianity. They drew scholarly attention to a country that developed an outstanding literary and religious culture in the early middle ages, a land of saints and scholars whose missionaries and teachers made a major contribution to the creation of Europe's Christian civilisation. Their work was particularly important because it provided a new set of symbols for Ireland. George Petrie edited a very important popular but high-quality magazine, the *Dublin Penny Journal*. It carried well-crafted articles on Irish antiquities and history, many written by himself. Sir Samuel Ferguson wrote in 1840 of its important role in 'bringing back to the light of intellectual day, the already recorded facts by which the people of Ireland will be able to live back, in the land they live in'. Later, Petrie established the *Irish Penny Journal* to inform the people at large of Irish cultural achievements in the past.

9.6. The approach of Thomas Davis in the 1840s was something new: cultural nationalism and the creation of an Irish identity in English. He took Ireland's past from the scholars and brought it to the people. He and his associates popularised Ireland's cultural heritage – in story, in history, in rousing ballads – to re-affirm 'the pedigree of her nationhood', to rekindle a pride in her history and language. The Young Ireland movement (and here Davis played a leading part, together with the Catholic journalist Charles Gavan Duffy and the Catholic barrister John Blake Dillon) was strongly influenced by wider European romantic nationalism. Young Ireland spread its ideas through *The Nation*, its weekly newspaper. The movement never won mass support, and its attempted rising in 1848 was doomed from the start. Nonetheless, its legacy is impressive. Later generations built on Young Ireland's concern for Irish culture – the Irish language, Irish music, art and history.

10. Catholicism after the Famine

10.1. The Great Famine was the most serious disaster of the century, an 'event of cosmic significance' during which superstition and fears were rife. Research suggests that the initial Catholic folk interpretation of the Famine was in terms of a supernatural judgement, God's wrath and divine punishment of the people's sins, a view apparently encouraged by the Church. It does indeed seem that the psychological shock of these years led to an increase in religious faith and practice. The loss of around two million of the poorest of its people ensured that the Catholic Church emerged from the period of Famine in a stronger position to carry out its pastoral role. Indeed, it has been claimed that the confidence and progress of Irish Catholicism between 1850 and 1875 was marked by a 'Devotional Revolution'.

10.2. A major factor in the shaping of the Church in these years was the leadership of Paul Cullen. He arrived in Ireland from Rome as papal delegate and archbishop of Armagh in 1850, was translated to Dublin in 1852, and became Ireland's first cardinal in 1866. As a reformer and ecclesiastical politician, Cullen created the modern Irish Catholic Church, regulated its clergy and its practices, and bound it closely to Rome. His work benefited from the progress made in the first half of the nineteenth century, and the changed conditions following the Famine. Cullen strengthened the relationship between a more devout people and a more disciplined clergy. The Synod of Thurles, convened by Cullen in 1850, marked the beginning of a more tightly controlled religious regime. The ratio of priests to people had been reduced to 1:1250. As a result of an increased government grant to Maynooth, after 1845, many of these priests were more likely to be from the lower ranks of Catholic society. Cullen's leadership was Rome-centred (Ultramontane) and he was keenly aware of the danger of an Irish-based nationalistic Catholicism (Gallicanism), of which Archbishop John McHale of Tuam was a volatile and outspoken advocate. Cullen, a skilled diplomat, easily outplayed him. Cullen was deeply hostile to the physical force tradition in Irish politics, and he strongly condemned the Fenian movement. However, he was primarily an ecclesiastical reformer, deeply committed to the papacy and anxious to make the Irish Catholic Church conform, to the fullest possible extent, to the ideal Roman model.

10.3. The results of these combined circumstances were already clear by the end of this period. The celebration of the sacraments in the home became a rare occurrence; confession and communion were much more frequent; the number of Sunday sermons increased; and more people than ever attended mass. Many new churches were built; and new Roman-style devotions flourished. Retreats and parish missions organised by the religious orders provided the opportunity for spiritual renewal and a proliferation of confraternities and sodalities encouraged religious practice amongst the laity. A massive increase in the numbers of religious orders influenced all levels of Catholic social life and religious practice. The number of nuns, which stood at 120 in 1800, had risen to 3,700 by 1870. Teaching orders of brothers, particularly the Irish Christian Brothers, also substantially increased in number. Through their work in schools in particular, this *para-clerical* church personnel had a powerful influence on the youth and did much to ensure the dominance of a strict Catholic ethos. As many have remarked, the sexually conservative nature of late nineteenth-century Ireland was one consequences of the Church's increased control, especially of the middle classes.

11. Post-Famine Protestantism

11.1. One of the few high points in nineteenth-century Protestant religious life occurred in Ulster in 1859. Known as the 'Second Great Awakening', this religious revival which swept over much of the province shows how Evangelicalism had infiltrated mainstream religion by the middle of the nineteenth century. Although the Presbyterian heartlands of Antrim and Down were most strongly affected, the counties of Londonderry and Tyrone also witnessed the 'miraculous manifestations, marvellous conversions and mysterious prostrations' that characterised the 'Great Revival'. Methodists and Anglicans were also affected, but Catholics remained largely immune.

11.2. Although the roots of the revival can be found in the gradual spread and growing acceptance of evangelical activity in all Protestant Churches from the beginning of the nineteenth century, this particular outbreak of religious excitement began amongst a group of young men who met together for prayer, and the laity played a key role in sustaining and spreading the movement. The original converts, on praying and preaching tours throughout the countryside, caused great excitement in churches and meeting houses. While many Protestant clergy welcomed what was claimed as a genuine outpouring of the spirit, some took a more cautious approach because of the physical phenomena that often accompanied dramatic conversions. The physical prostrations, faintings and 'strikings down', which were the most controversial characteristics of the 1859 revival, were felt by some to be fraud or delusion and, although they affected only a minority of converts, they caused considerable local excitement.

11.3. Promoters of the revival made great claims for its success, estimating that they had made around 100,000 converts in all. These statistics must, however, be treated with caution as many 'converts' were probably those on the periphery of church rather than drunkards, villains and the like. Another significant consequence of this period of revivalism was the growth of those denominations that required a more visible and positive commitment from their adult members; for example, the Plymouth Brethren particularly benefited. It is unlikely that the revival had such a direct effect on the lives of most ordinary men and women, though one would imagine that in small, close-knit communities the pressure to conform might be considerable. Most importantly, the revival gave a boost to Protestant confidence on the eve of further political assaults.

11.4. It is ironic that the Church of Ireland was being undermined by political events beyond its control just when administrative reform and evangelical zeal made its pastoral mission more efficient. But Disestablishment, the separation of church and state, an almost inevitable consequence of the Liberal government's attempts to deal with the problems of Ireland, united Protestants of all creeds against the perceived threat from Catholicism; for example, the Presbyterian leader Henry Cooke headed an emotional display of Protestant solidarity in Hillsborough in 1867. It was one of the major demonstrations against Gladstone's policy. Such instances of solidarity temporarily overcame narrower theological distinctions. However, when it came in 1869 (Irish Church Act), Disestablishment was on favourable terms. Protestant interests were looked after and proper provisions were made for the Church of Ireland's future. A Temporalities Commission was established to manage church revenue and the Representative Church Body was set up to deal with legal and administrative matters. It has been argued that the constitutional withdrawal of the British government from religion in Ireland left the Churches free to focus on their pastoral and spiritual mission.

12. Sectarianism

12.1. What really united the Protestant denominations was anti-Catholicism, and during the second half of the nineteenth century tensions between the broad religious communities frequently spilled over into violent sectarian conflict. In 1849, for example, at Dolly's Brae near Castlewellan in Co. Down, a clash between Ribbonmen and Orangemen resulted in several deaths.

12.2. While such rural conflicts had been common since the late eighteenth century, demographic shifts brought sectarianism to Belfast where it was to have lasting impact on culture, politics, and religion. The proportion of Catholics in the city, estimated at 16 per cent in 1808, had increased to 31.9 per cent by 1871 and, while religious riots in the town were rare before 1830, in the following decades sectarian clashes became more frequent and more violent. Competition for jobs and the activities of the Orange Order were contributory factors but so, too, were the popular and controversial outpourings of evangelical preachers. Anglican Thomas Drew and Presbyterian Hugh Hanna are prime examples of clerical leadership which, by graphically denouncing the 'errors' of Rome in open-air sermons, contributed to outbreaks of sectarian rioting. Thus the religious leadership, whether from Sunday morning pulpits or the speakers' platform at the Great Protestant meetings in Hillsborough, carried a weighty responsibility. Their sermons often determined the nature of local community relations.

13. Post-Famine culture

13.1. A major consequence of social change in these years was the decline of the Irish language. The regions and the social classes where Irish was most prevalent were hardest hit by the Famine, emigration, and the subsequent process of change. The language was increasingly seen as 'old-fashioned', here signifying poverty and ignorance rather than tradition and culture. The usual language of 'modern' everyday life – newspapers, schools, administration, and religion (whether Catholic or Protestant) – was English, and in a world where all these were becoming increasingly important the Irish language was bound to decline.

13.2. Although not solely responsible for the decline in the Irish language, the National System of Education did help to bring about mass literacy in English. When this was combined with changes in the methods of book production and in printing technology, the printed word in English became more readily available to all classes. Most medium-sized towns had at least one bookshop. In smaller towns and villages throughout the country, books could be bought, or even hired in the local grocery stores. Chapmen, itinerant small traders who plied their wares – clothing, combs, and small items of hard-ware – from door to door in country areas, also carried books. Reading materials were also available through a range of libraries. Despite the passage of the Public Libraries (Ireland) Act of 1855, rate-supported libraries were very slow to start. While subscriptions to commercial libraries were beyond the reach of many, landlords and clergy, intent on improvement, frequently established their own lending libraries.

13.3. The material available to the new reading public was diverse and generally reflected a culture beyond the shores of the island. Traditional tales such as *Aesop's Fables* or the *Arabian Nights*, tales of travel, adventure or disaster, and histories were all popular, as were cheap translations of French novels. Indeed the popularity of these was a matter of concern for religious bodies who themselves swamped the market with religious tracts and pamphlets. Specifically Irish material was more limited, though the theme of the Rebellion of 1798 did attract some writers, and collections such as *Irish Legendary Tales* and *Royal Hibernian Tales* were available. By mid-century, cheap editions of quality lit-erature were also being made available through series such as the *Parlour Library*. Newspapers were, of course, an important source of news, opinions, and information although until 1861 high taxation limited their circulation. However, they were widely read, they passed around in reading rooms and public houses, and their contents were discussed at length in a variety of venues.

13.4. In terms of culture more generally, a combination of secular and religious influ-ences had an effect on behavioural patterns during this period. Changes in farming methods, urbanisation, industrialisation, and a shift to a money economy led to the greater regularisation and organisation of leisure time. The influence of the Churches has already been noted. It seems that, generally speaking, a more 'respectable' and religious strong-farmer culture was replacing the old habits of the shebeens and riotous wakes. Nonetheless, weddings and funerals, hiring fairs and markets, the departure or return of emigrants, and harvest homes were all occasions of sociability, merriment, music, and dancing. In rural areas, 'crossroads' dancing was common on summer Sunday evenings while even in the Dublin slums, tenement families enjoyed gossip and regular 'hooleys'. Ballads and music, passed on from one generation to the next, were enjoyed in a range of venues, from humble cottages, to city streets to community gatherings of all kinds.

13.5. The new railway network was also important, enabling individuals, couples, and families to travel to the seaside or countryside for day trips, weekends, or even longer periods during Easter and summer holidays. While holidays were a rare luxury for the poor, they were a way of life for the wealthy and were made easier by the advances in travel. The London season was viewed in upper-class circles as an essential cultural and social opportunity – a time for the women to catch up on the latest fashions and for the men to renew acquaintances at their clubs, while both enjoyed the latest plays. Visits to the cultural centres of Europe were regular, and were seen as being particularly impor-tant educational experiences for upper-class young men and as providing the 'finishing' touches to the education of wealthy young women. 'Culture' was, of course, also available at home, and light opera was on offer at several venues. Between 1841 and 1867 twenty-two different music societies were founded for the middle and upper classes. Larger audiences enjoyed the programmes of *Grand National Concerts of Irish Music*, consisting of more popular tunes, such as *Moore's Melodies*.

13.6. While cultural, as well as religious experience, was diverse and multi-faceted, the influence of Ireland's dominant neighbour was strong. In the last decades of the nineteenth century, the nationalist challenge to this creeping Anglicisation, mostly the work of the Gaelic League (*Connradh na Gaeilge*), resulted in the resurgence of a Catholic Irish culture which, being both Gaelic and Catholic, would greatly strengthen one aspect of culture at the expense of a more inclusive diversity.

MYRTLE HILL

CHAPTER 4

The Great Famine, 1845–9

Malone: … My father died of starvation in Ireland in the black '47. Maybe you
heard of it?
Violet: The Famine!
Malone (with smouldering passion): No, the Starvation. When a country is full of
food, and exporting it, there can be no famine. Me father was starved dead;
and I was starved out to America in me mother's arms. English rule drove me
and mine out of Ireland …

George Bernard Shaw, *Man and Superman* (1903)

God sent a curse upon the land because her sons were slaves;
The rich earth brought forth rottenness, and gardens became graves;
The green crops withered in the field, all blackened by the curse,
And wedding gay and dance gave way to coffin and to hearse.

Anonymous poet, 1849

1. Famine in Ireland: comments of the Duke of Wellington (1830)

Famine is a failure in food supplies over a prolonged period in a whole society, or in a large
part of it. It was common in Ireland, as elsewhere, in the eighteenth and early nineteenth
centuries. Politicians were well aware of the underlying causes of scarcity and hunger though
they did little to tackle them. For example, on 7 July 1830 the Duke of Wellington wrote:

1.1. I confess that the annually recurring starvation in Ireland, for a period dif-
fering, according to the goodness or badness of the season, from one week to
three months, gives me more uneasiness than any other evil existing in the
United Kingdom.

1.2. It is starvation, because it is the fact that, although there is an abundance of
provisions in the country of a superior kind, and at a cheaper rate than the same
can be bought in any other part of Her Majesty's dominions, those who want in
the midst of plenty cannot get, because they do not possess even the small sum
of money necessary to buy a supply of food.

1.3. It occurs every year, for that period of time that elapses between the final consumption of one year's crop of potatoes, and the coming of the crop of the following
year, and it is long or short, according as the previous season has been bad or good.

Note these rough equivalents in estimating Famine donations: $1=€21; £1=€86; 1s.=€4.30; 1d.=€0.36 approx.
at 2009 values. There were 20 shillings/pound and 12 pence/shillling, and thus 240 pence/pound.

1.4. Now when this misfortune occurs, there is no relief or mitigation, excepting recourse to public money. The proprietors of the country, those who ought to think for the people, to foresee this misfortune, and to provide beforehand a remedy for it, are amusing themselves in the Clubs in London, in Cheltenham, or Bath, or on the Continent, and the government are made responsible for the evil, and they must find the remedy for it where they can – anywhere excepting in the pockets of Irish Gentlemen. Then, if they give public money to provide a remedy for this distress, it is applied to all purposes excepting the one for which it is given; and more particularly to that one, *viz.* the payment of arrears of an exorbitant rent.

1.5. However, we must expect that this evil will continue, and will increase as the population will increase, and the chances of a serious evil, such as the loss of a large number of persons by famine, will be greater in proportion to the numbers existing in Ireland in the state in which we know that the great body of the people are living at this moment.

[Wellington to Northumberland, 7 July 1830, in *Despatches*, vii, 111–12; repr. in P.S. O'Hegarty, *A history of Ireland under the Union* (London, 1952), 291–2]

2. The Great Famine

2.1. The Great Famine or 'Great Hunger' of 1845–9 is the most important event in modern Irish history. It was the worst catastrophe in modern European history before the twentieth century. If one judges famine by the percentage of the population that dies of it and its effects, it was the worst famine in modern times. It was caused, in the first place, by the failure of the potato on which about one third of the population depended for survival. The potato was attacked by the fungus *Phytophthora infestans*, previously unknown, which came to Europe from North America.

2.2. This caused a crisis that the government failed, in general, to cope with. The near complete failure of the potato crop made disaster on an unprecedented scale inevitable unless other food could be provided. As Cormac Ó Gráda writes:

> The Irish famine relief effort was constrained less by poverty than by ideology and public opinion. Too much was expected of the Irish themselves, including Irish landlords. Too much was blamed on their dishonesty and laziness. Too much time was lost on public works as the main vehicle of relief. By the time food was reaching the starving through the soup kitchens, they were already vulnerable to infectious diseases, against which the medical science of the day was virtually helpless. Too much was made of the antisocial behaviour inevitable in such crisis conditions. Too many people in high places believed that this was a time when, as *The Times* put it, 'something like harshness is the greatest humanity' ... Most important, public spending on relief went nowhere near the cost of

plugging the gap left by the failure of the potato … a shortfall of about £50 million (approx. €4.3 billion at 2009 values) in money … exchequer spending on
famine relief between 1846 and 1852 totalled less than £10 million (approx. €860
million).

[Cormac Ó Gráda, *Black '47 and beyond: the Great Irish Famine in history, economy, and memory*
(Princeton, NJ, 1998), 82–3]

2.3. The government's reaction to the crisis was slow. Food continued to be exported
from Ireland and arrangements for the importation of other foods were not effective.
The Revd Dr McEvoy, parish priest of Kells, wrote in October 1845:

On my most minute personal inspection of the potato crop in this most fertile
potato-growing locale is founded my inexpressibly painful conviction that one
family in twenty of the people will not have a single potato left on Christmas day
next. Many are the fields I have examined and testimony the most solemn can I
tender, that in the great bulk of those fields all the potatoes sizable enough to be
sent to table are irreparably damaged, while for the remaining comparatively
sounder fields very little hopes are entertained in consequence of the daily rapid
development of the deplorable disease. With starvation at our doors, grimly star-
ing us, vessels laden with our sole hopes of existence, our provisions, are hourly
wafted from our every port. From one milling establishment I have last night
seen not less than fifty dray loads of meal moving on to Drogheda, thence to go
to feed the foreigner, leaving starvation and death the sure and certain fate of the
toil and sweat that raised this food. For their respective inhabitants England,
Holland, Scotland, Germany, are taking early the necessary precautions – getting
provisions from every possible part of the globe; and I ask are Irishmen alone
unworthy of the sympathies of a paternal gentry or a paternal government? Let
Irishmen themselves take heed before the provisions are gone. Let those, too,
who have sheep, and oxen, and haggards. Self-preservation is the first law of
nature. The right of the starving to try and sustain existence is a right far and
away paramount to every right that property confers …

[*The Nation*, 25 October 1845; repr. in P.S. O'Hegarty, *A history of Ireland under the Union* (London,
1952), 293]

2.4. Others nearer the administration made similar complaints. The Mansion House
Committee, of which the Duke of Leinster and Lord Cloncurry were chairmen,
addressed a Resolution to the Lord Lieutenant of Ireland, Lord Heytesbury, in
November 1845:

We have ascertained beyond any shadow of doubt, that considerably more than
one-third of the entire potato crop in Ireland has already been destroyed by the
potato disease; and that such disease has not, by any means, ceased its ravages,
but, on the contrary, is daily extending more and more; and that no reasonable

conjecture can be formed with respect to the limits of its effects, short of destruction of the entire remaining potato crop ... our information on the subject is positive and precise and is derived from persons living in all the counties of Ireland, from persons of all political opinions and from clergymen of all religious persuasions. We are thus unfortunately able to proclaim to all the inhabitants of the British Empire, and in the presence of an all-seeing Providence, that in Ireland famine of a most hideous description must be immediate and pressing, and that pestilence of the most frightening kind is certain and not remote, unless immediately prevented ... That we arraign in the strongest terms, consistent with personal respect to ourselves, the culpable conduct of the present administration, as well in refusing to take any efficacious measure for alleviating the present calamity with all its approaching hideous and necessary consequences; as also for the positive and unequivocal crime of keeping the ports closed against the importation of foreign provisions, thus either abdicating their duty to the people or their sovereign, whose servants they are, or involving themselves in the enormous guilt of aggravating starvation and famine, by unnaturally keeping up the price of provisions, and doing this for the benefit of a selfish class who derive at the present awful crisis pecuniary advantages to themselves by the maintenance of the oppressive Corn Laws ... that the people of Ireland, in their bitter hour of misfortune, have the strongest right to impeach the criminality of the ministers of the Crown, inasmuch as it has pleased a merciful Providence to favour Ireland in the present season with a most abundant crop of oats. Yet, while the harbours are closed against the importation of foreign food, they are left open for the exportation of Irish grain, an exportation which has already amounted in the present season to a quantity nearly adequate to feed the entire people of Ireland, and to avert the now certain famine; thus inflicting upon the Irish people the abject misery of having their own provisions carried away to feed others, while they themselves are left contemptuously to starve ... *Signed* John L. Arabin, Lord Mayor of Dublin.

[John O'Rourke, *A history of the Great Irish Famine* (3rd ed., Dublin, 1902), 65–7; repr. in Colm Tóibín & Diarmaid Ferriter, *The Irish famine: a documentary* (New York, 2002), 47–8]

2.5. The statistics of modern scholars support these statements. In 1845 the excess of exported over imported grain was 485,000 tons; and in 1846 it was 87,000 tons. In 1847, however, Ireland became a net importer of grain, 763,000 tons; and in 1848, 125,000 tons.

3. How many died and who?

3.1. Because of poor data, historians arrive at different estimates of the number of famine fatalities. In the period 1846–51 between 1,000,000 and 1,500,000 people died: we cannot be certain of the number. Besides, births and marriages dropped significantly.

3.2. The upper and middle class, urban and rural, were virtually untouched by hunger. Those hardest hit were the agricultural labourers, the class that had increased most rapidly in numbers in the decades before the Famine. As Karl Marx stated, 'The Irish famine of 1846 killed more than 1,000,000 people, but it killed poor devils only' (*Capital*, i, pt vii, chapter 25). The poor were the first to die and they made up the majority of Famine victims. The unprecedented scale of deaths was not due to starvation alone: infectious diseases such as typhus, relapsing fever and cholera, killed very many.

4. Famine deaths and diseases

4.1. Starvation is a slow killer. First the body uses up all its deposits of fat. The metabolic rate sinks and physical and mental activity declines. Blood pressure falls. The internal organs, including the intestines, degenerate. The skin grows paper-thin, dull, grey, and blotchy. Fluid is retained in the body (famine oedema). Normally, one-third of body weight is lost before death occurs. The final stages are uncontrolled diarrhoea and cardiovascular collapse. Children under the age of five are particularly vulnerable. They suffer from muscle waste, a wizened and shrunken appearance that makes them look like old men and old women, swelling of the abdomen and lower limbs, lesions and darkening of the skin, and diarrhoea.

4.2. Contemporary reports describe these conditions:

> … a vast number of impotent folk, whose gaunt and wasted frames and ghastly, emaciated faces were too obvious signs of the suffering they had endured. The little boys and girls presented a hideous sight. In many instances, their heads had become bald and their faces wrinkled like old men and women of seventy or eighty years of age.
>
> [Thomas Armstrong, *My life in Connacht* (London, 1906), 13; repr. in L.A. Clarkson & E. Margaret Crawford, *Feast and famine: a history of food and nutrition in Ireland, 1500–1920* (Oxford, 2001), 140]

> We entered a cabin. Stretched out in one dark corner … were three children huddled together, lying there because they were too weak to rise, pale and ghastly, their little limbs … perfectly emaciated, eyes sunk, voices gone, and evidently in the last stages of actual starvation. On some straw … was a shrivelled old woman, imploring us to give her something, – baring her limbs partly, to show how the skin hung loose from the bone.
>
> [William Bennett, 'Extracts from an account of his journey in Ireland', *Transactions of the Central Relief Committee of the Society of Friends during the Famine in Ireland 1846 and 1847* (Dublin, 1852), 163; repr. Clarkson & Crawford, ibid.]

4.3. With hunger came the vitamin deficiency diseases such as scurvy, pellagra and xerophthalmia. These get worse the longer starvation continues. Scurvy is caused by lack of vitamin C. Symptoms are swollen bleeding gums with loosened teeth, soreness and stiffness of the joints and lower extremities, excruciating pain, bleeding under the skin and in deep tissues, and eventually death by haemorrhage. It had been rare in Ireland because potatoes have adequate vitamin C. During the Famine it became increasingly common and the sudden deaths of workers on relief schemes can be attributed to scurvy. Pellagra, caused by a lack of niacin (part of the vitamin B complex), is characterised by dermatitis, diarrhoea, and dementia. This was caused by malnutrition, mostly over-dependence on a relief diet of Indian corn. Xerophthalmia (Greek for dry eyes) is an eye disease associated with vitamin A deficiency and malnutrition in general. Children aged from three to five are particularly vulnerable. Symptoms are night blindness and, later, ulceration of the cornea, leading to blindness. All of these conditions were reported during the Famine.

4.4. In famines, most people do not die of hunger but of hunger-related fevers and diseases. The most important of these are typhus, relapsing fever, dysentery, and cholera.

4.5. Epidemic typhus is caused by the bacterium *Rickettsia prowazekii* which is carried by the human body louse (*Pediculus humanus*; Irish *míol cnis*). Lice become infected by feeding off an infected human. When infected lice feed, they defecate. When the person scratches the bite, the faeces (which carry the bacteria) are scratched into the wound or into the mucous membranes. Typhus can also be caught by inhaling the faecal dust of lice in bedding and clothing. The incubation period is seven days. Symptoms are headache, coughing, muscle pain; abrupt onset of high fever, chills, prostration; and mental confusion. By the sixth day, a rash appears on the trunk and spreads, and may become haemorrhagic and necrotic. Other common manifestations are delirium, photophobia, eye pain, kidney failure and enlargement of the spleen. Without modern treatments, nearly 100 per cent of patients die of the disease in epidemic conditions.

4.6. Louse-borne relapsing fever is caused by the spirochete bacterium *Borrelia recurrentis*. No animal reservoir exists. The human body louse is the carrier. The louse feeding on infected humans acquires the bacterium which then multiplies in the gut of the louse. The louse bite itself will not transmit the bacterium to another person. When an infected louse feeds on an uninfected human, the bacteria get in when the victim crushes the louse or scratches the area where the louse is feeding. *Borrelia recurrentis* infects the patient either through the scratches or through mucous membranes (including nasal ones) and then invades the bloodstream. The incubation period is 2–14 days. The patient develops a sudden-onset high fever. The initial episode usually lasts 3–6 days and is usually followed by a single, milder episode. The fever episode may end in a 'crisis' – shaking chills, followed by intense sweating, falling temperature, and low blood pressure. This stage may result in death. After several cycles of fever, patients may develop dramatic central nervous system symptoms such as seizures, stupor, and coma. The disease may also attack heart and liver tissues, causing inflammation of the heart muscle (myocarditis) and inflammation of the liver (hepatitis). Diffuse bleeding and pneumonia are other complications. Death rates from 30 to 70 per cent are usual in untreated patients during epidemics.

4.7. Typhus and relapsing fever spread rapidly where there is poor hygiene and where lice-infested starving people crowded together in workhouses, fever hospitals, feeding centres, and cramped ships without sanitation; and in the squalid, decrepit, and hideously over-crowded urban areas to which famine victims fled. Unwashed clothing and bedding are ideal for the proliferation of lice. Irish mortality rates are those typically reported for untreated typhus and relapsing fever epidemics.

4.8. Dysentery is an illness involving severe diarrhoea, often with bloody faeces, vomiting, septicaemia, and fever. It is caused by the bacterium *Shigella dysenteriae* and is highly contagious. It is a major threat in crowded areas with inadequate sanitation, poor hygiene, and bad water because it is spread by faecal contamination, whether by personal contact or water-borne. Epidemic dysentery is fatal in about 5–15 per cent of cases – particularly to children, the elderly, and the under-nourished. Deaths from dysentery rose sharply in 1846–7, and remained high until 1849.

4.9. Cholera appeared in 1849. It is an acute diarrhoeal disease caused by infection of the intestine by the bacterium *Vibrio cholerae*. When the infection is severe it is characterised by profuse watery diarrhoea, vomiting, and leg cramps. Rapid loss of body fluids leads to dehydration and shock. Without treatment, death can occur within hours. The disease is got by drinking contaminated water or eating contaminated food. In an epidemic, the source is usually the faeces of infected persons and cholera spreads rapidly where there is inadequate treatment of sewage and dirty drinking water. Its effects were most severe about the ports. It was the principal killer after typhus and relapsing fever.

4.10. Mortality from other diseases – especially tuberculosis, measles, and scarlet fever – rose rapidly in a population whose immune system was lowered by hunger and exposure.

5. Health care and workhouses

5.1. Medicine of the mid-nineteenth century had no real understanding of these diseases, and no therapy for most. Doctors could sometimes diagnose but hardly ever cure. Two hundred doctors died in 1847. Sadly, their medical attentions were mostly worthless, and sometimes harmful. Many landlords, clergy, workhouse officials and others who were in regular contact with the poor also died of contagious diseases.

5.2. In any case, most areas lacked hospitals and the health system was too uncoordinated to cope with the emergency. Relief of the poor was deficient. Until 1838 Ireland had no system of poor relief. The provision made in the poor relief system of 1838 (one workhouse per 62,000 persons) was inadequate even in good times: it collapsed when famine struck. Sadly, overcrowded and dirty fever hospitals and workhouses spread disease: they provided the ideal environment for the killer diseases, principally typhus, relapsing fever, and dysentery.

5.3. The workhouses were the nurseries of fever. The *Economist* reported of Castlerea Workhouse on 2 January 1847:

> … the dormitories resembled pig-styes more than habitations of human beings, and the effluvia from them was overpowering to the highest degree.

5.4. Here is a brief extract from a report on conditions in Fermoy Workhouse in March 1847, a building with accommodation for 800 and no fever hospital:

> A pestilential fever is now raging through the house, every room of which is so crowded as to render it impossible to separate the sick from the healthy … All the horrors of disease are aggravated by the foul air engendered by a multiplicity of impurities unavoidable where fifty patients are crowded into a room too small for twenty … On the first of January last, the number in the house was 1,377, from which date to the 8th of March inst. the admissions exceeded the discharges by 917, making a total of 2,294, of whom 543 died … By reason of this over-crowding of the house, the supply of bedding is so short as to render it necessary to place 4 or 5 in many of the beds, & on this day 30 children labouring under disease were found in 3 beds.
>
> [Minute Book, Fermoy Board of Guardians, 1847–8, 10 March 1847; cited in James S. Donnelly, *The land and the people in nineteenth century Cork* (London, 1975), 94]

5.5. Fever spread rapidly in the crowded understaffed under-equipped workhouses, as this extract shows:

> In Ballinrobe the workhouse is in the most awfully deplorable state, pestilence having attacked paupers, officers, and all. In fact, this building is one horrible charnel house [repository for the bones/bodies of the dead], the unfortunate paupers being nearly all the victims of a fearful fever, the dying and dead, we might say, huddled together. The master has become the victim of this dread disease; the clerk, a young man … has been added to the victims; the matron, too, is dead; and the respected esteemed physician has fallen before the ravages of the pestilence, in his constant attendance on the diseased inmates.
>
> This is the position of the Ballinrobe house, every officer swept away, while the number of deaths among the inmates is unknown; and we forgot to add that the Roman Catholic chaplain is also dangerously ill of the same epidemic. Now the Ballinrobe board has complied with the Commissioners' orders, in admitting a houseful of paupers and in striking a new rate, which cannot be collected; while the unfortunate inmates, if they escape the awful epidemic, will survive only to be the subjects of a lingering death by starvation!
>
> We have heard also of the inmates of the Westport workhouse and several of the officers being attacked by fever, but fortunately without any fatal results. Ballina and Swinford, too, have not escaped the dreadful contagion, and Sligo has been fearfully scourged. The Master – for many years a colours sergeant of

the 88th Regiment, who fought through many a bloody field unscathed – has fallen before dire disease, and the paupers are dying in dozens.

[*Mayo Chronicle*, 23 March 1847; repr. in Colm Tóibín & Diarmaid Ferriter, *The Irish famine: a documentary* (New York, 2002), 119]

5.6. Besides, some workhouses were without funds because they had more inmates than they could pay for, and they had to turn away the destitute and the starving. Prisons, too, became places of death.

6. Descriptions of the Famine

6.1. People died in their cabins and on the roadside and many were buried without coffins in mass graves. On 17 December 1846, Mr N.M. Cummins, absentee landlord and justice of the peace in Cork, gave eloquent expression to the miseries of the poor in a letter to the Duke of Wellington:

My Lord Duke, Without apology or preface, I presume so far to trespass on your Grace as to state to you, and, by the use of your illustrious name, to present to the British Public the following statement of what *I have myself seen within the last three days:*

Having for many years been intimately connected with the western portion of the County of Cork, and possessing some small property there I thought it right personally to investigate the truth of the several lamentable accounts which had reached me of the appalling state of misery to which that part of the county was reduced. I accordingly went on the 15th inst. to Skibbereen, and to give the instance of one townland which I visited as an example of the state of the entire coast district, I shall state simply what I saw there. It is situated on the eastern side of Castlehaven Harbour, and is named South Reen, in the parish of Myross. Being aware that I should have to witness scenes of frightful hunger, I provided myself with as much bread as five men could carry, and on reaching the spot I was surprised to find the wretched hamlet apparently deserted. I entered some of the hovels to ascertain the cause, and the scenes that presented themselves were such as no tongue or pen can convey the slightest idea of. In the first six famished and ghastly skeletons, to all appearance dead, were huddled in a corner on some filthy straw, their sole covering what seemed a ragged horse-cloth, and their wretched legs hanging about, naked above the knees. I approached in horror, and found by a low moaning they were alive; *they were in fever* – four children, a woman, and what had once been a man. It is impossible to go through the details – suffice it to say that in a few minutes I was surrounded by a least 200 of such phantoms, such frightful spectres as no words can describe. By far the greater number were delirious, either from famine or from fever. Their demoniac yells are still ringing in my ears, and their horrible images are fixed upon my brain.

My heart sickens at the recital, but I must go on. In another case – decency would forbid what follows, but it must be told – my clothes were nearly torn off in my endeavours to escape from the throng of pestilence around, when my neck-cloth was seized from behind by a grip which compelled me to turn. I found myself grasped by a woman with an infant, *just born*, in her arms, and the remains of a filthy sack across her loins – the sole covering of herself and babe. The same morning the police opened a house on the adjoining lands, which was observed shut for many days, and two frozen corpses were found lying upon the mud floor, *half devoured by rats.*

A mother, herself in fever, was seen the same day to drag out the corpse of her child, a girl about twelve, perfectly naked, and leave it half covered with stones. In another house within 500 yards of the cavalry station at Skibbereen, the dispensary doctor found seven wretches lying, unable to move, under the same cloak – *one had been dead many hours, but the others were unable to move either themselves or the corpse.*

To what purpose should I multiply such cases? If these be not sufficient, neither would they hear who have the power to send relief, and do not, even 'though one came from the dead.'

Let them, however, believe and tremble that they shall one day hear the Judge of all the Earth pronounce their tremendous doom, with the addition, 'I hungered and ye gave Me no meat; thirsty and ye gave Me no drink; naked and ye clothed Me not.' But I forget to whom this is addressed. My Lord, you are an old and justly honoured man. It is yet in your power to add another honour to your age, to fix another star and that the brightest in your galaxy of glory. You have access to our young and gracious Queen – lay these things before her. She is a woman, she will not allow decency to be outraged. She has at her command the means of at least mitigating the sufferings of the wretched survivors of this tragedy. They will soon be few, indeed, in the district I speak of, if help be longer withheld. Once more, my Lord Duke, in the name of starving thousands, I implore you, break the frigid and flimsy chain of official etiquette, and save the land of your birth – the kindred of that gallant Irish blood which you have so often seen lavished to support the honour of the British name – and let there be inscribed upon your tomb, *Servata Hibernia* ('Ireland was preserved by me').

[James Carty, *Ireland from Grattan's Parliament to the Great Famine (1783–1850)* (4th ed., Dublin, 1965), 172–3]

6.2. There are scores of similar reports from elsewhere. A local correspondent of the *Cork Examiner* reported from Tallow, Co. Waterford:

While I am writing these few lines in a miserable cabin there lie the gaunt and ghastly bodies of a mother and her son, found dead in each other's arms by the remaining little boy, who had gone out a day or two before to beg something for their relief. And this morning, before men had left their beds, the same sad postulant was at doors, begging therewith to purchase coffins to consign them to their mother earth.

[Des Cowman & Donald Brady (eds), *Teacht na bprátaí dubha: the Famine in Waterford, 1845–50* (Dublin & Waterford, 1995), 163; repr. in L.A. Clarkson & E. Margaret Crawford, *Feast and famine: a history of food and nutrition in Ireland, 1500–1920* (Oxford, 2001), 141]

7. Landlords and politicians

7.1. Many landlords did their best to provide relief and some suffered great financial hardship in doing so. Others refused to help. Some held that they were already paying enough in the rates that funded the new workhouses created by the Irish Poor Law Act (1838).

7.2. By early October 1845, the British government faced a major crisis in Ireland. This was made clear to it by Irish officials and by politicians such as Daniel O'Connell. In December 1845 O'Connell said:

It is melancholy and deplorable to think of the manner in which the government have delayed opening the ports for the reception of provisions from foreign countries; and see the inevitable result of this tardiness on their part. Other countries are receiving supplies of food from abroad, and securing themselves against threatened scarcity ... Ireland ... is situated in this peculiar position. There never was a richer or more abundant harvest of oats in Ireland than this year. The crop was decidedly more than average in quantity and most excellent in quality ... the produce of the oat harvest is superior to that of the last twenty years; and the breadth grown was unusually large. If our ports were closed against the exportation of this abundant supply of grain, see how advantageous and beneficial it would prove to the great bulk of the population ...

[*The Nation*, 6 December 1845; cited in P.S. O'Hegarty, *A history of Ireland under the Union* (London, 1952), 295]

7.3. On 17 January 1846, O'Connell raised the Famine in the House of Commons:

I have shown you our distress. I have shown you that there are no agricultural labourers, no peasantry in Europe, so badly off ... There are five millions of people always on the verge of starvation. I have shown you from government documents ... that its [Ireland's] people are threatened, that they are in the utmost danger of fearful famine, with its concomitant horrors ... I call upon all the members of this House to join in the most energetic measures to stop the impending calamity. You cannot be too speedy, you cannot be too extensive in your remedies ... death to an enormous amount will be the consequence of neglect.

[*Hansard*, 17 February 1845; repr. in P.S. O'Hegarty, *A history of Ireland under the Union* (London, 1952), 296]

8. Sir Robert Peel

8.1. The Prime Minister, Sir Robert Peel, declared that it was 'wise not to be too liberal' and that the 'greatest dependence must of course be on the spontaneous charity of the landed proprietors and others'. However, he knew well that the government had to act. His main relief measures were those used in earlier Irish famines.

8.2. He appointed a scientific commission to advise the farmers about the potato crop, but that was of no practical value. Peel set up food depots with secretly purchased Indian meal (the meal was known as 'Peel's brimstone'). Some £185,000 (approx. €16 million at 2009 values) was spent on the government's schemes, of which £135,000 (approx. €11.6 million) was recovered through sales of the food by local committees or private customers. Relief schemes were begun in March 1846, giving employment to about 140,000 in building roads, bridges, and piers to improve fishing. However, these schemes were badly run and often corrupt.

9. Lord John Russell and the Whigs

9.1. In the summer of 1846, coinciding with the second more devastating outbreak of the potato blight and the repeal of the Corn Laws (26 June 1846), Peel's government fell and he was replaced by Lord John Russell, who formed a Whig government.

9.2. Russell's government was deeply unsympathetic to Irish suffering. On 17 August 1846 Russell expressed government policy as follows:

> It appeared to the government that, while there should be public works, and these public works should be undertaken under due control, they should not defray the cost of these works from any Parliamentary grant, but that they should be defrayed from a loan to be repaid by the counties ... with reference to the supply of food, the government did not propose to interfere with the regular trade by which Indian corn and other grain food could be brought into that country [Ireland]. He proposed to leave the trade as much at liberty as possible. He believed that the markets would be best supplied without the interference of government ... He did not propose to interfere either with the wholesale or retail trade.
>
> [*The Nation*, 22 August 1846; repr. in P.S. O'Hegarty, *A history of Ireland under the Union* (London, 1952), 306]

10. Public works

10.1. The government's programme of public works proved to be a tragic error, especially in the bitter winters of 1846–7 and 1847–8. Workers were, by law, paid on piece-work, and bad weather reduced their income further. Piece-work also penalised the weak, the elderly, and the undernourished who were not able to labour effectively. Workers were poorly clothed and their health suffered from exposure. Besides, they were too badly fed to do heavy work, and many died of malnutrition. The average pay was 13 pence a day (but often less; for example, 8 pence per day in Skibbereen in December 1846) and not enough to sustain a family because of the steeply rising price of food. Besides, there was fraud, favouritism, and jobbing; and in some cases the truly destitute got little or nothing, as government inspectors themselves report.

10.2. Here is an extract from a report on relief work in Skibbereen, in December 1846:

> Yesterday morning at daybreak, I saw a gang of about 150, composed principally of old men, women, and little boys, going out to work on one of the roads near the town. At that time the ground was covered with snow, and there was also a very severe frost; seeing that they were miserably clad, I remarked to a bystander that it was a miracle that the cold did not kill them even though they had nothing to eat. In less than half an hour, one of them, an old man, named Richard Cotter, was brought on a man's back dying, and I had to give a cart to take him home. In the course of the day, I went out to visit this gang, who were opening a drain inside the fence on the Marsh road, and such a scene I hope I may never again be called upon to witness. The women and children were crying out from the severity of the cold, and were unable to hold the implements with which they were at work; most of them declared they had not tasted food for the day, while others said that but for the soup supplied by the Committee, they must starve. The actual value of the labour executed by these could not average two pence each per day, and to talk of task work to such labourers would be too ridiculous.
>
> [T.H. Marmion, *Cork Constitution*, 17 December 1846; repr. in Cormac Ó Gráda, *Black '47 and beyond: the Great Irish Famine in history, economy, and memory* (Princeton, NJ, 1998), 68]

11. Political economy: market economics and the Famine

11.1. The government's trust in the market was misplaced. Beginning in late 1846, there were widespread reports of profiteering in grain by merchants and retailers, particularly in the grain being imported from the United States. This large-scale profiteering was well known to the authorities. The Irish temperance reformer, Fr Theobald Mathew, worked closely with Famine victims. Writing from Cork on 16 December 1846 to Charles Edward Trevelyan, Assistant Secretary of the Treasury, Mathew stated:

> I deeply regret the abandonment of the people to corn and flour dealers. They charge 50 per cent to 100 per cent profit. Cargoes of maize are purchased before their arrival and are sold like railway shares, passing through different hands before they are ground and sold to the poor.
>
> [repr. in N. Marshall Cummins, *Some chapters of Cork medical history* (Cork, 1957), 114]

11.2. Writing from Limerick to Trevelyan, on 30 December 1846, Deputy Commissary-General Hewetson, an officer of the Relief Commission stated:

Last quotations from Cork: Indian corn, £17 5*s*. per ton *ex* ship; Limerick: corn not on the market; Indian meal £18 10*s*. to £19 per ton. Demand excessive. Looking to the quotations in the United States markets, these are really famine prices, the corn (direct … from the States) not standing the consignee [not costing the merchant] more than £9 or £10 per ton. The commander of an American ship, the *Isabella*, [come] lately with a direct consignment from New York to a [merchant] house in this city, makes no scruple … to speak of the enormous profits the English and Irish [merchant] houses are making by their dealings with the States. One house in Cork alone, it is affirmed, will clear £40,000 (approx. €3.5 million at 2009 values) by corn speculation; and the leading firm here will, I should say, go near to £80,000, as they are now weekly turning out 700 to 900 tons of different sorts of meal … there is so much cupidity abroad, and the wretched people suffering so intensely from the high prices of food, augmented by every party through whose hands it passes before it reaches them …

[John Canon O'Rourke, *The history of the Great Irish Famine of 1847 with notices of earlier Irish famines* (3rd ed., Dublin, 1902), 171; repr. in Colm Tóibín & Diarmaid Ferriter, *The Irish famine: a documentary* (New York, 2002), 182]

12. The poor, their betters and the survivors

12.1. The truly poor were an underclass, exploited and expendable. They could expect little charity from the Irish merchants, shopkeepers, officials, prosperous farmers, and small farmers. *The Nation* pointed out on 12 December 1846, that the widespread increase in arms sales, reported in the newspapers, was not for any revolution. The arms were being bought by comfortable farmers to defend their property and crops from attack and theft by the large numbers of the poor and unemployed who wandered the countryside in search of food.

12.2. It seems that many evicted small farmers and labourers had held sub-leases, not from landlords, but from head tenants and strong farmers who now turned them out. Under pressure from famine, grown children turned out their parents. Fearful of hunger and death, many saved themselves at the expense of neighbours, family, servants, and dependants. In the words of Gearóid Ó Tuathaigh, there was 'a failure of compassion'. People's actions were described by a Quaker observer in 1848 as 'the most unscrupulous … knavery, cunning & falsehood'.

12.3. The survivors' sense of guilt and shame led to 'famine denial' and a transfer of the whole responsibility for starvation and death to others – the government and the landlords. Few families admitted that any of their members died in the Famine or went to the workhouse. After the Famine many districts distanced themselves from the shame of famine: they claimed, wrongly, that they were unaffected, while other areas suffered.

12.4. The poor had long been spiritually neglected by a Roman Catholic clergy whose care was principally for the better-off elements in society. However, in the time of crisis, most clergy of all denominations (though there were exceptions), usually in an unwonted spirit of ecumenical co-operation, were effective advocates of their starving flocks, publicists on their behalf, and tireless helpers in the relief efforts. Besides, clergy of all churches suffered severe losses by ministering, in workhouses and parishes, to the fevered and the dying. In 1847, forty Protestant parish clergy died from famine fever, sufficient evidence of their selfless care for the distressed.

12.5. However, a small minority of Protestant clergymen, mostly evangelical New Reformers, engaged in proselytism, urging the people to change their religion in return for food. This was vigorously denounced by Roman Catholic priests in sectarian terms. The best known of these attempts is Revd Edward Nangle's Protestant colony in Achill, but there were many others. These attempts at conversion generally failed: most converts returned to Catholicism, as the 1861 Census shows, and English support for the Protestant mission in Ireland fell away.

13. Government policy

13.1. Sir Charles Wood, the Chancellor of the Exchequer, and Charles Edward Trevelyan, the Assistant Secretary of the Treasury, were in charge of government relief, such as it was. Both advocated *laissez faire*, and were determined to ensure that the government intervened as little as possible, and then only to help local efforts, not replace them. They believed that Irish landlords should bear the main cost of the relief and called for an end to government relief schemes and to the distribution of food.

13.2. Near-famine conditions throughout Europe led to rising food prices. In Ireland, even where food was available, the starving people could not afford to buy it.

14. Evictions

14.1. When tenants failed to pay their rents, they were evicted. Estimates of how many were evicted because of the Famine vary greatly. Timothy O'Neill estimates that 144,759 families (about 580,000 people) were evicted in the period 1846–54, and that 97,248 families were evicted in 1846–8 alone. Left without housing or means of subsistence other than charity or meagre government relief, eviction was a virtual death sentence for most. *The Times* (London) protested vigorously against the eviction of 300 tenants from the estate of Mrs Gerrard at Ballinglass, Co. Galway, on 13 March 1846:

> How often are we to be told that the common law of England sanctions injustice
> and furnishes the weapons of oppression? How long shall the rights of property

in Ireland continue to be the wrongs of poverty and the advancement of the rich be the destruction of the poor? [*The Times*, 31 March 1846]

14.2. However, as the Famine went on, sympathy lessened. Others sided with the evicting landlords and took harsh view of their hapless and impoverished victims. The *Illustrated London News* commented:

> The truth is that these evictions ... are not merely a legal but a natural process; and however much we may deplore the misery from which they spring, and which they so dreadfully aggravate, we cannot compel the Irish proprietors to continue in their miserable holdings the wretched swarms of people who pay no rent, and who prevent the improvement of property as long as they remain upon it ... it sounds very well to English ears to preach forbearance and generosity to the landowners. But it should be remembered that few of them have it in their power to be merciful or generous to their poorer tenantry ... They are themselves engaged in a life and death struggle with their creditors. Moreover, the greater number of the depopulators are mere agents for absent landlords or for the law-receivers under the courts acting for creditors.
>
> [*Illustrated London News*, 13 October 1849; repr. in Colm Tóibín & Diarmaid Ferriter, *The Irish famine: a documentary* (New York, 2002), 144]

15. Famine relief

15.1. The Poor Law system, never intended to deal with so dreadful a crisis, was completely inadequate. People were dying of hunger and fever in the workhouses, at their gates, and in the countryside. By the end of 1846 the Board of Works was collapsing under the strain. Government grain depots were opened in the West of Ireland in December. There, grain was offered to the starving at the market price plus 5 per cent. Many were too poor to buy it.

15.2. Private relief organisations were established during 1846. The Irish Relief Association raised £42,000 (approx. €3.6 million at 2009 values) and the General Central Relief Committee £63,000 (approx. €5.4 million). The Ladies' Work Association provided clothes. Major attempts to deal with the crisis in the West of Ireland were made by the Society of Friends whose organisers included William Edward Forster and James Hack Tuke. Another organisation, the British Relief Association, collected about £400,000 (approx. €34 million). Queen Victoria gave £2,000 (approx. €172,000).

15.3. Duties on imported corn were finally suspended in January 1847. The Temporary Relief of Destitute Persons (Ireland) Act, generally known as the Soup Kitchen Act, became law in February 1847.

A bitterly ironic ballad comments on the soup kitchens:

> Rejoice and make merry you'll hunger no more
> John Bull will soon send you all victuals galore;

A French cook to dress them, with boiler and pot
And a kitchen well heated, to keep the broth hot.
Two gallons of water, two ounces of drippin'
A quart of this soup with a biscuit to dip in
Will be doled out to stout men, the papers do say
To provide ample feeding throughout a whole day.
'Tis but to be feared they will all grow too fat
Unaccustomed to fare so nutritious as that;
While famine and fever and dysentery
With soup and the poor laws will vanish away.
For John Bull is bountiful, give him his due,
In dealing with others, just, generous too;
If he got our mutton, beef, butter and grain
He's now bringing meal for us over the main …

[*Fermanagh Reporter*, 1 April 1847; repr. in *Clogher Record*, 17 (2000–1), 78–9]

15.4. Although soup became the mainstay of the starving, there were too few soup kitchens and the soup itself was not nutritious. A report from Clones in March 1847 states:

The progress of the Famine in this neighbourhood, despite the various means that have been adopted to check it, is truly alarming. Its sad concomitants, fever and dysentery, are daily carrying off their victims; whole families in town and country are being carried away …. The soup kitchens, no doubt, afford great relief and are keeping many out of the jaws of death, but the number thus sustained when compared to those suffering the horrors of starvation is scarcely worth the naming. It is the very maximum if two out of any ten that are absolutely starving get relief in this way and even those wretched few only receive what is barely necessary to sustain life. If they have families, as is in most instances the case, they must either provide for them in some other way or suffer them to perish. These are simple unvarnished facts which every one in the neighbourhood who pays any attention at all to what is passing before him is fully aware of. It is a matter of almost daily occurrence to see some of these unhappy wretches who could no longer bear up under their afflictions falling in the street through absolute inanity. The police then endeavour to get them into the workhouse where, in general, they expire after a few days. Nor does the workhouse itself present a less frightful picture. The number of deaths in any day during the last week has not been so small as twenty within its walls. It has come to that state that among the living of the inmates there can scarcely be found as many in health as are able to bring to the grave and inter the dead, and while Famine is producing these dreadful effects – so dreadful that it is impossible to contemplate them without shuddering – the land of the poor is lying waste. No preparations are being made by them for another season and how, then, can we expect that next year will bring about a happier state of things? Alas! it seems but an idle hope.

[*Fermanagh Reporter*, 4 March 1847; repr. in *Clogher Record*, 17 (2000–1), 76]

15.5. Lord George Bentinck's bill for a state-aided railway building scheme to provide employment was heavily defeated in the House of Commons in February 1847. In June 1847, a separate Irish Poor Commission was set upon and put in charge of further assistance under the Poor Relief (Ireland) Act, which allowed Boards of Guardians of Workhouse Unions to give outdoor relief to the aged, infirm, and sick poor, and to poor widows with two or more dependent children. It also permitted the Boards to give food to the able-bodied poor for limited periods, but it excluded those holding more than a quarter-acre of land (the infamous 'Gregory Clause'). These were now forced to choose between meagre public relief and any hope that their paltry holding might provide for them.

15.6. Lord John Russell announced that there could be no more relief until the Irish Poor Law rate of five shillings in the pound was collected. Nearly £1 million (approx. €86 million at 2009 values) was raised, frequently by force. Violence increased during the unusually severe winter of 1847–8, especially attacks on rates and rent collectors. The government passed the Crime and Outrage (Ireland) Act in December 1847. A force of 15,000 troops was sent to Ireland and martial law was proclaimed in disturbed districts. Frightened property owners fled the country.

16. Young Ireland and the Irish Confederation

16.1. The more extreme members of Young Ireland, who had formed the Irish Confederation in January 1847, became more aggressive in tone. John Mitchel, a leader of the Confederation, in his newspaper the *United Irishman*, urged the starving people not to pay rents or rates, to resist eviction, to ostracise all who would not co-operate, and to arm themselves. In May 1848, Mitchel was arrested under the Treason-felony Act and sentenced to transportation to Van Diemen's Land (Tasmania, Australia).

16.2. The Confederation's attempt at revolution was farcical. It was led by an élite that was out of touch with the people and that did not understand them, or their mental and physical exhaustion. There were two affrays, both insignificant – 'the battle of Widow McCormack's cabbage patch' in July 1848 near Ballingarry, Co. Tipperary; and an attack on Cappoquin police barracks in September 1849. Membership of the Confederation was made an offence and, like Mitchel, many of its leaders were convicted of treason and transported to Van Diemen's Land. The rebellion fizzled out: the writings and memoirs of the gentlemen rebels were more important than their actions. As agricultural production rose and economic conditions improved, social order was restored.

17. Economic and social background to the Famine

17.1. The causes of the Famine are debated by historians. Its real context was that Ireland was vulnerable and its economy was fragile. By British standards Ireland was poor, and the Irish poor, a third or more of the population, were dangerously dependent on the potato for survival. It cannot be stored for more than a year, and thus good harvests could not compensate for bad. The Irish land system was inefficient and fragile. Relationships between landlord and tenant farmers were difficult, often hostile. Relationships between farmers on the one hand and the cottiers and rural labourers on the other were often bad. Agrarian violence, at different levels, rumbled below the surface.

17.2. The industrial revolution in England devastated cottage industries in Ireland in the 1830s and 1840s, especially the weaving and spinning of textiles, and many hundreds of thousands were left without employment. Thus the numbers dependent on the potato rose dramatically. Investment in the Irish economy was low, and therefore productivity was low. The poor had nothing to invest. Those who had money invested it elsewhere. Most landlords took little interest in the development of their estates, and invested little. British capital was not much invested in Ireland and Irish poverty tended to be seen as the result rather of Irish laziness, incompetence, and even immorality. When the natural disaster of the potato blight struck, Ireland lacked the resources to cope with the crisis by itself; it urgently needed government help.

18. Relations between Britain and Ireland

18.1. The relationship with Britain was problematical. Though both countries were united under the Act of Union and the whole of the United Kingdom was now a free trade area, Ireland was not really considered part of Britain. This point is made eloquently by Isaac Butt, professor of Political Economy at Trinity College Dublin:

> What can be more absurd, what can be more wicked, than for men professing attachment to an imperial constitution to answer claims now put forward for state assistance to the unprecedented necessities, by talking of Ireland being a drain on the *English* treasury. The exchequer is the exchequer of the United Kingdom … If the Union be not a mockery, there exists no such thing as an English treasury … How are these expectations to be realized, how are these pledges to be fulfilled, if the partnership is to be one of loss and never of profit to us? if, bearing our share of all imperial burdens – when calamity strikes upon us we are to be told that we then recover our separate existence as a nation, just so far as to disentitle us to the state assistance which any portion of a nation visited with such a calamity has a right to expect from the governing power? If Cornwall had been visited with the same scenes that have desolated Cork, would similar arguments have been used?
>
> [Isaac Butt, *Dublin University Magazine* 29 (April, 1847), 514; repr. in Colm Tóibín & Diarmaid Ferriter, *The Irish famine: a documentary* (New York, 2002), 185]

18.2. As the American economist and historian, Joel Mokyr, writes:

> Most serious of all, when the chips were down in the frightful summer of 1847, the British simply abandoned the Irish and let them perish. There is no doubt that Britain could have saved Ireland. The British treasury spent a total of about £9.5 million (approx. €817 million at 2009 values) on famine relief … Financed largely by advances from London, the soup kitchen program, despite its many inadequacies, saved many lives. When the last kitchen closed in October 1847, Lord Clarendon wrote in despair to the Prime Minister, Russell: 'Ireland cannot be left to her own resources … we are not to let the people die of starvation'. The reply was: 'The state of Ireland for the next few months must be one of great suffering. Unhappily, the agitation for Repeal has contrived to destroy nearly all sympathy in this country' … A few years after the Famine, the British government spent £69.3 million (approx. €6 billion) on an utterly futile adventure in the Crimea (the Crimean War, 1853–5). Half that sum spent in Ireland in the critical years 1846–9 would have saved hundreds of thousands of lives. It is difficult to reconcile this lavishness with claims that British relief during the famine was inadequate because the problem 'was too huge for the British state to overcome' … The contribution of Westminster to the relief of this horror was a pittance … It is not unreasonable to surmise that had anything like the famine occurred in England or Wales, the British government would have overcome its theoretical scruples and would have come to the rescue of the starving at a much larger scale. Ireland was not considered part of the British community.
>
> [Joel Mokyr, *Why Ireland starved: a quantitative and analytical history of the Irish economy, 1800–1850* (rev. ed., London, 1985), 291–2]

19. Populations and class

19.1. The Famine had many social and economic consequences. It greatly reduced the labouring classes in rural Ireland who had made up much of the population. They lost more to famine and famine fever than any other class.

19.2. Excess deaths, that is, deaths over and above the normal rate, for 1846–51 are reckoned at between a million and a million-and-a-half. The population declined by 2,225,000 in the period 1845–51 from a probable high of 8,200,000.

20. Migrants and economic refugees

20.1. The first Famine migrants fled to Dublin, Cork, and other cities and the bigger towns. They found no welcome. Famine victims, bringing famine fevers, crowded into Dublin. The cost of poor relief rose dramatically, stretching the city's Poor Law unions to their limits. In 1847 the North Dublin Union had to expand its capacity from 2,000 to 4,000. Rising crime filled the prisons, mostly with thieves and beggars (about eight out of ten beggars were from the country). A report of spring 1850 states that the Liberties were full of the fever-stricken from many parts of the country, especially Mayo, Galway and the western counties. Despite Famine deaths, Dublin's population rose from 232,726 in 1841 to 258,361 in 1851, an increase of 11 per cent. It has been argued that this Famine migration into Dublin drove down wages and swelled the pauper population of the city's slums.

20.2. Before the Famine there had been emigration of well over 100,000 a year. Now it rose greatly, and changed in kind. It remained a notable characteristic of Irish society long after the Famine – for much more than a century.

21. Emigration to Britain

21.1. Emigration to Britain, especially to the growing industrial cities, such as Liverpool, Manchester, and Glasgow, was well established long before the Famine; for example, 17.3 per cent of the population of Liverpool in 1841 were Irish. Here, in cities with rapidly expanding populations but without investment in housing, sanitation, and proper water supplies, the Irish were among the poorest and most despised unskilled workers, living in the squalid slums of the industrial revolution. Now, in the face of grim famine at home, migration rose dramatically: large numbers fled Ireland for Britain, most desperately poor and many already had typhus. The new steamers on the Irish Sea and cutthroat competition between the steamship companies reduced transit costs so that all but the truly destitute could afford the fare.

21.2. For many this was the first stage on their way to America. In 1847, more Irish left Liverpool for America than from all the Irish ports combined. For many more, Britain was their final destination. The average length of the Dublin–Liverpool passage was 12–14 hours, but bad weather could double the crossing time. Dublin was the principal port of departure, but most of the passengers came not from Dublin and its surrounds but from the famine-stricken West of Ireland.

21.3. The crossing was often an awful experience. The steamers were organised to carry corn and animals as food for Britain's growing industrial cities, not people. Most travelled on the open deck. This was cold and dangerous: there was no cover, no shelter from bad weather or rough seas, and little sanitation. There was chronic overcrowding. The migrants themselves were poorly clothed, often malnourished, and sometimes already ill. The steamship companies' only concern was profit.

21.4. The following newspaper extract give a flavour of the experiences of some:

> … a vessel called the *Wanderer* has just arrived here [Newport, South Wales] with nearly two hundred of the wretched famished creatures, chiefly from Skibbereen, huddled together in a mass of wretchedness unparalleled. On examining the crowded vessel, it was found that between twenty or thirty starving men, women, and children were lying on the ballast in the hold in dying condition. Their state

was most deplorable and had it not been that surgical and charitable aid was rendered the moment the vessel came alongside the wharf, it is said that many would have been brought ashore dead.

[*Cardiff & Merthyr Guardian*, 12 February 1847; repr. in Frank Neal, *Black '47: Britain and the Famine Irish* (Basingstoke & New York, 1998), 70]

21.5. The evidence of the Liverpool Medical Officers in charge of quarantine is horrendous:

As to the space available to each deck passenger, it may be observed that no portions of the vessels were set apart for such accommodation. The decks and holds were generally filled with cattle, so that even in an uncrowded state there was great difficulty in moving; but when passengers were in such numbers [i.e. 1,000], they were so jammed together in the erect posture that motion was impossible. One woman stated that she had been obliged to sit during the whole of the passage, from the want of room to save herself, while her children were placed under her legs for safety. The common offices of nature, including vomiting from sea-sickness, were consequently done on the spot … The passengers and cattle were therefore indiscriminately mixed together; the sea and urine pouring on their clothes from the animals, and they stood in the midst of filth and mire … The smell from the filth, mire, effects of sea-sickness and the engine, were most intolerable.

[Captain Denham's Report to the Board of Trade, 21 May 1849; repr. in Neal, op. cit., 77–8]

21.6. John Mesnard, the weighmaster of Cork, described the trade as 'disgraceful, dangerous and inhuman'. Appeals were made to the government, by the Liverpool authorities and many others, to regulate the chaotic and cruel passenger traffic between Ireland and England. These were ignored: government would not interfere with business.

Table 1: Irish arriving at Liverpool, 1847–54		
Year	*Passengers*	*Paupers*
1847	296,213	39%
1848	252,772	37%
1849	240,925	33%
1850	251,001	31%
1851	283,503	24%
1852	232,331	34%
1853	233,652	29%
1854	154,489	14%
Total	1,944,886	

(Source: Frank Neal, *Black '47: Britain and the famine Irish* (Basingstoke & New York, 1998), 61)

The Irish who settled in Britain were mostly paupers who had no choice but to live in the slums and survive on handouts and begging. Racked by typhus, relapsing fever, and dysentery, made worse by squalid crowded conditions and undernourishment, many died. Their British hosts treated them with a mixture of kindness, sympathy, contempt, and exasperation, but usually no better and no worse than British paupers. Local Boards of Guardians worked hard to relieve them; government did nothing. When the crisis ended, they were absorbed into the very lowest rank of the British industrial working class, but some rose as publicans and shopkeepers. In Liverpool, Manchester and some other cities, there was a growing Irish Catholic merchant and professional class that provided the leadership of Irish communities that were fed by continuing immigration. Writing in 1848 George Poulett Scrope MP, feared that Irish immigration might 'spread through Britain the gangrene of Irish poverty, Irish disaffection, and the deadly paralysis of industry …' (*How to make Ireland self-supporting* (London, 1848), 28). He need not have worried overmuch. Though there were conflicts and, for a time, 'Little Irelands', assimilation, intermarriage, and slow upward social mobility led to the absorption of most.

22. Emigration to North America

22.1. Emigration to North America had been mainly from Ulster but from 1847 emigrants came mostly from the south and west. Emigration was on a massive scale – about 100,000 in 1846, about 200,000 in 1847, almost 250,000 in 1851.

22.2. The haunting image of the coffin ships entered Irish history and Irish-American communal memory. Some recent historians argue that this is a myth: despite dreadful sufferings, misery, and many deaths, the great majority made it safely to the New World. However, Irish losses were far higher than those of emigrants from other European countries.

23. The voyage to North America: Canada

23.1. Deaths reached 20 per cent on the Canadian route in 1847 and about half the emigrants from Major Denis Mahon's Strokestown estates died in transit. British shipping regulations were lax; transit conditions were harsh; ships were often inferior, especially on the Canadian routes; many vessels were barely modified cargo ships in the British North American timber trade, not passenger ships. Many shipowners and agents were unscrupulous profiteers; 'passage brokers' hawked tickets at inflated prices and fraud was common. The crews were often callous; passengers were given inferior or very little food, and dirty or too little water; and the Famine passengers were very poor (though not the poorest) and were so riddled with disease that many were quarantined on arrival in North America.

23.2. Stephen de Vere, an Irish landlord from Curragh Chase, Co. Limerick, made the passage to Grosse Île in Canada, the quarantine station for Quebec, thirty miles below the city. He reported on the ship and its passengers:

Before the emigrant has been a week at sea he is an altered man. How can it be otherwise? Hundreds of poor people, men, women and children, of all ages from the drivelling idiot of 90 to the babe just born, huddled together, without light, without air, wallowing in filth, and breathing a foetid atmosphere, sick in body, dispirited in heart … the fevered patients lying between the sound in sleeping places so narrow as almost to deny them … a change of position … by their agonized raving disturbing those around them … living without food or medicine except as administered by the hand of casual charity, dying without spiritual consolation and buried in the deep without the rites of the church.

[cited in Cecil Woodham-Smith, *The Great Hunger* (London, 1962; repr. 1965), 221; repr. in Arthur Gribben (ed.), *The Great Famine and the Irish diaspora in America* (Amherst, MA, 1999), 137]

23.3. Some landlords, such as Lord Mounteagle, assisted emigration generously; others, like Lord Palmerston (later British Prime Minister) and Major Denis Mahon of Strokestown (assassinated in late 1847), notoriously shipped destitute tenants to North America. Here is an account by George Mellis Douglas, medical superintendent of Grosse Île, of the first ship of Mahon's tenants to arrive:

The *Virginius* sailed from Liverpool, May 28, with 476 passengers. Fever and dysentery cases came aboard this vessel in Liverpool, and deaths occurred before leaving the Mersey. On mustering the passengers for inspection yesterday, it was found that 106 were ill of fever, including nine of the crew, and the large number of 158 had died in the passage, including the first and second officers and seven of the crew and, the master and steward dying, the few that were able to come on deck were ghastly yellow looking spectres, unshaven and hollow cheeked, and, without exception, the worst looking passengers I have ever seen; not more than six or eight were really healthy and able to exert themselves.

[British Parliamentary Papers, *Colonies – Canada*, vol. 17, 385; repr. in Arthur Gribben (ed.), *The Great Famine and the Irish diaspora in America* (Amherst, MA, 1999), 142]

Nineteen more died while the ship lay at anchor, and ninety died in the quarantine sheds.

23.4. On 26 May 1847, there were 30 vessels with 1,000 emigrants waiting at Grosse Île; on 31 May 1847 there were 40 vessels waiting, stretched in a line two miles long down the St Lawrence river; there were 1,100 cases of fever in the sheds and tents of Grosse Île, short of bedding, sanitation and carers, and just as many ill in ships waiting to disembark; and another 45,000 emigrants were believed to be on the way.

23.5. Some 2,000 of the former tenants of Lord Palmerston, serving Foreign Secretary in Lord John Russell's government, were no better off: many were aged, destitute and almost naked, or helpless widows with young children. They had been misled by false promises of clothing and of between £2 (approx. €172) and £5 (approx. €430) a family on arrival in Canada. A shipload of them that had come in early winter, on 2 November 1847, to St

John, New Brunswick, were so miserable that the City Council protested vigorously against such behaviour by a member of Her Majesty's government. The protests of Mr Adam Ferrie, member of the Legislative Council of Canada, and of the Council of St John, were met with an arrogant and misleading answer from Palmerston's agent. That agent had been denounced by Ferrie as a 'worthless and unprincipled hireling, in whose bosom every principle of humanity and every germ of mercy had become totally extinct'.

24. Emigration to the United States

24.1. Emigration to the United States in an American ship was more expensive, the US Passenger Acts were stricter (and further tightened in spring 1847), and American ships were better crewed. In all, the experience of the emigrants was less grim. In the Atlantic states there were high charges for the admission of paupers and the infirm. Many Irish migrants evaded the rules by landing illegally or by landing in Canada and walking over the border into the US. New York City was the principal point of entry, and the Irish spread out from there into New York state and into the neighbouring states. However, many remained as slum dwellers and low-level labourers, seamstresses, and domestics in close communities in New York City. Three-quarters of the Famine immigrants settled in the US, mostly in the big cities.

24.2. A large Irish-American community came into existence, continuously fed by large-scale immigration from Ireland. Some were highly successful but most were semi-skilled, unskilled labourers, industrial workers, and domestic servants living in strongly Irish neighbourhoods. Because most were impoverished, without capital, education, skills or professions, their rise was slow. In time, they came to dominate the urban politics of New York, Boston and other large cities. Protestant Yankee bigotry kept the iron in their souls.

24.3. Because of the Famine, many Irish-Americans bore a deep hatred of English government in Ireland and they supported every subsequent Irish nationalist movement – cultural, political, and military. Irish-Americans funded the Fenians, Home Rule, the Land League, Connradh na Gaeilge, Sinn Féin, the Irish War of Independence, and other activities. In the post-Famine understanding of things, the British government and the Irish landlords were alone held responsible for the Famine. In the words of Kerby Miller, 'As a result, Catholic Ireland and Irish America emerged from the Famine's terrible crucible more vehemently and unanimously opposed to Protestant England and its Irish representatives than ever before'.

25. Long-term effects of the Famine on Ireland's population

25.1. Dramatic changes in Irish population brought about by the Famine and consequent emigration repositioned Ireland in the scale of European countries: from being a medium-sized one, in terms of population, it became a small one, and getting smaller.

25.2. As Cormac Ó Gráda writes:

> One the eve of the famine, Ireland comfortably out-peopled the whole of Scandinavia, and also contained more people than Benelux. By 1914, both Scandinavia and Benelux would contain more than three times as many people as Ireland. Portugal and Scotland, with fewer people than Ireland in 1845, would contain more in 1914. The population of England and Wales, less than double that of Ireland in 1845, was eight times as high in 1914.
>
> [Cormac Ó Gráda, *Black '47 and beyond: the great Irish Famine in history, economy, and memory* (Princeton, NJ, 1998), 29–30]

26. Social and economic changes

26.1. The Famine brought about major social and economic changes in Ireland. The larger farmers grew more prosperous but landlords' incomes fell. Landlords began to take a closer interest in balancing their rent books than they had done before, and estate management improved. They moved against middlemen who had paid a fixed rent on long leases, and who were largely responsible for the sub-division of land before the Famine. Middlemen and sub-tenants were removed from the land system.

26.2. Some landlords were bankrupted by the Famine. In consequence, the government passed the Encumbered Estates Act in 1848 so that bankrupt landlords (about 10 per cent of them) could sell some or all of their entailed and debt-ridden estates on the open market. This created a market in land; and £20,000,000 (approx. €1.7 billion at 2009 values) worth of land was sold, mostly to new speculator landlords who were no improvement on their predecessors, and many were worse.

26.3. The Famine greatly speeded up the transition from the labour intensive tillage to more profitable livestock farming. One farm in four disappeared between 1845 and 1851, mostly holdings less than 15 acres. The average size of a farm increased: by 1851 about 51 per cent of farms were more than 15 acres, and holdings under 5 acres fell from 24 per cent in 1845 to 15 per cent in 1851. Many historians accept that this was a good thing, but not all.

27. Cultural changes

27.1. The Famine hastened the decline of the Irish language. The areas where Irish was strongest suffered most from famine and emigration. That the proselytising Protestant clergy gave up using Irish in their missions by 1854 is a strong indicator of the rapid decline of the language. The strong farmers were turning to English which they saw as the language of progress and of the future, the passport to positions in the British Empire for their sons and daughters. The Catholic Church was hostile to traditional religious beliefs, 'patterns', and rites at holy wells, enshrined in Irish prayers and devotions to the Irish saints. These had no place in the ultramontane vision of Archbishop Paul Cullen and his likes. The Catholic Church was also hostile to a salty anti-clericalism in Irish songs and folk culture. The Irish-speaking evangelical missionaries, armed with the Irish Protestant translation of the bible, had provoked the bitter hostility of the Catholic clergy, to Irish as well as to their missions. Increasingly, the Irish Catholic Church saw itself as a church with a mission to promote Catholicism throughout the English-speaking world, and in so doing it turned its back on the Gaelic world. Priests preached in English to wholly Irish-speaking congregations and Catholic education for Irish speakers was provided wholly in English.

27.2. Ireland was becoming the land of the 'bold tenant farmer'. Increasingly, he had a dominating influence on the style and attitudes of the countryside (and therefore on the social, political and religious life of the nation as a whole). His careful opinions, cautious politics, orthodox religious beliefs (purged of any troublesome deviant notions), mercenary marriage settlements, unbendingly conservative outlook, and that most dynamic of all desires – the desire to better himself – gave post-Famine Irish society its distinctive traits.

DONNCHADH Ó CORRÁIN

CHAPTER 5

Private responses to the Great Famine

1. Private relief, abroad and at home

1.1. One of the remarkable aspects of the Great Famine was the amount of private relief collected on behalf of the Irish poor, especially following the second crop failure in 1846. Although this money is difficult to quantify, it amounted to at least £2,000,000 (approx. €172 million at 2009 values). A small part of the money was sent to the Scottish poor because the potato crop had also failed in the Highlands of Scotland. During earlier food shortages, in 1822 and 1831, charitable bodies had been set up to provide relief at a local level. Remarkably, the relief given after 1846 was international: donations came from all over the world, even from people who had no connection with Ireland. It cut across religious, national, and economic differences. Help came from groups who were themselves poor, including former slaves in the Caribbean and Native Americans in the United States. Heads of states were also involved – for example, Queen Victoria, the Sultan of the Ottoman Empire, and the President of the United States.

1.2. There was extensive fund-raising in Ireland from all sections of society. Resident landlords were generally involved, although many absentees were criticised for their indifference. Even children were fund-raising; for example, pupils in a school in Armagh City started a subscription for the local poor in 1847. Most private donations and charitable bodies came to an end at the harvest of 1847, partly because donations had started to dry up, but also because people believed the Famine was over. Though private charity was short-lived, it played a vital role in saving lives.

2. Relief organisations

2.1. When the potato blight came back private relief committees were formed in Ireland and Britain. While this was a customary response to distress, the scale of fund-raising by the committees formed after 1846 was unusual. The most important ones were the British Relief Association, the General Central Relief Committee, the Irish Relief Association and the Mansion House Committee. Some committees that had helped in the food shortages of 1822 and 1831 were revived.

2.2. The British Association for the Relief of Distress in Ireland and the Highlands of Scotland (the British Relief Association) was one of the most successful private relief

---

Note these rough equivalents in estimating Famine donations: $1=€21; £1=€86; 1s.=€4.30; 1d.=€0.36 approx. at 2009 values. There were 20 shillings/pound and 12 pence/shillling, and thus 240 pence/pound.

bodies. It was formed in London on 1 January 1847 by Lionel de Rothschild, a Jewish banker and philanthropist, later the first Jewish MP. Of the money that the Association raised, five-sixths went to Ireland and one-sixth to Scotland. A Polish count, Paul de Strzelecki, was appointed to oversee the distribution of money in Ireland. He refused to take any pay for his work and was knighted for his services. One of his most successful schemes was the feeding of children in schools in the West of Ireland. The scheme came to an end in 1848 when the funds of the British Relief Association ran out.

2.3. Some private relief organisations were also set up in Ireland, particularly in Belfast and Dublin. The General Central Relief Committee, formed in Dublin on 29 December 1846, was one of the largest. By the end of 1847, it had given 1,871 grants, ranging from £10 to £400 and it had distributed £61,767 (approx. €5.3 million) in all. It included many prominent and influential people. Two of its trustees were the Marquess of Kildare and Lord Cloncurry. It included the Catholic Archbishop of Dublin, Daniel Murray; the Marquess of Abercorn; the Dean of St Patrick's; the Earl of Erne; Daniel O'Connell MP; and William Smith O'Brien MP. Charitable organisations were formed in Belfast, for example, the Belfast General Relief Fund founded by leading members of the local Church of Ireland and Presbyterian clergy.

3. Fundraising in Ireland

3.1. In folk memory, Irish landlords have generally been condemned for their callous attitude towards their poor tenants. However, the response of landlords was very varied. While some used the distress to evict their tenants, others gave relief in different ways. When the blight came a second time some landlords lowered their rents by 10 per cent. These actions tended to be short-term, especially because landlords themselves had financial problems when taxes rose steeply and income from rents fell.

3.2. Most of the charitable efforts of Irish landlords were concentrated on the early months of 1847. The Marquess of Sligo, a liberal landlord, was chairman of a committee that set up a private soup kitchen in Westport in January 1847. He made an opening donation of £100 (approx. €8,600 at 2009 values) and promised a subscription of £5 a week. Other local gentry and Church of Ireland clergy contributed, and the opening donation rose to £255 (approx. €22,000). In Co. Down, Lord Roden, a landlord well known for his evangelical views and his involvement in the Orange Order, opened a soup shop on his estate where a soup, made of rice and meal porridge, was sold at a penny a quart and potato cake was sold at 12 ounces a penny. Some landlords, such as the Earl of Shannon, also resold soup at less than cost. In Skibbereen, which had been infamous for the sufferings of the people, the Church of Ireland minister, the Revd Caulfield, gave 1,149 people one free pint of soup each day. In Belfast, a privately funded relief committee in Ballymacarrett gave soup to over 12,000 people daily, about 60 per cent of the local population. On some estates rent was reduced or employment provided.

Daniel O'Connell, who owned estates in Co. Kerry, gave his tenants a 50 per cent reduction in rent. Lord and Lady Waterford financed a soup kitchen on their estate, and Maria Edgeworth in Edgeworthstown provided free seed to her tenants. The Earl of Devon sent £2,000 (approx. €150,000) and the Duke of Devonshire £100 to help the tenants on their Irish estates. But not all landlords were generous. The absentee landlord, James Robinson, donated £1 to the Waterford Union for its soup kitchen. Lord Londonderry, one of the ten richest men in the United Kingdom, who owned land in counties Down, Derry, Donegal and Antrim, in addition to property in Britain, was criticised for his meanness: he and his wife gave £30 (approx. €2,600) to the local relief committee, but spent £150,000 (approx. €13 million) renovating their house.

3.3. Within Ireland, some groups and individuals were very actively involved in fundraising. The Irish Art Union organised an exhibition of Old Masters and the proceeds were given to various relief organisations. The Irish Benchers gave £1,000 (approx. €86,000) to the General Relief Fund and the Irish Coast Guards raised £429. The brewer Arthur Guinness made two separate donations of £60 (approx. €5,200) and £100 (approx. €8,600).

4. The Society of Friends (Quakers) and relief

4.1. The Famine attracted assistance from a wide variety of religions, ranging from Hindus in India to Jews and Baptists in New York. The main Protestant churches in Ireland (Church of Ireland and Presbyterian) were actively involved in collecting and distributing relief. The Society of Friends (Quakers) distinguished themselves in charitable work and are warmly remembered for their Famine relief.

4.2. By the mid-nineteenth century, the Quakers had become a predominantly middle- and upper middle-class body, prominent in textiles, shipping, railways, and retailing. The efforts of Irish and English Quakers such as Jonathan Pim and James Hack Tuke to organise relief works were widely praised. Jonathan Pim (1806–85), was the owner, with his brother William Harvey Pim, of the Dublin firm of Pim Brothers, drapers and textile manufacturers. Jonathan Pim was Liberal MP for Dublin, 1865–74, and the first Irish Quaker to sit in Parliament. James Hack Tuke (1819–96), was a banker and was very active in the distribution of relief in Ireland in 1847 and again in 1880. On both occasions he published widely-read and influential accounts of what he had seen. His experiences in 1847 are recorded in *A visit to Connaught in 1847*, where he wrote: 'The culminating point of man's physical degradation seems to have been reached in Erris'. He was accompanied on his relief mission by his fellow Quaker W.E. Forster (later Chief Secretary for Ireland, 1880–2).

4.3. The Quakers were motivated by simple Christian charity and their interventions saved many lives. Like many others, they became involved when the blight returned. In November 1846, at the suggestion of Joseph Bewley, the Central Relief Committee of the Society of Friends was established in Dublin. Joseph Bewley and the Bewley family were tea and coffee merchants who went on to found their well-known Oriental cafes in Dublin and elsewhere. During the Famine, Bewley was joint secretary with Jonathan Pim, of the Central Relief Committee. In the following month, a sister committee was set up in London. Both committees worked closely with their co-religionists in the United States. Though the Quakers in Ireland were small in number – there were only about 3,000 – they played a most important role in providing relief, particularly through soup kitchens. When the government decided to use soup kitchens as the main form of relief in the spring of 1847, the Quakers provided the boilers to make the soup.

4.4. They were particularly effective in informing newspapers in Dublin and Britain of the true situation in the West of Ireland, emphasising the extent of suffering. At the beginning of 1847, the Committee warned that unless more food was made available millions of lives would be lost and it stated that 'those who are guilty of neglect in these particulars will be responsible before man, and we venture to add, before an all-just Providence'.

4.5. The Quakers were also successful in raising money outside Ireland, especially in Britain and the United States. Unlike many other charitable bodies, their involvement did not end in 1847. Their donations amounted to over £83,000 (approx. €7.1 million). Almost 2,000 individual grants ranging from £10 to £400, were distributed through Protestant and Catholic clergymen. The largest grants, over £20,000 (approx. €1.7 million), were made in Connacht, although over £11,000 (approx. €945,000) was donated to Ulster, principally Cavan and Donegal. At the end of 1847, as donations dried up, the committee wound down its activities. It did not accept (as the government said) that the Famine was over but it felt that charity towards Ireland had dried up.

4.6. In 1848, however, the Quakers decided that instead of providing direct relief to the poor, they would concentrate on providing longer-term assistance, such as fishing tackle, seeds, and farm implements. In response to the deepening distress after the harvest failure in 1848, the committee reconvened in May 1849. It raised and distributed over £4,000 (approx. €340,000) within two months. Money was allocated only to clergymen in the south and west. This reflects the geographical shift in the need for relief. In July 1849 they appealed in newspapers, including *The Times*, for financial support to enable them to respond to the 200 outstanding applications.

4.7. Quakers themselves were personally involved in distributing Famine relief, and this took a high toll. At least fifteen Quakers died as a result of Famine-related diseases. Jonathan Pim collapsed from overwork, and the premature deaths of Joseph Bewley, Jacob Harvey and William Todhunter were attributed to exhaustion. During one year, the Quakers had distributed approximately £200,000 (approx. €17.2 million). Their work was particularly important because it was direct, was based in the communities where it was required, and had no ideological or religious agenda.

5. The involvement of the Catholic Church

5.1. The churches played an important part in the distribution of government and private relief. Local priests and ministers were widely praised for their role in helping the poor. Some churches also established their own relief committees to raise funds. The two Catholic bishops who were particularly involved were Archbishop Murray of Dublin and Archbishop MacHale of Tuam. Catholic aid continued beyond 1847, when many other forms of private relief had dried up. The amount collected is hard to quantify but it was probably more than £400,000 (approx. €34.5 million). Most of this was distributed by local priests in the distressed areas. This avoided much of the expense and the delay that marked government relief.

5.2. Because of its overseas network, the Irish Catholic church was able to attract money. Some of the largest amounts were raised by the Catholic parishes in Britain and the United States. The *Tablet*, the leading English Catholic newspaper, offered to act as a channel for English Catholics to send money to Ireland. By March 1847, Bishop John Bernard Fitzpatrick of Boston had raised almost $20,000 (approx. €420,000 at 2009 values), mostly from local Catholics, though it was meant for distribution to all creeds in Ireland. Apart from donations from outside Ireland, priests in Ireland donated money for the famine poor. James Maher, the Rector of the Irish College in Rome, sold his horse and gig for this purpose. The staff and students of Maynooth College made a donation of over £200.

5.3. A committee for the Irish poor was established in Rome on 13 January 1847. Pope Pius IX donated 1000 Roman crowns from his own pocket. In addition to personal financial assistance, he also offered spiritual and practical support. In March 1847, he took the unprecedented step of issuing a papal encyclical to the international Catholic community, appealing for support for the victims of the Famine. As a result, large sums of money were raised by Catholic congregations: the Vincent de Paul Society in France raised £5,000 (approx. €430,000); the diocese of Strasbourg collected 23,365 francs (approx. €90,000); two priests in Caracas in Venezuela contributed £177 (approx. €15,000); Father Fahy in Argentina sent over £600; a priest in Grahamstown in South Africa sent £70; and the Catholic community in Sydney in New South Wales sent £1,500. Despite the unprecedented intervention by Pope Pius IX, the Irish bishops failed to thank him for his donation or for the encyclical letter until forced to do so by Dr Paul Cullen. Cardinal Fransoni, an adviser to the Pope, was also angry because of the laziness of the Irish bishops in fund-raising for the poor, though he had given them official permission to do whatever was needed to be done. The thanklessness of the Irish bishops and their wrangling with one another lost them further vital support in Rome. The Pope's concern and support for Ireland came to an abrupt end in 1848 when the revolutionary struggle in Italy forced him to flee Rome. Nevertheless, his brief interest had a major effect in urging the international Catholic community to support relief in Ireland. But things could be difficult: as the letter from the Bishop of Augsburg demonstrates, transferring money to Ireland could be complicated.

6. The contribution of women

6.1. Women were particularly involved in the collection and distribution of private relief. They were encouraged by the early action of Queen Victoria who donated £2,000 (approx. €172,000) to the British Relief Association in January 1847. This made her the largest single donor to Famine relief. More important, Victoria published two 'Queen's Letters', the first in March 1847 and the second in October 1847, asking people in Britain to donate money to relieve Irish distress. The first was printed in the main newspapers and read out in Anglican churches. Following its publication, a proclamation announced that 24 March 1847 had been chosen as a day for a 'General Fast and Humiliation before Almighty God', and the proceeds were to be distributed to Ireland and Scotland. The Queen's first letter raised £170,571 (approx. €14.7 million) but the second raised only £30,167 (approx. €2.6 million). In fact, the second letter was widely condemned in Britain, and this indicates a hardening in public attitudes towards the giving of private relief to Ireland.

6.2. Following the second appearance of the blight, ladies' associations were formed in Ireland and England, such as the Ladies' Relief Association in Dublin and the Belfast Ladies' Association. The Society of Friends also established separate ladies' committees. Asenath Nicholson, an American evangelist who visited Ireland during the Famine, praised the Belfast women for their hard work and she contrasted their efforts with the laziness of the ladies of Dublin.

6.3. One of the most successful of the women's groups was the Belfast Ladies' Association. It held its first meeting on 1 January 1847 at the Commercial Buildings in Belfast. It was described as being attended by 'a large and influential assemblage of Ladies, of all religious denominations'. One of the oldest members was Miss Mary Ann McCracken, whose brother, Henry Joy McCracken, had been executed as a rebel in 1798. At the first meeting, resolutions were passed and three treasurers, three secretaries, and five sub-committees were appointed. The sub-committees were a Corresponding Committee (to contact the distressed districts), a Collecting Committee (to appeal for subscriptions and donations), an Industrial Committee (to provide employment), a Clothing Committee (to supply clothing and blankets), and a Bazaar Committee (to hold a sale of ladies' work at Easter).

6.4. Initially the Association was formed for the relief of distressed districts in the west of the country but increasingly during 1847 it became clear that there was famine elsewhere, even in industrial towns such as Belfast. The Association was organised under the direction of the Revd John Edgar, a noted temperance advocate and Professor of Divinity in the Royal College of Belfast. The Society attempted to counteract the effects of the Famine in the West of Ireland by trying to 'improve, by industry, the temporal condition of the poor of the females of Connacht and their spiritual [condition] by the truth of the bible'. By 1849, it had collected £15,000 (approx. €1.3 million) which was used to establish industrial schools in 'wild Connacht', where skills such as knitting and needle-work could be taught. By 1850, the Association had employed thirty-two schoolmistresses within the province who worked under the direction of the resident ladies. In the same year, the Association claimed to have offered employment and education to over 2,000 poor girls and women. Its members tried to change the habits and morality of the poor in general by influencing the behaviour of women.

6.5. The tragedy of the Famine spurred many women into action. An extraordinary range of activity was carried on by women of all denominations. Food kitchens were set up. Committees of women organised the distribution of relief and collected money. Nuns nursed in fever hospitals and fed the starving at their convents. Women philanthropists tried practical solutions to poverty by creating employment for the female poor in cottage industries. Generally, this type of philanthropy was not carried on by charitable societies but depended on the enthusiasm of individual women. The teaching of needlework became an integral part of the education given by nuns to poor children and many laywomen acted as teachers and benefactors in schools where needlework was taught. Some 902 children had been taught these skills in schools by 1851. This kind of education was particularly prevalent in Cork; for example, Mrs Meredith opened the Adelaide school in the city, which employed 'young persons of limited means or reduced circumstances'. Similar work was carried out by the Ladies' Industrial Society of Ireland, founded at the height of the Famine in 1847 to 'carry out a system for encouraging and developing the latent capacities of the poor of Ireland'. Other smaller ladies committees were formed, modelled on the Belfast Society, such as the Newry Benevolent Female Working Society, which provided employment for women in spinning, knitting and needlework.

7. The contribution of the United States

7.1. The United States, which had strong connections with Ireland, provided very significant private relief – in excess of $2,000,000 (approx. €42 million at 2009 values). A large part was in cash, food, clothing, and blankets. One of the first relief committees was established in Boston at the end of 1845, although most of the relief efforts came after the second failure of the potato crop. The Boston committee, which included many members of the local Repeal Association, blamed the Famine on British misrule in Ireland.

7.2. In 1847, members of the American government, including George Dallas, the Vice-President, were involved in giving assistance to Ireland. Jacob Harvey, who co-ordinated relief donations in New York, estimated that in January and February 1846, Irish labourers and servants had sent $326,410 (approx. €7 million) to Ireland in small bank drafts. By January 1847 the payments totalled over $1,000,000 (approx. €21 million). There was a more widespread response to the second failure of the potato crop, helped by the fact that the United States had enjoyed a bumper harvest. An attempt was even made by the American Senate to provide $500,000 (approx. €10.5 million) to Irish relief, though it ultimately failed. The President, James Polk, made a $50 (approx. €1,000) donation: a Boston newspaper declared scornfully that it was too small and had to be 'squeezed' out of him.

7.3. One action of the relief committees in Boston that got great publicity was the sending of two ships (the sloop-of-war, USS *Jamestown* and the naval frigate USS *Macedonian*) full of supplies to Cork. The *Jamestown* completed the journey to Queenstown (now Cóbh) in record time. A portion of the food on the *Macedonian* was distributed in Scotland. Both ships were crewed by volunteers. That the United States was in the middle of a war with Mexico made the government's grant of permission more noteworthy. In reply to criticisms of the government for permitting a warship to be used for the benefit of another country, Captain Forbes of the *Jamestown*, declared: 'it is not an everyday matter to see a nation starving'. A Boston newspaper described the mission of the *Jamestown* as 'one of the most sublime transactions in the nation's history'. Some Cork newspapers used the arrival of the *Jamestown* to contrast the generosity of the people of the United States with the meanness of the British government. In total, over 100 vessels carrying 20,000 tons foodstuffs, came from the United States to Ireland in the wake of the *Jamestown*. Although many high-ranking officials became involved in relief, donations came, too, from people who were themselves poor and disadvantaged, such as the Choctaw Indians in the United States. Their contribution of $170 (approx. €3,600) was made through the American Society of Friends.

8. Worldwide aid

8.1. The response of people overseas, particularly those of Irish descent but also of people who had no ties with Ireland, was an important part of private relief. The first donation was raised in India at the end of 1845, on the initiative of British troops serving in Calcutta. It was followed by the formation of the Indian Relief Fund in January 1846 that appealed to British people living in India to start similar collections. They raised almost £14,000 (approx. €1.2 million). The Freemasons of India contributed £5,000. A contribution of £3,000 was raised in Bombay in one week.

8.2. The government of Barbados gave a donation, partly inspired by a donation given by Ireland to them some years earlier. In 1847–8, committees in Australia raised over £10,000 (approx. €860,000). Money was set aside to assist emigration from Ireland to Australia, but was eventually returned to the donors because the committee could not agree about the kind of emigrants to help, whether paupers or able-bodied emigrants. Other donations came from South Africa (£550); St Petersburg, Russia (£2,644); Constantinople (£620); the islands of Seychelles and Rodriguez (£111 and £16); and Mexico (£652), showing that the Famine had become an event of international significance.

9. Private relief: proselytism and 'souperism'

9.1. Private charities provided essential relief but the activities of a few were controversial. This is because some private relief was associated with proselytism, that is, missions to convert poor Catholics to Protestantism. Those who changed their religion in return for relief were given disparaging names: 'soupers', 'jumpers', or 'perverts'. A few charitable bodies read the bibles to the poor to whom they gave food.

9.2. In the genuine belief that they were saving souls, a small number of Protestant evangelicals used the hunger of the Catholics as a means to convert them. In the West of Ireland, famine missionaries, such as the evangelicals the Revd Hyacinth Talbot D'Arcy and the Revd Edward Nangle, tried to win converts in this way. Some evangelicals believed, no doubt sincerely, that the British government had really caused the Famine by giving a grant to Catholic education, to Maynooth College, in 1845: 'It is done, and in that very year, that very month, the land is smitten, the earth is blighted, famine begins, and is followed by plague, pestilence and blood'. On the near total failure of the potato crop in 1846 there was a quick rise in demand for the services of these missions and by the spring of 1847 they were employing over 2,000 labourers and feeding 600 schoolchildren each day. By 1848, the number of schoolchildren attending the mission schools had increased to over 2,000, and 3,000 adults were employed carrying out relief works, out of a total population of 7,000.

9.3. Another well-known missionary who worked in the West of Ireland was Michael Brannigan, a convert from Catholicism to Presbyterianism and a fluent Irish speaker. In 1847 he established 12 schools in counties Mayo and Sligo, and by the end of 1848 they had grown to 28, despite 'priestly opposition'. Attendance soon dropped when the British Relief Association began providing each child with a half-pound of meal every day, but this ended on 15 August 1848 when funds ran out.

9.4. The worries of the Catholic clergy are well described in a letter from Fr William Flannelly of Ballinakill, Co. Galway, to Daniel Murray, Archbishop of Dublin, on 6 April 1849:

> It cannot be wondered if a starving people would be perverted [converted from Catholicism] in shoals, especially as they [the missionaries] go from cabin to cabin, and when they find the inmates naked and starved to death, they proffer food, money and rainment, on the express condition of becoming members of their conventicles.

The *Freeman's Journal* condemned this as 'nefarious unchristian wickedness'. Pope Pius IX was worried enough to urge the Catholic hierarchy to oppose the work of missionaries and, on one occasion, he reprimanded the bishops for not doing enough to protect their flocks.

9.5. By 1851 the main missions claimed that they had won 35,000 converts and they were anxious to win more. Shortly afterwards, 100 additional preachers were sent to Ireland by the Protestant Alliance. Well-provisioned missionary settlements in such destitute areas as Dingle and Achill Island attracted many converts. These missions were generally opposed by the Church of Ireland. The impact of the missions was, in the end, slight and tended to be localised. Some charitable organisations (including orders of nuns) believed that the distress gave them an opportunity to teach the Irish peasantry 'good' habits of hard work. The missions, and even more so the negative reaction of the Catholic clergy, tended to encourage sectarianism. Besides, many converts had to go elsewhere because of hostility and contempt in their own communities.

10. After the Famine

10.1. There were further crises in Ireland from time to time, and famine threatened again in 1860–62 and 1879–80. Again, international private relief proved essential and saved many lives. However, private relief to Ireland was viewed by some nationalists as another consequence of British injustice. When Charles Stewart Parnell, the leader of the Home Rule movement, visited the United States at the end of 1879 he asked that donations be sent to Ireland. But he also accused England of failing to assist Ireland during the Great Famine, and he alleged, wrongly, that Queen Victoria was the only sovereign in Europe who gave nearly nothing from her private purse.

10.2. There was one important long-term political consequence. The descendants of those who fled to the United States from famine-stricken Ireland kept alive in the Irish-American community a deep feeling of bitterness towards the British government and towards British rule in Ireland. As a result, Irish-Americans were a fertile source of funding for all Irish nationalist movements, parliamentary and military, in the late nineteenth and twentieth centuries.

CHRISTINE KINEALY

CHAPTER 6

Private responses to the Great Famine: documents

1. William Balch in Ireland, 1848

1.1. *Introduction.* The Revd William Balch was an American Universalist minister who travelled to Ireland when the effects of the Famine were still striking. He arrived by ship at Queenstown (now Cóbh), Co. Cork, on 17 May 1848. By the following week he had travelled to Tralee from where he recorded the awful sense of despair, a 'horrid picture' of poverty and starvation. Balch was surprised at the relative affluence to be found only a few miles down the road. He provides a powerful and moving account of a class utterly degraded. He later published *Peculiar people, or, reality in romance* (1881). SOURCE: William Steven Balch, *Ireland as I saw it: the character, condition, and prospects* (New York, 1850), 161–5.

1.2. Tralee is situated in the bottom of a delightful valley … on the south, stretching off to the west, is a range of abrupt hills, covered with brown heather, and dotted with white cabins and patches of tilled ground far up towards their summits. The town itself shows many signs of thrift I had not expected to see, in this part of the country. Some of the streets are spacious and regularly laid out, and many houses are new and handsome, and the grounds about them are tastefully decorated. A fair proportion of the inhabitants are well dressed and genteel in their manners.

1.3. I noticed many very handsome women sitting by their windows, reading, walking in the streets, or present in the church. I was surprised at such marks of refinement, so unlike the character of the people we have seen since leaving Cork. I am sorry to be compelled to add, however, that we also saw specimens of destitution, and misery, more horrid than any before described.

1.4. In one place we saw an old woman lying on a sort of bed, which had been made of old rags, upon some boxes, by the side of a yard fence. Two sticks were stuck in the ground, on the top of which was placed an old door, the other side resting on the fence. This formed her only shelter. A ragged quilt was spread over her, which she wrapped closer about her as we came near. A dirty cap was on her head; beneath it her shrivelled, cadaverous face, faintly tinged with a hectic fever, one hand, withered to a skeleton, lay by her cheek on the coarse pillow of straw, which must have been gathered from the stable near by. Close to her sat a middle

Note these rough equivalents in estimating Famine donations: $1=€21; £1=€86; 1*s.*=€4.30; 1*d.*=€0.36 approx. at 2009 values. There were 20 shillings/pound and 12 pence/shillling, and thus 240 pence/pound.

95

aged, and more decently dressed female, who might have been her daughter. She begged of us, in the name of God, of the blessed Saviour, and the Holy Virgin, in strong words which seemed familiar to her, bartering freely the rewards of heaven, for one poor ha'-penny, for the sick, and dying woman. The old lady muttered some words in answer to our inquiries, which were scarcely intelligible; indicating, however, that it was the 'will of God', and apparently trying to submit, as well as she could, to what she seemed to regard a dire necessity.

1.5. One or two younger women, and some small children, gathered around us, perfect pictures of destitution, the most abject and loathsome. It was impossible for us to contemplate this scene of misery. We had not the nerve to listen to their tale of woe. What we saw was enough – too much almost, for human credulity. It was more, by far, than we believed possible in a Christian land; in a town of twelve thousand inhabitants, and the capital of Kerry county, close by the elegant mansions of opulent merchants and landholders, where fashion and luxury make a fair display; and only a few rods from churches of various denominations, where God is professedly worshipped, in the name of the merciful Redeemer, who gave it as a witness of the divinity of his mission that 'the poor have the Gospel preached to them,' and made the standard of acceptance to the honours he came to bestow, 'I was hungered, and ye gave me meat; thirsty, and ye gave me drink; naked, and ye clothed me; a stranger, and ye took me in; I was sick, and ye visited me'; assuring them, that inasmuch as they had done it unto one of the least of his brethren, they had done it unto him.

1.6. Mark our further astonishment, when, as we turned away from this place, we saw posted up, close by, and in many other places about the town, notices of a sermon and a collection for that day, to take place in the Methodist church, in aid of 'Foreign Missions'. My God! Thought I, is it come to this, that these poor creatures – thy children – are to be laid on boards in the street, and left to starve, while Christians are called upon, in the name of religion, and the hopes of heaven, to give their substance to help convert the heathen? …

1.7. Here is a prolific soil, a genial climate, and every physical ability which a bountiful God could bestow; and yet what heart-rending scenes of starvation and misery! What wails of oppression! What appalling horrors; what stoic indifference on the part of the better – some times the religious portion of the community; what inhuman neglect on the part of government, which pretends to exercise royal protection over her colonies!

1.8. We turned from this horrid picture, and went away to seek some object to divert our minds, and relieve us from the painful feelings which had overwhelmed us. We did not succeed. The elegance of some of the public buildings, the court-house, the church, the Catholic chapels, the meeting houses of

Presbyterians and Methodists, the hospitals, the Union workhouse, the infantry barracks, the Green park, the fine bay – nothing could eradicate the impressions of that wretched family, which inhumanity suffered to remain in the open street, under circumstances which appealed so forcibly to every generous and Christian feeling for sympathy and relief. More than once I turned to go back and cut short my means of travelling, by contributing sufficient to make them all comfortable. But then I felt what an insufficient thing is individual charity, where there is so much poverty and suffering. I cannot avert the evil, turn back the tide, or check the streams which are swelling constantly the flood of pauperism already spread so widely over this land. The root is deeper than I can reach, and useless is the effort of a stranger to do more than give a drop of comfort as he passes by.

2. Asenath Nicholson in Ireland

2.1. *Introduction.* Asenath Nicholson (1792–1855), was born in eastern Vermont, USA. A teacher, writer, and traveller, she first visited Ireland in 1844 for nearly a year. She returned and spent the period from May 1846 until September 1848, visiting the destitute in the West of Ireland. A devout Christian, Nicholson was committed to the conversion of the Catholic Irish. However, she was no crude proselytiser, but a very caring woman who was deeply affected by the misery that she witnessed all around her. In the first extract, dated 17 April 1849, Nicholson describes what she witnessed in the locality of Louisburgh, Co. Mayo. In the second, she gives her view of Quaker involvement in relief. In her third she praises the Belfast women for their hard work and contrasts their efforts with the laziness of the ladies in Dublin. SOURCE: Asenath Nicholson, *Annals of the Famine in Ireland, in 1847, 1848 and 1849* (first published 1851; 2nd ed. by M. Murphy (Dublin, 1998), 136–8 (extract I), 179 (extract II), 57 (extract III)

I

2.2. With a sister of Peter Kelly I went to 'Old Head', and was first introduced into one of the dreadful pauper schools where ninety children received a piece of black bread once a day. It was a sad sight; most of them were in a state of rags, barefooted, and squatted on the floor waiting for a few ounces of bread, with but here and there a fragment of a book. The clean schoolmaster, on a cold day, was clad in a white vest and linen pantaloons, making the last effort to appear respectable, labouring for the remuneration of a penny a week from each family if by chance the family could furnish it. These ninety all belonged to Mrs Garvey's tenantry, and there were others looking on who had come in likewise, not belonging to her lands, who wistfully stood by without receiving one morsel. I looked till my satiated eyes turned away at a pitiful sight like this. Neither the neat cottage, the old sea, nor my favourite Croagh Patrick could give satisfaction in a wilderness of woe like this. When will these dreadful scenes find an end?

2.3. Naught but desolation and death reigned; and the voice of nature, which was always so pleasant on the sea-coast, now united with the whistling of the wind, seemed only to be howling in sad response to the moans and entreaties of the starving around me. The holy well … is near this place. In years gone by this well was a frequented spot where invalids went to be healed. It is now surrounded by stone, covered with earth, and a path about gives the trodden impress of many a knee where the postulant goes round seven times, repeating a Paternoster at every revolution, and drops a stone which tells that the duty is performed. A hole is shown in a stone where the holy St Patrick knelt till he wore the stone away. A poor peasant girl, in the simplicity of her heart, explained all the ceremonies of the devotees and virtues of the well, regretting that the priests had forbidden the practice now. A company soon entered the churchyard and set down a white coffin, waiting till the widow of the deceased should bring a spade to open the grave; and while the dirt was being taken away she sat down, leaning upon the coffin, setting up the Irish wail in the most pathetic manner. She, by snatches, rehearsed his good qualities then burst into a gush of tears, then commenced in Irish, as the meagre English has no words to express the height of the grief, madness or joy. The ground was opened but a few inches when the coffin of another was touched. The graveyards are everywhere filled so near the surface that dogs have access, and some parts of the body are often exposed.

2.4. A debate was now in progress respecting good works and the importance of being baptised into the true church. Mrs G., who professed to be a papist, disputed the ground with them, till the contest became so sharp that I retired, for their darkness was painful. It seemed like the valley and shadow of death, temporally and spiritually.

2.5. The little town of Louisburgh, two miles from Old Head, had suffered extremely. An active priest and faithful Protestant curate were doing their utmost to mitigate the suffering, which was like throwing dust in the wind; lost, lost forever – the work of death goes on, and what is repaired today is broken down tomorrow. Many have fallen under their labours. The graves of the Protestant curate and his wife were pointed out to me in the churchyard, who had fallen since the Famine in the excess of their labour; and the present curate and his praiseworthy wife, unless they have supernatural strength, cannot long keep up the dreadful struggle. He employed as many labourers as he could pay at four pence a day, and at four o'clock these 'lazy' ones would often be waiting at his gate to go to their work. He was one day found dining with the priest, and the thing was so novel that I expressed a pleasant surprise, when he answered

> 'I have consulted no one's opinion respecting the propriety of my doing so. I found on coming here, this man a warm-hearted friend to the poor doing all

the good in his power, without any regard to party, and determined to treat him as a neighbour and friend, and have as yet seen no cause to regret it.'

This same priest was not able to walk, having been sick, but he was conveyed in a carriage to Mrs Garvey's and most courteously thanked me for coming into that miserable neighbourhood, and offered to provide some one at his own expense to convey me into the Killery mountains, to see the 'inimitable scenery and the wretched inhabitants that dwell there'.

2.6. In company with the wife of the curate and the physician, I went there. The morning was usually sunny, but the horrors of that day were inferior to none ever witnessed. The road was rough, and we constantly were meeting pale, meagre-looking men, who were on their way from the mountains to break stones and pile them mountain-high for the paltry compensation of a pound of meal a day. These men had put all their seed into the ground, and if they gave up their cabins they must leave the crop for the landlord to reap, while they must be in a poorhouse or in the open air. This appeared to be the last bitter dreg in Ireland's cup of woe!

2.7. 'Why', a poor man was asked, whom we met dragging sea-weed to put upon his potato-field, 'do you do this, when you tell us you expect to go into the poor-house, and leave your crop to another?' 'I put it on, hoping that God Almighty will send me the work to get a bit'. We met flocks of wretched children going to school for the bit of bread, some crying with hunger, and some begging to get in without the penny which was required for their tuition. The poor little emaci-ated creatures went weeping away, one saying he had been 'looking for the penny all day yesterday, and could not get it'.

2.8. The doctor who accompanied us returned to report to the priest the cruelty of the relieving office and teacher, but this neither frightened or softened these hard hearts. These people are shut in by mountains and the sea on one side, and roads passable only on foot by the other, having no bridges and the paths entirely lost in some places among the stones. We left our carriage and walked as we could; and though we met multitudes in the last stages of suffering, yet not one through that day asked charity, and in one case the common hospitality showed itself, by offering us milk when we asked for water. This day I saw enough, and my heart was sick, sick.

II

2.9. ... with all the zig-zag movements in the Famine there were some redeem-ing qualities, there were some things carried on and carried through, which were not accused of sectarianism, for the simplest reason – none was manifest ... The Society of Friends justly merit this acknowledgement, and they have it most heartily from every portion of Ireland. Not belonging to the Society, my opportunity of testing the true feelings of the poor was a good one, and when in a school or soup-shop the question was put – 'Who feeds you?' or 'Who sends you these clothes?' – the answer was: 'The good Quakers, lady, and it's they that have the religion entirely.'

III

2.10. July 6th. [1847], I took the steamer for Belfast. *Here* was work going on, which was paramount to all I had seen. *Women* were at work; and no-one could justly say that they were dilatory or inefficient. Never in Ireland, since the Famine, was such a happy combination of all parties, operating so harmoniously together, as was here manifested. Not in the least like the women of Dublin, who sheltered themselves behind their old societies – most of them excusing themselves from personal labour, feeling that a few visits to the abodes of the poor were too shocking for female delicacy to sustain; and though occasionally one might be prevailed upon to go out, yet but for a few days could I ever persuade any to accompany me. Yet much was given in Dublin, for it is a city celebrated for its benevolence, as deservedly so, as far as giving goes. But *giving* and *doing* are antipodes in her who has never been trained to domestic duties.

3. Letter of Charles Edward Trevelyan to Thomas Spring-Rice, Lord Mounteagle

3.1. *Introduction.* Charles Edward Trevelyan, Assistant Secretary to the Treasury in London (1840–59), held firmly to the doctrine of *laissez faire* (that state intervention in society and economy should be minimal), and persisted in this opinion in the face of calamitous famine in Ireland. He blamed the Irish landlords for the chronic distress in Ireland. But he went further in seeing the Famine as the result of a failure in the Irish character, and as the judgement of God on the Irish. In this letter, dated 9 October 1846, to the Lord Mounteagle, a concerned Irish landlord, he set out his views about the Famine, and about the minimal role of the government in relief. SOURCE: Dublin, National Library of Ireland, Mounteagle, MS 13,397; edited in Noel Kissane, *The Irish Famine: a documentary history* (Dublin, 1995), 51.

3.2 My Dear Lord,
I have had the pleasure of receiving your letter dated 1 inst., and before proceeding to the subjects more particularly treated in it, I must beg of you to dismiss all doubt from your mind of the magnitude of the existing calamity and its danger not being fully known and appreciated in Downing Street.

3.3. The government establishments are strained to the utmost to alleviate this great calamity and avert this danger, as far as it is in the power of government to do so; and in the whole course of my public service, I never witnessed such entire self-devotion and such hearty and cordial co-operation on the part of officers belonging to different departments met together from different parts of the world, as I see on this occasion.

3.4. My purchases are carried to the utmost point short of transferring the famine from Ireland to England and giving rise to a counter popular pressure here, which it would be the more difficult to resist because it would be founded on strong considerations of justice.

3.5. But I need not remind your lordship that the ability even of the most powerful government is extremely limited in dealing with a social evil of this description. It forms no part of the functions of government to provide supplies of food or to increase the productive powers of the land. In the great institutions of the business of society, it falls to the share of government to protect the merchant and the agriculturist in the free exercise of their respective employments, but not itself to carry on these employments; and the condition of a community depends upon the result of the efforts which each member of it makes in his private and individual capacity …

3.6. In Ireland the habit has proverbially been to follow a precisely opposite course, and the events of the last six weeks furnish a remarkable illustration of what I do not hesitate to call this defective part of the national character. The nobility and the gentry have met in their respective baronies, and beyond making presentments required by law, they have, with rare exceptions, confined themselves to memorials and deputations calling upon the government to do everything, as if they have themselves no part to perform in this great crisis of the country. The government is expected to open shops for the sale of food in every part of Ireland, to make all the railroads in Ireland, and to drain and improve the whole of the land of Ireland, to the extent of superseding the proprietor in the management of his own estate, and arranging with his tenants the terms on which the rent etc. is to be adjusted …

3.7. I must give expression to my feelings by saying that I think I see a bright light shining in the distance through the dark cloud which at present hangs over Ireland. A remedy has already been applied to that portion of the maladies of Ireland which was traceable to political causes, and the morbid habits which still to a certain extent survive are gradually giving way to more healthy action. The deep and inveterate root of social evil remains, and I hope I am not guilty of irreverence in thinking that, this being altogether beyond the power of man, the cure has been applied by the direct stroke of an all-wise Providence in a manner as unexpected and unthought as it is likely to be effectual. God grant that we may rightly perform our part, and not turn into a curse what was intended for a blessing. The ministers of religion and especially the pastors of the Roman

Catholic Church, who possess the largest share of influence over the people of Ireland, have well performed their part; and although few indications appear from any proceedings which have yet come before the public that the landed proprietors have even taken the first step of preparing for the conversion of the land now laid down to potatoes to grain cultivation, I do not despair of seeing this class of society still taking the lead which their position requires of them, and preventing the social revolution from being so extensive as it otherwise must become.

Believe me, my dear lord, yours very sincerely,
C.E. Trevelyan. Treasury.

4. Contributions of landlords, clergy, and others

4.1. *Introduction.* Several newspapers reported donations made and actions taken by landlords, clergy, and others to alleviate distress. Here is a selection. SOURCE: Sources are listed after each item.

4.2. A meeting for establishing a soup kitchen was held in the poor house of Westport on 16 December [1847]. The Marquess of Sligo was the chairman. The subscriptions included:

Marquess of Sligo: donation £100 (approx. €8,600 at 2009 values), weekly subscription £5. Marchioness of Sligo: donation £10, weekly subscription £3. William Levyston Esq. donation £50, weekly subscription £2. George Glendinning donation £50, weekly subscription £3. The Revd Patrick Pounden donation £10, weekly subscription £1. M. MacDonnell: donation £25, weekly subscription £1. Very Revd Bernard Burke: donation £10, weekly subscription 10 shillings (*The Globe & Traveller*, London, 1 January 1847).

4.3. The result of my experiments enables me to sell at the village cook shop, one-and-a-half pound of excellent rice and meal porridge, seasoned, for one penny; one quart of soup for one penny; 12 ounces of potato cake for one pence (Address of Lord Roden, Tollymore Park, Co. Armagh, to resident gentry of Ireland) (*The Globe & Traveller*, 1 January 1847).

4.4. Viscount Lorton, the chairman of the Boyle Union, is giving his tenants free seed (*Roscommon & Leitrim Gazette*, 2 January 1847).

4.5. Lord and Lady Waterford have given £30 for Dungarvan Soup Kitchen (*Roscommon & Leitrim Gazette*, 9 January 1847).

4.6. Mr [Daniel] O'Connell has allowed his tenants a 50 per cent reduction in rents (*The Globe & Traveller*, 12 January 1847).

4.7. Sir Montague Chapman of Clonmellon, Westmeath, sent 120 emigrants to Australia to colonise his estate near Port Adelaide (*Roscommon & Leitrim Gazette*, 20 March 1847).

4.8. Archbishop MacHale gave £100 to the Roman Catholic clergy of Westport for the relief of the destitute (*Roscommon & Leitrim Gazette*, 24 April 1847).

5. Belfast Ladies' Association

5.1. *Introduction.* The Belfast Ladies Association was one of the most successful women's fund-raising groups. It held its first meeting on 1 January. At this meeting, treasurers, secretaries, and sub-committees were appointed, and resolutions were passed (described below). SOURCE: *First Report of the Committee of the Belfast Ladies' Association for the Relief of Irish Destitution, 6 March 1847* (Belfast, 1847).

> **5.2.** *Resolutions.* That this meeting do form itself into a Society, for the purpose of raising a fund, by subscription, and otherwise as may be resolved upon, to be applied to the relief of such of the afflicted districts throughout Ireland as may appear to the Committee, now to be appointed, most in need of relief, being guided by the urgency of the case without reference to religious distinctions …
>
> That a subscription list be opened, for the above purpose; and that the Committee do divide the Town into districts, and appoint Collectors, to solicit subscriptions to their funds, from those who have not already subscribed …
>
> **5.3.** *Report* … Since the formation of the Association, a great change has taken place in the aspect of our town and neighbourhood. When our operations commenced, little was apprehended, with regard to the sufferings of the poor of this large and commercial town: but the misery of other districts has driven in a large number of poor creatures for shelter and food here, who could find none in their own bare and bleak homes. In addition to this, our own poor have been gradually getting worse and worse, till, at last, an effort must be made for rescuing them from the fate that has followed many in other localities. Under these circumstances, some members of the Association formed themselves into a Committee, specially for the purpose of looking after our own poor, and have been joined by a large body of ladies, of all sects and parties.

6. Cork Ladies' Relief Society

6.1. *Introduction.* The Cork Ladies' Relief Society was one of several relief organisations established by women in this period. Such organisations generally had affluent landed women as patrons. Many aimed to provide support to the female members of a family by providing work. It was expected that these industrious women would benefit the family as a whole and not become a burden to the state in the long-term. SOURCE: *Cork Constitution*, 30 January 1847.

6.2. Patroness, the Countess of Bandon; Patronesses, the Marchioness of Thomond; Dowager Countess Mountcashel; the Countess Listowel; Dowager Lady Bernard; Lady H. Bernard; Lady A. Bernard; Lady H. Bernard (Cheltenham); Lady Jane Moore; Lady Mary Berehaven; Lady L. Aldworth; Lady Katherine Boyle; Hon. Mrs C. Bernard; Hon. Mrs White Hedges; Lady Beecher; Lady Chatterton; Mrs General Turner; Mrs Colonel Meade; Mrs Beamish; Mrs Newman (Deanery); Mrs D. Freeman (Castle Cor); Mrs Sarsfield; Mrs Penrose; Mrs R.B. Tooker; Mrs Ormsby; Mrs Lombard; Mrs St George; Mrs Herbert; Mrs Morgan (Tivoli); Mrs Captain Spread; Mrs Woodroffe; Miss Gibbings (Lapp's Island); Miss Crawford; Miss M. Crawford; Miss Warren; Mrs Beasley.

6.3. *Committee of Management.* Mrs Sarsfield; Mrs Ormsby; Mrs Beasley; Mrs R.B. Tooker; Miss Crawford; Miss M. Crawford; Miss Warren; Miss Wheatley, secretary, 2 Albert Place, Cork; Miss A. M. Lee, treasurer, 3 Mount Verdon Terrace, Cork.

6.4. The treasurer looks forward to the Christian public to aid the infant and parochial schools in the city and county of Cork, by giving breakfasts to the most destitute children, and assisting their mothers to supply them with food. Also, to give relief to the widows and orphans, who have lost the men of their families by starvation. If funds admit, or are supplied by the sister country [England], where the treasurer has applied for contributions, she hopes to add clothing, but for the urgent wants of nature, food to save the lives of thousands of children and poor families is absolutely necessary in the starving districts in the country parishes. The secretary will be happy to receive any contributions …

6.5. The following queries are to be answered by applicants soliciting relief from the Cork Ladies' Relief Society for the South of Ireland, and returned to the committee of management, addressed to the secretaries of the county associations:

Table 2: Questionnaire

I.   Has a Ladies' Relief Association been formed in your parish or locality?

II.   What is the name of the county, district, parish, and the nearest post town?

III.   What is the extent of the district and the number of inhabitants?

IV.   What is the state of the females, widows etc., as regards sickness, poverty, age and infirmity, and how many are unable to work for their own support?

V.   Have subscriptions been entered into, and to what amount in your vicinity; or has relief been received from any other source?

VI.   What schools are in the parish, infant or parochial, and how many children attend, and do the Ladies' Committee visit them?

VII.   Have soup kitchens been opened throughout the district, and have the schools been supplied gratuitously with bread or soup, or if sold, at what rate?

VIII.   Is there any public or private employment for the women, boys, or girls in the country farms, to assist the men by their industry?

IX.   Have the poor in the country gardens – and do they require seed to encourage them to cultivate their ground?

X.   Have you any objection that any of your statements be published or forwarded to the London Committee?

All letters from the country to be addressed to Miss Wheatley, secretary, No. 2 Albert Place, Cork.

7. Elizabeth Smith's response

7.1. *Introduction.* Elizabeth Smith (née Grant), diarist, was born on 7 May 1797 at 5 Charlotte Square, Edinburgh. She was the eldest child of the local laird [landowner], Sir Peter Grant, a lawyer and MP and his wife Jane, daughter of Edmund Ironside, Rector of Houghton-le-Spring. Most of her childhood was spent in London and on the family estate on Speyside. The family went to live in Edinburgh at the end of the Napoleonic wars and spent time in Holland, Belgium and France in 1819. In 1820, her spendthrift father faced with financial ruin, decided to return to the Highlands. In 1827, the family went to India, where Elizabeth's father was appointed a judge in Bombay. While in India, Elizabeth married the Irishman, Colonel (later General) Henry Smith of Baltiboys, Co. Wicklow, seventeen years her senior. When her husband inherited the neglected Co. Wicklow estate, they went to Ireland, to restore the house and develop the farms. Elizabeth also established a school. Her diaries cover the full range of society, with shrewd, amusing. and often important insights. Smith's attitude to the Irish poor was typical of her class. The following extract is taken from the journal she kept while living in Co. Wicklow. Here she recounts her own reactions to the increasing distress in 1847. SOURCE: Patricia Pelly & Andrew Tod (eds), *The Highland lady in Ireland: Elizabeth Grant of Rothiemurchus* (Edinburgh, 1991).

> **7.2.** December 1846. ... The Poor Houses are full, therefore now I believe in the destitution cry. The people are starving I believe. Cold and nakedness and discomfort of every kind they are indifferent to, provided they can fill their stomacks [*sic*], stuff them rather with the lowest quality of food, its bulk is what they look for, for years the failure of the potato crop has been expected, yet no preparations were made to meet this coming evil. They have no forethought. If they get a shilling they must spend it. They can't make 11*d.* [eleven pence] do and save the penny; they have no store for the rainy day, then when it comes they rail at all the rest of the world for not stepping forward to their relief instantly as if they deserved the quicker aid because they never helped themselves. There is no energy, no honesty, no industry among them. Already good effects have been

produced. The Poor House will improve their habits, the dearness of provisions has driven many of the idle hangers-on at home out into the world to earn the food no longer to be had by grubbing for it. So we must live in hope that, happen what may, things can never again be so wretchedly bad as they have been.

7.3. 12 January 1847. Alas! the Famine progresses; here it is in frightful reality to be seen in every face. Idle, improvident, reckless, meanly dependent on the upper classes whom they so abuse, call the bulk of the Irish what we will, and no name is too hard almost for them, here they are starving round us, cold, naked, hungry, well nigh houseless. To rouse them from their natural apathy may well be the work of future years. To feed them must be our business this year. Baltiboys is in comfort, few of our people in real distress, some in want of assistance and they get it, others in need of nothing. My habit of going constantly about among them keeps me pretty well acquainted with their condition, but lest I should mis-calculate I am taking the whole estate regularly through at this time. Two days of visiting introduced me to no distress, only to two cases of struggling – that expressive word. I mean to make a catalogue raisonné* of our population to leave among our family archives as a curiosity for future squires and a guide to us now.

7.4. Hal has killed a beef for our poor and we make daily a large pot of good soup which is served gratis to 22 people at present. It is ready at one o'clock and I thought it quite a pretty sight yesterday in the kitchen: all the workmen coming in for their portion, a quart with a slice of the beef; half of them get this one day for a dinner with a bit of their own bread; the other half get milk and the cheap rice we have provided for them. Next day they reverse the order. The Colonel is giving them firing [fuel] too; so they are really comfortable; there are twelve of them and ten pensioners, old feeble men and women, or those with large fami-lies of children; some of them no longer living on our ground yet having been once connected with us we can't desert them.

7.5. So far well; but beyond our small circle what a waste of misery; how are we to relieve it? Such a dense population squatted here and there upon neglected properties, dying with want, wretched every year, but ruined this. At the relief committee yesterday it was resolved to institute soup kitchens at proper stations for general relief, to be supported by subscription, each subscriber to have a cer-tain number of tickets. I think the gentlemen are doing this, the ladies must combine for a clothing fund. The rags are scarcely coverings for decency; beds and bedding there are none, among the mob, I mean; such misery crushes hope, yet hope I will …

*The catalogue raisonné was a document compiled by Smith in early 1847 listing all the people living and working in Baltiboys.

8. Letters of Queen Victoria

8.1. *Introduction.* Queen Victoria was the largest individual donor to Famine relief. She published two 'Queen's Letters', in 1847 seeking donations to relieve Irish Famine victims. The first was published in the newspapers and read out in Anglican churches. A Proclamation announced that 24 March 1847 was to be a day of 'General Fast and Humiliation before Almighty God'. Funds collected were to go to Famine relief in Ireland and Scotland. The first Letter raised the large sum of £170,571 (approx. €14.7 million). Here is the text. SOURCE: *The Times* (London), 22 January 1847.

8.2. Victoria Regina,

Most Reverend Father in God, our right trusty and right entirely beloved councillor, we greet you well. Whereas a large portion of the population in Ireland, and in some districts in Scotland, is suffering severe distress, owing to the failure of the ordinary supplies of food; and whereas many of our subjects have entered into voluntary subscriptions for their relief, and have at the same time humbly prayed to us to issue our Royal Letters, directed to the Lord Archbishop of Canterbury and the Lord Archbishop of York, authorising them to promote contributions within their respective provinces for the same benevolent purpose.

8.3. We ... being always ready to give the best encouragement and countenance to such humane and charitable undertakings, are graciously pleased to condescend to their request; and we do hereby direct that these letters be by you communicated to the several Suffragan Bishops within your province, expressly requiring them to take care that publication be made hereof on such Sunday in the present or ensuing month, and in such places within the respective dioceses, as the said Bishops shall appoint; and that upon this occasion the ministers in each parish do effectively excite their parishioners to a liberal contribution, which shall be collected the week following at their respective dwellings by the churchwardens or overseers of the poor in each parish; and the ministers of the several parishes are to cause the sums so collected to be paid immediately into the hands of the Bank of England, to be accounted for by them, and applied to the carrying on and promoting of the above mentioned good designs.

And so we bid you very heartily farewell. Given at the Court at St James, the 13th day of January 1847, in the tenth year of our reign.

9. Opposition to Queen Victoria's letters

9.1. *Introduction.* By the end of 1847 the British public had grown tired of the seemingly endless requests for aid for Ireland. The second letter raised £30,167 (approx. €2.6 million). In fact, the second letter was widely censured in Britain, indicating a fall-off in support for Irish relief. Here is a harsh extract from one of the many letters from the public printed in *The Times*. SOURCE: *The Times* (London), 19 October 1847.

9.2. A wise Providence has put a check upon the brute creation to prevent an excessive increase, but man has been left to be guided by reason. These Irish, however, seem to have none; nothing but a mere brute instinct and appetite totally unguided by reason or foresight. What commiseration can we have for these people, and why should we be called on to support them? To do so is, in effect, a premium for recklessness and improvidence.

10. Relief work in Dungarvan

10.1. *Introduction.* Dungarvan, Co. Waterford, had been a centre of disturbances in the early months of 1846. At the end of September, about 4,000 people protested in the local town and plundered stores to discourage merchants from exporting grain. When troops fired on the crowd, several were injured and two killed. The workhouses were full by the end of 1846, and the closing of relief works resulted in an additional 2,000 people seeking admission. No alternative was provided by the government. Local bakers intervened: they gave unemployed workers bread in an attempt to protect their shops from being ransacked. This document refers to the relief efforts of some women in Dungarvan in January 1847. It reveals much about society's attitude to women and their role as 'benevolent' carers. SOURCE: *Cork Examiner*, 1 January 1847.

10.2. Dungarvan, Dec. 27: The resolve of the ladies to establish these depots [soup kitchens] is a noble one and their exertions to carry it out in the most useful and effective manner are decidedly unprecedented.

10.3. Woman, true to the instincts of her own beautiful – almost spiritual – nature, saw that there was one great necessity, which male relief committees, or the desultory employment afforded by public works, could not possibly remedy, and she immediately proceeds to supply it. She, by that more refined and subtle perception, that heart-touching sensibility so peculiarly her own, felt, and truly felt, that there was many a hapless creature who, in this awful passage in our calamitous history, was forced, whether through the pride which belonged to better days, or by reason of decrepitude or old age, to shrink away, forgotten by the world, into squalid and miserable domiciles [houses], located in dark and filthy lanes, there to die, with hunger, and not one friendly hand to extend relief … many a poor widow and helpless female, with no person to earn a shilling for her sustenation …

10.4. And what can be so delightful as to find these gentle beings leaving their drawing rooms, their perfumed chambers, their refined and elegant amusements, their lulling music, etc., to enter the house of poverty and wretchedness and rags and multiform misery, where every sight is almost loathsome; every scent pestiferous; every sound the moans of the creature stretched in a bedless dormitory, reduced to a skeleton by emaciating poverty and starvation; and bringing with them the nourishment afforded by these depots? To find them exploring these haunts of misery and hunger for the purpose of alleviating them is, indeed, a scene for angels to smile on … There is in it a thousand times more of the heroine than in deeds which may sound far higher, but which could not affiliate with the wretched poor.

10.5. These benevolent ladies have thrown aside every distinction, which in ordinary times the conventionalities of society may, perhaps, act out from them. They feel fully the pressure of the times, the necessity for action, and since the formation of their plan, no exertion has been spared by them in carrying it out. Their only emulation is who can do the most good …

10.6. Already the ladies of Dungarvan have collected a sum exceeding £130 (approx. €11,000) for their fund. The Marquess of Waterford has subscribed £20 to it, and Lady Waterford £10 …

11. Contribution of Pope Pius IX

11.1. *Introduction.* A committee for the Irish poor had been established in Rome on 13 January 1847. The pope donated 1,000 Roman Crowns (approx. €19,000) from his Privy Purse. SOURCE: *The Times* (London), 20 May 1847.

11.2. Among the many instances of public and private liberality which the distress in Ireland has called forth, it will be interesting to hear the following one of the present distinguished and excellent Pope Pius IX who, on being asked for an autograph to be exhibited at one of the numerous bazaars held in this country for the relief of the suffering, wrote a letter, *scritta di sua mano* [in his own handwriting] for that purpose, accompanying it with a beautiful rosary of agates, and a carnelian medallion, engraved with the head of our Saviour, pendant from it.

12. The Encyclical Letter of Pope Pius IX

12.1. *Introduction.* Besides personal financial assistance to Ireland, Pius IX issued a papal encyclical to the universal Church, 25 March 1847, seeking aid for the victims of the Irish Famine. This document bears the mark of Paul Cullen, friend and advisor of the Pope. Consider the remarkable references to the 'Irish Nation' and the 'Kingdom of Ireland', and this is a deliberate use of sensitive terms by the papal chancery. The Pope's message is heartfelt. It contains a rich tapestry of references to scripture and to the writings of the ancient saints of the Church, and needs to be studied very carefully as an example of papal diplomacy. As a result of the Pope's appeal, large sums of money were raised by Catholics worldwide. Despite his unprecedented intervention the Irish bishops neglected to thank him and this and their infighting lost them vital support in Rome. The Pope's concern ended abruptly in 1848 when revolution in Italy forced him to flee Rome.

SOURCE: Pius IX, *Praedecessores nostros*, Encyclical to the Universal Church requesting aid for Ireland (25 March 1847), in Anne Fremantle, *The Papal Encyclicals in their historical context: the teachings of the Popes from Peter to John XXIII* (New York, 1963).

12.2. To all Patriarchs, Primates, Archbishops and Bishops.

Venerable Brothers, We give you Greetings and Our Apostolic Blessing.

You know from your study of the Church's history, that our predecessors in the Roman Pontificate assiduously assisted Christian nations. You know, too, that this zeal included not only spiritual benefits conferred on the Christian people, but also disaster relief whenever calamity struck. This fact is confirmed by documents of ancient (Eusebius of Caesarea, *Ecclesiastical history*, book iv, 23, Letter of Dionysius, Bishop of Corinth to Soter I, Bishop of Rome) and more recent times, as well as by Our own recollection of recent events. Who indeed could, or should, more fittingly display this fatherly concern of spirit than those whom the Catholic faith teaches 'are the Fathers and Teachers of all Christians'? (Council of Florence, *definitio fidei*). And to whom should afflicted peoples have recourse but to those who have proved by actual deeds over a long period of time that they are sympathetic benefactors?

12.3. Inspired by this notable example of our predecessors, and at the behest of our own will, we immediately made every effort, as far as we could, to bring help to the Irish Nation in its time of peril. Therefore, as soon as we learned that the Kingdom of Ireland was suffering a great dearth of food, both grain and other provisions, and that the Nation was hard pressed by a series of dreadful diseases caused by this dearth of food, we immediately came to its aid. We proclaimed that public prayers should be made to God in this city of ours; we exhorted the Roman clergy and people, as well as the rest of Rome's residents, to come to the aid of Ireland and to pray for it. By contributing ourselves and by collecting money in Rome, we were able to send a contribution to Our Venerable Brothers, the Archbishops of Ireland. They distributed it among those in need.

12.4. But letters reach us daily from Ireland, bringing news of a worsening calamity. We are distressed and again want to help that Nation. Ireland deserves our aid for so many reasons. The clergy and people of Ireland have always revered the Apostolic See. Indeed, that Nation has persevered in professing the Catholic religion in all distressful times, and the Irish clergy have worked industriously to spread the Catholic religion in the farthest parts of the earth. Finally, the Irish Nation zealously honours and accepts the blessed Peter whose humble representative we are, and whose dignity, to quote the words of Leo the Great, 'does not fail in the person of an unworthy heir' (Leo the Great, *Sermon* 2).

12.5. So, having carefully weighed this grave matter and having ascertained also the view of several cardinals on the implementation of our plan, we have decided to write this letter to you, Venerable Brothers, so that we may provide for the needs of the Irish People.

12.6. In this matter we advise you all in the Dioceses and districts subject to your jurisdiction to proclaim three days of public prayers in churches and other holy places, as has previously been done in Rome. Do this in order to beseech God, the Father of Mercies, to free the Irish People from this great disaster, and to prevent such a misfortune befalling the other kingdoms and lands of Europe as well. To encourage these prayers, we grant an indulgence of seven years to those who are present at these prayers on any occasion; and, in addition, on those who attend the prayers for the entire three days and who also within a week receive the Sacraments of Penance and of the Most Blessed Eucharist, we bestow by Our Apostolic authority a Plenary Indulgence.

12.7. In addition, we urge you to exhort the people under your jurisdiction to give alms for the relief of the Irish Nation. You know the power of almsgiving and the rich fruits which proceed from it. You know the noteworthy praises showered on almsgiving by the holy Church Fathers and especially by St Leo the Great in many of his sermons. And you readily recall the well-known letter of St Cyprian, Martyr and Bishop of Carthage, to the Bishops of Numidia (*Epistle* 60) which contains clear evidence of his people's zeal in generous almsgiving for those Christians who needed help. You can, furthermore, remember the words of St Ambrose, Bishop of Milan (*Epistle* 2, to Bishop Constantius) that 'the beauty of wealth lies not in the manner of life of the rich but in food given to the poor; wealth is more resplendent among those who are weak and in want; Christians should learn to use money in looking not for their own good but for Christ's, so that Christ in turn may look after them'. When you recall these and other words of praise, we hope that you will vigorously assist the poor to whom we refer.

12.8. We could indeed end our letter here. But since you are about to proclaim public prayers, we must add, Venerable Brothers, that of which 'Our daily urgency, the care of all the Churches' (St Paul, 2 Cor 2:28) warns us day and night: that is, the furious, savage storm that we have seen for a long time raised up against the whole Church. Our spirit shrinks to recall 'how greatly his enemy hates the Holy One' (Ps 73:3) and what evil scheming now goes on 'against the Lord and His Christ' (Ps 3:2). Therefore, we strongly recommend that when you proclaim public prayers for Ireland, you ask your people to beseech God at the same time for the whole Church.

Meanwhile, Venerable Brothers, We most lovingly impart to you Our Apostolic Blessing.

Given in Rome at St Mary Major on the 25th of March 1847, in the first year of Our Pontificate.

13. Fundraising by German Catholic bishops

13.1. *Introduction.* This is a letter, in reply to previous correspondence, from Peter von Richarz, Archbishop of Augsburg, to Daniel Murray, Archbishop of Dublin, describing the outcome of fund-raising undertaken by him and by the Archbishop of Munich & Freising. He details the transmission of the monies and states that the funds will be available in a Dublin bank account in the New Year (1848). SOURCE: Letter from Peter von Richarz, Bishop of Augsburg to Dr Daniel Murray, Archbishop of Dublin. Dublin Diocesan Archives, Drumcondra, Co. Dublin.

13.2. Augsburg, 25 December 1847

To the Most Reverend Dr Daniel Murray,

My Lord,

According to Your Lordship's letter of the 11 November, I took great care to find a banker here who would undertake to transmit to You by Your appointed way the money collected in my Dioceses for the relief of the Destitute Poor of Ireland, which I mentioned in my letter of the 29th. October past.

In the meantime, the Most Reverend Archbishop of Munich and Freising, Count Charles Augustus of Reisach, had also sent to me the voluntary contributions collected for Ireland in his Archdiocese in an amount of 153 florins [approx. €1,200] desiring me to send you this money together with the collected sum of my Dioceses.

This money counted to the sum, which was collected in my Dioceses, gives exactly the sum of 13,196 florins (approx. €145,000) which a few days ago the Banker, Augustus Frommel of this place accepted in such a manner that after the deduction of postages and other expenses, there still remained the sum of 13,144 florins for being sent to Your Lordship.

This said, Banker A. Frommel has procured Bills of Exchange upon London and after the receipt of the money he intimated to me to have written to Messrs Coutts & Co., Bankers in London, that after the deduction of their expenses they should lodge the above mentioned sum of 13,144 florins in your favour in the Bank of Ireland, Dublin. The Bills of Exchange will be payable in the middle of the next month of January circa.

Your Lordship may please to give me in a few lines an acknowledgement of having received the money, and You will distribute it between the Destitute Poor of Ireland in a manner which may seem to You most suitable.

Recommending myself and my Diocesans to Your Lordship's and the Irish Catholics' fraternal prayers. I am with the greatest respect and veneration.

My Lord, Your Lordship's humble servant and Brother in Christ
Peter Richarz
Bishop of Augsburg.

14. American reactions

14.1. *Introduction.* The United States sent more than two million dollars' worth of private relief to Ireland, in the form of cash, food, and clothing. The Boston Relief Committee, one of the first, dates to the end of 1845. The following five documents offer a sampling of the reporting of the Famine in the press in Boston and Washington, the vigorous American reaction, and the pressure brought on the political elite, including the President, the Vice-President, and Congress, to organise and contribute to relief for Ireland.

1. Meeting of the Friends of Ireland
SOURCE: *Boston Pilot*, 12 December 1845.

14.2. On Monday evening one of the most numerous and enthusiastic meetings that we ever attended assembled in the Odeon to consider the best ways and means of contributing to alleviate the distress which now threatens the people of Ireland, in consequence of the failure of the Potato Crop. The Odeon, capable of holding three thousand persons, was thronged throughout ...

14.3. It appears by undoubted evidence, recently arrived among us, that the British government neglects to provide for the inevitable famine which impends over the Irish people by refusing to shut the Irish ports against the further exportation of the Grain grown upon the soil, which belongs by the laws of God to the Irish people, but on the contrary, induces the export of Irish Grain to England, by keeping up the inhuman Corn Laws, and forbidding the reception of foreign Wheat, Flour, or Corn into the United Kingdom, unless on payment of an agricultural duty ...

14.4. Resolved. That with a view to alleviate in some degree that Famine, which we deem to be inevitable, we now enter into a subscription towards the purchase of provisions either in Ireland or here, to aid to the utmost limits of our means our suffering brethren beyond the Atlantic ...

14.5. Resolved. That we call upon our fellow citizens from Maine to Texas, without distinction of creed or party, nation or color, to come forward at this dreadful crisis in the fate of a suffering people, and aid us in rescuing them from the horrors of famine.

14.6. Resolved. That we call from this spot, and on this occasion, upon the dormant Repeal Associations throughout America to revive their activity in the cause of Ireland and so co-operate with us and the patriots of Ireland in a vigorous effort to restore that great nation to her place among the communities of Europe, where her children shall be masters of their own rich soil, and be thereby abundantly supplied with every accessory of life.

2. Meeting in Washington
SOURCE: *Daily National Intelligencer* (Washington), 8 February 1847.

14.7. The undersigned, in view of the fearful ravages of the famine now prevailing in Ireland, hereby call a public meeting of members of Congress and all others at the seat of government who will co-operate in the movement, for the purpose of devising some general efficient plan whereby the charities of the people of the United States may be concentrated for the relief of that unhappy country from the horrors of death by starvation.

3. The Washington Public Meeting
SOURCE: *Daily National Intelligencer* (Washington), 10 February 1847.

14.8. Held last night in Odd Fellows' Hall, for giving an impulse to a national movement for the relief of Ireland, was the largest meeting of the kind which ever took place in this city. The Hon. George M. Dallas, Vice-President of the United States, presided, assisted by a large number of Vice-Presidents, Senators and Representatives. The meeting was earnestly and impressively addressed by the Vice-President, by the Hon. Daniel Webster, the Revd Dr Dewey, the Hon. Mr Maclay, the Hon. Mr Owen, the Hon. Mr Crittenden, and other gentlemen; and sundry resolutions for organising a general system of relief, and an eloquent address, were adopted.

4. Aid from Boston
SOURCE: *Boston Pilot* (Boston), 6 March 1847.

14.9. We are delighted to state to our readers that the work of the relief for Ireland is progressing beyond all expectation. The Right Revd Bishop Fitzpatrick has already remitted nearly twenty thousand dollars. This speaks well for the zeal of the Irish and Catholics of Boston, and there is no doubt that the same amount will again be collected and sent over ere long. To those who may feel curious to know why money was remitted instead of breadstuffs, and how it will be distributed, we would inform them that *immediate* relief being required, it was thought best to send the money, as it will be conveyed in less than half the time that it would take to send over the produce … We furthermore understand that the above and all subsequent remittances will be placed into the hands of the Archbishops of Ireland, and by them distributed in accordance with the wants of the various localities, and without distinction of creed.

5. Loss of the Bill for the Relief of Ireland
SOURCE: *Boston Pilot* (Boston), 13 March 1847.

14.10. Washington. As I anticipated, the Bill appropriating $500,000 for the relief of the starving poor of Ireland has been allowed to die a natural death contrary, I would venture to say, to the expectations and wishes of three-fourths of the people of this country. It passed the Senate by a very respectable majority, some of the most distinguished members of that body voting in its favour and thereby sanctioning the constitutionality of the measure … But the wiseacres of the House thought differently, and acted accordingly … A meeting of the Cabinet was held a few days afterwards. There it was learned that James Buchanan (Secretary of State) had subscribed $100 and how would it look if the President refused to give a cent! Here policy got the better of economy. That yellow-covered book was now sent for, and the name of James Polk stands recorded upon the *third* page opposite to which is subscribed the sum of $50.

15. American donations

15.1. *Introduction.* Here are excerpts from several contemporary sources, detailing aid provided by private sources from within the United States. The first document describes the efforts of the Irish Relief Fund in New York; and the second the cargo of provisions of two American naval ships, the USS *Jamestown* and USS *Macedonian*, for the relief of Ireland and Scotland. The third and fourth documents refer to the donation from the Choctaw Nation and an American response to it. These latter documents throw more light on American racism than the notable generosity of the Choctaw.

1. Irish Relief Fund, New York
SOURCE: *New York Sun*, quoted in *The Times* (London), 19 March 1847.

15.2. The Irish Relief Fund is swelling up. New York has contributed nearly $40,000 (approx. €800,000) in all; and the same energetic movement is going forward in Boston, Albany, Utica, Philadelphia, Baltimore, Washington, Cincinnati, New Orleans etc. It is impossible for us to give every instance of individual charity in the various cities. We shall endeavour to keep the run of contributions in this city, and eventually we hope to receive from the relief committee full lists of all the donations made in the city and neighbourhood for Ireland and Scotland. At the city of Newark, New Jersey, a meeting has been held, $1,500 (approx. €31,000) subscribed, and measures adopted to send out a ship laden with grain for the Irish poor. Mr M.H. Grinnel, the shipping merchant, has made arrangements to deliver in Ireland, at his own expense, 1,000 bushels of corn presented by Mr James Wadsworth of Genessee, Livingston County, New York. A lady in this city has sent $1,000 (approx. €21,000) to the relief committee, but she modestly withholds her name. The New York relief ship *Victor*, now loading at this city, was chartered some time ago, when freights were cheap, by Messrs Dulilh and Cousineri, who cheerfully transferred their favourable bargain to the relief committee. At Cincinnati, Ohio, $3,000 (approx. €63,000) was subscribed in one evening, and committees appointed to increase the sum. At New Bedford, Massachusetts, Mr Rotch, jun. gave $400 (approx. €8,400); and Mr E. Harris, of Woonsocket, Rhode Island, $500. Rochester has contributed $1,000. The Catholic Church at Boston has contributed $5,387 (approx. €113,000).

2. Jamestown and Macedonian cargo
SOURCE: Charles Edward Trevelyan, *The Irish crisis* (London, 1848), 50–1.

15.3. Two United States ships of war, the *Jamestown* and *Macedonian* were manned by volunteers, and sent to Ireland and Scotland with the following charitable supplies, for which no claim for freight was made …

Table 3: USS *Jamestown* cargo

Wheat	4 qrs*
Barley	3 qrs 4 bsh
Oats	2 qrs 4 bsh
Rye	9 qrs 2 bsh
Peas	30 qrs
Beans	279 qrs 3 bsh
Indian Corn or Maize	339qrs 2bsh
Wheatmeal/Flour	96cwt 1 qr
Barley/Oatmeal	19 cwt 2 qrs 16 bsh
Indian Corn Meal	4,229 cwt 3 qrs
Rice	154 cwt 1 qr 4 bsh
Bread and Biscuit	1,048 cwt 3 qrs 21 bsh
Potatoes	61 cwt 1 qr 1 bsh
Apples, dried	6 bsh
Pork	707 cwt 0 qr 16 bsh
Hams	291cwt 3qr 4bsh
Fish	4cwt
Clothing	10 cases, 18 barrels.

Table 4: USS *Macedonian* cargo

Indian Corn Meal	1,043,504 lbs
Rice	145,824 lbs
Beans	19,424 lbs
Peas	11,388 lbs
Indian Corn	lbs 3,800
Wheat	100 lbs
Salt Pork	200 lbs
Clothing	13 boxes, 3 bales, 3 barrels.

*Note on converting 1847 Imperial dry measures to metric. 1 quart=1.136 litres; 32 quarts=1 bushel or 36 litres; 1 quarter (qr)=12.75kg; 1 cwt (hundredweight)=50.8kg; 20 cwt (hundredweight)=1 ton=1016kg; 2.2lbs=1kg

3. Donation from the Choctaw Nation
SOURCE: Minute of M. Van Schiack, Chairman of the Quaker Relief Committee, New York, May 1847.

> **15.4.** Among the contributions last received is a sum of $170 (approx. €3,500 at 2009 values) of which the largest part was contributed by the children of the forest ... these distant men have felt the force of Christian sympathy and benevolence and have given their cheerful aid in this good cause, though they are separated from you by miles of land and an ocean's breadth.

4. Response to the Choctaw donation
SOURCE: *Arkansas Intelligencer* (Arkansas, USA), 3 April 1847.

15.5. What an agreeable reflection it must give to the Christian and philanthropist, to witness this evidence of civilisation and Christian spirit existing among our red neighbours. They are repaying the Christian world a consideration for bringing them out of benighted ignorance and heathen barbarism. Not only by contributing a few dollars, but by affording evidence that the labours of the Christian Missionary have not been in vain.

16. Relief and proselytism: charity in Connacht

16.1. *Introduction.* The Belfast Ladies' Association was organised under the direction of the Revd John Edgar, the noted temperance advocate and professor of Divinity in the Royal College of Belfast. By 1849, it had collected £15,000 (approx. €1.3 million) which was used to establish industrial schools in Connacht. By 1850, the Association had employed thirty-two schoolmistresses. In the same year, the Association claimed to have offered employment and education to over 2,000 poor girls and women. The extract from Edgar's letter below sketches the difficulties faced by him in his daily work. SOURCE: *The Banner of Ulster*, 9 January 1849.

> **16.2.** But the great lesson which has been taught us by those persons who have so nobly devoted themselves to the advancement of their countrymen, is the vast capacity for improvement which exists in the Irish people ... The following extract, from a most valuable communication ... by the Revd John Edgar, D.D., professor of Divinity in the Royal College of Belfast, forcibly illustrates this truth:–

> **16.3.** 'I am doing a little work in wild Connacht; will you help me with a little publicity, to induce some of the generous and strong to come to my aid? During the famine I was the means of getting collected some fifteen thousand pounds. Excellent ladies, of different denominations, assisted me in getting and spending part of it; and when the cry of hunger was hushed, they resolved to devote themselves to the same object which engages your pen and heart now – industry and general reformation ...

16.4. We have to encounter many difficulties – utter ignorance of order, punctuality, manufacture or manufacturing implements – want driving our pupils, before well-instructed, to the poor-house – lying, thievish habits, dark houses unfit for work, irregularity of means of conveyance, ignorance of the English language – but, over and above all, the opposition, with a few exceptions, of the Romish priests, of which I could tell strange tales.

16.5. The latter difficulty, we presume, is occasioned by the rule of the schools, which makes the reading of the Bible a part of the daily business, coupled, as we understand, with some religious teaching or devotional exercise.

17. Relief and proselytism: an appeal

17.1. *Introduction.* Michael Brannigan, a convert from Catholicism to the Presbyterian Church, was a well-known proselytiser who worked in the West of Ireland. He was fluent in Irish. In 1847 he established 12 schools in counties Mayo and Sligo, and by the end of the next year there were 28, despite the opposition of the Catholic priests. Here is a heartfelt letter to the Protestant children of Britain about his work and difficulties. SOURCE: *The Banner of Ulster*, 12 January 1849.

17.2. To the children of the Protestant Churches in England, Ireland and Scotland.

Dear Children,

Another year has rolled by since I last wrote to you. No doubt many of you are now looking for news about the children of poor Connacht, to whom you cheerfully divided a portion of the gifts last year.

… On looking at my letter of last year, I find that the number of schools that I had then under my care only amounted to twelve; it pleased the Lord to enable those to weather the storm of famine and priestly opposition during the last twelve months and to increase them to twenty-eight … The twelve schools that I had under my superintendence in December 1847 were attended by a thousand scholars, whilst in the twenty-eight now in operation, there are not more than one thousand one hundred and twenty. The average attendance, you will perceive, is greatly reduced. This was not caused by priestly denunciation, for of such the children are not afraid, but by the famine which, alas, has driven many of the scholars of our schools into the workhouse, where they are deprived of a Scriptural education … Many were so uncharitable as to conclude that is was the food, and not the Bible, that the children loved, and that so soon as they were deprived of the one, they would reject the other; experience has shown us, however, that such was not the case … they are not happy in that place of confinement [workhouses] – they have no Bibles there – no catechism, except the one belonging to the Church of Rome … They will then be registered as children of

Roman Catholics – be entirely deprived of all Scriptural education – be trained up in degrading subjection to the priest, and habituated to the soul-destroying service of the mass …

I am, my dear children, yours in the Lord,

Michael Brannigan, Missionary of the General Assembly of the Presbyterian Church in Ireland.

18. Central Relief Committee

18.1. *Introduction.* The General Central Relief Committee, formed in Dublin on 29 December 1846, was one of the most important private relief agencies. It had offices at 36 College Green and was well funded because of the influential people who were its trustees and committee members – the leading clergy, Catholic and Anglican; aristocrats such as the Marquess of Kildare, Lord Cloncurry, and the Earl of Erne; Daniel O'Connell MP; and William Smith O'Brien MP. In total, it distributed £61,767 (approx. €5.3 million). SOURCE: *Report of the Proceedings of the General Central Relief Committee for all Ireland from its formation on the 29th December to the 31st December 1847* (Dublin, 1848), 1–5.

18.2. A General Central Relief Committee for all Ireland was formed on 29 December, 1846, and held its first meeting on the 31 December, when the following Resolutions were agreed to as the basis on which to act:–

18.3. *Resolved.* That thoroughly acquainted as we are with the state of Ireland, we do feel it a solemn duty to warn the friends of humanity of the awful deficiency of food for subsistence in this country, for even a short period, the deficiency being so great as to threaten with certain death, hundreds of thousands of our fellow creatures; and unless the most active, prompt, and persevering exertions be made to augment in an almost indescribable degree, the quantity of food at present in Ireland, famine and pestilence will desolate the land …

18.4. Those parties who applied to the Committee were furnished with forms of queries, the answers to which were submitted to the consideration of the Committee that sat from day to day, investigating with great pains and patience every application for relief which during the whole year was brought under their notice …

18.5. About the beginning of September, the extreme pressure having abated, and the early harvest commencing, the Committee ceased allocating, except in a few instances of a peculiar nature, and finally, in October, altogether suspended their operations …

18.6. The Committee have the satisfaction of being enabled to state, that very general and cordial unanimity prevailed among the clergy of the different religious denominations in their united labours for the relief of the destitute.

19. British Relief Association

19.1. *Introduction.* The British Association for the Relief of Distress in Ireland and the Highlands of Scotland (the British Relief Association) was formed in London in January 1847 by Lionel de Rothschild, Jewish banker and philanthropist. Funds reached it from many sources, inside Britain and outside – from royalty and from private citizens of all classes and creeds. SOURCE: *Report of the British Association for the Relief of the Extreme Distress in Ireland and Scotland* (London, 1849), 10–11.

> **19.2.** The Committee which was formed in London to supply this deficiency [of food], was composed of men of every variety of opinion, religious and political. It commenced its operations by the publication of an address, setting forth the objects for which the Association had been formed, and the principles which would guide the Committee in the distribution of the monies raised.

> **19.3.** The response which this appeal received was as prompt as the emergency required. Her Majesty the Queen immediately directed that her name should be placed at the head of the list of donors for a contribution of £2,000 (approx. €172,000), with a most gracious promise of such further amount as the exigency might demand; and the example was liberally followed by every member of the Royal Family, including His Majesty the King of Hanover.

> **19.4.** A circular, issued by the Right Hon. the Lord Mayor of London (John Kinnerlsey Hooper) to the chief magistrates of the provincial cities and boroughs of England and Wales, met with an equally ready response. Public meetings were called in several important towns; subscription lists were opened at nearly all the Banks and principal mercantile establishments of the country; and these lists afford conclusive evidence of the anxiety of Englishmen, whatever their sphere or station, to contribute, to the utmost extent of their means, towards the relief of their suffering fellow-subjects.

> **19.5.** At a subsequent period, the subjects of the Crown of Great Britain, scattered not only in the colonies, but in foreign states, entered into public subscriptions for the same purpose. Nor were the subscriptions limited to British subjects. In the list of donors will be found the name of His Imperial Majesty the Sultan, a subscriber of £1,000 (approx. €86,000), whose munificent example was followed in his own and other states by many, whose sole ties with the people of Great Britain were those of sympathy, humanity, and the brotherhood of mankind.

20. Worldwide donations

20.1. *Introduction.* Listed below are some of the largest donations given to the British Relief Association to help alleviate famine in Ireland. The amount contributed through the British Association was £263,251 (approx. €22.6 million). SOURCE: Charles Edward Trevelyan, *The Irish crisis* (London, 1848), 86–7.

20.2. The following are some of the most remarkable contributions:–

Her Majesty the Queen – £2,000
H.R.H. Prince Albert – £500
H.M. the Queen Dowager – £1,000
His Majesty the King of Hanover – £1,000
His Imperial Highness the Sultan – £1,000
The East India Company – £1,000
The Corporation of the City of London – £1,000
The Bank of England – £1,000
The Duke of Devonshire – £1,000
The Worshipful Company of Grocers – £1,000
An Irish landlord, for Skibbereen – £1,000
Manchester and Salford Committee – £7,785
Newcastle and Gateshead Committee – £3,902
Hull Committee – £3,800
Leeds Committee – £2,500
Huddersfield Committee – £2,103
Wolverhampton – £1,838
York Committee – £1,770
Cambridge University and Town – £2,706
Oxford University and City – £1,770
Proceeds of a ball given in Florence – £891 17s. 2d.
St Petersburg – £2,644
Constantinople – £620
English Church in Amsterdam – £561
Parish priests in Denmark – £504
Malta and Gozo – £720
British Guiana – £3,000
House of Assembly, Nova Scotia – £2,915

21. Lord Clements in the House of Lords

21.1. *Introduction.* Lord Clements spoke in the House of Lords of the monies held unclaimed in dormant Irish charities that could be used for Famine relief. SOURCE: Debate in House of Lords, 5 February 1847, reported in the *Vindicator* (Belfast), 10 February 1847.

21.2. Lord Clements wished to call the attention of Her Majesty's Government to the Irish charities which were at present lying dormant. He would name a few of these charities. There was the Irish Peasantry Society, and the British and Irish Ladies' Society, both of which had received subscriptions to a very large amount. The British and Irish Ladies' Society had received the sum of £12,300 (approx. €1 million) from the subscriptions of 1822, when the last famine visited Ireland. There was another society which had received subscriptions to a similar amount. There was also a handsome subscription collected in the city of Dublin, by a society, which afterwards dissolved itself, leaving a large balance in the Bank of Ireland. Now, these funds could not be touched, unless by an act of parliament, and when they were called upon for an advance to meet the destitution which prevailed in Ireland, he wished Her Majesty's Government to look after the funds. One society, called the Reproductive Society, had a large sum in their account.

22. Overseas aid: British and foreign

22.1. *Introduction.* The overseas response, especially from those of Irish descent, but not limited to them, was generous and significant. British India contributed well over £22,000 (approx. €1.9 million), but much smaller British possessions gave generously as did many foreign states. Here are five short extracts on the actions of Barbados, Tobago, Antigua, and the Ottoman Sultan.

1. Relief from Barbados
SOURCE: *The Liberal* (Barbados), 15 February 1847.

> **22.2.** The harrowing accounts of the daily increased numbers of deaths from starvation in the above countries [Ireland and Scotland] have caused in London the establishment of the British Relief Association – an auxiliary committee has been formed in Barbados to aid in carrying out the benevolent objects of the British Association. It is hereby notified to the public that subscriptions have been opened at the office of the Colonial Treasury and at the Colonial and West Indies banks where the donations of the charitable are most earnestly supplicated.

2. The House of Assembly, Barbados
SOURCE: Editorial, *The Liberal* (Barbados), 15 February 1847.

> **22.3.** A Bill will be introduced in the House of the Assembly at its next meeting to grant a sum of money for the same purpose [giving aid to Ireland]. We trust the amount will be worthy of our legislation, and of the occasion for which it is to be granted. As a correspondent has stated, Barbados owes Ireland a great deal of gratitude for substantial aid in distress. The princely sum of £20,000 was contributed by the citizens of Dublin for our relief after the dreadful hurricane of 1780. What would that amount do at present? ... Let us suggest to our country friends, small cultivators and labourers, that food is the article most needed in Ireland, and more valuable at the moment than gold ... They are without food. A yam, a quart of corn – anything that will be eaten and will reach Ireland will

be acceptable ... And in this way, the poorest of our labouring friends may contribute to the wants of the destitute and starving brethren in Ireland. Oh how we should rejoice to see a ship sail out of Carlisle Bay with a cargo of our native provisions, contributed as a free will offering of Christian amity, by the free peasants of Barbados to their distressed brethren in Ireland.

3. Donations from Tobago

SOURCE: From Lieutenant Governor Graeme to Earl Grey, Colonial Secretary, Government House, Tobago, in Parliamentary Papers, *Copies of Despatches to the Secretary of State from the Governors of Her Majesty's Colonial Possessions,* 53, 1847, p. 15, 4 May 1847.

22.4. My Lord, in pursuance with the sixth resolution, unanimously adopted at a public meeting held in this island for the purpose of taking into consideration the destitution which prevails in Ireland and parts of the Highlands of Scotland. I do myself the honour to place in the hands of your lordship the first of two sets of exchange notes for £150 (approx. €13,000 at 2009 values) and £160 3s. 5d., making a total of £310 3s. 5d. Although this is only a mite in comparison with the gigantic efforts made by the other provinces for the relief of our destitute fellow countrymen, Your Lordship will learn with pleasure that the negro population of Tobago have come forward on this occasion with much liberality and good feeling.

4. Donations from Antigua

SOURCE: From Governor Higginson to Earl Grey, Colonial Secretary, *Parliamentary Papers, Copies of Despatches to the Secretary of State from the Governors of Her Majesty's Colonial Possessions,* 53, p. 16, 11 May 1847.

22.5. I have the honour to report, for the information of your lordship, that the private subscriptions collected in this island for the relief of the distressed Irish and Scotch, amounted to £646 2s. 3d. sterling, of which £444 12s. 3d. was remitted to Messrs Latouche, Co. Dublin, for the former, and £200 10s. 0d. to Henry Brook Esquire, Banker, Glasgow, for the latter. It was gratifying to observe that many of the emancipated race [slaves in British colonies who were liberated after 1833] readily united with the other classes of the community in contributing to this charitable object. Subscriptions for the same purpose have also been raised in other islands, but I have not been informed of the sums realised.

5. The Sultan of the Ottoman Empire

SOURCE: *The Times* (London), 17 April 1847.

22.6. A letter from Constantinople mentions an act of liberality on the part of the Sultan which does him great credit. Upon hearing of the suffering of the Irish, the Sultan caused to be handed to the Honourable Mr Wellesley, £1,000, to be disposed of by him in the best way towards their alleviation.

23. Belfast Relief Fund

23.1. *Introduction.* This is a brief account of the proceedings of the committee administering the Belfast General Relief Fund in January 1849. SOURCE: *The Banner of Ulster*, 5 January 1849.

> **23.2.** A public meeting of this Society was held on Wednesday, at one o'clock, in the Town Hall, the Mayor presiding. The attendance was not numerous. After some preliminary conversation, the Revd Dr Drew read the Society's report. The document set out by stating the reasons for the formation of the Society, and according to Dr Edgar a tribute of grateful acknowledgement for the assiduity with which he entered the task of enlisting the sympathies and bounty of the Belfast contributors on behalf of the nation's wants. It then details the various meetings of the Society, with the business transacted in each, particularly the rules laid down to be acted upon – first, that the relief be afforded to alleviate the present distress in Ireland without restrictions to any locality – secondly, that the sum raised be entrusted to a committee, to be elected from the subscribers – and thirdly, that this sum be expended solely in supplying food. The amount thus raised was £7,073 1s. 9d. (approx. €600,000) – the sub-committee who inquired into the applications for grants being engaged in their duties for seven hours in the day.

24. Destitution in the West of Ireland, 1849–50

> **24.1.** *Introduction.* Sidney Godolphin Osborne (1808–89), clergyman and philanthropist of distinction, wrote on many matters: education, sanitation, women's rights, and cholera. In 1849 and again in 1850, he visited Ireland. This left a deep and lasting impression on him: 'In these pages, [readers will] find a ready source of reference to those facts, on which I ground my appeal for the consideration of all who love mercy and justice, to the oppression, and the suffering, of the people of this part of the Queen's dominions'. He makes clear his disgust and his shame at the seeming failure of the British government to alleviate the suffering of the poor. Here he describes his journey through Clifden in 1850 and his visit to the workhouse there. SOURCE: Sidney Godolphin Osborne, *Gleanings in the West of Ireland* (London, 1850), 74–80.

> **24.2.** There was a yard, with a day ward in it, of about 30 ft by 15 ft [9.14 × 4.57 metres], with open roof, in which were about 160 small children; in one corner there was a child with the small-pox out upon it; at least 30 of the others had not been vaccinated … The state of these children's clothing was quite shameful; if possible, they were in this respect worse than the same class at Limerick. Many of them were mere skeletons. They were walked out into the yard for me to see them better; as they passed us, one child actually, whether of herself, or by order,

put her hand across to hold the rags together in front of the poor thing who walked with her, that we might not be more shocked ... they looked in the yard so cold, so comfortless, so naked, and such a libel on humanity, that I was glad to have them called in again to the close and infected atmosphere of the crowded day room; they were, I believe, all girls, though such is the nature of pure rag attire, that the dress often ceases to be any guide, as to the sex, amongst the young.

24.3. There were two underground places, which the architect meant for lumber rooms, which we, however, found inhabited; they were damp and chilly, unventilated, and utterly unfitted for the purpose to which they were applied. There were some adult women in one of them, crouched upon the cold floor, looking just as such beings, so starved, so clad, would look in such a place; they were new admissions. There was little about the whole house out of keeping with what I have described: want of space, want of clothing, in a refuge crowded by those who come in starving and naked, must defy anything like the order and decency which should characterise every public establishment professing to be under the guardianship of the laws.

24.4. We now went to an Auxiliary [overflow building], just occupied by a class of able-bodied women, called the 'Police Barrack'. The day rooms of this wretched building had no sashes in the ground-floor windows; they were, however, covered with iron lattice; immediately under them was a mass of stinking filth of the most miscellaneous character. Passing through a narrow dirty passage, we turned out of a confined yard, in which some masons were at work building up a wall, into two day rooms, i.e. what had been two rooms; the partition door, however, had been removed, though the division walls, or some of them remained. The rooms were measured in my presence, and the result, on a drawing in my notes, records, that the area of both inclusive of 21 ft by 12 ft [6.4 × 3.65 metres]; in this space, we found 32 women in the inner room, 35 in the outer, being 67 adult women in a space of 21 ft by 12 ft! The ceiling was not, I believe, nine feet from the ground. In another small room, 9 ft by 11 ft [2.74 × 3.35 metres], twelve grown-up women lived, i.e. existed. In a loft, of dimensions not larger than the first-mentioned rooms, the roof coming down at an acute angle to the floor, twenty-six adult women were said to sleep; I believe more did sleep.

24.5. No power of pen can describe the state of the clothing of this seething mass of female pauperage; there were some, that the others, for shame's sake, would not let stand up before us; some I felt ashamed to ask to do so, though with more rags on. The smell of the rooms was intolerable; that of the yard, from an unmistakable source, no improvement on it. I can hardly conceive anything more thoroughly brutalising than the herding of this mass together at night; for if they do not sleep in their dirty rags, they must at all events, I presume, be disentangled from them when they lie down, in the place where they lie down; this rag heap, then, redolent of many days or weeks' wear in this confined space, must add its share to that offence to every sense, which, without it, the masses so herded on the floors would produce.

24.6. There were altogether 150 inmates in this house. The day room looks through the lattice into the public street; how such a place, for such a number of persons, could ever have been sanctioned, I cannot understand; if they escape a pestilence, which shall destroy life, they cannot escape an amount of moral disease, which must so brutalise, as to painfully affect it.

24.7. We now went to another Auxiliary, in which were between 40 and 50 infants, with their mothers, many of these small morsels of misery were absolutely naked; their mothers, generally speaking, clothed only so far as a small allowance of filthy rags, can be called clothing. Of course they were crowded far more than was in any way justifiable. In another Auxiliary, there were 2 or 300 able-bodied females; still the same want of dress, or rather the same insufficiency of rags; packed closely at night in two or three dormitories; by day, their only shelter was one room, of the same area as any one of the said dormitories; but its size reduced by the tables for dining; they were sitting in heaps, in idleness, about the yard. The Auxiliary for the boys was some miles off, so that I did not see it; I can only hope it is no worse than those I did see, though that were scarcely possible.

24.8. This Clifden Union had poor rates in course of collection at the end of the quarter, terminating 30th of last March, to the amount of £2,287 (approx. €197,000); it had received relief from the rate-in-aid in that quarter, to the amount of £2,115; its net liabilities at the same period, over balance at the Bank, were £6,292 (approx. €540,000). The weekly average mortality per 1,000 inmates, for the four weeks ending March 30th, 1850, was 1:8!

24.9. It is awful to contemplate, as in the case of this Union, to what one's fellow creatures can be exposed, when the scene of infliction is in one of these out of the way corners of Her Majesty's dominions. There is a chance, in a place like Limerick, of some stray traveller, or some local party of sufficient courage and humanity, rising up, to publicly protest against such treatment of our fellow subjects, in establishments, supported under legal enactment, and supposed to be under official supervision; but here, I believe, anything might be done, and the chances of exposure be small. The people of all ranks are so now accustomed to scenes of misery and tyranny, that they have ceased to be shocked or roused by them; they say, 'the potato rot' brought it about, 'potato plenty' will heal it. The intermediate misery is counted as a small thing for humanity to notice; humanity, I fear, has been so taxed, that it has become blind to anything, which might increase its burden.

24.10. I know no justifiable excuse, however, for such wanton contempt of life and decency; I do not know why the 'rate-in-aid' Bill was passed, but to obtain the efficient working of the Poor-law, in bankrupt Unions; it is folly to call this make-shift make-shame system Poor-law administration. In England one-fiftieth part of such conduct, would so rouse the indignation of the public, that a speedy end would be put to the abuse, and I have no doubt, pretty severe rebuke dealt on all who connived at, or promoted it. I have yet to learn, that Ireland is not an integral part of Great Britain; I have yet to learn, that doings so disgraceful can exist is Ireland, and not be a shame and disgrace to England.

24.11. My friend here again indulged himself in large investments in bread, to feed the poor wretches he found in the street, and with the customary result; he soon being forced from the pressure, to make a retreat at the rear of the shop. I cannot wonder at the perseverance he displayed; he was new to Ireland; less hardened than myself. From a window we got an opportunity of seeing, ourselves unseen, some of the bread he had given consumed; there was no deceit in the way it was devoured; more voracious reality, it would be hardly possible to conceive; to see the fleshless arms grasping one part of a loaf, whilst the fingers – bone handled forks – dug into the other, to supply the mouth – such mouths too! With an eagerness, as if the bread were stolen, the thief starving, and the steps of the owner heard; it was a picture, I think neither of us will easily forget.

24.12. … No sooner was our car under weigh, than a pack of famished creatures of all descriptions and sexes, set off in full chase after us; the taste of fresh bread, still inflamed the spirit of some; the report of it put others in hot hungry pursuit; the *crescit eundo* [it grows as it goes] is ever realised in the motion of an Irish mob. Our driver did his best, but our pursuers had us at advantage; for our road was up a very steep long hill; they gained on us, and we were soon surrounded by the hungry pack; the cry of the regular professional mendicant, the passionate entreaty of the really destitute, the ragged, the really starving; the whining entreaties of the still more naked children, still more starved – in a famine the weakest ever suffer soonest. The quickness and volubility of Irish national mendacity, sharpened by hunger, and excited by the rare chance of appeasing it, all combined to give voice to the pack. No two luckless human beings were ever so hunted; no ravening wolves ever gave more open expression of their object – food. A little coaxing – my friend's; a little violence – my own; a little distribution of copper coin from both of us, at last rid us of the inconvenient, but natural result of an Englishman with money in his pocket, and a baker's shop near, wishing in Ireland to feed some starving people.

25. The Ladies' Hibernian Female School Society

25.1. *Introduction*. The Ladies' Hibernian Female School Society, established in 1824, encouraged Irishwomen to open schools in their localities. A parent body arranged to collection and distribute funds. The women themselves were not paid for their work. By 1845 it claimed to have over 230 schools under its patronage. Many of the women were condemned by the Catholic Church which saw them as potential proselytisers. Here a Sligo lady writes to thank donors for their charity. SOURCE: *Christian Ladies' Magazine*, London, March 1847.

25.2. *14 December 1846.* As you enjoy so much the luxury of doing good, you may form some right conception of my delight yesterday, after having 100 articles of dress made in the school, and distributing with them fifty more with my own hands to our children. Think of the joy and gladness with which each little one returned to her own home. It was a jubilee indeed. Oh! What a gracious God we have to do with! Who serves him for nought! I received your second welcome half note to-day. When a supply comes, I think I am passing rich; but, to my surprise, I find myself, on the arrival of a new announcement, actually in need!

25.3. *5 January 1847.* How good God is in thus bringing into such active operation the benevolence of comparatively unknown friends. I include in this remark the £5 (approx. €430) of your last remittance, and all the other marks of God's tender pity through the instrumentality of our humane and munificent English sympathizers. It is amazing the regularity with which my charity purse is supplied. When I begin to calculate on withholding my hand, as its contents begin to run to a close, I am that very day put to shame for my unbelief, by the delivery of some new packet of help. My God, where shall I thy praise begin?

CHRISTINE KINEALY AND TOMÁS O'RIORDAN

AN

A C T

FOR

The Union of *Great Britain* and *Ireland.*

FRIDAY THE FIRST DAY OF AUGUST, ONE THOUSAND EIGHT
HUNDRED, ROYAL ASSENT GIVEN.
JOHN GAYER, D. CLER. PARL.

DUBLIN:

Printed by George Grierson,

PRINTER TO THE KING'S MOST EXCELLENT MAJESTY.

1800.

1. The title page of the Act of Union (1800), from a contemporary printing.

2. Dublin's first great Palladian building, the Parliament House in College Green (now Bank of Ireland). Designed by Sir Edward Lovett Pearce (1699–1733), and built 1728–39. A 1767 engraving by the cartographer and surveyor, (Peter) Bernard Scalé, (1739/40–1826). (Courtesy of the Irish Architectural Archive.)

3. St Patrick's Day (1844), military parade at Dublin Castle, watercolour by Michelangelo Hayes (1820–77). The culmination of the Castle social season on 17 March each year began with an inspection of the guard by the Viceroy and military manoeuvres. Here we see the 11th Hussars in the foreground, with trumpeters of the 3rd Dragoon Guards and infantry of the 16th Regiment. A grand banquet and St Patrick's Ball followed. (Courtesy of the OPW.)

4. The Lord Lieutenant or Viceroy was the monarch's representative in Ireland. The Viceroy's offices were in Dublin Castle; the Vice-Regal Lodge (now Áras an Uachtaráin) in Phoenix Park was his official residence. The Lord Lieutenant, James Hamilton, first Duke of Abercorn (1811–85), is pictured seventh from the right c.1866.

5. Portrait of Daniel O'Connell as a young counsellor. *Dublin Magazine*, March 1813. Attributed to a member of the Brocas family.

6. Daniel O'Connell's funeral procession drew immense crowds. His remains were brought early in August 1847 to the Catholic Church in Marlborough Street, Dublin. He was buried on 5 August at Glasnevin cemetery, Dublin, first in a temporary grave, and from 1869 in a vault beneath a magnificent 165 feet high replica round tower.
(*Illustrated London News,* August, 1847.)

7. Sir Robert Peel (1788–1850) as a young man. Peel had considerable experience of governing Ireland. As Conservative prime minister in 1845–6, his secret purchase of Indian corn helped prevent widespread famine.

8. Arthur Wellesley, 1st Duke of Wellington (1769–1852), after a portrait by Sir Thomas Lawrence.

9. An engraved portrait of Henry William Paget, 1st Marquess Anglesey (1768–1854), in earlier life, after the original by Sir Thomas Lawrence.

10. Engraved portrait of George III (1738–1820), King of Great Britain and Ireland (1760–1820). Published in 1809, after the original by Sir William Beechy.

11. 'Dr Arthur and his man Bob giving John Bull a Bolus'. Cartoon of 1829 showing Wellington and Peel forcing Emancipation down the throat of a reluctant John Bull.

12. Anti-Emancipation cartoon, depicting Wellington, Peel and the Lord Chancellor of England, Lord Lyndhurst, receiving absolution from a band of Catholic prelates. They had been given authority by George IV to consider bringing forward Emancipation as a government measure.

13. 'The Apostates and the Extinguisher …', by Williams, 23 February 1829. The cartoon depicts the capitulation of British politicians to Catholic agitation. Wellington is shown kissing the Pope's toe and professing loyalty to Rome, while Home Secretary Peel offers up the Anglican liturgy and the crown to the pontiff. The prime minister prepares to set the papal tiara on both of them, thereby extinguishing the flame of Protestantism in Britain. On the right the (papal) bull gores a docile and muzzled (British) pit bull. (Courtesy of the British Museum, London.)

ANNO DECIMO

GEORGII IV. REGIS.

****

An Act for the Relief of His Majesty's Roman Catholic Subjects. [13th *April* 1829.]

WHEREAS by various Acts of Parliament certain Restraints and Disabilities are imposed on the Roman Catholic Subjects of His Majesty, to which other Subjects of His Majesty are not liable: And whereas it is expedient that such Restraints and Disabilities shall be from henceforth discontinued: And whereas by various Acts certain Oaths and certain Declarations, commonly called the Declaration against Transubstantiation, and the Declaration against Transubstantiation and the Invocation of Saints and the Sacrifice of the Mass, as practised in the Church of *Rome*, are or may be required to be taken, made, and subscribed by the Subjects of His Majesty, as Qualifications for sitting and voting in Parliament, and for the Enjoyment of certain Offices, Franchises, and Civil Rights: Be it enacted by the King's most Excellent Majesty, by and with the Advice and Consent of the Lords Spiritual and Temporal, and Commons, in this present Parliament assembled, and by the Authority of the same, That from and after the Commencement of this Act all such Parts of the said Acts as require the said Declarations, or either of them, to be made or subscribed by any of His Majesty's Subjects, as a Qualification for sitting and voting in Parliament, or for the Exercise or Enjoyment of any Office, Franchise, or Civil Right, be and the same are (save as herein-after provided and excepted) hereby repealed.

Acts relating to Declarations against Transubstantiation, repealed.

II. And be it enacted, That from and after the Commencement of this Act it shall be lawful for any Person professing the Roman Catholic Religion, being a Peer, or who shall after the Commencement

Roman Catholics may sit and vote in Par-

14. Extract from the 'Act for the Relief of His Majesty's Roman Catholic Subjects', taken from *Statutes passed in the Tenth Year of King George the Fourth* (1829).

15. 'Brother, Brother, we're both in the wrong.' *Punch*, 15 June 1844. This cartoon features Queen Victoria and Tsar Nicholas I of Russia reflecting on their roles in the affairs of Ireland and Poland respectively. Victoria admits Britain's culpability in Irish injustices and suggests that Nicholas is responsible for similar wrongs in Poland. The Vienna settlement of 1815 established a reduced (and largely Catholic) Poland as a separate kingdom ruled by the much resented Tsar.

RAILWAY VIADUCT. ATHLONE. 2926. W.L.

16. Athlone Railway viaduct was built to cross the Shannon in 1850. It is approximately 165m (540ft) in length with a central span of 37m (120ft). The engineer was G.W. Hemans, and the contractors were Fox and Henderson. (Courtesy of the National Library of Ireland.)

17. Thomas Francis Meagher (1796–1874), second from right, and William Smith O'Brien (1803–64), seated, under guard at Kilmainham Gaol, Dublin, before being deported to Van Diemen's Land (Tasmania), Australia, in 1848. (Courtesy of Kilmainham Gaol.)

18. The linen industry strengthened the economic position of Ulster tenants. Profits from flax cultivation helped raise farm incomes and could increase the value of the tenant right in a holding when sold under the 'Ulster custom'. This 1859 sketch shows the flax being spread on the ground in sheaves. *Illustrated London News*, 24 September 1859.

19. Photograph of Lord John Russell (1792–1878), dated *c.*1864. Russell was the Whig Prime Minister during the Famine (1846–52). Although not unsympathetic to Ireland, he was deeply ignorant of conditions in the countryside. (Courtesy of Sean Sexton.)

20. Albumen portrait of Sir Charles Trevelyan (1807–86), London, *c.*1860. As Assistant Secretary to the British Treasury during the Famine, he has been associated more than any with the inadequate relief policies of the Whig Government. He was, nevertheless, knighted by Queen Victoria in 1848 for his services to Ireland during the Famine. (Courtesy of Sean Sexton.)

21. Illustration of an emigrant ship leaving Liverpool in 1850. Between 1815 and 1845, between 750,000 and 1,000,000 emigrants left Ireland for North America. *Illustrated London News*, 6 July 1850.

22. 'Deaths by Starvation'. This vicious caricature from 1847 shows the devil presiding over a clerical feast while the people starve, a view of the Famine that contrasts sharply with that of *Punch*. It depicts the Anglican clergy as parasites, living off tithes, while the people suffer. Satan presides over the obscene feast on an Irish bull, holding a pig, a lamb and a loaf of bread. A waiter with a demon's tail carries in more decanters of port. The scene of excess and revelry contrasts starkly with the ghoulish carpet of emaciated cadavers beneath the diners' feet. Artist unknown. (Courtesy of the British Museum, London.)

23. 'Monster meeting' in August 1843 at Tara, royal site of the ancient High Kings. It was the largest of about forty such events that year. Supporters of Repeal often exaggerated the size of the crowds, but they were among the biggest political gatherings ever held in Ireland. *Illustrated London News*, 26 August 1843.

24. An ambrotype portrait photograph of an Irish labourer *c*.1850s. Images of labourers in their working clothes from this time are rare. (Courtesy of Sean Sexton.)

25. Portrait of Paul Cardinal Cullen (1803–78). *Harper's Weekly*, 30 November 1878.

26. From a portrait of Paul Cardinal Cullen in St Patrick's College, Drumcondra, Co. Dublin.

27. The Synod of Thurles in Session, September, 1850. *Illustrated London News,*
14 September 1850.

THE STATION.

UR readers are to suppose the Reverend Philemy M'Guirk, parish priest of Tir-neer, to be standing upon the altar of the chapel, facing the congregation, after having gone through the canon of the Mass; and having nothing more of the service to perform, than the usual prayers with which he closes the ceremony.

"Take notice, that the Stations for the following week will be held as follows :—

28. A 'station' mass in a private house. In the late eighteenth and early nineteenth centuries this was common. Illustration from *Traits and stories of the Irish peasantry* (1830), by William Carleton (1794–1869).

29. 'The Fenian Guy Fawkes' by Sir John Tenniel (1820–1914), senior cartoonist on *Punch* for over forty years. He plays on old anti-Catholic prejudices in his new take on the Gunpowder Plot, depicting an apish Irishman sitting on a barrel on gunpowder surrounded by innocent women and children. *Punch*, 28 December 1867.

TAKING THE (IRISH) BULL BY THE HORNS.

30. The Liberal Prime Minister William E. Gladstone (1809–98) found the Irish land question difficult. This *Punch* cartoon of 1870 shows him wrestling with the horns of an Irish bull, one a tenant, the other a landlord. Many felt that his 1870 Landlord and Tenant (Ireland) Act did not go far enough. *Punch*, 26 February 1870.

31. Engraving of Queen's College Cork (now University College Cork) c.1880s. The College (Ireland) Act provided for the foundation of three new colleges of Higher Education at Cork, Galway and Belfast. The Queen's Colleges opened to students on 30 October 1849.

32. Powerscourt House, Enniskerry, Wicklow, seat of the Viscounts Powerscourt, designed for Richard Wingfield by the gifted German architect Richard Cassels (1690–1751), in 1740. By the 1870s, the Viscount Powerscourt owned nearly 41,000 acres in Wicklow and 12,000 acres in Wexford and Dublin. Their estates were generally well managed and free of the destitution witnessed in parts of southern and western Ireland.

CHAPTER 7

The campaign for Catholic Emancipation, 1823–9

'I would rather give up my throne and beg from door to door throughout Europe than consent to such a measure', *George III*

1. Introduction

1.1. The Catholic question – political equality for Roman Catholics – was the most divisive issue in British domestic politics in the first thirty years of the nineteenth century. Such concessions aroused profound fears for the constitutional stability of the state and arose from a deep religious prejudice. However, the pressing need to pacify Ireland and a more liberal climate of opinion in England in the late 1820s ensured that any legislation would, in time, be pushed through.

1.2. Catholic Emancipation was finally granted by the Roman Catholic Relief Act of 13 April 1829 (10 Geo. IV, c. 7). It provided a new oath of allegiance, enabling Catholics to enter Parliament. Catholics were allowed to belong to any corporation and to hold certain positions that they were previously barred from, namely, many high-ranking governmental, administrative and judicial offices. The Act applied to the whole of the United Kingdom.

2. Background to the campaign

2.1. After the Reformation and the establishment of the Anglican Church, the British government enacted laws discriminating seriously against non-Anglicans, that is, Catholics and Dissenters. This was particularly serious in Ireland where over 80 per cent of the population were Catholic and about 4 per cent were Dissenter. Catholics were viewed as potential traitors, as un-British, and having divided loyalties. The situation worsened in the early eighteenth century when the Irish Parliament passed further and more seriously discriminatory laws against Catholics: they were subject to punitive taxation, not allowed to possess weapons, and discriminated against in terms of access to education, employment, property rights, and freedom of worship.

2.2. Educated Catholics began to agitate humbly for concessions in the eighteenth century, and with some success. These concessions came in the form of 'Relief Acts' in the latter half of the eighteenth century. The Bogland Act of 1772 (11 & 12 Geo. III, c. 21) allowed Catholics to take 61-year reclamation leases of bogland. The Act of 1774 (13 & 14 Geo. III, c. 35) made it possible for 'subjects of whatever persuasion' to take the Oath of Allegiance to the Crown. However, this should be seen in the context of the generous concessions made to Catholics in Canada in the same year through the Quebec Act (14 Geo. III, c. 83 [G.B.]), which allowed Quebec Catholics free exercise of religion and exempted them from the Oath of Supremacy. The Catholic Relief Act of 1778 (17 & 18 Geo. III, c. 49 – Luke Gardiner's Act), enabled Catholics to inherit in the same way as Protestants and to take out leases for up to 999 years. Further relief measures in 1782 allowed Catholics to purchase and inherit freehold land (except in parliamentary boroughs), to 'teach in school', and act as guardians. From April 1791, they were allowed to practise law, and Sir Hercules Langrishe's Act of 1792 (32 Geo. III, c. 21) opened the way for them to become barristers and solicitors. Although much opposed, the Catholic Relief Act of 1793 (33 Geo. III, c. 21 – Robert Hobart's Act), gave Catholics the right to bear arms, enabled them to hold some civil and military offices, to attend Trinity College, and conceded a parliamentary franchise. By the end of the century, only exclusion from Parliament and some of the higher offices remained.

2.3. A minority of liberals and radicals in Parliament supported the campaign for Catholic Emancipation. In Ireland, Emancipation was an extremely contentious issue because many Protestant Anglo-Irish believed that Catholics were inferior. More importantly, as a minority they feared that they would lose their power and status if Catholics were given political rights. Roman Catholicism had been seen as a threat to the English constitution for three centuries following the Reformation. A virulent hatred and fear of popery was widespread in Parliament and among the people. At the beginning of the nineteenth century, when Europe was in revolutionary turmoil, Britain's stability and safety were seen to depend on defending the Protestant constitution. To many this meant continuing to exclude Catholics from political and public life. Many ordinary Britons who signed anti-Catholic petitions in 1828–9 saw themselves, as part of a native tradition of resistance to Catholicism which stretched back for centuries. In Surrey, an anti-Emancipation pamphlet called *Queen Mary's Days* was circulated, containing images of the burnings of Protestants at Smithfield. As many as 3,000 anti-Emancipation petitions poured in from the counties – places that had never petitioned Parliament before, or that Londoners had probably never heard of – such as Ysceifiog in Flintshire, Screveton in Nottinghamshire, and Troedyraur in Cardiganshire. In Kent, as many as 60,000 people assembled at a monster anti-Catholic meeting on Penenden Heath. While such actions showed an intense dislike of Catholicism (rather than anti-Irishness), the lack of violent protest in 1829, in contrast to the Gordon Riots which followed the Catholic Relief Act (1778), showed that many Britons no longer feared Catholicism as much as their ancestors.

2.4. William Pitt, leader of the Conservatives, and his Irish secretary, Lord Castlereagh, claimed to support Emancipation and promised that Catholics and Protestants would have equal rights in the Houses of Parliament as a condition of the Act of Union in 1800. King George III refused to sanction the promised Bill. Pitt and Castlereagh resigned from government and the question was shelved. Petitions seeking full civil and political rights for Catholics were presented to Parliament but were rejected by large majorities in 1805 and 1808. Nevertheless, there was a gradual but steady increase in support for Catholic relief. An Emancipation Bill introduced in 1819 by Henry Grattan, the foremost Irish politician, was defeated by only two votes. Another Bill introduced by William Conyngham Plunket in 1821 passed the House of Commons but was defeated in the House of Lords, which remained staunchly opposed to it.

3. The Catholic Association: origins and organisation

3.1. The campaign for Emancipation was mainly restricted to élites until Daniel O'Connell took up the cause in the 1820s and made it an issue for the people at large. A Kerry landlord and a lawyer by profession, O'Connell saw the problems of the Irish poor at first hand and genuinely wanted to alleviate their condition. He believed that a limited form of self-government for Ireland was the answer to its social, economic, and political ills. He realised, however, that the government would never concede this unless there were more Irish, and in particular, Catholic representatives in Parliament. O'Connell planned, then, to win Catholic Emancipation in the first instance.

3.2. In 1823, O'Connell and Richard Lalor Shiel, another prominent advocate of Irish interests, founded the Catholic Association to campaign for an end to discrimination against Catholics, and to attain religious equality and political rights. This marked a new and most significant phase in the campaign for Catholic rights. Initially, O'Connell and Shiel intended the Association to comprise the leaders of Catholic Ireland. Seventy members enrolled at the outset and voted on a constitution that committed them 'to adopt all such legal and constitutional measures as may be most useful to obtain Catholic Emancipation'. Members paid a subscription fee of one guinea per annum (£1 1s. 0d. = €90 at 2009 values), and attended meetings each Saturday, with a quorum of ten members. To allay any fears of revolutionary intent or activity, the Association decided to conduct all its business openly and in public. It allowed reporters or other interested parties (who were not members of the Association) to attend its meetings and consult its minute books and lists of members.

3.3. Despite the ability and dedication of its leaders, the Catholic Association made little impression on government, Parliament, or the public in its first few months. Support was weak, even from members. Meetings were often cancelled because there were less than ten members present. Critics of the new Association ridiculed and dismissed the 'Roman Catholic Popish Parliament of Ireland' as insignificant. Its leaders, however, were able and dedicated. O'Connell and Shiel were celebrated orators. Shiel, a prominent lawyer and son of a Waterford merchant, was an efficient organiser and a first-rate propagandist, in print and in speech. He devised the Association's census project (see §5 below), and was largely responsible for mobilising and co-ordinating Catholic priests. Shiel also kept the foreign press, especially in sympathetic France, up-to-date about the campaign for Catholic Emancipation. Frederick William Conway, editor of the *Dublin Evening Post*, was another prominent leader of the campaign. A Protestant committed to the Catholic cause, Conway was one of the earliest and most active members of the Association, and promoted its aims through his well-regarded newspaper. Thomas Wyse, head of one of the great Catholic landowning families of Waterford, quickly became one of the most important members of the Catholic Association which he joined in 1826. He was almost solely responsible for the successful election of the Association's candidate in Waterford in 1826. Wyse also wrote a best-selling history of the movement, *A historical sketch of the late Catholic Association of Ireland* (1829), which is still an invaluable source for its activities.

4. Campaign tactics: Catholic rent

4.1. O'Connell was interested in American and French campaigns of resistance and movements for reform, cases where a majority of the people united to force government to accept their demands. Influenced by these examples, O'Connell modelled his tactics on theirs. He planned to transform the Dublin-based elite group into a nationwide popularly-based organisation. In February 1824, ten months after its foundation, he proposed that every Catholic in Ireland should become an associate member by subscribing a penny a month. This was soon called the 'Catholic Rent'. O'Connell's appeals to Irish Catholics, rich and poor, to take up the cause of Emancipation had impressive results. Within weeks, Catholic lawyers 'on the circuit' (working in provincial courts), businessmen, and clerics brought his plan to the countryside. In all parts of the country, public meetings were held, often in town halls or local churches, and people were appointed to organise the collection of the 'Catholic Rent'. Prominent members of the Association commonly attended these meetings and their passionate speeches on justice and equality caused great excitement. The public responded with overwhelming enthusiasm and the Association became the first mass populist movement in Ireland. Rank-and-file members, mainly poor or middle class, had little to lose and everything to gain by joining the Association.

4.2. As well as establishing a nationwide network of local branches, the Dublin-based Central Committee continued to hold weekly meetings and members of the public were invited to attend. At these the Association debated topical issues and discussed tactics. As numbers increased the Association had to move to larger premises in the Corn Exchange. This building, with office accommodation, a committee room, and a drawing room, met all its needs. Its central room, a large hall filled with benches like the House of Commons, could accommodate several hundred. It had another unexpected advantage. The coal porters who worked beside the Corn Exchange acted as a guard for members of the Association and protected them from agitated Orangemen who tried to disrupt the meetings. In later years, O'Connell often declared that it was Dublin's coal porters who 'carried' Emancipation.

4.3. The most important element in uniting Catholics in the campaign was the penny subscription or 'Catholic Rent'. When O'Connell first proposed the scheme in February 1824, he declared that it would provide the Association with at least £50,000 (approx. €4.25 million at 2009 values) a year and give every Catholic in Ireland an interest in the campaign. This figure was not reached but the Association had a secure income, and (as O'Connell hoped), it helped to unite Catholics. In each county, a treasurer, secretary, and committee were appointed to organise regular collections and to send the returns to the Central Committee in Dublin. People generally volunteered their services and agreed to work in pairs and collect in given areas. In some rural areas, especially where landlords were hostile to the Association, collectors did not visit homes and instead collected the Rent outside chapels, after Sunday mass, once a month. Although there were some complaints of intimidation or harassment by collectors, contemporaries remarked on the great eagerness amongst Catholics throughout Ireland to contribute to the campaign.

4.4. The Catholic Rent was used to finance the Association, pay for meetings, speakers, travel, and publications, and to compensate tenants who were evicted because of their membership. William Gregory, Under-Secretary in Dublin Castle, described the minimal fee as 'the most efficient mode that could be devised for opening direct communications between the popish Parliament and the whole mass of the Irish population'. James Doyle, Bishop of Kildare and Leighlin, described the Rent in 1824 as 'the most efficient measure ever adopted by any Catholic body'. At the end of its first year, the Association had an income of £1,000 (approx. €85,000) per week (that is 960,000 pennies each month, there being 240 pence in the pound), and savings of £10,000 (approx. €850,000).

5. Census gathering

5.1. Another important strategy, proposed by Shiel, encouraged people, with clerical help, to co-operate with the government's census. Previously, people were suspicious because they thought the government used the census to impose more taxes. The result greatly encouraged the Association because it showed the extent to which Catholics outnumbered Protestants and the degree of discrimination against Catholics.

5.2. Wyse described the importance of the census in convincing Catholics of the justice of their claims to equal civil and political liberties:

> Whole parishes were stated to exist where it was not possible to meet a single Protestant; rich rectorships were discovered without a single parishioner; teachers were mentioned to have been paid out of lavish parliamentary grants who had not a single scholar; churches were allowed to fall to ruin by their opulent incumbents, that they might be rebuilt by a starving people, while within a few miles' distance, flocks of thousands might be found with no other chapel than a thatched hovel to shelter them from the visitation of the elements … Till the

period of its [the census] introduction, the details of Catholic grievance and Catholic strength were comparatively unknown (Thomas Wyse, *Historical sketch of the late Catholic Association of Ireland*, 2 vols, London 1829).

6. Petitions

6.1. Local branches of the Catholic Association, as well as the Central Committee in Dublin, lobbied politicians in Parliament, drew up petitions for government and the Crown, organised legal assistance for poor farmers victimised by landlords, and encouraged freehold tenants (the wealthier ones) to register properties to qualify them to vote.

6.2. The Catholic Association kept up pressure on government by raising Irish grievances at every opportunity in Parliament. It did this primarily through petitions, drawn up by local branches of the Association, and signed by hundreds of thousands of people throughout Ireland. Before the establishment of the Catholic Association, petitions were mainly polite requests for Emancipation or for even lesser concessions. The Association planned to plague Parliament with constant complaints and with forceful demands for change. O'Connell explained this policy at a large meeting in Dublin in July 1824: 'No act of oppression should occur from the Giant's Causeway to Cape Clear, but they should drag it before Parliament'.

6.3. During the six years of its campaign, the Association petitioned for reforms in many areas other than its ultimate goal, Emancipation: an end to corrupt administration of law and order; an end to the dominance of the Established Church; abolition of tithes (obligatory payments by all, regardless of religion, to support the Established Church) and other unfair taxes; repeal of the remaining Penal laws, of the Act of Union, and the of Act suppressing the Catholic Association; suppression of Orange lodges; government assistance for Catholic education; relief and welfare for the most needy (Poor Laws); and a general investigation into bad conditions in Ireland and measures to improve them. In 1829, the last year of the campaign, about 1,700 petitions were sent to each House of Parliament. By this time, the Central Committee in Dublin had worked out a system to help country branches to prepare petitions. It sent examples of petitions, some specifically for Emancipation and some against local grievances, to parish priests and committee members to distribute locally. Volunteers brought petitions from house to house or priests announced them from the altar commonly on Sundays when tables were set up outside chapels where people were presented with pens and ink to sign. This petition campaign had some success. Its direct effect was to provoke heated debates in Parliament, and publicity in the press, which increased sympathies for Irish demands in the House of Commons and prepared the groundwork for Emancipation Bills in 1825 and 1829.

7. The Catholic clergy

7.1. Catholic clergy quickly took a leading role in the Association, a new and fateful departure in Irish politics. Previously, the Catholic Church had been reluctant to play an active role in politics. Now priests throughout Ireland became committed members of the Association and were instrumental in the growth and organisation of its campaign. Clergy were commonly the most energetic and enthusiastic collectors of the Catholic Rent. Some priests, according to contemporary reports, threatened or denounced from the pulpit parishioners who refused to pay. This did not mean, however, that Catholics were unwitting victims of dictatorial priests. In some places, people threatened to boycott priests who refused to assist the campaign. This had serious practical as well as spiritual implications for clerics whose income was solely dependent on voluntary contributions from parishioners.

7.2. Catholic bishops, for the most part, helped promote the cause. For example, James Doyle, Bishop of Kildare and Leighlin, one of the most influential, was instrumental in rallying clergy at the outset of the campaign, and continued to be amongst its most vocal supporters. In the autumn of 1823, Doyle published a pamphlet entitled: *A vindication of the religious and civil principles of the Irish Catholics*. Over 8,000 copies were circulated by priests to promote the campaign. Other bishops helped the cause by providing the Association with lists of clergy in their diocese and appealing publicly to priests and people to support the campaign. Clerical support helped to mobilise parishioners and many people considered the campaign to be as much about religion as civil rights.

7.3. According to Thomas Wyse, clerical support gave the campaign a crusade-like quality:

> A sort of religious sanction was thus communicated imperceptibly to a cause, which to those not immediately engaged in its promotion appeared purely and altogether political: the very principle upon which the exclusion had originally been founded was religious; and the late crude efforts at proselytism by the opposite church had enhanced not a little this conviction in the mind of a large mass of the population, that the whole struggle was religious.
>
> [Thomas Wyse, *Historical sketch of the late Catholic Association of Ireland* (2 vols, London, 1829)]

8. Popular and official responses to the campaign

8.1. Passions ran high in Ireland in the 1820s. O'Connell was a constitutional nationalist and opposed in principle the use of force to achieve political ends. He insisted from the beginning that the campaign could only succeed if it were non-violent. Nevertheless, the threat of violence was still very much present at the beginning. Secret societies waged a bloody campaign against high rents, tithes, and evictions. The government responded with coercion: trial without juries, curfews, and martial law. William H. Gregory, one of the longest serving Civil Under-Secretaries of Ireland (1812–31) favoured just such a policy of repression over concession. He served under five Lord Lieutenants and six Chief Secretaries and he formed close personal ties with Robert Peel. O'Connell described Gregory as the real ruler of Ireland at this time and the 'very demon of Orangeism at the Castle'. The son of a Galway landowner, he had been educated at Harrow, Cambridge, and the Inner Temple. He married into one of Ireland's most powerful Ascendancy families and while he had an interest in promoting the welfare of the Irish population, his views were largely uncompromising and rigidly Protestant. As Under-Secretary, Gregory was continuously resident in Dublin, and he was responsible to the Chief Secretary for the routine workings of the whole Irish Administration. He handled most of the incoming correspondence to the Irish government at Dublin Castle and corresponded with the Chief Secretary, often absent from Dublin, advising him on events in Ireland. As the centre of communication within the government, Gregory came to exercise great authority during his long tenure in the Castle. Thomas Wyse wrote that Gregory 'held in his hands the destinies of Ireland'. He strongly opposed Catholic Emancipation, believing that the 'menacing rebels' should be subdued before any concessions were offered.

8.2 O'Connell denounced intimidation and violence by agrarian secret societies – as well as by Orangemen – and appealed to their members to give up violence. While insisting that political agitation was the only way to achieve civil liberties, O'Connell forcefully expressed the grievances of the discontented masses. From 1824, the rates of agrarian crime decreased. O'Connell claimed, with reason, that the Catholic Association had restored calm to the countryside by giving country people a constitutional means of expressing their demands. Police officials and administrators backed up reports that the Catholic Association had pacified Ireland.

8.3. As well as condemning violence, O'Connell argued that most people were peaceable by nature. He denied that Irish Catholics were inherently rebellious or instinctively hostile to Britain, its government, or the Crown. He emphasised continuously that Irish Catholics were loyal and wanted to strengthen the link with Britain, not destroy it. The Association frequently began petitions for reform with a declaration of loyalty to the throne and its representatives in Ireland. It even placed a portrait of George IV in its meeting rooms. The Association argued that to end agitation in the countryside and ensure the continued loyalty of Irish Catholics the government must end discrimination against them and treat them justly.

8.4. In spite of the Catholic Association's stress on its loyalty, many were very suspicious of its activities and motives, and worried about its popularity in the countryside. They feared that the country people could turn violent very easily, inflamed by fiery speeches about discrimination and injustice. These fears were sharpened by reports about people drilling as if for war, and by rumours about the possibility of foreign intervention by France or the United States. Both countries followed developments carefully and were obviously sympathetic to Catholic demands. Irish-Americans had founded societies in many towns and cities in the United States to raise money and support for Emancipation and this was a great help to the Catholic Association.

8.5. The government, as well as Protestant and Anglo-Irish observers, were particularly and increasingly concerned about the ability of the Catholic Association to rally hundreds of thousands of people at short notice. This was powerfully demonstrated on Sunday, 13 January 1828, at a series of simultaneous meetings in over 1,600 parishes nationwide. In Ulster, there were numerous clashes between thousands of assembled Catholic Association supporters and angry Protestants. By 1828, many liberal Protestants in Ireland, who had supported the Catholic Association, withdrew. Ultra-Protestants, predominantly in Ulster, reacted more forcefully by founding Brunswick Clubs to oppose Emancipation by all means necessary, and the old cry of 'No surrender' was heard again. Tensions were raised by reports that tenants were threatening to withhold rents and tithes. To try to improve the situation, the Catholic Association sent thousands of letters to the most disturbed areas, especially Tipperary, urging people to stay calm. In a public letter, O'Connell urged people in the south-west to call off all meetings in the short-term, and two 'pacificators' were sent to the south to reinforce this appeal. These measures helped restore quiet. Indeed, the journey of the two Catholic Association delegates became an occasion of great public celebration in Tipperary, Clare, and Limerick. People drew their carriages themselves through the streets and turned out in huge numbers with torches and lanterns to welcome them.

8.6. In this uneasy period of calm, Emancipation remained a source of constant and fierce debate in Britain. Liberal party members and voters generally supported Catholic demands for reform. Conservatives, whose party was in government, denounced the Association as radical, even revolutionary, and demanded its suppression. Anglo-Irish opponents of Emancipation inflamed passions by warning of immediate catastrophe. The government responded by declaring the Catholic Association illegal. On 4 February 1825, the government announced that it would outlaw political organisations that existed for more than fourteen days.

9. The Emancipation Bill of 1825 and the 'Wings' controversy

9.1. To soften its suppression of the Catholic Association, the government agreed to consider a Catholic Relief Bill and O'Connell was invited to negotiate the terms with its architect, Sir Francis Burdett MP. In order to win as much support as possible in Parliament, O'Connell agreed to some government demands: to accept state payment of Catholic clergy and to raise the property qualification for franchise. These concessions, known as the 'Wings' to the Bill, caused uproar in Ireland. Many people were deeply opposed to the 'Wings' because they feared it would compromise the Catholic clergy and too many tenants, the 'forty-shilling freeholders', as they were called (who formed a large part of the electorate), would lose the vote.

9.2. Sir Francis Burdett's Emancipation Bill of 1825 was passed by the House of Commons but rejected by the Lords, by 178 to 130. The defeat damaged O'Connell's reputation. For a while there was intense popular opposition to the Bill and mass indignation at O'Connell for having agreed to such objectionable terms. The controversy convinced O'Connell not to make such compromises again.

9.3. To repair the damage done by the 'Wings' controversy and to regain popular confidence, O'Connell focussed on rebuilding the Catholic Association and reuniting its members. In its Suppression Bill, the government prohibited societies from discussing political matters for more than fourteen days. It did not, however, prevent organisations from meeting to discuss non-political matters. O'Connell, undaunted, changed its name and declared that he would continue to do so. Although flouting the law, O'Connell argued that the laws themselves were morally wrong and that Catholics were therefore justified in opposing them. Thus, in July 1825, O'Connell established the 'New Catholic Association' to work for 'public peace and harmony', to promote 'a liberal and religious system of education, to conduct a census of the Catholic population, to encourage charitable activities and such other purposes as are not prohibited by the said statute'.

9.4. In spite of the 'Wings' controversy, the movement for Emancipation grew in strength. People continued to hold mass demonstrations throughout the country and the first annual provincial meetings were held in Munster, Leinster and Connacht in 1825. In the Ulster counties there was a significant Protestant population generally opposed to the movement. In the other three provinces, however, these annual meetings became a crucial part of the campaign. Towns competed with each other for the privilege of hosting them and the successful bidder planned the programme for months in advance. O'Connell, Shiel or other prominent leaders of the Association addressed these day-long events that attracted hundreds of thousands from surrounding counties.

10. The campaign for votes and electoral victories, 1826

10.1. Under the Act of Union, Ireland was represented in the House of Lords by four Church of Ireland bishops and twenty-eight members of landed gentry (known as 'temporal peers'). The latter were elected for life by Irish peers in the House of Commons. These 'Lords' voted against Emancipation, two to one, and were often openly hostile to Irish demands. The representatives in the House of Commons, including one hundred Irish MPs were, for the most part, more sympathetic. Over a half of the Irish representatives were pro-reform and the rest voted against Emancipation.

10.2. Irish Catholics who had property worth at least forty shillings (£2) per annum had been given the right to vote in 1793. There were over 100,000 of these registered in the 1820s, the most numerically significant group of voters in Ireland and crucially important, therefore, in elections. Landlords were dependent on the votes of forty-shilling freeholders and used influence or intimidation to ensure the tenants voted for them.

10.3. The year 1826 was one of mass meetings and increasing excitement about the coming elections. O'Connell realised that a greater show of strength in the country and in Parliament was essential to force the government to grant Emancipation. Leaders of the Catholic Association appealed to its members to vote for pro-Emancipation candidates only. The campaign was a success. The Catholic Association candidate in Waterford was elected and the landlords' dominance was broken. Further successes followed in Cavan, Monaghan, Westmeath, and Louth when large numbers of forty-shilling freeholders went against their landlords to vote for pro-Emancipation candidates. The most dramatic victory was in Clare in 1828. O'Connell's overwhelming success there finally persuaded government that Emancipation could no longer be denied. These elections were the most important elements in the campaign from 1823 to 1829.

10.4. Catholics were an overwhelming majority in the Waterford constituency, with forty-one Catholics to every Protestant. Thomas Wyse had organised a committee in Waterford in August 1825 to defeat the Beresfords who had dominated politics in the county for over seventy years and were staunchly opposed to Catholic reforms. Wyse's central committee, based in Waterford city, co-ordinated the branch committees in every barony. They compiled lists of electors and reported on progress throughout the county. They canvassed the freeholders of Waterford urging them to ignore pressure from landlords to vote for the sitting MP, Lord George Beresford, and to support the Emancipation candidate, Villiers Stuart. Members of the committee went out to the parishes and addressed the people in chapels for eight Sundays before the elections. The Central Committee of the Association in Dublin was doubtful at the start about success. Reports from Waterford, however, were encouraging and Wyse's committee believed that they could persuade people to go against their landlords and break the Beresford hold on power. On 13 June 1826, ten days before the election, they made a fervent appeal to the people of Waterford and O'Connell announced plans to visit Waterford on Villiers Stuart's behalf. Crowds poured into the city to enjoy pre-election activities, all carefully controlled by the butchers of Ballybricken, one of the oldest areas of the city where markets and public events were commonly held. There were daily rallies in favour of both candidates and speeches by leading members of the Catholic Association, including O'Connell, who attracted hundreds of thousands of people. Commentators described the excitement in the city. People everywhere carried green flags or wore green ribbons, handkerchiefs, or hats to demonstrate colourfully their support for Villiers Stuart. Even those most bitterly opposed to the Catholic cause remarked how well conducted the assemblies were, in spite of popular expectations (given that election rallies were quite frequently scenes of riotous celebration or conflict).

10.5. When voting began the electors of Waterford showed their independence of spirit and voted overwhelmingly for the Catholic Association candidate. Beresford got 528 votes, Villers Stuart, 1,357. Richard Power, the other pro-Catholic candidate and a standing MP, was returned to parliament with 1,424 votes. As polling drew to a close, Beresford accepted his total defeat and withdrew from the election. At this time, Villiers Stuart and Power had enough votes to make their victory certain and 700 freeholders were still waiting to give both these candidates their vote.

10.6. The election in Waterford took the country by surprise. Ascendancy land owners realised that they could no longer dominate politics or expect to be re-elected to parliamentary seats that their families had controlled for decades. The government realised that the Catholic Association was a powerful force that could bring about a peaceful revolution if it could get pro-Emancipation candidates elected in other counties. O'Connell was well aware of the vital importance of the forty-shilling freeholders.

11. 1828: victory in Clare and crisis in London

11.1. In January 1828, a Conservative government, led by the anti-Emancipation Prime Minister, Arthur Wellesley, 1st Duke of Wellington (1769–1852), was returned to power. The campaign was stepped up. On 13 January, the Catholic Association held simultaneous meetings all over the country to demonstrate its strength. O'Connell claimed that over 100,000 met in Dublin, and almost five million in the countryside, and defiantly warned the government against suppressing the movement:

> If they pass an Act, preventing any three men from meeting to discuss Catholic affairs, we will take off our gloves, and hold up our hands in the street, declaring that we are not speaking on Catholic affairs (*cheers*). We will talk of them at dinner; if they prevent us from speaking at our meals, we will proclaim a fast day, and in prayer we shall talk of Catholic politics. We will speak of them whilst we sip our tea and coffee. I defy them to prevent us – if they prevent us from talking politics, why we will whistle or sing them (*loud cheers*). We shall implicitly submit to the letter of the law – but that shall be the extent of our obedience.

11.2. The government realised that it would be impractical, if not impossible, to suppress the movement and did not attempt to do so. In July, the Association dropped the 'New' from its title and resumed all its old activities, stronger than ever: 10,000 full members, over three million associate members, and a weekly income of over £2,000 (approx. €170,000 at 2009 values). Much of this money paid Catholic lawyers to defend Catholics in court. The Association also set up arbitration boards in the country to act as local courts in opposition to the official courts. The Association believed, however, that Emancipation and equality at law could only be won through parliament.

11.3. In 1828, O'Connell decided to run himself as a candidate for the House of Commons when a surprise election was announced in Co. Clare. The MP for Clare, William Vesey Fitzgerald, had to stand for re-election because he had been appointed to a government position (President of the Board of Trade) which carried a salary.

O'Connell decided to stand against him to test the government's resolve. He was allowed to stand as a candidate for election but would not be allowed to take his seat in parliament if he won because he was Catholic.

11.4. Vesey Fitzgerald, an Anglican, was a moderate in politics and supported the campaign for Emancipation. Nevertheless, O'Connell felt it was the right time to put the question to the people and to increase pressure on the government. He called on people in Clare to vote for him and for Emancipation and to force the government to act. Under-Secretary Gregory wrote from Dublin Castle on 7 July that 'whatever fears may be entertained from the excited feelings of the Catholics, I apprehend greater danger from the sullen indignation of the Protestants'. O'Connell was elected MP for Co. Clare in 1828 with a huge majority, which Peel described as 'an avalanche'. This was the crisis O'Connell hoped for. On 12 August 1828, George Dawson MP for Londonderry, was heckled by a hostile crowd during his speech at the annual Orange dinner held to commemorate the lifting of the Siege of Derry (1689). Previously an unbending defender of the Protestant Ascendancy, he now believed that the only alternative to crushing the Catholic Association was to 'look at the question [of Emancipation] with an intention to settle it'. News of Dawson's speech soon reached London. Peel was furious and reported to Wellington that 'The King has a deeper *tinge* of Protestantism than when you last saw him'. In January 1829, Peel wrote to Under-Secretary Gregory in Dublin Castle arguing that Catholic Emancipation seemed the only practicable course to take:

> Will I advise *the King* to take the only remaining course – I myself shrinking from the sacrifices and responsibility that it entails – or will I remain at my post – setting the example of sacrifice to others and abiding for myself the issue be it what it may? I have chosen the last alternative, painful as it is to me. I may be wrong – but at any rate I am prepared to make sacrifices which will prove that I think I am right.

After much persuasion, dithering, and some tears, King George IV finally consented to the measure. He himself had stated in July 1828 that 'Ireland could not remain as it is.' In order to prevent a serious revolt in Ireland the government was pressed to act. The British Parliament finally enacted the Roman Catholic Relief Bill in April 1829. It granted Catholic Emancipation and enabled O'Connell, after some delay, to take his seat. The Irish Parliamentary Elections Act, 1829 (10 Geo. IV, c. 8), which came into force at the same time, raised the county freehold franchise from 40 shillings to £10. This reduced the electorate from 230,000 to approximately 14,000. The franchise in the towns was left untouched, and the electoral changes applied to Protestants as well as Catholics.

11.5. Thus, the Tory administration was able to defuse the threat of civil war in Ireland. However, a country that was garrisoned by five-sixths of the infantry force of the United Kingdom could not be regarded as an equal partner in that Kingdom. While 1829 was the end of an era, O'Connell was correct when he said that Emancipation would never have been conceded except under the compulsion of necessity. As such, the measure was deprived of all grace and effect. Since the Act was not retrospective, O'Connell was presented with the old Oath, which he refused to take. This and the denial of his seat for the time being were viewed as an affront to him and to Ireland.

11.6. While Emancipation did not bring peace, prosperity, or an end to sectarian tensions in Ireland, it did open the way for further political, social, and economic reforms. It demonstrated that public pressure could be brought to bear on the government without resort to violence. Indeed, the English radical reformers looked for, and received, O'Connell's support and advice. Emancipation also opened the way for the Disestablishment of the Church of Ireland. Catholics, however, were still excluded from the throne. They continued to be excluded from the oldest universities and the highest legal offices. Catholics that were employed by the state still had to swear they would not 'disturb or weaken the Protestant religion or Protestant government in this Kingdom'. Electoral prejudice also remained. Practising Jews were not admitted to Parliament until 1858, and Scotland would not return a Catholic MP to Westminster until the 1890s. William Lamb, Lord Melbourne (1779–1848), twice British Prime Minister in the 1830s, observed that, on the question of Catholic Emancipation, 'all the wise men had been proved wrong and all the damned fools right'.

GILLIAN M. DOHERTY AND TOMÁS O'RIORDAN

CHAPTER 8

Catholic Emancipation: documents

1. O'Connell's reaction to the suppression of the Catholic Association, 1825

1.1. *Introduction.* The subject of Emancipation was a constant and extremely controversial topic of debate in England in the early decades of the nineteenth century. Whig-Liberal party members and followers generally supported Catholic demands for reform. The Tories, whose Conservative party was in government, denounced the Association as radical, even revolutionary, and demanded its suppression. The government responded to these fears by declaring the Catholic Association illegal. On 4 February 1825, it intended to outlaw political organisations that existed for more than fourteen days. O'Connell, undaunted, changed its name and declared that he would continue to do so for as long as necessary and the Association continued just as before. Here is a punchy excerpt from a speech of O'Connell's, 8 January 1825. SOURCE: John O'Connell (ed.), *The select speeches of Daniel O'Connell* (2 vols, Dublin, 1854), ii, 469.

> **1.2.** But I am told we are to have a parliamentary interference for suppression. Well, should they be displeased at the formation of this room, or our meeting in it, why we can build another; if they object to the denomination [title] we have given ourselves, why we can change it with that of board, or committee, or even directory. If they prohibit our meeting, surely they cannot prevent our assembling to dine together. This Association is the creature of the Penal Code, and as long as Catholic disabilities exist, so long must some organ have its being through which to convey our complaints, to proclaim our grievances and to demand our redress.

2. The 'Catholic Rent', I

2.1. *Introduction.* Catholic Rent was the name given to the subscription paid by associate members of the Catholic Association. The initial subscription of one guinea (£1–1s.–0d.; approx. €90 at 2009 values) per year was lowered from February 1824 (on the suggestion of O'Connell) to a minimum of one penny a month (approx. €0.36 cents) for 'associate membership'. This helped to rid the association of its elitist image and gave ordinary people a sense of belonging to the movement. The collection of the Catholic Rent also helped create a valuable network of committees and agents around the country. Thomas Wyse (1792–1862), one of the Catholic Association's main organisers, noted that the rent amounted to 'an Irish revolution'. Here is Daniel O'Connell's plan for the systematic collection of this small monthly subscription throughout Ireland and his listing of the objects on which the money should be spent. SOURCE: The *Dublin Evening Post*, 19 February 1824.

143

2.2. ... Catholic people of Ireland ... do not dare to despair. They know that their cause is just and holy. It is the cause of religion and liberty. It is the cause of their country and of their God. It never can be abandoned by the Catholics of Ireland ... But in order effectually to exert the energies of the Irish people, pecuniary resources [funds] are absolutely necessary. Your committee have a just and entire confidence that such resources can be procured with facility, and that it requires nothing more than a reasonable portion of exertion on the part of a few individuals to secure abundant pecuniary means [funds] to answer every legitimate object ... Your committee respectfully submit that the following purposes are of obvious and paramount utility; and that no doubt does or can exist of their being perfectly legal.

2.3. To forward petitions to parliament, not only on the subject of Catholic Emancipation but for the redress of all local or general grievances affecting the Irish people. Under this head should be included a salary for a permanent parliamentary agent in London. Your committee conceive that a sum of £5,000 (approx. €425,000 at 2009 values) per annum would cover all the expenses under this first head.

2.4. To procure legal redress for all such Catholics, assailed or injured by Orange violence, as are unable to obtain it for themselves; to prevent, by due course of law, Orange processions and public insults; to bring before the high courts of criminal justice all such magistrates as should participate in or countenance the illegal proceedings, processions, etc., of the Orange faction; and to arrest, by the powerful arm of the law, that career of violence by which principally in the north, but occasionally in the south, so many Catholics have been murdered by Orangemen, many of whom are entrusted with arms by the government for far different purposes – and, in fine, to prosecute the Orange murderers where we cannot prevent the murders. There is also another head of legal relief of great importance. It is to procure for the Catholics the actual enjoyment of all such rights in the several corporations in Ireland to which they are by law entitled, and which have for thirty years past been perseveringly withheld from them by interested bigotry. To this important object your committee would in the first years devote £15,000 (approx. €1.3 million) per annum.

2.5. To encourage and support a liberal and enlightened press, as well in Dublin as in London – a press which could readily refute the arguments of our enemies and expose the falsehood of their calumnies upon us and our religion – a press which would publish and explain the real principles of the Catholics, and by the irresistible force of truth, either silence or at least confound our calumniators. For the last two centuries the British press ... has teemed with the most unfounded calumnies and the grossest falsehoods on the subject of the religion and principles of the Catholics. The popular writers of the present day, even those who support our claims to emancipation, affect an air of candour by joining our worst enemies in traducing our most sacred religion. It is time that this grievous mischief should be checked; and your committee conceive that a less sum than £15,000 (approx. €1.3 million) per annum ought not to be dedicated to this most useful purpose.

2.6. To procure for the various schools in the country cheap publications by means of which the Catholic children may attain knowledge without having their religion interfered with, or their social virtue checked by anything unchristian or uncharitable. The money given by parliament for this purpose is shamefully misapplied; and the necessity of a resource of this description is daily felt by the Catholic prelates and pastors, who have the greatest anxiety to promote the education of their flocks but are unable to afford sufficient sums of money for that purpose.

2.7. Your committee would in the first instance expend £5,000 (approx. €425,000) per annum to remedy this evil; they would recommend that all the savings on the foregoing heads of expenditure (which they trust will be considerable) should be applied then to advance education. Your committee would respectfully submit the propriety of aiding the resources of the Irish and other Catholics in North America, to procure for them a sufficient number of priests. The number of Catholics in the United States is great and daily increasing. The want of Catholic clergymen is felt as an extreme evil; and it is thought that a sum of £5,000 a year could not be better applied than in remedying in some measure this deficiency.

2.8. Besides, the Catholics in Great Britain are multiplying almost beyond hope. The French Revolution supplied the English Catholics with clergymen for many years. That resource is now gone; and it would be suited to the charity and piety of the Irish people to supply their haughty and erratic neighbours with the means of instruction in that ancient faith which, since the first days of Christianity, always was, and still is, and while the world lasts, will be the genuine source of every Christian and social virtue.

2.9. Having detailed these five distinct objects, your committee beg leave to state that as they conceive that after exhausting those purposes, there ought to remain a sum of at least £5,000 per annum at the disposal of the Association – they would recommend that such sum should be allowed to accumulate in the public funds, and that out of such accumulation the Catholic Association should from time to time be at liberty to dedicate, in fair and reasonable proportions, in contributions towards erecting schools, building Catholic churches, and erecting and furnishing dwelling-houses for the clergy in the poorer parishes, and ameliorating in other respects the condition of the Catholic clergy in Ireland.

2.10. Your committee confidently hope that if the plan which they are about to suggest be adopted, such accumulation will greatly exceed £5,000 per annum and may be five times that sum, and thereby afford means of doing great and permanent good to the most estimable, laborious, learned, and pious clergy with which it has ever pleased the eternal wisdom to bless a faithful and suffering people. The basis of our plan is founded on the extent of the Catholic population of Ireland. We may expect a good deal of assistance from the liberal portion of our Protestant fellow countrymen, but our reliance for success must be placed upon the numbers and patriotism of the Catholic people of Ireland …

2.11. The detail of the plan of your committee is this. They purpose –

1st. That a monthly subscription should be raised throughout Ireland, to be denominated 'the monthly Catholic Rent'.

2nd. That the Association should forthwith appoint two of its members [as] a secretary and [an] assistant in order to collect such subscriptions throughout Ireland.

3rd. That such secretary and assistant should immediately open an account with each parish in Ireland and enter therein the particulars of all monies subscribed by such parish[es].

4th. That the Association should adopt the most speedy means of nominating, in conjunction with the inhabitants of each parish, and if possible with the privity of the Catholic clergyman, a number of persons not to exceed twelve, nor less than three, in order to collect the subscriptions.

5th. That monthly returns be procured from such persons or from as many of them as possible, and that a monthly report, in writing, of the progress made in each parish be given in by the [parochial] secretary for the subscriptions to the secretary of the Catholics of Ireland, to be by him laid before the Association.

6th. That care be taken to publish in, or at least as near, each Catholic chapel as may be permitted by the clergy, the particulars of the sums subscribed in such parishes, with the names of each subscriber, unless where the individuals shall choose to insert the subscription under the heading of anonymous.

7th. That accounts of subscriptions, debtor and creditor, be published annually for the satisfaction of the subscribers and the public at large.

8th. That all subscriptions be paid, as soon as transmitted to Dublin, into the hands of the treasurer to the association.

9th. That an efficient committee of 21 members be appointed to superintend and manage the collection and expenditure of the subscription money, to be styled and to act as a committee of accounts.

10th. That no monies be expended without an express vote of the Association upon a notice regularly given.

11th. That the amount expected from each individual shall not exceed one penny per month, but that each individual shall be at liberty to give any greater monthly sum he pleases, not exceeding in the entire two shillings per month.

12th. That the guinea (£1 1s. 10d.) paid by each member of the Association on his admission be deemed and taken as part of the entire of the contribution of the individual to the subscription thus proposed, and that each member be requested to allocate his guinea to some particular parish.

13th. That each subscriber be at liberty to allocate his subscription either to the fund generally or to any particular object heretofore specified, and that such allocation be in every respect, strictly and without any deviation, attended to.

14th. That Daniel O'Connell, Esq., be appointed secretary for subscriptions, and James Sugrue, Esq., his assistant.

2.12. Your committee submit that if only one million of the six millions of Catholics which this country contains will contribute the small sum of one farthing (one-quarter of a penny) a week each, the resources of the Association will exceed the estimate of expenditures heretofore detailed. They cannot doubt the readiness with which the subscription will be raised if proper means are taken to apply for it universally.

2.13. Your committee cannot conclude without expressing their decided conviction that if this plan shall be carried into complete operation, all the difficulties in the way of our emancipation will be speedily removed – and we shall have the glory as well as the advantage of carrying into effect the Christian principle of liberty of conscience.

Daniel O'Connell, Chairman

3. The 'Catholic Rent', II

3.1. *Introduction.* This is an account of the 'Catholic Rent', written by Thomas Wyse. He explains itse importance in unifying Catholics behind the campaign for Emancipation. Young and old, rich and poor, responded to O'Connell's calls for 'a penny a month', and although individual contributions were small, each person who subscribed to the Rent felt involved personally in the movement. Wyse describes how local people volunteered to collect the Rent and organised committees to administer the funds. These formed, in effect, branches of the Catholic Association and acted as a link between the Central Committee in Dublin and the network of branches around the country. According to Wyse, the Rent was the means of transforming an elite movement into a mass democratic one, a means of politicising people throughout the countryside, and of giving them a stake in the campaign for Emancipation. SOURCE: Thomas Wyse, *Historical sketch of the late Catholic Association of Ireland* (2 vols, London, 1829), i, 208–10.

3.2. The contribution of a penny per month was proposed by Mr O'Connell: it was instantly adopted; every man hurried to cast his mite into the treasury of a body, from which he felt assured it would return to him in tenfold good. Every peasant in Ireland, every Catholic inhabitant, from the child of seven to the grandfather of seventy, was invited to contribute; and thus arose in a few weeks the *'Catholic Rent'*. The name was strange; the collection at first awkward and ill-organised; the amount fell far below the calculations of the proposers; but the great point was the principle, and that was fully discovered ...

3.3. It was not only that positive suffering was removed or that Catholic power was augmented by so large an accession of its funds; a new means of binding the people in an open and visible fraternity, which extended from one end of Ireland to the other, was obtained. Every farthing [one-quarter of a penny] paid added a link to the chain. The Rent was first organised in the towns; it then spread, though slowly, to the neighbouring parishes; and from thence, by degrees, to the most remote parts of the country. The Collectors at first volunteered;—formed a committee;—divided the town into walks for collection—and transmitted their funds, through their secretary, to the Association. As they increased, and improved their system, they enlarged considerably its objects. They took rooms,—held their meetings weekly,—not only received reports of rent and remittances to the Association, &c. but discussed every subject of public policy connected with the general question; and, in most particulars, exhibited a close analogy to the great body with whom they were in relation. In the towns, the consequences were very conspicuous. The Rent proceeded rapidly; and with it a corresponding passion for political discussion, which pervaded every body and every class of society. The various dinners of charitable societies, trades &c. soon were made vehicles of this universal passion. It penetrated:—it clung to every thing. The most indifferent action took its colour from the one principle: the most casual conversation invariably terminated in the Catholic question. But the county parishes continued more or less inert. Up to the very eve of dissolution, the towns generally furnished in a double proportion to the counties.

4. The 'Catholic Rent', III

4.1. *Introduction.* This is a detailed account of the Catholic Rent by county, and in total for 1826. It amounted to over £14,896 (approx. €1.26 million at 2009 values). The total raised by early 1829 was almost £52,000 (approx. €4.4 million). SOURCE: Thomas Wyse, *Historical sketch of the late Catholic Association of Ireland* (2 vols, London, 1829), ii, appendix.

4.2. Table 5: Catholic Rent: details of receipts and expenditure for the year 1826

County of	£.	s.	d.
1. Antrim	138	5	9
2. Armagh	113	6	3
3. Cork	2,824	13	0
4. Clare	428	10	2
5. Carlow	239	9	5
6. Cavan	792	0	0
7. Donegal	76	2	9
8. Down	240	8	1½
9. Dublin	1954	19	5
10. Meath	604	14	5½
11. Fermanagh	72	17	8
12. Galway	635	15	7
13. Kerry	381	15	7½
14. Kildare	567	4	10½
15. Kilkenny	749	19	10
16. King's County (now Offaly)	549	3	3½
17. Leitrim	148	2	9
18. Louth	689	2	8½
19. Limerick	548	8	11
20. Longford	168	7	1
21. Londonderry	144	2	0
22. Monaghan	194	15	0
23. Mayo	293	6	½
24. Queen's County (now Laois)	257	0	5½
25. Roscommon	166	7	0
26. Sligo	164	14	3½
27. Tipperary	1,648	7	6½
28. Tyrone	65	10	7
29. Westmeath	526	19	9
30. Wicklow	174	14	7
31. Wexford	504	1	0
32. Waterford	738	11	4½
	£16,895	18	11½
Subscriptions	£2,224	4	5
Interest on government securities	£144	0	0
	£19,228	3	4½
Sundry expenses (Dec. 31, 1824, to March 18, 1825)	£4,331	11	6½
TOTAL: (Approx. €1.25 million at 2009 values)	**£14,896**	**11**	**10**

(Note these rough equivalents in estimating 1826 donations. £1=€84; 1s.=€4.20; 1d.=€0.36 cents approx. at 2009 values)

5. Daniel O'Connell in Waterford, 1826

5.1. *Introduction.* Daniel O'Connell often wrote to his wife while campaigning in Waterford in the summer of 1826. On 19 June 1826, he wrote from Dromana, Cappoquin, Co. Waterford, home of Villiers Stuart, the successful O'Connellite candidate in the Waterford election. The 'scene' he refers to is in Lady Morgan's (Sydney Owenson), third novel, *Florence McCarthy: an Irish tale* (London, 1818). The landlord mentioned as being on the 'adverse interest' is Wray Palliser (1789–1862), Kilcomragh Lodge, Co Waterford. He was a lieutenant colonel in the Waterford Militia 1810–62. O'Connell goes on to describe his visits to Kilmacthomas and Dungarvan, and the great welcome he received from the tenants, despite the obvious opposition from the Beresford and Devonshire estates. SOURCE: Letter from Daniel O'Connell to his wife about campaigning in Co. Waterford, 19 June 1826, *Irish Monthly*, 12 (1884), 216.

5.2. Dromana, Co. Waterford, 19 June 1826.

> My own sweet Love
> Here I am at this lovely spot. I believe it is that which Lady Morgan makes the scene of many of the incidents in *Florence McCarthy*. It is really a beautiful situation. As to yesterday, *first*, I wrote to you from Waterford and enclosed you a cheque for £35; next, sweetest, we heard an early mass at Waterford and then started for Dungarvan. We breakfasted at Kilmacthomas, a town belonging to the Beresfords but the people belong to us. They came out to meet us with green boughs and such shouting you can have no idea of. I harangued them from the window of the inn, and we had a good deal of laughing at the bloody Beresfords. Judge what the popular feeling must be when in this, a Beresford town, every man their tenant, we had such a reception. A few miles farther on we found a chapel with the congregation assembled before mass. The Priest made me come out and I addressed his flock, being my second speech. The freeholders here were the tenants of a Mr Palliser, who is on the adverse interest, but almost all of them will vote for us. We then proceeded to Dungarvan on the coast. There are here about four hundred voters *belonging* to the Duke of Devonshire. His agents have acted a most treacherous part by us, and our Committee at Waterford were afraid openly to attack these voters lest the Duke should complain of our violating what he calls his neutrality. But I deemed that all sheer nonsense, and to work we went. We had a most tremendous meeting here; we harangued the people from a platform erected by the walls of a new chapel. I never could form a notion of the great effect of popular declamation before yesterday. The clergy of the town most zealously assisted us. We have, I believe, completely triumphed, and I at present am convinced we shall poll to the last man of these voters. We then had a public dinner and great speeching. We broke up about nine, and Wyse and I came here with Mr [Villiers-] Stuart in his carriage. We arrived about half after ten, and are going this day to Lismore on another mission.

6. What is Emancipation?

6.1. *Introduction.* Henry Robert Westenra, MP for Co. Monaghan, discusses in the letter below how differently various people understand 'Emancipation'. He has a level-headed and 'step-by-step' view of Emancipation. It is also likely that he was influenced by electioneering motives since the names he mentions (Lord Cremorne, and Coote) were influential political figures in the county. Monaghan had a fairly denominationally and politically mixed population and electorate, where the Orangemen were powerful and where Emancipation politics could be a liability. His 'step-by-step' view was, therefore, a safe one. During the 1826 general election, Westenra was a keen supporter of Emancipation. O'Connell helped him to victory with a circular letter sent to the parish priests and other notables in the constituency. As in Waterford and elsewhere, Emancipation played a dramatic and important part in the Monaghan constituency during the 1826 election. There was a gradual increase in support for it. This was reflected in the numbers of Emancipation MPs elected between 1807 and 1820 for Irish constituencies. Between the general elections of 1807 and 1812, of the 34 Irish MPs elected, 28 supported Emancipation; in the 1812 parliament the figure was 35 out of 40; and by 1820, 45 out of 52 Irish MPs supported Emancipation. Organised Catholic electioneering had clearly helped to win converts to Emancipation. Westenra was alleged to have taken a pledge in support of Emancipation during his first election for Monaghan in 1818. During 1819 Henry Grattan presented several petitions in favour of Catholic Emancipation. In May of that year he put forward his motion for a Committee* to inquire into laws affecting Catholics, but it was defeated by a majority of just two in the House of Commons. The Duke of Norfolk (Henry Charles Howard, 1791–1856), a Roman Catholic, was admitted to his office of Hereditary Earl Marshal of England by a Speical Act of Parliament in 1824. Prior to this Act, Protestant deputies were required when the Earl Marshal was a Roman Catholic. The Earl Marshal was the eighth of the Great Officers of State – traditional Crown ministers, who either inherit their positions or are appointed to exercise certain largely ceremonial functions. After the Emancipation Act was passed in 1829, the Duke of Norfolk became the first Roman Catholic since the Reformation to take the oaths and take his seat in the House of Commons. SOURCE: From a letter from the Hon. Henry Robert Westenra, MP for Co. Monaghan, to his father, Lord Rossmore, 15 October 1824. Belfast, Public Record Office, Northern Ireland (T.2929/3/75).

6.2. … I have all through denied being pledged to any man or party. I did not understand it in that light … nor do I now, nor ever did.

6.3. Cremorne's letter was immediately forwarded to me after the famous motion Grattan brought on for going into a Committee* on the Roman Catholic claims.

*Committees are small groups of Members of Parliament which are set up in order to discuss, examine or advise upon specific public policy issues or pieces of legislation. The political membership of each committee is in proportion to the state of the parties in the whole House, so the government will always have a majority.

On that subject, I have always expressed my opinion that the only way in which I would enter on the subject would be by taking it step by step. I have always said I was no exclusionist; I did not want to exclude persons professing the Roman Catholic faith from all office, quite the reverse; but that there were some offices, the kingly office, for instance, the office of Lord High Chancellor and many others, such as the heads of most of the principal offices of the government department[s], to which I considered them totally inadmissible. I think so still, and am by no means prepared to retract one inch of my former declarations. I asked Cremorne myself, would you admit Roman Catholics to such offices, would you like to see a Roman Catholic King on the throne, or a Chancellor of that creed on the bench? Certainly not, was his answer, and Coote said the same; and I own I was surprised to receive afterwards a letter from him arraigning my conduct in having opposed Grattan's motion for going into a Committee* on the question.

6.4. If you vote for going into a Committee, it is generally understood you vote for the principle of the bill. To the principle of the bill, *viz.* granting them all their claims, I was decidedly averse, and therefore I would not go into a Committee on the question. From this I have never swerved, and see no reason at present to alter my course; nor until it is proved to me that this is not a Protestant government essentially and integrally, and that any country governed by a Roman Catholic King and government is at all as free, I cannot change.

6.5. I am told there are many minor offices from which Roman Catholics are excluded. Let them, in God's name, bring in a bill to admit them into such. See how easily the Duke of Norfolk was admitted into the office of Grand Marshal. But as to people finding fault with me for not voting for Roman Catholic Emancipation, why, it is as great a humbug as the name is. What are they to be emancipated from? People don't know what they are speaking about for the most part. They have some general terms to which they apply particular meanings of their own, and they confound and confuse everything, and then blame me and everyone else for the errors which their own ignorance makes them commit …

7. Clare by-election

7.1. *Introduction.* An outstanding orator, Daniel O'Connell toured the country, attracting tens of thousands of enthusiastic followers. When the government moved to suppress the Catholic Association, O'Connell renamed it the New Catholic Association and continued the campaign unabated. The first major success of the organisation came in the Waterford by-election of 1826 when the powerful Beresford family were defeated by Henry Villiers Stuart (1st Baron, 1803–74). There was a by-election in Clare in 1828 when the wealthy landowner, William Vesey Fitzgerald (1783–1843) had been appointed

President of the Board of Trade by the Prime Minister, the Duke of Wellington. Under the terms of the Place Act, he had to seek re-election. A popular landlord and clearly on the side of Emancipation, he had sat without opposition for Clare for nearly ten years. Despite this, the Catholic Association put Daniel O'Connell forward to contest Co. Clare, although, as a Catholic, he could not take his seat in Parliament. O'Connell's victory (2,057 to 982 votes) marked the last stage of the fight for Emancipation – it was granted a year later. The dramatic circumstances of Vesey Fitzgerald's defeat resulted in O'Connell's most vocal critic, Robert Peel, and the Duke of Wellington, admitting defeat. They realised that the government had to concede Emancipation sooner rather than later; getting rid of the Irish forty-shilling freeholders was more important than continuing to resist the inevitable. The government found Vesey Fitzgerald another seat (Newport, Cornwall) and he was re-elected for Ennis in 1831. The derogatory reference in his letter to 'the Catholic parliament' is to the Catholic Association. SOURCE: Extract from the letter from William Vesey Fitzgerald, Ennis, Co. Clare, to the Lord Lieutenant, the Marquess of Anglesey, 5 July 1828, reporting his defeat by O'Connell in the Clare by-election. Public Record Office, Northern Ireland (D.619/32K/40).

7.2. Ennis July 5

The priests have triumphed, and through them and their brethren, the Catholic parliament will dictate the representatives of every county in the south of Ireland. I know that your Excellency has been kept aware of all the circumstances which have occurred during this contest. I need not characterise them, but it is impossible to contemplate them without the deepest anxiety and alarm. I could not have formed a notion of the extent and power of Catholic organisation.

The poll closed tonight. It was hopeless from the first day, and I looked on the contest as desperate from the account of the defection of the first great interest. I have kept it open, however, until I had received the vote of any gentleman in the county who could poll, and now I hardly know how my number has been made [up] for I had incredibly few forty-shilling freeholders. What a convulsion for any man to throw the county into, to satisfy his own vanity and to obtain what he cannot use ...

8. Daniel O'Connell's election address, 1828

8.1. *Introduction.* In this speech, O'Connell appealed to the freeholders (those entitled to vote because they owned property) in Co. Clare to support him as a Catholic candidate. It is, of course, a highly political statement and a deeply partisan description of Vesey Fitzgerald. This address to the voters was published in newspapers and on broadsheet posters. SOURCE: *Dublin Evening Post*, 24 June 1828.

8.2. Councillor O'Connell's Grand Address to the Freeholders of Co. Clare

Fellow Country men – Your county wants a Representative – I respectfully solicit your suffrages to raise me to that station,

8.3. It is true that as a Catholic, – I cannot, and of course never will take the oaths at present prescribed to Members of Parliament, but the authority which created these oaths – the Parliament, can abrogate them, and I entertain a confident hope that if you elect me, the most bigoted of our enemies will see the necessity of removing from the chosen representative of the people an obstacle which would prevent him from doing his duty to his King and his Country.

8.4. The oath at present required by law is – 'That the sacrifice of the Mass and the Invocation of the blessed Virgin Mary and other Saints, as now practiced in the Church of Rome, are impious and idolatrous'. Of course I never will stain my soul with such an oath; I leave that to my honourable opponent, Mr Vesey Fitzgerald. He has often taken that horrible oath; – he is ready to take it again and asks your votes to enable him so to swear. I would rather be torn limb from limb than take it. Electors of the County Clare, choose between me, who abominates the oath, and Mr Vesey Fitzgerald, who has sworn it full twenty times!

8.5. I do not like to give the epitome of his political life, but I cannot refrain. – He first took office under [Prime Minister Spencer] Perceval, who obtained power by raising the base, bloody, and unchristian cry of 'No popery' in England.

He voted for the East Retford Bill*, for a measure which would put two violent enemies of the Catholics into Parliament. In the case of the Protestant Dissenters in England, he voted for their exclusion, that is, he voted against the principle of Freedom of Conscience – that principle on which we found our right to Emancipation.

Finally, he voted for the suppression of the Catholic Association of Ireland!

And after this, Sacred Heaven! he calls himself a friend of the Catholics.

He is the ally and colleague of the Duke of Wellington, and Mr Peel; and is their partner in power.

8.6. If you return me to Parliament, I pledge myself to vote for every measure which can strengthen the right of every human being to unrestricted and unqualified freedom of conscience.

To vote for every measure favourable to radical reform in the representative system, so that the House of Commons may truly, as our Catholic ancestors intended it should do, represent all the people.

---

*The East Retford Disfranchisement Bill. East Retford was a notoriously 'rotten' or corrupt borough. The usual treatment for a Borough which had perpetual bribery was to expand its boundaries and franchise into an area free of corruption. East Retford was disfranchised by the House of Commons but reprieved twice due to the political instability in the years 1827–30. William Huskisson's resignation as Colonial Secretary and Leader of the Commons was followed by those of Lord Palmerston as Secretary of War, Charles Grant as President of the Board of Trade, and William Lamb (later Lord Melbourne) as Irish Secretary.

To vote for every measure of retrenchment and reduction of the national expenditure, so as to relieve the people from the burthen of taxation &c.

Electors of the County Clare, choose one who has devoted his early life to your cause – who has consumed his manhood in a struggle for your liberties, and who is ready to die for the Catholic faith.

9. Meeting between Anglesey and O'Connell, 1828

9.1. *Introduction.* Henry William Paget, 1st Marquess of Anglesey, served two terms as Lord Lieutenant of Ireland, 1828–9, 1830–3. He supported Catholic Emancipation and reforms in education and tithes. He tried to assure the King by claiming that he was neither Protestant nor Catholic and would always try to act impartially. By 1828, rebellion was openly feared in Ireland. Daniel O'Connell was returned at the Co. Clare by-election and £14,000 (approx. €1.2 million) in 'Catholic Rent' was collected in just one week for his election fund. Anglesey, however, was determined that 'the first moment of tranquillity be seized'. Wellington wrote privately that he thought Anglesey had been bitten by 'a mad Papist or instigated by the love of popularity.' On 26 July 1828, Anglesey informed Peel that O'Connell had requested an interview with him to discuss law and order. Anglesey found it difficult to refuse but took the precaution of having a witness present, Lord Forbes. The blunt but eloquent Anglesey was very well able to use his powerful personality in such interviews. He described his tactical approach to Peel: 'It will be my business to be very patient, very guarded, but not severely reserved, and whilst he is endeavouring to penetrate me, to try if I can make anything out of him'. However, it seems likely that Peel would have strongly disapproved of Anglesey's frankness with O'Connell about his own personal position, and the apology he offered for the conduct of Peel and Wellington. However, Anglesey was able to ascertain from the tête-à-tête that O'Connell would be willing to yield on disfranchising the forty-shilling freeholders (which he did next year). When Anglesey questions O'Connell's sincerity, it is presumably because he wanted to point out to him that his strong language and tactics were liable to damage the Catholic cause and raise the hackles of the anti-Emancipation camp. The words 'without quibble' refer to the many devices used by O'Connell to get around the Unlawful Societies (Ireland) Act of 1825 which curtailed the activities of Catholics and Orangemen alike (and outlawed the Catholic Association). SOURCE: Extract from the 'Memorandum by Lord Anglesey of the conversation he has had with O'Connell about the Catholic Association, Emancipation, &c., 29 July 1828', Public Record Office of Northern Ireland (D.619/37).

> **9.2.** … Mr O'Connell … with much mark of respect and peculiar calmness and mildness of manner expressed great regret at the unhappy state of the country which, he humbly suggested, was kept up by the frequent and unnecessary interference of the police and by the Protestants being generally armed.

9.3. He feared he might have been much misrepresented to me; that he was most anxious for the tranquillity of the country; that no effort should be wanting on his part to preserve it; that the Catholics were driven to the course they were now pursuing by the ungenerous treatment they had received; that they were sensible that the progress they had made in their cause was solely attributable to the state of agitation and excitement that had been kept up; that they could now unhappily look to no other chance of success, and that it was therefore natural and to be expected that they should persevere in their course; that the object of the Association was to gain such an influence over the population as to secure the return to parliament of men devoted to their cause and who, by constantly agitating the question and bringing it before the House of Commons, would drive ministers from their station or compel them to grant Emancipation.

9.4. I told Mr O'Connell that I should speak frankly and hold to him precisely the language that I did to everyone, of whatever persuasion he might be; that I was quite free from prejudice either in religion or in politics; that what I thought, the world might know; but that I might be misrepresented or misunderstood; that as therefore he and I were not upon an equal footing, in as much as he had his meetings and his press to resort to, whereas I had not a single newspaper in my interest, or a man to stand up to point out mis-statements that might be made, it were better that whatever might pass in conversation should be held to be of a private nature. He entirely acquiesced in what I proposed and, putting his hand upon his heart and obsequiously bowing, assured me on the honour of a gentleman that, whatever might occur, it should not transpire through him.

I proceeded to say that I deeply deplored the state of Ireland, in whose welfare I took a peculiar interest, etc, etc, etc. I differed with him respecting to the employment of the police, whose forbearance and moderation was generally the theme of praise; that they were frequently driven to the use of their arms to save their lives, and that in every instance the closest investigation of their conduct took place; that they were always amenable to the civil power; that the Protestants had, indeed, arms to a certain extent, but that they were prohibited from using them, and that the Catholics were under similar circumstances; that in point of fact no distinction existed as to regulation on that head.

9.5. I gave him full credit for desiring tranquillity and being willing to use his efforts to preserve it, but I observed, when a very sensitive and half barbarous people were brought into great excitement, no one ought to presume that he had the power of controlling them. I admitted my belief that perseverance and agitation had gained for the Catholics the ground upon which they stood; that no one was more anxious than myself for the success of their cause – not even he whose language and conduct had indeed often led me to doubt if he was sincere; that so far from discouraging the agitation of the question, the presenting of petitions, its frequent discussion, I would advise a continuance in the same course, that the cause should be advocated by the ablest members of both Houses of Parliament; that I did not even object to the meeting of the Association for the furtherance of their objects by every fair legal means (without quibble); yet I could not but think it might be well worth trying the experiment of discontinuing them for a time, in the hope that such a proof of forbearance and acquiescence in the wishes of many of the warmest friends of the Catholics, might produce a very advantageous effect. I expressed my doubt of the justness of his expectations from the manner in which he hoped that Ireland would be represented; that if it were attempted to carry on future elections in the spirit of that of Clare, he might depend upon a great reaction in England; that it would become a 'no popery' question, and that many of the present supporters of the Catholics would lose their seats in England.

9.6. Mr O'Connell seemed extremely anxious to impress upon my mind his abhorrence of insurrection and his conviction that none was to be expected. I assured him that I had no apprehensions; that I could not bring my mind to believe persons could be found hardy enough to attempt to resist the law and break the peace; yet that I felt bound to be prepared – that I was in fact prepared; and that, happen what might, I felt perfectly confident of being able to put down insurrection in an instant. I spoke of my determination to act upon all occasions with the greatest forbearance – of the reluctance with which I should draw the sword, of the horror I had of the sanguinary consequences which must be dreadful if I began; that so convinced was I of the propriety and the necessity of adjusting the Catholic question, that if left to my own judgement, I would not lose a moment in effecting it; that even in the event of disturbances I would, upon their suppression (provided I could effect it with my troops) still concede all reasonable points; but that I could not shut my eyes to the possibility of the most appalling of all cases – that of my being compelled in aid of the King's troops, to arm the Orange population. What, said I, must be the dreadful consequences of such a measure – war to extermination and the total extinction of all hope to the Catholics! For how could any government which had called for the energy of Protestants to put down Catholic rebellion, ever propose to the former to receive into the Constitution, upon an equality of rights, those whom they had been called upon to assist in subduing from open rebellion?

9.7. This appeared to strike Mr O'Connell very forcibly. He quite acquiesced in the observation, and said, not only would such an event put off to an immeasurable term the adjustment of the question, but in the event of insurrection (which he again assured me was not to be apprehended) even the power I possessed (and he thought it great) would not enable me to suppress the rising of the Orangemen. I assured him that most peremptory orders of precaution against all excesses had been given; that I never had considered and never would consider from what quarter infraction of the law and of the peace came; that nothing could be more certain than that an equal measure of justice would be dealt out to all …

9.8. I have omitted to state that, previously to entering into conversation I desired Mr O'Connell to understand that whatever I said or should thereafter say, was purely upon my own account; that I had no authority to discuss, much less to negotiate upon, the subject of Emancipation; that negotiation in fact was inadmissible; and that whenever anything should be done, it must be done by the legislature without treaty, although of course communications of a private character might pass between individuals interested.

9.9. The conversation now turned upon the practicability of making such arrangements as might pacify the country and satisfy all parties. I said I feared there would be great difficulties. He assured me that on the part of the Catholics there would be none; that he offered himself to assist by every means in his power, and pledged himself to overcome such as might, however, be started. He at first said that all the bishops would be ready to confer with me, but shortly afterwards he insinuated that he who so intimately knew them all and all the bearings of every part of the case, might be more useful than perhaps any other. He talked of the facility with which the court of Rome might be engaged to make similar arrangements to those made with the Kings of Prussia and of the Netherlands. He seemed to hold quite cheap any doubt as to the management of the priests.

9.10. I did not think it advisable to go directly to the elective franchise question, but I went so near the wind as to be perfectly persuaded in my own mind, from the manner in which he took my observations, that the forty-shilling freeholders would never stand in the way of an adjustment.

9.11. I now took occasion to give a pretty strong lecture upon the conduct of the Association and, more particularly, upon its language towards the Duke of Wellington. I told him that the Duke had been greatly calumniated; that he was placed in a most difficult situation; that he was supported by all the ultra Protestants; that there were, perhaps, strong feelings (at which O'Connell had himself hinted) in another quarter [King George IV]; that these were all to be managed; and that, however the Duke might be inclined to acquiesce in the policy of removing all penal enactments and disqualifications, he could not be expected to be able to carry the measure at once and by main force. I told him I had not a particle of authority to announce the Duke's conversion, but that my belief was he would willingly set it at rest by fair concession. At all events, I said, the Duke, I firmly believe, is the only man who can carry that question, and I do not despair of his attempting it; but much in my mind depends upon tranquillity and moderation in Ireland.

9.12. If we can approach the next session of parliament without any previous violent manifestation of party violence, if the Association assumes a less offensive tone, still more if its meetings were to be discontinued – I should augur most favourably of the result. But if the same insulting language is held, if the public authorities continue to be vilified, if the attempts to overawe public opinion are persevered in, then I shall despair of the cause. It can only be carried as a measure of government, and no government will be found to attempt it under such forbidding circumstances.

9.13. Here the conversation ended. Mr O'Connell appeared much pleased with his reception. Lord Forbes left the room with him, and perhaps Mr O'Connell's exclamation the moment they reached another room is the most remarkable and satisfactory of all that took place. He said, I see but one difficulty. It is the forty-shilling freeholders. We cannot *all at once* give them up. We must have time!

9.14. O'Connell is the vainest of men and the easiest taken by a good bait … My firm belief is that O'Connell is perfectly sincere. I should be laughed at for my gullibility, but I repeat that I believe him sincere; that he has a good heart and means well and means indeed always what he says; but that he is volatile and unsteady and so vain that he cannot resist momentary applause.

10. Discrimination against Catholics, 1829

10.1. *Introduction.* Thomas Wyse (1791–1862), a Catholic landowner and prominent member of the Catholic Association, was to the fore in the campaign for enfranchisement of the forty-shilling freeholders. He wrote a history of the movement for Catholic rights that illustrated the extent and practice of sectarian discrimination. As well as public offices from which Catholics were excluded, as seen in the extract below, Wyse recorded offices relating to trade, industry and commerce, education, charity, medicine, law enforcement, and the universities which enforced similar prohibitions. SOURCE: Thomas Wyse, *Historical sketch of the late Catholic Association* (2 vols, London, 1829).

10.2. It is necessary to bear in mind the proportions of the Irish population, which may be fairly estimated as follows: Catholics: 7,000,000; Protestants and Dissenters of all descriptions: 1,100,000.

Table 6: Offices of Civil Rank, or of honour, from which Catholics are excluded by Law in Ireland.

Lord Lieutenant	1
Chief Secretary	2
Peers of Parliament	28
Members of the House of Commons	100
Lord Chancellor	1
Keeper of the Privy Seal	1
Vice-Treasurer	1
Teller of the Exchequer	1
Auditor-General	1
Governors of Counties	73
Custodes Rotulorum (Keeper of the Rolls)	32
Secretary to the Lord Lieutenant	1
Members of the Privy Council	63
Attorney-General	1
Postmasters-General	1
Sheriffs	48
Provost and Fellows of Trinity College, Dublin	25
Officers of Corporations	400
TOTAL	780

Table 7: Offices to which Catholics are eligible by Law in Ireland.

	Number of Offices	*Number of Catholics*
In Chancery	73	0
Insolvent Court	10	1
King's Bench	28	3
Common Pleas	32	1
Exchequer	56	2
Assistant Barristers of Counties	32	2
Clerks of the Crown	39	0
Crown Solicitors	12	0
Officers of Towns/Corporations	8	0
Inspectors-General of Prisons	100	0
Jails, Local Inspectors, officers of Co. Prisons	151	0
Chief Magistrates of Police	4	0
Chief Constables of Police	350	20
Valuation Commissioners	4	0
Police Magistrates of Dublin	18	0

To these should be added the long and most important list of Justices of the Peace, and Grand and Petit Jurors, and the army of Constables, in which, could they be procured, the same proportions would be found to exist; as the persons whose right it is to appoint to those offices, almost uniformly act upon the same spirit of exclusion and intolerance as that from which their own nomination emanated.

11. Henry Goulburn's letter to Archbishop Beresford

11.1. *Introduction.* Henry Goulburn (1784–1856), Conservative politician, had been appointed as Chief Secretary for Ireland, 1821–7, under Richard Colley Wellesley (Lord Lieutentant, 1821–8). He was unpopular in Ireland because of his earlier opposition to the Catholic Disability Removal Bill (1821). He had also introduced the Irish Tithe Composition Act in 1823. In the spring of 1825, he carried a bill for the suppression of unlawful societies, which O'Connell's Catholic Association managed to elude by dissolving itself and re-forming in July. Goulburn supported the Prime Minister, the Duke of Wellington, and Sir Robert Peel in their opposition to the granting of Catholic Emancipation. In the general election of 1826, he had been returned for an Irish constituency, Armagh City (having failed to secure Cambridge University). The Archbishop of Armagh, Lord John George Beresford (1773–1862), who controlled the borough, placed it at the disposal of the government. However, a recent convention, established in 1801, reserved the Armagh seat for someone who was prominent in the opposition to Emancipation. Archbishop Beresford was strongly opposed to Catholic Emancipation, on the grounds that it 'would transfer from Protestants to Roman Catholics the ascendancy of Ireland.' It is not surprising, therefore, that Goulburn felt it necessary to write this lengthy letter of explanation to Beresford. He clearly had deep respect for the Archbishop which is in stark contrast to the brusque treatment of the Archbishop by Wellington (see §19). Clearly, Beresford must have been satisfied with Goulburn's argument, as he was again returned for Armagh in the 1830 general election. The other names mentioned are: Robert Dundas, 2nd Viscount Melville, First Lord of the Admiralty (1812–27, 1828–1830); John Charles Herries, Master of the Mint under the Duke of Wellington (1828–30); Edward Law, 1st Earl of Ellenborough, President of the Board of Control on four occasions and later Governor-General of India (1841–4); George Hamilton-Gordon, 4th Earl of Aberdeen, Foreign Secretary under the Duke of Wellington (1828–30) and later Prime Minister (1852–5); and Sir George Murray, Lieutenant General of the Ordnance from 1824 and Commander-in-Chief in Ireland, 1825–8. SOURCE: Memorandum by Henry Goulburn, Chancellor of the Exchequer in the Wellington ministry and MP for Armagh, 28 January 1829, justifying to Archbishop John George Beresford his decision to remain a member of a government that was committed to passing Catholic Emancipation. Public Record Office of Northern Ireland (T.2772/7/10B).

11.2. … I have been, for some time past, impressed with an opinion that it was necessary to alter the principle on which the government has been formed ever since the death of Mr [Spencer] Perceval, namely that of professed neutrality upon the Roman Catholic question. Each day gives rise to questions affecting Ireland, in all of which the Roman Catholic question more or less enters, and these questions cannot be put aside or be left undecided without increasing inconvenience and danger to important interests of the country, and without a dereliction of duty on the part of those to whom its administration is entrusted. I am satisfied that the system of compromise which has, necessarily, grown out of the division of the government has been, and is daily becoming more, unfavourable to the authority of the Crown and of Parliament …

11.3. Hence I have come to the conclusion that it is essential to form a united government, either on the principle of resisting all further concession to the Roman Catholics, or on that of conceding. From communication with other members of the government whose opinions on the Roman Catholic question coincide with my own, I find that they participate in similar feelings.

11.4. The first subject of consideration is the practicability of forming a government united in resistance to the Roman Catholic claims. Such a government would be that to which I should be disposed to give a preference. But is it practicable to form it? The Duke of Wellington would, of course, be looked to as the head of such, or of any very effective administration which could be formed from the members of the present government. But he has expressed himself decidedly in favour of a settlement of the Roman Catholic question, although he thinks it might, for a time, be postponed with advantage. It would obviously be difficult therefore for the Duke to place himself at the head of an administration formed upon the principle of settled and permanent resistance to concession. The Chancellor also is not disinclined to concession with proper guards and securities. With such feelings, he could add but little strength to an exclusive government. Lords Melville, Aberdeen, and Ellenborough, Sir G. Murray and Mr V[esey] FitzGerald could not, from their known opinions, be members of such an administration. There would only then remain in the House of Commons, Mr Peel, Mr Herries and myself, who had held Cabinet office. The subordinate offices of the government are mostly held by young men who are favourable to concession. Little assistance therefore could be looked for in that quarter in filling the higher departments of the state with persons competent to discharge effectually the business of them.

11.5. But when I look at the state of the House of Commons, I see no prospect, even if such a government could be formed, of commanding a majority of the House. The House decided last year in favour of the consideration of the Roman Catholic claims. The majority was not great, but it was a majority in a House recently elected – at a period when Protestant feeling was by no means dormant, and it was obtained at a moment when, from the recent change of government, a display of Protestant feeling might have been expected. The changes which have since taken place have given no accession to Protestant strength. On the contrary, some of those who, on the last occasion, voted against concession, have since pledged themselves to support it in future, and others have expressed their opinion that a settlement ought to take place, and have intimated an indisposition any longer to oppose it. In the present House of Commons, therefore, there is no hope that a government formed on the principle of resisting concession could secure a majority. There is still less hope that such a government could carry those measures which, without reference to the Roman Catholic question, are indispensably necessary to the security of Protestant interests and for carrying which a united Protestant government is mainly desirable. Of these measures, the restriction of the elective franchise in Ireland admits of no delay, yet in this House of Commons, an attempt to regulate it effectually unaccompanied by concession must fail, and failure on such a question would decide the fate of the administration.

11.6. But a dissolution and an appeal to the people on Protestant principles might make a change in the House of Commons. The effect of a dissolution then comes next to be considered. It is probable that an election would add to the number of English members opposed to concession. Not, however, to any great extent. The educated classes of this country (with the exception of the clergy) are much divided in opinion. Elections are expensive. The supporters of Catholic views are rich. The population of the great towns is also much divided in opinion. The attempts which have been made to excite an expression of popular opinion have not been so general or so completely successful as might have been anticipated, nor such as to authorise an opinion that great additional strength to the Protestant interest would be the consequence of a new election.

11.7. In Scotland, there is no reason to calculate upon alteration of the relative proportion of the supporters and opposers of concession.

11.8. But in Ireland, the effect of a general election would be to remove every member for a county or large town (with the exception perhaps of four or five) who had either resisted concession or supported the government. It would do more. It would substitute for those who had moderately supported it the violent and radical demagogues of the day, men without connection, without the sympathies of gentlemen, devoted to an opposition to the government by all means fair or unfair. The result would be an accession of from sixty to seventy members representing, in fact, the priests and the Association, acting under their orders and opposed to government, both in the abstract and in detail. Whatever numbers, therefore, might be gained in England on a dissolution would be more than counterbalanced by the introduction of such a body from Ireland.

11.9. I therefore see no mode of enabling a united Protestant government to stand. I am forced then to contemplate the consequences of its formation and its failure. The most immediate would be to transfer the government to an administration not merely favourable to concession, but pledged to carry Roman Catholic Emancipation on Roman Catholic principles, regardless of securities, because they have pronounced them to be unnecessary, prepared therefore to place at hazard the interests of religion, of the Church and the Protestants of Ireland …

11.10. I feel, as I ever have felt, the risk of admitting Roman Catholics to political power. I know the difficulty of devising adequate securities. But I cannot conceal from myself that, owing to the past division of the government, political power has actually devolved on the Roman Catholics. It is exercised by them in the worst possible form, in the command of the whole Irish representation, and will, by a continuance of that division, be consolidated and increased. I think it therefore better, in the absence of any hope of a united Protestant government, to join in a settlement which shall rid us of the impending dangers, and raise up an effective barrier against Roman Catholic encroachment in future.

11.11. If the Roman Catholic Association and other similar bodies be immediately and permanently suppressed; if the elective franchise be rescued from the hands of the priests, and effectually regulated; if the Roman Catholic religion be placed in such a subordinate relation to the religion of the state as shall prevent competition and conflict; if, in addition to these necessary securities, the union of the government shall secure towards the clergy the property and the privileges of the United Church, the constant support to which they are entitled; and if such a government carry with it the support of parliament, much will be done to countervail the possible evils of concession. In continuing a member of a government determined to attempt a settlement, I do so in full confidence and on a perfect understanding that these objects are to be attained, and when attained, I think that the power which Roman Catholics may acquire by admission to parliament and to office, under certain limitations, will become less hazardous than that which they at present exercise over parliament in defiance of the law and of the government, and to the prejudice of both …

12. Sir Thomas Wyse on 'moral force'

12.1. *Introduction.* Thomas Wyse reflected on the campaign for Catholic Emancipation and the importance of 'moral force' in achieving it. Moral force meant rejecting violence outright and bringing about change by rallying the masses to demand their natural rights. It is the belief that Catholics would eventually succeed in forcing the government, by peaceful means, to concede their demands because their cause was just and ethical. Based on a firm and optimistic belief in the power of good to triumph over evil, Wyse confidently asserted that people will always, and inevitably, overcome injustice without violence, if they put their minds to it. SOURCE: Thomas Wyse, *Historical sketch of the late Catholic Association of Ireland* (2 vols, London, 1829), I, 7–9.

12.2. Catholic Emancipation, it will be seen, has not been achieved by a *coup de main* [i.e. an armed surprise attack]; liberty has not come to the Catholic by accident; nor is it, as has been falsely surmised, the gift of a few leaders; but its seeds have, year after year, been plentiful sown in the mind of a whole people, until the appointed moment for the sure and abundant harvest had fully arrived. The moral force of patient and unceasing effort in a just cause, confiding fully in the God of justice and its own might, has been adequately proved: the certainty of final triumph, when truth and reason are the combatants, is placed beyond a doubt: and if this great lesson, and no other, had been taught by the late struggle, it would have been well worth all the sacrifice and delay. Every day, the chance of regenerating a nation by the coarse expedients of physical force is, thank God! becoming less and less. There is every day a greater confidence in the power and efficacy of mere mind; there is every day a more firm assurance in the strength and sufficiency of unassisted reason ...

12.3. To confer the greatest share of human blessing on the governed by means the most general, the most simple, and the most permanent, is surely a glorious art. An Englishman should not now have to learn it; he ought to be the first to teach it to all mankind. The suppression of restrictions on personal liberty, on the liberty of the press, the amelioration of the elective code, new guarantees for the rights of publicity and opinion, a more popular municipal organisation, are portions of the same system in France, of which the approaching Emancipation of the Catholics is a still greater portion in England ... In order to be free, there is one thing necessary, and only one—strongly, deeply, and perseveringly, to *will* it.

13. Provincial meetings of the Catholic Association

13.1. *Introduction.* In these reports of provincial meetings, Wyse gave an impressive description of the excitement they caused, and their importance in rallying people. He explained how towns competed for the honour of hosting meetings. At these the 'leading class', that is, educated and comfortable elites, Catholics and Protestants, met to discuss the campaign and to address the many thousands who came from all over the county and further afield. Although deeply committed to improving the lives of the poor, Wyse, himself a wealthy landowner, believed that the privileged elites were the natural and best leaders of the people. In the same spirit, he was committed to ending sectarian hatreds and promoting harmony between Catholics and Protestants. Thus, Wyse praised local organisers of meetings who helped to unite all classes and creeds in their shared goal of civil and political liberty. He paid tribute in particular to prominent members of the Catholic Association who travelled throughout Ireland to promote the cause. Finally, he observed that the poorer classes zealously attended these meetings and talked about the events and speeches for months after. SOURCE: Thomas Wyse, *Historical sketch of the late Catholic Association of Ireland* (2 vols, London, 1829), i, 226–7, 241, 245.

13.2. Each province of Ireland was summoned by requisition; the Catholics invited their Protestant friends; both met on an appointed day, in a town chosen in rotation, in one or other of the counties of the province. They generally remained sitting for two days, and dined together on the second or the third. The result was most important. It was not only another convention … but it was a convention of Catholics and Protestants. It familiarised both sects with each other … The people also incalculably benefited. It was not only a spectacle of great and stirring interest … but it was really a series of impressive public lectures on their grievances and their rights, which left behind them thoughts which burned for many months afterwards in the hearts of the peasantry, gave them a visible and sensible connexion with the leading class of their countrymen, and taught them that upon the co-operation and union of all orders depended mainly the chance by which they might have a future restoration to their rights …

13.3. In the country, such an event is an epoch which fills a great portion of the peasant's existence; it is the hope of his entire family for months before, and the boast for months after: the speeches are read and re-read with the utmost assiduity, learned by heart, discussed, and cited, with an earnestness and sympathy unintelligible to a mere citizen …

13.4. The day and town in which the gathering was to take place were often contested with anxiety. It was a matter of local, almost of personal pride, to exhibit, under the most striking forms, the pretensions, the wealth, the intelligence, the enthusiasm, of the favoured county … The Provincial meeting thus travelled round the entire province in four or five years, and each town and each succeeding year vie in the numbers it could assemble, in the magnificence of its preparations, in the boldness of its resolutions, in the spirit which it generated, with its predecessors. Men whose names had long been familiar through the public prints to the ear of their fellow-countrymen thus became personally known one after the other to them all; the leaders grew really such; and the Association, viewed through such a medium, had an influence (what power is stronger than such an influence?) scarcely equalled by the government itself.

14. The retreat of Wellington, 1829

14.1. *Introduction.* Lord Francis Leveson-Gower (1800–57) was a protégé and friend of Wellington. He was spokesman for the Irish administration in the House of Commons, and was in favour of Catholic Emancipation. In Parliament (1822–46) he supported the liberal Tory policies, becoming an early exponent of Free Trade. He was Chief Secretary for Ireland, 1828–30. Lord Anglesey was a soldier (he had commanded the cavalry at the Battle of Waterloo under Wellington). Appointed Lord Lieutenant of Ireland in 1828, his short time in Ireland convinced him of the pressing need for Catholic Emancipation. Lord Leveson-Gower says a good deal in his letter to him. He was not in a position to tell Anglesey all he knew of Wellington's intentions, but he hinted that the Duke would not continue to resist Catholic Emancipation. Wellington had already made a declaration in the House of Lords in June which indicated his willingness to concede such a measure, but he was vague about how and when. On 28 September, Wellington wrote privately to Anglesey indicating that he wanted to make Emancipation a reality but he had to first reconcile the King to it. Until that was done, Anglesey should not talk about it. Lord Anglesey had not been a member of Cabinet while serving as Lord Lieutenant of Ireland (1828–29) and he complained that he was being kept in the dark. However, Wellington, perhaps revealed more than he should have. In August 1828, the King finally relented and acceded to Wellington's request to be able to discuss the matter with Peel and the Chancellor. It was only in January 1829, that the King gave him authority to discuss the matter with the Cabinet. SOURCE: Lord Francis Leveson-Gower to Lord Anglesey. Public Record Office, Northern Ireland (D.619/31H/12).

14.2. Irish Office, July 19th 1828

My dear Lord Anglesey,

I think it may be convenient to you to receive from time to time any scraps of information in my knowledge as to what passes on this side of the water …

… There are persons here who are inclined to think, or at least to fear, that the Duke takes too soldier-like a view of the state of Ireland, and that he looks to putting things down by force – a short struggle, an easy victory …. I do not think that, as a soldier or a politician, he will choose to fight on his present ground a battle for the existence of the Protestant Church and the connection of the two countries. We have, I think, now little security that we shall not ultimately have to fight this battle, but I am sure Emancipation will give us the best position for doing it. This is the point which I have uniformly pressed in conversation with him.

The danger I now conceive to be a premature commencement of this odious conflict, and I have accepted my situation with the hope of being humbly instrumental in preventing such a result. I should hardly venture to hope that Mr Peel would stay in office and lend his assistance to any final arrangements. I think the loss of his liberal tone of politics on Irish questions, such for example as education, etc, would be severely felt. Any temporary loss, however, would be cheaply purchased by a good arrangement …

Believe me, my dear Lord, very faithfully yours,

F. Leveson-Gower

15. Correspondence on Catholic Emancipation, 1828–9: letter from Wellington to Anglesey, 19 November 1828

15.1. *Introduction.* Daniel O'Connell wrote (somewhat unfairly) in the spring of 1830:

> … in the annals of history there never was anything so undignified as the resistance of the Duke of Wellington to Emancipation, save and except the manner in which he yielded to it. Recollect his letter to Dr Curtis, his tin-case letter to the Duke of Leinster – above all, his letters to that gallant and excellent nobleman, the Marquess of Anglesey.

The following letter is taken from the acrimonious correspondence between Wellington and Anglesey. It is one of a number of letters in which the Prime Minister complains about Anglesey's conduct, and particularly his close relations with members of the Catholic Association. Anglesey later made many of the letters public in his own defence. O'Gorman Mahon (Charles James Patrick Mahon, 1800–91) and Thomas Steele (1788–1848) were prominent members of the Catholic Association, whom Wellington had wanted dismissed as Justices of the Peace (JPs) because of their political activities. Anglesey's aide-de-camp, Baron de Tuyll, and his son, Lord William Paget, had attended Catholic Association meetings. SOURCE: Public Record Office of Northern Ireland (D.619/26C/32).

> **15.2.** … It is perfectly true that till I had occasion to write to you on the 11th instant respecting Mr Mahon and Mr Steele, I did not mention to you the King's feelings upon affairs in Ireland. I did not do so because I was in hopes that in the progress of events the King might see reason to change his opinions, and because it is really very painful to notice matters which would be of a private nature if they had not a bearing upon public affairs. I might have at an earlier period expressed the pain I felt at the attendance of gentlemen of your household, and even of your family, at the Roman Catholic Association. I could not but feel that such attendance must expose your government to misconstruction, but I was silent, because it is painful to notice such things.

> **15.3.** But I have always felt that, if these impressions upon the King's mind should remain – and I must say that recent transactions have given fresh cause for them – I could not avoid to mention them to you in a private communication, and to let you know the embarrassment which they occasion. I may be blamed for not communicating sooner that they existed, but considering their continued existence and the renewed cause for them, I should be still more blamed if I did not mention them to you at all.

Ever, my dear Lord Anglesey,
Yours most sincerely,
Wellington

16. Correspondence on Catholic Emancipation, 1828–9: letter from Wellington to Patrick Curtis, Catholic Primate of All Ireland, 11 December 1828

16.1. *Introduction.* Wellington went behind Anglesey's back when he wrote to Dr Patrick Curtis, the Catholic Primate stating that he was 'sincerely anxious' to see the Roman Catholic question settled but stressed the difficulties that he faced and the need to 'bury it in oblivion for a short time'. Curtis forwarded this letter to Anglesey. Curtis had known Wellington for many years. While Rector of Salamanca College in 1811, during the Peninsular War, he was arrested by the French as a spy, and it was only the entry of the British forces into the war that saved his life. This is when he first met Wellington, to whom (it is said) he supplied valuable intelligence. Wellington is said to have shown his gratitude to Curtis by recommending him highly to the Spanish authorities and by encouraging the Pope to make him Primate. Curtis had actually written to Wellington first. However, the contents of the letter reveal no more than what Wellington had already put on the record in the House of Lords in June 1828. SOURCE: *The Annual Register, or, A view of the history, politics, and literature of the year 1828* (London, 1829), 149–50.

> **16.2.** … I have received your letter of the 4th instant, and I assure you that you do me justice in believing that I am sincerely anxious to witness the settlement of the Roman Catholic Question, which, by benefiting the state, would confer a benefit on every individual belonging to it. But I confess, that I see no prospect of such a settlement.
>
> **16.3** Party has been mixed up with the consideration of the question to such a degree, and such violence pervades every discussion of it, that it is impossible to expect to prevail upon men to consider it dispassionately. If we could bury it in oblivion for a short time, and employ that time diligently in the consideration of its difficulties on all sides (for they are very great), I should not despair of seeing a satisfactory remedy …

17. Correspondence on Catholic Emancipation, 1828–9: letter from Anglesey to Patrick Curtis, Catholic Primate of All Ireland, 11 December 1828.

17.1. *Introduction.* Wellington was well aware that only his personal authority, particularly with the Tory majority in the House of Lords, would get an Emancipation Bill through. Anglesey's actions had provoked angry reaction. His reply to Curtis arguing that all constitutional means should be used to 'forward the cause' and its later publication led to his being ordered home immediately. Wellington had to drop him in order to dispel the illusion that Anglesey's advice had influenced his decision. The French politician Charles de Talleyrand told Lord Palmerston that 'he saw that the Duke had determined on conceding the Irish Catholic claims, and that he did not mean anyone else to have the credit'. Anglesey here admits that he disagreed with Wellington about burying the question in oblivion for a time because that would be impossible; but he pointed out that Wellington was more likely than anyone else to be able to overcome any prejudices that stood in the way of a settlement; and he urged that the Duke should not be abused or impeded in any way. Anglesey told Curtis that his letter was to be regarded as secret. However, he changed his mind a week later when news of his dismissal began to spread through Dublin. He had the letter published on New Year's Day, 1829. SOURCE: *The Annual Register, or, A view of the history, politics, and literature of the year 1828* (London, 1829), 149–50

17.2. … I hasten to acknowledge the receipt of your letter of the 22nd, covering that which you received from the Duke of Wellington, of the 11th instant, together with a copy of your answer to it. I thank you for the confidence you have reposed in me. Your letter gives me information upon a subject of the highest interest. I did not know the precise sentiments of the Duke of Wellington upon the present state of the Catholic Question. Knowing it, I shall venture to offer my opinion upon the course that it behoves the Catholics to pursue.

17.3. Perfectly convinced that the final and cordial settlement of this great question can alone give peace, harmony, and prosperity to all classes of His Majesty's subjects in this kingdom. I must acknowledge my disappointment on learning that there is no prospect of its being effected during the ensuing Session of Parliament. I, however, derive, some consolation from observing, that his Grace is not wholly adverse to the measure; for if he can be induced to promote it, he, of all men, will have the greatest facility in carrying it into effect.

17.4. If I am correct in this opinion, it is obviously most important that the Duke of Wellington should be propitiated; that no obstacle that can possibly be avoided should be thrown in his way; that all personal and offensive insinuations should be suppressed; and that ample allowance should be made for the difficulties of his situation. Difficult it certainly is, for he has to overcome the very strong prejudices, and the interested motives of many persons of the highest influence, as well as to, allay the real alarms of many of the more ignorant Protestants.

17.5. I differ from the opinion of the Duke, that an attempt should be made to 'bury in oblivion' the question for a short time. First, because the thing is utterly impossible; and next, if the thing were possible, I fear that advantage might be taken of the pause, by representing it as a panic achieved by the late violent reaction, and by proclaiming, that if the government at once and peremptorily decided against concession, the Catholics would cease to agitate, and then all the miseries of the last years of Ireland will be re-acted.

17.6. What I do recommend is, that the measure should not be for a moment lost sight of – that anxiety should continue to be manifested – that all constitutional (in contradistinction to merely legal) means should be resorted to, in order to forward the cause; but that, at the same time, the most patient forbearance – the most submissive obedience to the laws, should be inculcated; that no personal and offensive language should be held towards those who oppose the claims.

17.7. ... Let the Catholic trust to the justice of his cause – to the growing liberality of mankind. Unfortunately, he has lost some friends, and fortified his enemies, within the last six months, by unmeasured and unnecessary violence. He will soonest recover from the present stagnation of his fortunes by showing more temper [moderation], and by trusting to the legislature for redress.

17.8. Brute force, he should he assured, can effect nothing. – It is the legislature that must decide this great question; and my greatest anxiety is, that it should be met by the Parliament under the most favourable circumstances, and that the opposers of Catholic Emancipation shall be disarmed by the patient forbearance, as well as by the unwearied perseverance of its advocates.

17.9. My warm anxiety to promote the general interests of this country is the motive that has induced me to give an opinion, and to offer advice. ...

18. Correspondence on Catholic Emancipation, 1828–9: letter from Wellington to the Duke of Leinster, 12 January 1829

18.1. *Introduction.* This is Wellington's laconic and cold reply to a letter from various Irish Protestant notables acknowledging his receipt of their pro-Emancipation address. Among many other matters, the danger that the King would refuse to allow Emancipation had yet to be got over and discretion was the best policy. SOURCE: Public Record Office of Northern Ireland (D.3078/3/20/2).

18.2. London, January 12, 1829

My Lord Duke,

I have had the honour of receiving this morning your Grace's letter of the 7th inst., and a tin case containing the declaration of certain Protestants in Ireland respecting what is called Roman Catholic Emancipation, and the list of the names of the persons who have signed the same.

I have the honour to be, my Lord Duke, your Grace's most obedient humble servant,

Wellington

19. Correspondence on Catholic Emancipation, 1828–9: letter from Wellington to Lord George Beresford, Anglican Archbishop of Armagh, 1 April 1829

19.1. *Introduction.* Archbishop Beresford, who strongly opposed Catholic Emancipation, took the unconstitutional course of asking the King to veto the Emancipation Bill. He seconded the motion of the Archbishop of Canterbury in the House of Lords, arguing that the Bill would 'transfer from Protestants to Roman Catholics the ascendancy in Ireland'. His speech on that occasion was printed in 1829. By his reference to the Privy Council in this letter to Beresford, Wellington meant that Beresford and the other Archbishops had sworn the Privy Counsellor's oath, part of which bound them 'to do as a faithful and true servant ought to do to His Majesty'. Here Wellington coldly declines to present to the King an anti-Emancipation address from Beresford and various bishops of the Church of Ireland. SOURCE: Public Record Office of Northern Ireland (D.664/A/51).

19.2. London, April 1, 1829

My Lord Archbishop,

I have had the honour of receiving your Grace's letter of the 30th March, in which your Grace has enclosed a copy of the address which certain of the Archbishops and Bishops of Ireland propose to present to his Majesty on Saturday.

By the last paragraph of that address, his Majesty is to be implored to withhold his royal sanction from the measures now under the consideration of Parliament. Your Grace, the Lord Archbishop of Dublin and the Lord Archbishop of Tuam are Privy Counsellors in his Majesty's Privy Council in Ireland, and must be the best judges whether it is fit that the advice that that paragraph contains ought to be given to His Majesty.

I cannot so far concur in and sanction this advice as even to be the channel of laying before His Majesty a copy of the address in which it is to be conveyed. I have the honour to be, my Lord Archbishop, Your Grace's most obedient, humble servant,

Wellington

20. Sir Robert Peel's speech on Emancipation

20.1. *Introduction.* There was considerable support for Emancipation in the House of Commons, though it had been firmly opposed by those in high office: the King, the Prime Minister (Wellington), the Secretary of State (Sir Robert Peel), and a majority of peers. Peel had spent much time on the Irish question. As Chief Secretary for Ireland (1812–18), he saw at first hand the operation of the remaining legal restrictions on Catholics, and heard constant Irish complaints about them, in particular the ban on Catholics sitting in Parliament. In 1823–9, he received, as Home Secretary, regular reports about the Catholic Association and had a bulky correspondence with Irish officials and English politicians about how best to end their agitation without granting their demands. O'Connell's overwhelming victory in Clare and the fear of revolution persuaded Peel and the strongest opponents of Emancipation that change was necessary. Wellington's meeting with George IV at Windsor (27 February 1829) lasted five hours. The Duke explained in detail to the King his proposals for Catholic relief, and why it was necessary. The King became very agitated, and agonised about his conscience and his coronation oath. He brought up the possibility of abdicating and, after breaking down in tears, he finally relented and accepted the legislation. People began gathering outside the House of Commons at ten o'clock on the morning of 5 March 1829. The doors were not opened until after six, when all the seats in the chamber were filled in a matter of minutes. Peel managed the House of Commons with consummate ability and his speech (regarded as the best he ever made) went on for over four hours. In it, he explained why the government had decided to grant Catholic Emancipation 'in the spirit of peace' and to prevent war. Notice how formal his language is and how carefully his dramatic change of mind is expressed. This shows how divisive the issue still was and it conceals the violent opposition of the King. He gave a long and detailed account of the history of the 'Catholic Question' and defended the legislation from the criticism that it conceded too much and with too few safeguards. He called for an end to mutual jealousies of Catholics and Protestants and expressed the hope that if the measure was passed that 'armed with the consciousness of having done justice and of being in the right,' they [Protestants] would attain the moral high ground. Peel carried the House with him, and was frequently interrupted by enthusiastic cheers. The debate continued next day and went on until the early hours of 7 March. The government's proposals were finally approved by 348 votes to 160, and in the following month the Catholic Relief Bill passed into law. Here is a substantial extract from Peel's lengthy speech. SOURCE: 'Measure for the Removal of the Roman Catholic Disabilities', House of Commons, 5 March 1829, *Hansard*, XX (February–March 1829), 727–80 (extract).

The Clerk of the House of Commons read as follows:

20.2. The state of Ireland has been the object of His Majesty's continued solicitude. His Majesty laments that, in that part of the United Kingdom, an Association should still exist, which is dangerous to the public peace, and inconsistent with the spirit of the Constitution; which keeps alive discord and ill-will amongst His Majesty's subjects; and which must, if permitted to continue, effectually obstruct every effort permanently to improve the condition of Ireland. His Majesty recommends that when this essential object shall have been accomplished, you shall take into your deliberate consideration the whole condition of Ireland, and that you should review the Laws which impose Civil Disabilities on His Majesty's Roman Catholic subjects. ...

Mr Secretary Peel then addressed the House as follows:

20.3. Mr Speaker, I rise as a minister of the King, and sustained by the just authority which belongs to that character, to vindicate the advice given to His

Majesty by a united Cabinet to insert in his gracious Speech the recommenda-
tion which has just been read respecting the propriety of taking into consideration the condition of Ireland, and the removal of the civil disabilities affecting
our Roman Catholic fellow-subjects. I rise, Sir, in the spirit of peace, to propose
the adjustment of the Roman Catholic question – that question which has so
long and so painfully occupied the attention of Parliament, and which has distracted the councils of the King for the last thirty years.

20.4. I rise, Sir, to discuss this great question in the spirit inculcated in one of those
simple and beautiful prayers with which the proceedings of this House were on this
day auspicated. In that solemn appeal to the Almighty Source of all wisdom and
goodness, we are enjoined to lay aside all private interests, prejudices, and partial
affections, that the result of our councils may tend to the maintenance of true religion and justice; the safety, honour, and happiness of the King; the public wealth,
peace, and tranquillity of the realm; and the uniting and knitting together of the
hearts of all persons and estates within the same in true Christian charity.

20.5. Sir, I approach this subject, almost overpowered by the magnitude of the
interests it involves, and by the difficulties with which it is surrounded. I am not
unconscious of the degree to which those difficulties are increased by the peculiar situation of him on whom the lot has been cast to propose this measure, and
to enforce the expediency of its adoption. But, Sir, through all these difficulties
(be they of a public or a personal character, however disproportionate to my
capacity, or galling to my feelings) I am supported by the consciousness that I
have done my duty towards my Sovereign and towards my country; and that I
have fulfilled the obligations of the solemn oath to His Majesty which I have
taken as his responsible minister, namely, 'That I would in all matters to be
treated and debated in Council, faithfully, openly, and truly declare my mind and
opinion, according to my heart and conscience'.

20.6. According to my heart and conscience, I believe that the time is come
when less danger is to be apprehended to the general interests of the empire, and
to the spiritual and temporal welfare of the Protestant Establishment, in attempting to adjust the Catholic Question, than in allowing it to remain any longer in
its present state. I have stated on a former occasion, that such was my deliberate
opinion; such the conclusion to which I found myself compelled to come by the
irresistible force of circumstances and I will adhere to it, and I will act upon it,
unchanged by the scurrility of abuse – by the expression of opposite opinions,
however vehement or however general; unchanged by the deprivation of political confidence, or by the heavier sacrifice of private friendships and affections.
Looking back upon the past, surveying the present, and forejudging the prospects
of the future, again I declare that the time has at length arrived when this question must be adjusted.

20.7. I have been called upon to state the reasons which have swayed me in the adoption of the course I now advocate, and which is in opposition to that which I have so long pursued. And for the satisfaction of those who have made this appeal to me, and for the satisfaction of the people of this country, I will endeavour to make out the case I have been challenged to establish.

20.8. I am well aware, Sir, that I speak in the presence of a House of Commons, the majority of which is prepared to vote in favour of an adjustment of this question, upon higher grounds than those on which I desire to rest my arguments. To them it is needless to appeal. But I trust that, in what I shall think it necessary to say, less with the personal object of self-vindication than with a view to satisfy the great body of the people of this empire; those who require no reasoning to convince them, will bear with me while I go through the details of an argument which has pressed on my mind with the force of demonstration.

20.9. Sir, I have for years attempted to maintain the exclusion of Roman Catholics from Parliament and the high offices of the State. I do not think it was an unnatural or unreasonable struggle. I resign it, in consequence of the conviction that it can be no longer advantageously maintained; from believing that there are not adequate materials or sufficient instruments for its effectual and permanent continuance. I yield, therefore, to a moral necessity which I cannot control, unwilling to push resistance to a point which might endanger the Establishments that I wish to defend.

20.10. Does that moral necessity exist? Is there more danger in continued resistance than in concession accompanied with measures of restriction and precaution? My object is to prove, by argument, the affirmative answer to these questions. In that argument, I shall abstain from all discussions upon the natural or social rights of man. I shall enter into no disquisitions upon the theories of government. My argument will turn upon a practical view of the present condition of affairs, and upon the consideration, not of what may be said, but what is to be done under circumstances of immediate and pressing difficulty. Sir, the outline of my argument is this: we are placed in a position in which we cannot remain. We cannot continue stationary. There is an evil in divided cabinets and distracted councils which can be no longer tolerated ...

20.11. ... Let us cast a rapid glance over the recent history of Ireland, trace it from the Union, the period when the retirement of Mr Pitt from the King's councils brought more prominently forward the differences of public men in regard to the Catholic Question. What is the melancholy fact? That for scarcely one year, during the period that has elapsed since the Union, has Ireland been governed by the ordinary course of law. In 1800, we find the *Habeas Corpus* Act suspended, and the Act for the Suppression of Rebellion in force. In 1801, they were continued. In 1802, I believe, they expired. In 1803, the Insurrection for which Emmet suffered broke out: Lord Kilwarden [Arthur Wolfe] was murdered by a savage mob, and both acts of Parliament were renewed. In 1804, they were continued. In 1806, the West and South of Ireland were in a state of insubordination, which was with difficulty repressed by the severest enforcement of the ordinary law. In 1807, in consequence chiefly of the disorders that had prevailed in 1806, the act called the Insurrection Act was introduced. It gave power to the Lord Lieutenant to place any district by proclamation out of the pale of the ordinary law, it suspended trial by jury – and made it a transportable offence to be out of doors from sunset to sunrise. In 1807, this act continued in force, and in 1808, 1809, and to the close of the session of 1810. In 1814, the Insurrection Act was renewed; it was continued in 1815, 1816, and 1817. In 1822, it was again revived, and continued during the years 1823, 1824, and 1825. In 1825, the temporary act intended for the suppression of dangerous associations, and especially the Roman Catholic Association, was passed. It continued during 1826 and 1827, and expired in 1828. The year 1829 has arrived, and with it the demand for a new act to suppress the Roman Catholic Association …

20.12. We cannot replace the Roman Catholics in the position in which we found them, when the system of relaxation and indulgence began. We have given them the opportunities of acquiring education, wealth, and power. We have removed, with our hands, the seal from the vessel, in which a mighty spirit was enclosed – but it will not, like the genius in the fable, return within its narrow confines, to gratify our curiosity, and enable us to cast it back into the obscurity from which we evoked it. If we begin to recede, there is no limit which we can assign to our recession. We shall occasion a violent reaction – violent in proportion to the hopes that have been repeatedly excited. It must be coerced by new rigours, provoking in their turn fresh resistance. The re-enactment of the Penal Laws, even if practicable, would not suffice.

20.13. Now look at the population of Ireland, and then determine whether such a system of government is, in the present state of the world, maintainable. According to the Census of 1821, the population of Ireland was computed to amount to nearly seven millions of persons. Of them, by a calculation formed by my right honourable friend [Mr Leslie Foster], deduced from the numbers of children educated in Ireland, five millions are Roman Catholics – two millions Protestants, including the members of the Established Church and every branch of Protestant dissenters. Can the local government of Ireland be conducted through the exclusive instrumentality of two millions out of seven of the population? Surely government, civil government, means something more than the rigid enforcement of penal law, the suppression of breaches of the peace, and the apprehension of notorious offenders …

20.14. … These circumstances being duly considered, again I ask, how is the civil and criminal process of the law to be equably and regularly conducted throughout Ireland, supposing the withdrawing of the powers and privileges already granted to the Roman Catholics to have the effect which I anticipate from it – namely that of dividing the population into two distinct classes – one favoured by the law, the other totally estranged from it? It may be said, and truly said, that reliance can be placed upon the army and upon the police; but will England patiently bear the enormous expense of enforcing every civil right of property, of supporting every legal claim for rent or for tithes, by the agency of such expensive instruments? …

21. The Catholic Relief (Emancipation) Act, 1829

21.1. *Introduction.* Ever since the Reformation, restrictive legislation imposed on Roman Catholics aimed to protect the Protestant state. While Protestant Dissenters were mostly regarded as loyal subjects, Catholics were thought to have divided loyalty, between king and pope. Many believed that they should not, therefore, enjoy the privileges of full citizenship. Roman Catholicism was viewed as an intolerant, proselytising and authoritarian religion. In 1688, and again in 1714, the strict rules of succession were set aside so that a Roman Catholic monarch could not succeed. The Act of Settlement (1701) provided that the throne should pass to Sophia (1630–1714), Electress of Hanover, and her Protestant descendants. Sophia was a grand-daughter of James I, and a niece of Charles I. Only her descendants that were Protestant and had not married a Roman Catholic, could succeed to the throne. Catholics were therefore (and still are) 'uncapable to inherit, possess, or enjoy the crown and government of this realm'. Sophia died just weeks before Queen Anne (1665–1714), and more than fifty individuals who were closer in blood to Anne (but Catholic) were passed over, in favour of Sophia's son, George Ludwig of Hanover. He was crowned King George I of Great Britain and Ireland, and reigned from 1714 to 1727.

21.2. From the 1770s on support for a relaxation of the penal laws had powerful advocates within government circles. By the early nineteenth century religious zeal and intolerance amongst ordinary Britons was diminishing. Following the Act of Union (1801), support for further Roman Catholic relief measures grew: in 1805 some 336 MPs had voted against it, after 1812 this dropped to 250, and in 1819, a relief measure failed by just two votes. The long agitation for civil rights for Catholics culminated in the passing of the Catholic Relief Act (10 Geo. IV, c. 7) which became law on 13 April 1829. The Act repealed the declarations against transubstantiation [the change by which, in Catholic belief, the substance (though not the appearance) of the bread and wine in the Eucharist becomes Christ's body and blood], and against the saints and the Mass until now required of elected representatives before taking their seats in Parliament. Instead of the Oaths of Allegiance, Supremacy and Abjuration there was substituted a simple Oath of Allegiance to the King and the Hanoverian succession which declared that the Pope had no right to depose heretical monarchs (section II). Irish Catholics undertook to accept the land settlement of the seventeenth century; and undertook never to use any privilege to disturb or weaken the Protestant religion or government in the United Kingdom. This oath was later abolished by the Promissory Oaths Act, 1871 (34 & 35 Vic., c. 48).

21.3. Furthermore, Roman Catholics were entitled to hold all civil and military offices except those of Regent, Chancellor, and Lord Lieutenant. The disqualification regarding the office of Lord Chancellor of Ireland (section XII) was later removed by the Office and Oath Act, 1867 (30 & 31 Vic., c. 75). Catholics were finally allowed to hold the office of Lord Lieutenant of Ireland (section XII) under the provisions of the government of Ireland Act, 1920 (10 & 11 Geo. V, c. 67). Catholics continued to be excluded from certain specified ecclesiastical offices limited to members of the Established Church, and from using titles associated with it. Other restrictions applied to the use of robes of office and the exercise of Roman Catholic rites or ceremonies except in Roman Catholic places of worship (section XXV). Since the Act carried none of the 'Wings', such as the royal 'veto' on the appointment of bishops, or the payment of clergy, which had been attached to earlier bills, it left the Catholic clergy free of state control. Jesuits were required to leave the kingdom, and other religious orders were to be made incapable of receiving charitable bequests. SOURCE: 10 George IV, c. 7; *A Collection of Public General Statutes* ... (London, 1829), 105–15.

AN ACT FOR THE RELIEF OF HIS MAJESTY'S ROMAN CATHOLIC SUBJECTS

I. WHEREAS by various acts of parliament certain restraints and disabilities are imposed on the Roman Catholic subjects of His Majesty, to which other subjects of His Majesty are not liable, and whereas it is expedient that such restraints and disabilities shall be from henceforth discontinued, and whereas by various acts certain oaths and certain declarations, commonly called the declarations against transubstantiation and the invocation of saints and the sacrifice of the mass, as practised in the church of Rome, are or may be required to be taken, made, and subscribed by the subjects of His Majesty as qualifications for sitting and voting in parliament and for the enjoyment of certain offices, franchises, and civil rights, be it enacted ... that from and after the commencement of this Act all such parts of the said acts as require the said declarations, or either of them, to be made or subscribed by any of His Majesty's subjects as a qualification for sitting and voting in Parliament or for the exercise or enjoyment of any office, franchise, or, civil right, be and the same are (save as hereinafter provided and excepted) hereby repealed.

II. And be it enacted that ... it shall be lawful for, any person professing the Roman Catholic religion, being a peer, or who shall after the commencement of this Act be returned as a member of the House of Commons, to sit and vote in either House of Parliament respectively, being in all other respects duly qualified to sit and vote therein, upon taking and subscribing the following oath, instead of the oaths of allegiance, supremacy, and abjuration: I, *A. B.*, do sincerely promise and, swear that I will be faithful and bear true allegiance to His Majesty King

George the Fourth and will defend to the utmost of my power against all conspiracies and attempts whatever, which shall be made against his person, crown, or dignity. And I will do my utmost endeavour to disclose and make known to His Majesty, his heirs and successors, all treasons and traitorous conspiracies which may be formed against him or them. And I do faithfully promise to maintain, support, and defend, to the utmost of my power, the succession of the Crown, which succession, by an Act entitled *An act for the further limitation of the Crown and better securing the rights and liberties of the subject,* is and stands limited to the Princess Sophia, Electress of Hanover, and the heirs of her body, being Protestants; hereby utterly renouncing and abjuring any obedience or allegiance unto any other person claiming or pretending a right to the Crown of this realm. And I do further declare that it is not an article of my faith, and that I do renounce, reject, and abjure the opinion that princes excommunicated or deprived by the pope or any other authority of the see of Rome may be deposed or murdered by their subjects or by any person whatsoever. And I do declare that I do not believe that the pope of Rome, or any other foreign prince, prelate, person, state, or potentate, hath or ought to have any temporal or civil jurisdiction, power, superiority, or pre-eminence, directly or indirectly, within this realm. I do swear that I will defend to the utmost of my power the settlement of the property within this realm as established by the laws, and I do hereby disclaim, disavow, and solemnly abjure any intention to subvert the present church establishment as settled by law within this realm, and I do solemnly swear that I never will exercise any privilege to which I am or may become entitled, to disturb or weaken the Protestant religion or Protestant government in the United Kingdom. And I do solemnly, in the presence of God, profess, testify, and declare that I do make this declaration and every part thereof in the plain and ordinary sense of the words of this oath, without any evasion, equivocation, or mental reservation whatsoever. So help me God …

V. And be it further enacted that it shall be lawful for persons professing the Roman Catholic religion to vote at elections of members to serve in Parliament for England and for Ireland, and also to vote at the elections of representative peers of Scotland and of Ireland, and to be elected such representative peers, being in all other respects duly qualified, upon taking and subscribing the oath hereinbefore appointed and set forth …

X. And be it enacted that it shall be lawful for any of His Majesty's subjects professing the Roman Catholic religion to hold, exercise, and enjoy all civil and military offices and places of trust or profit under his Majesty, his heirs or successors; and to exercise any other franchise or civil right … upon taking and subscribing … the oath hereinbefore appointed …

XII. Provided also, and be it further enacted that nothing herein contained shall extend or be construed to extend to enable any person or persons professing the

Roman Catholic religion to hold or exercise the office of guardians and justices of the United Kingdom or of Regent of the United Kingdom, under whatever name, style, or title such office may be constituted, nor to enable any person, otherwise than as he is now by law enabled, to hold or enjoy the office of Lord High Chancellor, Lord Keeper or Lord Commissioner of the Great Seal of Great Britain or Ireland, or the office of Lord Lieutenant, or Lord Deputy, or other Chief Governor or governors of Ireland, or His Majesty's High Commissioner to the General Assembly of the Church of Scotland.

XIV. And be it enacted that it shall be lawful for any of His Majesty's subjects professing the Roman Catholic religion to be a member of any lay body corporate, and to hold any civil office or place of trust or profit therein, and to do any corporate act or vote in any corporate election or other proceeding, upon taking and subscribing the oath hereby appointed and set forth, instead of the oaths of allegiance, supremacy, and abjuration, and upon taking also such other oath or oaths as may now by law be required to be taken by any persons becoming members of such lay body corporate …

XVI. Provided also, and be it enacted that nothing in this Act contained shall be construed to enable any persons, otherwise than as they are now by law enabled, to hold, enjoy, or exercise any office, place, or dignity of, in, or belonging to the United Church of England and Ireland, or the Church of Scotland, or any place or office whatever of, in, or belonging to any of the ecclesiastical courts of judicature of England and Ireland respectively, or any court of appeal from or review of the sentences of such courts, or of, in, or belonging to the Commissary Court of Edinburgh, or of, in, or belonging to any cathedral or collegiate or ecclesiastical establishment or foundation, or any office or place whatever of, in, or belonging to any of the universities of this realm, or any office or place whatever, and by whatever name the same may be called, of, in, or belonging to any of the colleges or halls of the said universities … or any college or school within this realm; or to repeal, abrogate, or in any manner to interfere with any local statute, ordinance, or rule, which is or shall be established by competent authority within any university, college, hall, or school, by which Roman Catholics shall be prevented from being admitted thereto or from residing or taking degrees therein …

XXIV. And whereas the Protestant Episcopal Church of England and Ireland, and the doctrine, discipline, and government thereof, and likewise the Protestant Presbyterian Church of Scotland, and the doctrine, discipline, and government thereof, are by the respective Acts of Union of England and Scotland, and of Great Britain and Ireland, established permanently and inviolably, and whereas the right and title of archbishops to their respective provinces, of bishops to their sees, and the deans to their deaneries, as well in England as in Ireland, have been settled and established by law, be it therefore enacted that if any person after the commencement of this Act, other than the person thereunto authorised by law, shall assume or use the name, style, or title of archbishop of any province, bishop of any bishoprick, or dean of any deanery in England or Ireland, he shall for every such offence forfeit and pay the sum of £100 (approx. €8,500).

XXV. And be it further enacted, that if any person holding any judicial or civil office, or any mayor, provost, jurat [municipal officer], bailiff, or other corporate officer, shall after the commencement of this Act, resort to or be present at any place or public meeting for religious worship in England, or in Ireland, other than that of the united church of England and Ireland, or in Scotland, other than that of the church of Scotland, as by law established, in the robe, gown, or other peculiar habit of his office, or attend with the ensign or insignia, or any part thereof, of or belonging to such his office, such person shall, being thereof convicted by due course of law, forfeit such office, and pay for every such offence the sum of £100.

XXVI. And be it further enacted, that if any Roman Catholic ecclesiastic, or any member of any of the orders, communities, or societies herein-after mentioned, shall, after the commencement of this Act, exercise any of the rites or ceremonies of the Roman Catholic religion, or wear the habits of his order, save within the usual places of worship of the Roman Catholic religion, or in private houses, such ecclesiastic or other person, shall being thereof convicted by due course of law, forfeit for every such offence the sum of £50 (approx. €4,250) ...

XXXIV. And be it further enacted, that in case any person shall, after the commencement of this Act, within any part of this United Kingdom, be admitted or become a Jesuit, or brother, or member of any other such religious order, community, or society as aforesaid, such person shall be deemed and taken to be guilty of a misdemeanour, and being thereof lawfully convicted shall be sentenced and ordered to be banished from the United Kingdom, for the term of his natural life ...

XXXVII. Provided always, and be it enacted, that nothing herein contained shall extend or be construed to extend in any manner to affect any religious order, community, or establishment consisting of females bound by religious or monastic vows.

22. 'A bloodless revolution'

22.1. *Introduction.* The Catholic Relief Act (10 Geo. IV, c. 7) received the royal assent on 13 April 1829. Now that the restrictions against which he had fought so long had at last been lifted, Daniel O'Connell felt an overwhelming sense of personal liberation. He wrote to his friend James Sugrue the following day, 14 April, describing the relief bill as a 'bloodless revolution'. He was anxious that nothing should mar their peaceful victory and sent word that the Catholics of Dublin should not celebrate by illuminating the city in case it should provoke a disturbance. He confidently expected to take his seat in the House of Commons after the Easter recess. On Friday, 15 May, O'Connell appeared before a crowded House of Commons. He refused to take the Oath of Supremacy and in his turn was refused the right to take the new oath. O'Connell's subsequent speech at the bar of the House was favourably received, but the Commons accepted, by 190 votes to 116, the Solicitor-General's motion that he should be excluded unless he took the Oath of Supremacy. The government argued that the Relief Act was not retrospective and therefore O'Connell could not benefit from it. Nevertheless, he was re-elected, unopposed, for Co. Clare on 30 July 1829. SOURCE: Maurice R. O'Connell (ed.), *The correspondence of Daniel O'Connell* (8 vols, Dublin, 1972), iv, 180–1.

22.2. The First day of Freedom!

4 April 1829

My dear friend, – I cannot allow this day to pass without expressing my congratulations to the honest men of Burgh Quay [the Catholic Association] on the subject of the Relief Bill.

It is one of the greatest triumphs recorded in history – a bloodless revolution more extensive in its operation than any other political change that could take place. I say *political* to contrast it with *social* changes which might break to pieces the framework of society.

This is a good beginning, and now, if I can get Catholics and Protestants to join, something solid and substantial may be done for all.

It is clear that, without gross mismanagement, it will be impossible to allow misGovernment any longer in Ireland. It will not be my fault if there be not a 'Society for the Improvement of Ireland,' or something else of that description, to watch over the rising liberties of Ireland.

I am busily making my arrangements respecting my own seat. As soon as they are complete you shall hear from me.

I reckon with confidence on being in the House on the 28th instant, the day to which the adjournment is to take place. I think my right now perfectly clear and beyond any reasonable doubt.

Wish all and every one of the 'Order of Liberators' joy in my name. Let us not show any insolence of triumph, but I confess to you, if I were in Dublin, I should like to laugh at the Corporators.

I am writing a congratulatory address to the people. It will appear, I hope, on Easter Monday in Dublin.

Believe me, &c.,
Daniel O'Connell.

GILLIAN M. DOHERTY AND TOMÁS O'RIORDAN

CHAPTER 9

The Synod of Thurles, 1850: discipline and education

1. The summoning of the Synod

1.1. The first national synod of the Catholic hierarchy held in Ireland since the middle ages opened on Thursday, 22 August 1850, at Thurles, Co. Tipperary. Its goal was to reform the Catholic Church, root and branch, and to ensure that it conformed in everything to the standards of the universal Catholic Church as set by Rome. Pastoral care and preaching were sometimes fitful, attendance at mass was irregular, and the administration of the sacraments (including baptism) was inadequate. It is true, there had been a great deal of church building – 20 before 1800, 60 between 1800 and 1830, 170 between 1830 and 1850 – but in the eyes of Paul Cullen, the whole church was in need of an overhaul. The Synod was called by Cullen, the newly appointed Archbishop of Armagh and Primate of All Ireland (head of the Catholic Church). He had recently returned from Rome as Apostolic Delegate, a papal office that gave him complete control over the Catholic Church in Ireland. He used his powers to reform it. Rome was concerned about the administration of the Church in Ireland. An 'ultramontanist', Cullen believed that every national church should follow the Roman model exactly, in practice, in teaching, and in discipline. This was in the fullest measure obtained. He was utterly opposed to local or popular religious expressions and determined to end these in Ireland. The Synod marked the beginning of this process.

1.2. Under Cullen's strict control, the Irish hierarchy discussed popular religious beliefs and practices, considered how these differed from those of Rome, decided what to keep, what to suppress, and what to change, in order to make the Catholic Church in Ireland conform exactly to Roman standards. The Synod was also concerned with contemporary social, economic, and political problems, particularly those thought to involve moral issues, and which therefore required the attention of the bishops.

1.3. The Synod of Thurles attracted much attention from the public and the government because of one major matter, the University Question. In 1845, five years before the Synod, the government had introduced the Colleges (Ireland) Act to establish a new system of university education (the Queen's Colleges), and this was one of the reasons why the Synod met. The government had acted in response to a successful campaign for educational reform. This Act was extremely controversial because prominent politicians and clerics had opposed it, and split public opinion. The Irish bishops, as well as the priests and the laity, were deeply divided on the issue. The Synod was to resolve their disputes and agree on a single policy about University education for Catholics.

2. Educational problems: primary education

2.1. The bishops had been divided about the state-supported national schools system established in 1832. There was opposition from Protestants and Catholics who wanted the government to establish exclusively religious schools run by the Churches. The Archbishop of Dublin, Daniel Murray, and eighteen other bishops, supported the national school system because they believed that it was the best that the British government would give. However, ten bishops followed John MacHale, Archbishop of Tuam, in opposing the system.

2.2. MacHale and his followers believed that government schools might be used to convert Catholic children to Protestantism, and they insisted that the Catholic hierarchy have control of Catholic education to safeguard Catholic faith and morals. Unable to resolve their differences, the Irish hierarchy appealed to Rome in 1839 for guidance. The Holy See responded in 1841 that each bishop was to decide for his own diocese whether or not to support the national schools.

3. Educational problems: university education

3.1. This Vatican decision resolved the debate about non-denominational education for a while but the issue flared up again over university education. Catholics were allowed to attend Trinity College Dublin, the only University in Ireland, but were not entitled to the same honours and privileges as Protestants. Furthermore, the teaching staff of the University had to be in Anglican Holy Orders, that is, had to be ordained Protestant clergymen. Sir Thomas Wyse, a landed Catholic from Waterford city, and others interested in education, were concerned about the lack of educational facilities for the middle and upper classes, and especially for Catholics. They praised the government for providing a national and universal primary system of education for all children but urged it to provide progressively better facilities for the more privileged classes who would later govern the country. They lobbied the government for state-supported second and third level institutions.

3.2. On 9 May 1845, the Colleges (Ireland) Bill was introduced in the House of Commons: it proposed to establish provincial Colleges to be granted University status once opened. The government was to finance the establishment and maintenance of the Colleges and the Crown was to be responsible for appointments and dismissals. Its core principle was that the Colleges were to be non-denominational: no religious test was required of staff, and religion was not to be taught as a university discipline. The Colleges (Ireland) Bill was passed on 10 July and became law on 31 July 1845. The Act stipulated that it 'shall be lawful' to assign lecture rooms 'within the precincts' so that each student may 'receive religious instruction according to the creed which he professes to hold' from recognised religious teachers. The Act established provincial Colleges on the model of University College London (founded in 1826), providing non-sectarian, non-residential, low-fee, third-level education.

4. Public and episcopal conflict

4.1. The public was deeply divided. Protestant loyalists, for the most part, supported the Act. Members of the Young Ireland party, Protestant and Catholic, hoped 'mixed' education would help reconcile Protestants and Catholics and unite them in the campaign for Repeal. Sir Thomas Wyse was the most important figure in educational reform in Ireland, and many middle-class Catholics who campaigned with him, supported the Act. However, Daniel O'Connell, and many in his Repeal movement were against the Colleges, because of the opposition of influential bishops. Many Catholic bishops were hostile to the idea of so-called 'godless colleges' and pressed the government to make provision for religious appointments and instruction. The government hoped to appease Protestants who were opposed to government grants for Catholic education, and to assure Catholics that the Colleges were not intended to convert them to Protestantism.

4.2. There were disagreements, however, amongst bishops and clergy. Archbishop William Crolly (1780–1849) stated at a public meeting in Armagh that he was satisfied with the government amendments and would give his approval for a College in his diocese. Crolly was impressed by the government's assurances that it would not discriminate against Catholics in the Colleges and he hoped that it would grant more concessions in the future. He was concerned about proposals to leave the College in Ulster to Presbyterians, and those in the rest of the country to Anglicans and Catholics. He hoped to persuade the government to establish the proposed college in Armagh rather than in Belfast (a largely Presbyterian city). He was confident he would have more influence on it in Catholic Armagh, his cathedral city. Besides, Crolly believed that Catholics would attend the Colleges no matter what their bishops said, and thought that such a challenge to his authority would weaken his influence with the government. The Archbishop's letter led to serious controversy amongst clergy and laity. Crolly was accused by some of abandoning the Catholic souls in his care, praised by others for accepting the best measure that could be had. In his defence, Crolly referred to the Papal ruling of 1841 that bishops could decide as they judged best about national schools in their own diocese.

4.3. A majority of bishops opposed Crolly and argued that university was very different from national schools because College students, living away from home, would not have their parents and local priests to look after their religious instruction. Crolly's claim to make decisions for his own diocese was challenged by bishops who argued that the Catholic hierarchy should act as a body because the three Colleges served the entire country and affected all bishops. It was felt that the bishops would weaken their position with the government by disagreeing in public and thereby lessen their chances of getting a better deal.

4.4. Crolly convened a meeting of the bishops to discuss the Bill in Dublin on 21 and 23 May 1845. Following heated debate, the bishops agreed that they should resolve their differences and issue a joint statement. First, they condemned the proposed colleges as 'dangerous to the faith and morals of the Catholic pupils'. Nevertheless, they wished to co-operate with the government to provide University education for Catholics 'on fair and reasonable terms' if the government accepted their demands. These were: that a propor-tion of the professors and teachers in the Colleges should be Catholic, and that these should be sanctioned by the bishop of the diocese; that Catholics should hold the pro-fessorships in history, logic, metaphysics, moral philosophy, geology, and anatomy; that Catholic bishops should be members of the Boards of Trustees responsible for appoint-ments and dismissals; and, finally, that Catholic chaplains should be appointed to look after the interests of Catholic students.

4.5. The government rejected all the bishops' demands but promised to uphold Catholic interests. Government ministers and members of parliament, who were deeply opposed to proselytism, tried to allay people's fears. The government made a slight change to the Bill to allow religious instruction in Colleges if paid for by private endowment. Full con-trol of the Colleges, however, still remained with government.

4.6. In spite of reassurances and concessions, the bishops, as a body, refused to compro-mise on their demand for Catholic Colleges for Catholics. They explained that they did not suspect the intentions or motives of the government but argued that there were no safeguards against the abuse their powers in the future by governments and College authorities. MacHale sent a letter to O'Connell to be read in Parliament and O'Connell backed the bishops' notion that the government would not intervene in the Colleges' affairs to protect Catholic rights and interests. He said:

> You tell me that you will protect the Catholics. You say, that if a professor
> preaches infidelity [Protestant attempts to convert Catholics], you will dismiss
> him. I am not satisfied with that. I mean you no disrespect, but I will not take
> your word for it. The bishops insist on having a power lodged in them for find-
> ing out the infidelity, and of having some voice at least in the dismissal of pro-
> fessors who might inculcate it.

4.7. Many bishops opposed the Colleges Bill as one for 'godless colleges' and called on the government to make provision for religious appointments and instruction. The gov-ernment amended the Bill to enable the Colleges to offer classes on religious studies, but only if they were financed privately. This did not satisfy the bishops.

4.8. In spite of the bishops' seeming unity, however, they were still deeply divided. Archbishop Crolly, in particular, was strongly in favour of the Colleges. To show their opposition to Crolly, nineteen bishops made a statement on 13 September repeating their opposition to the Act, in spite of changes. Some of these had supported the national schools a few years earlier. Archbishops MacHale of Tuam and Slattery of Cashel sent an appeal to Rome for assistance through Dr Paul Cullen, Rector of the Irish College in Rome and a staunch opponent of the University Act. They included the memorial to the Lord Lieutenant, and the resolutions of the bishops. The Holy See did not respond until

October 1847 – because of political disturbances in Rome – and repeated its previous decision against any co-operation with the Colleges. It suggested an alternative: the establishment of a Catholic University and urged unity amongst the hierarchy.

4.9. In the meantime, Ireland had experienced two years of devastating famine, O'Connell had died, Sir Robert Peel's Conservative government had been replaced by Lord John Russell's Liberals, who seemed initially more favourable to Catholics. After consultation with Dr Murray, Archbishop of Dublin, Lord Clarendon, the Lord Lieutenant, prepared a revised copy of the College statutes for the consideration of the Pope, and reiterated the government's commitment to giving Catholics proper representation on College boards and staff. MacHale protested strongly against Murray's intervention and went to Rome with a statement signed by seventeen bishops to the effect that the altered University Act did not grant any more concessions to Catholics. Having heard Clarendon's case, Rome issued a statement on 11 October 1848 denouncing, once again, the government Colleges, and calling for the establishment of a Catholic University. It instructed that future meetings of the Irish hierarchy should be organised according to canon law and should send their decisions to Rome for approval.

4.10. The government had by now established Colleges in Galway, Cork and Belfast, which had 400 students on opening in autumn 1849. A priest was appointed first President of Queen's College Galway, and a prominent Catholic scientist, Sir Robert Kane, first President of Queen's College Cork. Catholic deans of residence were appointed with the approval of the resident bishops. However, a majority of the hierarchy were still dissatisfied because of the small number of Catholics appointed as teaching staff.

4.11. Archbishop Crolly's death of cholera in April 1849, was a blow to those who supported the Queen's Colleges. Rome appointed Dr Paul Cullen as his successor. He returned to Ireland with yet another rescript that forbade priests to hold offices in the Colleges. On 30 May 1850, Cullen issued a letter summoning the bishops to a synod to be held in Thurles in August.

5. The opening of the Synod of Thurles

5.1. The bishops issued pastoral letters to explain the objects of the Synod and urged people to pray for its success. They avoided the controversy that prompted it, and stated that synods appeared unusual only because they had been banned during the penal era. However, most people understood the importance of the University question and awaited the outcome with keen anticipation. Newspapers took up the cause with vigour. The government was displeased at Cullen's refusal to discuss the issue with it, although it attempted to conciliate the bishops as much as possible in public.

5.2. The Synod opened in Thurles with great ceremony and lasted almost three weeks. Some 10,000 people gathered to witness the procession of bishops and clergy from St

Patrick's College to the Cathedral where Cullen celebrated High Mass to open the proceedings. Laurence Forde, master of ceremonies, reported that:

> the mass was celebrated by the Primate himself with full solemnity – all the arrangements were modelled as far as possible on the plan of the Papal Chapels, the music too was Ecclesiastical, the Mass was the old Irish College Mass in four parts quite in the Palestrina style.

5.3. Four Irish archbishops and twenty-three Irish bishops were entitled to attend. Three of the bishops were incapacitated by age or illness and were represented by procurators [deputies]. Besides the archbishops, bishops, and their procurators, the mitred abbot of Mount Melleray and the provincials and heads of the various religious orders also assisted at the Synod. Each bishop and procurator was attended by a theologian, except the primate, who in his capacity as Apostolic Delegate was entitled to two theologians. There were also three secretaries who were responsible for keeping the minutes and recording the resolutions and propositions voted upon. There were, of course, numerous other clergy who assisted at the public ceremonies but were not entitled to attend the regular sessions of the Synod, which were held in private. Two sessions or congregations were held each day, morning and afternoon, except Sundays, and the participants were all formally bound to secrecy. At the morning sessions, the entire Synod assembled to listen without comment to the opinions of the theologians on the various propositions to be considered. At the afternoon sessions, only those who had votes – the bishops, procurators, and mitred abbot, twenty-eight in number – met to discuss and decide by majority vote the various matters to be considered. The secretaries took minutes and recorded the votes. The actual debates of the Synod were held in private and their decisions were to remain confidential until approved by Rome.

5.4. In the first week of the Synod there was little contention, and the work of the ecclesiastics proceeded briskly. The early agenda consisted mainly of propositions concerning the rules by which the Synod would be conducted; matters of faith; the administration of the sacraments; the life and character of the clergy; the duties of the bishops, parish priests, and curates; ecclesiastical property; and the establishing of archives.

6. The Queen's Colleges: heated debate

6.1. When the propositions regarding the Queen's Colleges were introduced, however, the harmony was shattered. The press and public also had a keen interest in the debates on the Queen's Colleges. On 27 August 1850, the *Dublin Evening Post*, a strongly conservative and Unionist paper, announced that the Queen's Colleges had received royal assent for University status. A few days later, the government announced its list of Visitors to sit on the Boards of Trustees. These included nine laymen for the three Colleges, with two Catholic and two Protestant bishops for each College.

6.2. A huge crowd attended the second public session of the Synod, a mass held in the Cathedral in Thurles on 29 August 1850 at which MacHale gave the sermon. MacHale did not make a direct attack on the government, however, but emphasised the Catholic Church's claims to protect the interests of Catholics. The reports of the proceedings of the Synod, now available in Roman archives, show that party lines were sharply drawn. One of the secretaries of the synod, Fr Dominic O'Brien, described the opening of the debate on the Queen's Colleges:

> The Archbishop of Dublin rose and declared that he received the rescripts of the Holy See with the most obsequious respect; but that, none the less, he would never act contrary to his conscience, whether out of respect for the Holy See, or for any other reason. The Archbishop said also that he would never oppose the rescripts, but that, while receiving them with the most respectful silence, he would never do anything to put them into effect. He would never impose any censure or ecclesiastical penalty on any priest or other ecclesiastic who sought or accepted any office in these Colleges; he would not prevent them being appointed deans of residence; he would not procure the removal from office of those already appointed; and he would not exhort the faithful to stay away from these Colleges, or to keep their sons away from them.

6.3. This uncompromising declaration set the tone for what followed. Two decrees excluding priests from the Colleges under pain of suspension were approved by 14 bishops and opposed by 13. Another decree, admonishing the laity to 'reject and shun' the Colleges, was approved by 15 and opposed by 12. The papal party seems to have been surprised at the extent to which their opponents were prepared to flout the clear wishes of the Holy See. Archbishop Cullen later commented that the Archbishop of Dublin exhibited 'an obstinacy that was remarkable'. Bishop Cantwell of Meath wrote that 'during the Synod his Grace of Dublin and his adherents evinced a most fractious and disobedient spirit', and added that the Synod was brought to a satisfactory conclusion only 'by the mildness, rare tact and great talent of Dr Cullen'.

7. Continuing disagreement and its resolution

7.1. The majority were surprised at the attitude of their opponents in the Synod, and astonished at their continued resistance afterwards. As soon as the Synod had dispersed, the thirteen bishops of the minority appealed to Rome against the decrees on the Queen's Colleges. Archbishop Murray had this published in the press, although the proceedings of the Synod were confidential. Thus on 5 September 1850, the *Dublin Evening Post* reported that the Synod opposed the Universities by a majority of only one vote. Next day, the *Cork Examiner* reported that Dr Cullen was going to compel priests to break all links with the Colleges. Complaints from the majority poured into Rome. 'The question now is whether Pius IX or the English government is to govern the Catholic Church in Ireland', wrote Archbishop Slattery of Cashel. Archbishop Cullen declared:

The real question to be decided is whether one ought or ought not to obey the decision of the Holy See; whether the Pope ought to rule the Church in Ireland through the majority of bishops, or whether, on the other hand, the English government ought to rule it by means of the Archbishop of Dublin.

7.2. By the end of 1850 there seemed to be a crisis in the Irish Church. Relations between the two parties in the Irish hierarchy were never worse. Within a few months things changed. In September 1850, the Pope set up an English Catholic hierarchy of archbishops and bishops to rule the Catholic Church there. This caused much resentment among English Protestants because it seemed to flaunt the rapid progress of Catholicism in England. The government's reaction was provocative. In 1851, it introduced and carried the Ecclesiastical Titles Bill, which made it a penal offence for Catholic bishops to use territorial titles.

7.3. This played right into the hands of Cullen and his supporters. They had always said that the British government was an enemy of the Catholic Church; the Ecclesiastical Titles Bill seemed to prove their point. In the weeks of its passage through Parliament there was a stampede away from the government by the Catholics who had supported it until now. Archbishop Murray issued a pastoral condemning the government's action. The Catholic members of the Bar – of all sections of the Catholic community the one reputed to be the most devoted to the government's interests – issued a protest against its legislation. The Ecclesiastical Titles Act was never enforced and was quietly repealed by Gladstone in 1871. However, the moderate party was badly shaken. They could no longer believe that the attitude of British statesmen to the Catholic Church was, on the whole, one of good will.

8. Summary of the decisions of the Synod of Thurles

8.1. *Education*: The Synod condemned the Queen's Colleges and resolved to establish a Catholic University. It called on priests to increase the number of schools and to direct 'those pious associations for the diffusing of catechetical knowledge and the caring of the poor'. It accepted that each bishop should have discretion in relation to primary education in his diocese.

8.2. *Administration*: The Synod discussed the canon law in the different dioceses and decided on a uniform system, in particular relating to the administration of sacraments outside the church. During the eighteenth century and because of the penal laws, baptisms, marriages, and confessions took place mostly in private houses. These practices still remained in the early nineteenth century. The bishops wanted to end them in order to bring the Irish Church into line with the discipline of the universal Catholic Church but they did not wish to force change on people too abruptly. They ruled that marriages and baptisms were henceforth to take place in churches, apart from exceptional cases. A register of marriages and baptisms was to be kept in each church. Marriages between

Catholics and non-Catholics were to be discouraged. The Church's disapproval of such unions was to be shown by withholding much of the normal marriage ritual. They did not ban the 'stations', that is, masses in private houses at which priests heard confessions, because they anticipated great opposition to this. The legislation showed, in fact, that there were no serious differences between Catholicism in Ireland and on the Continent.

8.3. *Organisation and discipline*: Priests were instructed to attend retreats and to keep themselves informed about theological matters. They were prohibited from going to public houses, horse races, and theatres. Each parish was to have a parochial house. Parish priests were not to have more than fifteen acres of land, and curates were forbidden to hold any land without the consent of the bishop. Priests were forbidden to denounce people or movements from the altar, or to say mass after noon. It was also decreed (Decr. 5):

> … in the administration of certain sacraments, let the parish priests beware lest anything be done that may savour of simony or avarice. Let the sacraments never be denied under the pretext that offerings have not been made; otherwise the delinquents may be disciplined according to the bishop's judgement.

Catholic clergy were not to engage in public disputes with members of other religions, and the laity were forbidden to engage in discussions with non-Catholics. A provision was also made for the establishment and preservation of diocesan archives.

8.4. *Proselytism and Conversions*: Measures were recommended to counter the work of proselytisers who tried to convert people to Protestantism by sermons, publications, and rewards. Special attention was paid to the dangers faced by emigrants, and those who lived or worked in Protestant environments such as with landed families or in the armed forces. To combat this, specially commissioned preachers were to be invited to give retreats. Sodalities were to be established for the laity, and Catholic books were to be published to help strengthen the faith.

8.5. *Secret societies*: Secret societies were condemned.

8.6. *Matters in dispute*: Questions on which the bishops could not agree were to be referred to Rome.

9. The conclusion of the Synod

After two weeks of intense private discussions amongst the hierarchy, interrupted by lavish public masses and ceremonial processions that attracted thousands of people from all the country, the Synod of Thurles ended on 9 September, 1850 with High Mass. The Synod then forwarded its decrees to Rome. It could not make its findings public until they had received papal approval.

10. The University Question again

10.1. On its last day of sitting, the Synod sent a letter to the government, declining to accept any positions on the Colleges' Board of Trustees which, according to many reporters, was evidence that the hierarchy had decided against any co-operation with the Colleges. The bishops' pastoral letter, issued on the 14 September, 'read in full Synod and unanimously adopted', condemned the Colleges as

> ... an evil of a formidable kind against which it is our imperative duty to warn you with all the energy of our zeal and all the weight of our authority. In pointing out the dangers of such a system we only repeat the instructions that have been given to us by the Vicar of Jesus Christ ... [who] has pronounced this system of education to be fraught with 'grievous and intrinsic dangers' to faith and morals ... The successor of Peter has pronounced his final judgement on the subject. All controversy is now at an end – the judge has spoken – *the question is decided.*

10.2. The bishops also published the rescripts from Rome, issued in 1847, 1848 and again in April 1850, which declared that priests were not allowed hold office in the Colleges. The pastoral address also announced that the bishops planned to establish a University for Catholics. It also referred to the Famine, sympathised with 'victims of the most ruthless oppression that ever disgraced the annals of humanity', and condemned the 'desolating track of the exterminator ... in those levelled cottages and roofless abodes'. The Prime Minister and other members of Government were angered at this attack on landlords 'which could excite the feelings of the peasant class against those who were owners of the land'.

10.3. Many prominent Catholics withdrew their support from the Colleges after the publication of the bishops' pastoral. The *Dublin Evening Post*, on 17 September 1850, reported that some bishops objected to the pastoral because the Synod's decrees had not yet been approved by Rome, that the bishops were almost evenly divided about the issue, and that there was only a majority of one opposed to the Colleges. The Prime Minister denounced the statement issued by the hierarchy at the end of the Synod.

11. The Synod's decrees come into force

11.1. The *Decreta Synodi Plenariae Episcoporum Hiberniae* ('Decrees of the Plenary Synod of the Bishops of Ireland') were approved by the Vatican and published in Dublin in 1851. They came into force for the Irish Catholic Church on 23 May 1851, but some time passed before they were accepted. They were not popular with the clergy, and three years after the Synod, Cullen complained that the decrees were not observed even in Thurles. Though the clergy were instructed to keep out of politics, this ruling had little effect on their political activities in the nineteenth and twentieth centuries.

11.2. At the beginning of January 1852, however, Cullen was able to report to Rome that the decrees were in force in every diocese except Galway. A fortnight later MacHale wrote to say that Galway had fallen into line. The final blow to the moderate party was the death of their leader, Archbishop Murray, in February 1852. Murray had been the one bishop of distinction on the moderate side. None of the survivors had his qualities of leadership. His successor at Dublin was Archbishop Cullen, who was translated from Armagh. Now the moderate party virtually ceased to exist. The mild Gallicanism of certain professors at Maynooth continued to worry Cullen for some years to come, but among the bishops the reconciliation between the two parties seemed to be complete.

12. A landmark in church history

12.1. The Synod had generated remarkable excitement because it was the first Synod held for hundreds of years. It was also the first public formal meeting of the Catholic hierarchy, and the first public expression of its power and influence, since the relaxation of the anti-Catholic Penal Laws of the eighteenth century. People today may find it difficult to understand the extent of interest in the rulings of the Synod amongst all shades of political opinion in Ireland, and in Government offices in Dublin and in London. Leading newspapers had written lengthy daily editorials to try to influence the bishops in Synod.

12.2. Within ten years of the Famine, church building had fully recovered its momentum, in particular the provision of cathedrals. The joint pastoral of the Catholic bishops, November 1859, stated (with some exaggeration): 'in every part of the country we see churches rising up that rival in beauty of design and elegance of execution the proudest monuments of the zeal, piety, and the taste of our forefathers'. The Synod marked an important stage in the rising confidence of the Catholic Church and its leaders and shaped Irish Catholicism for well over a century to come.

12.3. Church attendance increased dramatically from about 33 per cent before the Famine to over 90 per cent by the century's end. This renewed devotion was helped by the increase in religious vocations, the expansion of church building since the 1840s, and the decline of the Irish population after the Great Famine. In the two decades following Cullen's arrival in Ireland the number of priests increased by nearly a quarter, to a total of about 3,200. This equates to one priest for every 1,250 people in 1870. Between 1850 and 1870, the number of nuns in Ireland increased from 1,500 to over 3,700, or one nun for every 1,100 people. By 1900, there were over 14,000 priests, monks, and nuns, equating to one religious for every 235 people. Catholic lay people now had more access to clergy and churches than at any other time in modern Irish history.

12.4. An ultramontane, authoritarian, puritanical, and pietistic Catholic Church was created in Ireland and henceforth it had a powerful influence on education, public morality, social life, and national politics, though it professed to be non-political. Irish missions and migrants brought this type of Catholicism to the English-speaking world – to Britain, the British Empire and the United States of America. It was influential: nearly 30 per cent of the 730 bishops at the first Vatican Council, 1869–70, were either Irish or of Irish descent.

GILLIAN M. DOHERTY AND TOMÁS O'RIORDAN

CHAPTER 10

The Synod of Thurles, 1850: documents

1. Report of the opening of the Synod

1.1. *Introduction.* The following is taken from a description of the opening of the Synod of Thurles in *The Times* (London) in August 1850. It is unsympathetic to the Catholic bishops. It sees the bishops who opposed the Queen's Colleges as backward and bigoted persons whose attitudes will be swept away by progress and a Catholic population that will not be told what to do by bishops. It is deeply unsympathetic to the proposed reforms of the Catholic Church and is ill-informed about them, or pretends to be; in fact, the Synod is treated with a disdain that masks disquiet. SOURCE: *The Times* (London), 22 August 1850.

1.2. The day 'big with the fate of Rome' has arrived, and all Irish eyes are now directed to the town of Thurles, where there is just now assembled in convocation a goodly array of Roman Catholic prelates and their adjuvants [helpers], who will have to pronounce the Papal decision *in re* [in the matter of] the bigots *versus* the Queen's Colleges, as well as take into consideration other weighty matters connected with the discipline of the Roman Catholic Church in Ireland. These latter, it is said, will include the questions of extra fastings and vigils throughout the year, the re-imposition of exploded holydays, and the return of the priesthood to the primitive costume worn by the several orders in connexion with the Church of Rome. The proceedings will extend over several days, and accredited reporters have been despatched to the scene of action by nearly all the Roman Catholic journals in the country.

1.3. A moderate Dublin journal (rather a rare commodity) thus refers to the approaching deliberations of the Synod: – 'The fanatical journals, to whom the denunciation of the "Godless Colleges" has afforded an ample subject for weeks past, announce, with the air of authority, that the condemnation of the colleges has already been decided on by a majority of the prelates, and that they are merely to meet in the Synod to formally announce that decision. Whether this may be the case or not we have no means of knowing; but this rumour is not entitled to much credence, coming from so unscrupulous a source. If the assembled bishops come to a decision hostile to mixed education, and thereby use their influence to perpetuate the ignorance of the people, we feel assured that the advancing spirit of the age will resist any such attempt to trammel the wheels of progress, and that the educated portion of the Roman Catholic population will declare, in language not to be mistaken, that the days of such dictation are at an end'.

1.4. The *Freeman's Journal* of this morning has a vivid description of the appearance yesterday of the town of Thurles, its streets crowded with the clergy of all ranks, from the
mitred archbishop down to the 'friar of order gray', besides a strong muster of strangers
from all parts anxious to be spectators – on the payment of a handsome fee – of the first
day's ceremonials, which, on the conditions specified, are to be thrown open to the
public gaze. Upon subsequent days the Synod will, of course, sit with closed doors
strictly. At 3 o'clock yesterday, the *Freeman's* reporter writes, the bishops went into pre-
liminary council, and after remaining for more than an hour in conference the theologians and *apparitores* [attendants, clerks] entitled to assist them in the deliberations were
summoned to attend, and after another hour being thus spent in private, the prelimi-
nary council separated at 5 o'clock.

2. The opening procession

2.1. *Introduction.* The Catholic Church has always been keen to distinguish itself from
other faiths. Its insistence on pageantry, ritual, and grand symbolism is one of its most
important ways of doing so. Few religions in the nineteenth century could compete with
the Church of Rome's talent for self-promotion, grand organisation, and colourful dis-
plays. The following extract describes the show of public piety before the official opening of the Synod in the normally quiet market-town of Thurles – the zealous faith of the
ordinary people, the huge influx of visitors, the elaborate preparations. The scenes of
mass popular religious devotion at the Synod were like those of the 31st International
Eucharistic Congress in 1932 and the visit of Pope John Paul II to Ireland in 1979. Note
the stress of the *Freeman's Journal* on the dignity and good order of the great crowds, the
elegance of the scene, and the splendour of the clerical arrangements. SOURCE: The
Freeman's Journal, August 1850.

> **2.2.** … From the earliest dawn vast crowds of people began to arrive from all
> parts of the surrounding vicinity. Each succeeding train arriving at Thurles, either
> from the north or south, came fully laden with visitors, both clergy and laity. The
> hotels in the town were crowded from the day previous, and temporary accom-
> modation was eagerly sought after. Even the private houses of the townspeople
> were put in requisition for the purpose of accommodating the crowds who could
> not obtain room in the hotels. The shops and warehouses were closed, and the
> aspect of the principal street indicated the observance which is usual on the occa-
> sion of the high festivals of the church, or at times of great public solemnity. The
> street-way leading through the town in the direction of the college presented
> during the morning a continuous tide of people coming in from the adjoining
> country parishes, and proceeding to the spot where it was known that the pro-
> cession would pass on its way to the church. The weather was beautiful. The
> morning sun shone warmly and brightly on the scene, which even previous to
> the commencement of the procession wore an aspect of solemnity.

2.3. The usual street noises, the loud laugh and the passing jest, so usual in the street of a country town, were all hushed, and the fine-looking peasantry, clad in their Sabbath costume, might be seen either proceeding with quiet and subdued demeanour, or standing in groups conversing in low and restrained voices about the coming ceremony. The Catholic Chapel, as may be expected, was surrounded from the earliest hour with dense crowds of people. The gates of the chapel yard were kept closed, and a strong guard of constabulary were drawn up around them for the purpose of preserving order and preventing any confusion which might arise from the people's anxiety to witness the procession.

2.4. At the opposite side of the road, directly fronting the chapel, the gates of the college were seen, guarded in like manner by a body of police. From this gate stretches a smooth and tastefully kept carriageway, nearly a quarter of a mile in length, extending to the hall steps and vestibule of the collegiate edifice. This roadway divides equally the beautiful lawn which extends in front of the building. From the gate to the front door of the vestibule there were stationed, at a few paces distant from each other, privates of the constabulary force, armed and accoutred as for parade or duty, who were placed there to secure the line of procession from casual interruption.

2.5. At a few minutes after ten o'clock the appearance of some of the attendant officials at the front of the vestibule gave indication that the procession was about to issue forth, and the gaze of the assembled thousands was eagerly fixed on the doorway. The great mass of people were congregated outside on the road between the college gates and the gate of the church, occupying also platforms temporarily erected so as to command a view of the line of procession. Every window in the neighbouring houses was crowded with spectators, and within the gates some groups of the gentry obtained permission to station themselves so as to enjoy uninterrupted sight of the prelates and clergy in their progress from the college. The large bell of the chapel and the chimes of the convent were now heard at intervals, and notwithstanding the immense crowds outside, so complete was the stillness and respectful silence that prevailed that even at a considerable distance within the college gates, the solemn pealing of the noble organ of the chapel could be heard.

2.6. At length the glittering cross, borne aloft by the crucifer, was seen issuing from the college vestibule. From where we stood the view from without of the spacious hall inside was grand and solemn indeed. The entire vestibule was filled with priests in white surplices and crimson stoles which, flashing in the red light of the waxen tapers, as contrasting with the bright sunlight outside, presented as effect indescribably beautiful. Through the open valves of the great entrance a glimpse was afforded of the grand staircase, down which rank after rank in almost countless array, the body of white robed priests were seen descending, whilst long before the front rank of the procession issued from the vestibule the voices of the clerical choir could be heard chanting that glorious and soul-thrilling hymn *Veni Creator spiritus*. Then the procession issued forth.

3. Paul Cullen, first letter to Monsignor Barnabò

3.1. *Introduction.* After making the arrangements for the Synod at the end of May, Paul Cullen returned to Drogheda, where for the next two months he was busy with pastoral duties and diocesan matters. He preferred to live in Drogheda for several reasons. First, he could commute easily to Dublin by rail. Second, he found Drogheda religiously more congenial than Armagh. There was a splendid convent of Presentation Sisters (with about a thousand pupils) and the people were also 'very Catholic and good'. The first letter Cullen wrote to Monsignor Alessandro Barnabò, Secretary of Propaganda (later Cardinal Prefect), dated 16 May 1850, written shortly after his return to Drogheda from Armagh, shows how he dealt with the Roman authorities. He reports on the state of his diocese and his flock, and looks forward to the Synod. SOURCE: Rome, Archives of the Society for the Propagation of the Faith, *Scritture riferite nei congressi, Irlanda* (S.R.C.), volume 30, folios 419–24; edited in Emmet Larkin, *The making of the Roman Catholic Church in Ireland, 1850–60* (Chapel Hill, NC, 1980), 22.

3.2. Drogheda, May 16 1850

> I wrote a few lines to acknowledge the receipt of several briefs and letters that your Excellency has sent me through Monsignor Raffaele Fornari. I have already spoken with the Archbishop of Dublin and several other prelates, and all are perfectly satisfied with the way in which matters have been arranged for the future synod.

> **3.3.** After my arrival here in Ireland I have been continually ill because of the extreme cold of the season. I have however made a long tour through this diocese, which took me to Armagh to take possession of the cathedral which is nothing other than a hovel hardly twenty feet high. The last archbishop began a new building and has spent about £15,000 towards completing the edifice. Still the wretchedness among the Catholics is very great, and the population is reduced by a third from what it was six years ago.

> **3.4.** Famine, disease, and emigration have produced this very extraordinary reduction. The Catholics have suffered much more than the Protestants because the latter are very well off, while the greater part of the former are very wretched.

> **3.5.** The diocese of Armagh is very long, but extremely narrow, whence it is necessary to travel about ninety miles to pass from one end to the other. The city of Armagh is handsome, and there is an ancient cathedral built in Catholic times, but now belonging to the Protestants. The Anglican archbishop has a magnifi-

cent palace and a country house that compares to the Villa Borghese with £25,000 (approx. €2.4 million at 2009 values) annual income. The Catholic archbishop, it may be said, is without a cathedral, without a home, and without an income. Truly in this whole province the Church is very badly provided for, and everything still remains to be done. Let us hope that God will help us make some beginning to the good work that is [only] awaiting a fruitful result from the synod, which will be probably celebrated on the Feast of the Assumption of the Blessed Virgin, but it will require much time and patience to put things in order here.

4. Paul Cullen, second letter to Monsignor Barnabò

4.1. *Introduction.* The two most vehement enemies of Queen's Colleges – John MacHale, Archbishop of Tuam, and William O'Higgins, Bishop of Ardagh – took no part in the full-dress debate at the Synod beyond saying that their views were so well known that there was no need to repeat them. When the discussion ended, voting on the nine propositions before the Synod began on Saturday, 31 August 1850. The fifth, that the laity were obliged to reject and avoid the Queen's Colleges because of grave and intrinsic dangers to faith and morals, was carried by sixteen votes to twelve. The sixth proposition, that in order to avoid harm to the laity the bishops should issue a synodal letter warning the laity of the dangers of the Colleges, was approved by only fifteen votes to thirteen. Cullen declared in a letter to Tobias Kirby, Rector of the Irish College in Rome on 31 August 1850, that 'The Holy See must vindicate her authority, otherwise the faith is lost in Ireland'. Rather scandalised by the bishops who had supported the 'Godless' Colleges, Cullen wrote that evening to Monsignor Barnabò, enclosing the decisions of the Synod. SOURCE: Rome, Archive of the Irish College, Kirby Papers, folio 205; edited in Emmet Larkin, *The making of the Roman Catholic Church in Ireland, 1850–60* (Chapel Hill, NC, 1980), 31.

> **4.2.** I hasten to send you the propositions and rules that the synod of Thurles has at this moment adopted concerning the Queen's Colleges. The Decrees of Propaganda were read for the Synod, and the subject was examined with all possible patience and care. The Archbishop of Dublin repeatedly declared he received the said Decrees, but that he believed that the Pope did not understand the nature of the Colleges; but that he believed them to be good and useful, and that he would never do anything to prevent the young people from attending them. About eleven other Bishops expressed themselves in the same terms of disregard for the instruction of the Holy See. I am sorry to be obliged to declare with pain that these Bishops have not demonstrated the deepest respect for the decisions of the Holy See. The Archbishop of Dublin is so bound up with the government that he will never oppose any project that emanates from that Government, and he always carries several other Bishops with him. I am still very shocked at the way in which these several prelates have expressed themselves.

5. Paul Cullen, letter to Sir Thomas Redington

5.1. *Introduction.* Cullen, in a letter written from Dublin on 16 September 1850, to Sir Thomas Redington, Under-Secretary (the British Administration's chief civil servant) in Ireland, conveyed to him, and indirectly to Clarendon, the Lord Lieutenant, his views on the controversial Queen's Colleges and the prerogatives of the Pope in Ireland. He declined the offer to be a Visitor of the Queen's College, Belfast. SOURCE: Peadar Mac Suibhne (ed.), *Paul Cullen and his contemporaries, with their letters, 1820–1902* (5 vols, Naas, 1961–77), ii, 60.

> **5.2.** Dublin, September 16, 1850
>
> … There is a further reason which renders it imperative on me to follow the course I have adopted. The Pope in his quality of Supreme Pastor of the Church, whose duty it is to lead the faithful to good pastures and to drive them away from poisonous ones, was consulted by all the bishops of Ireland on the question whether the education proposed to be given in the Queen's Colleges could be considered safe and whether the Catholic youth of Ireland could frequent them without endangering their religious principles, and the answer the bishops received was that those establishments were grievously and intrinsically danger-ous and that no Catholic prelate was at liberty to take a part in carrying them into operation. The experience, the wisdom, the authority of the Holy See leaves me no alternative but to follow its instructions.

6. Canon Cooper, letter to Dr Tobias Kirby

6.1. *Introduction.* Cullen was determined to have the decrees of the Synod quickly approved by Rome. He wished to quell any fears of Dr Tobias Kirby, Rector of the Irish College Rome, that Rome's intervention might result in serious division or a schism in the Irish Church. Cullen and his supporters argued that most of the people were sound, and the more radical middle classes in the larger cities and towns were few in number and had little influence. When Peter Canon Cooper, St Mary's, Dublin, wrote to Kirby on 9 October 1850, he gave his own biting portrait of this middle class. Cooper had gone to Rome in 1840 to receive a doctoral degree. He returned to Ireland a convinced Ultramontanist, determined to resist those clergy opposed to the increase of Roman authority in the Irish Church. He is bitter about the small educated Irish middle class and sees them as traitors, as 'Castle Catholics' misleading the general public. SOURCE: Rome, Archive of the Irish College, Kirby Papers; edited in Emmet Larkin, *The making of the Roman Catholic Church in Ireland, 1850–60* (Chapel Hill, NC, 1980), 47.

> **6.2.** It is what is called, and self-called, the *aristocratic* and *respectable* class that is recalcitrant. This class is both conceited, ill-informed, and merely subservient to our heretical Government. It lives on the smiles of Court and on the hopes of

Court preferment for its own. It is an eminently venal class; no wonder that in it should be found many a Judas to sell J. Xst [Jesus Christ] over again in the person of His Church. But beyond this class or clique there is in Ireland little disposition to rebel. However, though small, or rather because small, they try to multiply themselves by their activity and violence. And since the simple people cannot understand the merits of the question it is in the power of this unscrupulous party by means of sophistry and especially under favour of some Episcopal names, to agitate and mislead the multitude.

7. John R. Corballis, letter to Archbishop Murray

7.1. *Introduction.* On 2 October 1850, the *Dublin Evening Post* published an exchange of letters between Archbishop Murray and John R. Corballis, a successful Dublin barrister and Commissioner of the National System of Education. His letter to his friend Murray is an able and forceful statement in favour of the Queen's Colleges. He questions the wisdom of Catholics withdrawing from Trinity College. Murray went on to reveal to Corballis the existence of the minority party petition that had been sent to the Pope. The Archbishop of Cashel, Dr Michael Slattery, is the member of the Synod who was a graduate of Trinity College. The sly reference to this was obviously intended to embarrass Slattery, a keen supporter of Cullen. SOURCE: *Dublin Evening Post*, 2 October 1850.

7.2. Rosemount, Roebuck, September 30

My dear Lord,

May I respectfully ask your Grace as well for my own information as for that of some other Roman Catholics of your diocese who have sons either in Trinity College, or in the course of preparation for it, or for the newly established Queen's Colleges, how we are to understand the late Synodical Address on the subject of these Colleges? Are we thereby actually prohibited from sending our children to these Colleges? And, if so, how far is such a provision actually binding on us *in foro conscientiae* [upon our conscience]? To many of us it appears altogether inexplicable that, after petitioning, in the days of persecution, for admission into Trinity College, after being permitted, with the tacit sanction of your Grace, and your eminent predecessors and colleagues … for upwards of half a century, to receive our education there, and seeing that one of the members of that very Synod, most distinguished for rank, is actually a graduate of the University, it does appear strange that in the year 1850, education in Trinity College, or even in any of the Colleges recently established on such a liberal footing as regards us should be unequivocally condemned, and that without one reason being assigned for this sudden change, or any provision in the meantime being made for affording a suitable education to our children. I need not say that this subject is of intense interest to the Roman Catholic gentry of your Grace's diocese, as well as to the Roman Catholic middle classes of Ireland generally, and I therefore, my dear lord, take the liberty of entreating such an answer from your Grace as I may make known to the numerous persons who have spoken to me upon it; and which if it do not calm our apprehensions, at least may guide our future course of action on this all important point.

8. Paul Cullen, letter on the Catholic University to Dr Tobias Kirby

8.1. *Introduction.* The Fathers of the Synod appointed a committee (four archbishops and four bishops) to look into the establishment of a Catholic University. They hardly realised how big the task was. Cullen had managed to get all the bishops to ratify the synodal address to the clergy and the faithful which brought the Synod to an end on 9 September 1850. However, Archbishop Murray was quite willing to question Cullen's view that only a Catholic University could protect the faithful young people of Ireland from the evil literature in which the world abounded. The publication of John Corballis's letter spurred the university committee into action. In early October 1850 the committee was broadened to give it a mix of ability and respectability. Each of the bishops was to co-opt a priest and a layman and the enlarged committee was given the vital task of raising funds. Cullen invited Murray to join it: he thought he would do less harm inside than out. Murray then co-opted his dean and vicar-general, Dr Meyler, a keen advocate of the Queen's Colleges. Meyler carried on an irregular opposition to Cullen whenever he could, especially in the matter of education. But Cullen had packed the committee with his own supporters. Murray attended the first meeting and no more. Cullen wrote in Italian to Dr Tobias Kirby, Rector of the Irish College Rome, describing the first meeting in Dublin. SOURCE: Rome, Archive of the Irish College, Kirby Papers; edited in Emmet Larkin, *The making of the Roman Catholic Church in Ireland, 1850–60* (Chapel Hill, NC, 1980), 49.

8.2. Yesterday we held a meeting to take steps to launch a Catholic University. The Archbishop of Dublin from the beginning of the meeting spoke strongly against the project. The Vicar-General of Dublin, Dr Meyler, spoke even more strongly against it. But all the others that were present did not pay any attention to their words and were determined to go ahead. We began at once by making a collection. Up to the moment a sum of about £2,000 (approx. €190,000 at 2009 values) has been received – nearly 10,000 Roman scudi – and about £150 in anonymous contributions. The Archbishop of Dublin and his Vicar refused to contribute. It was decided to place the money received in the names of the four Archbishops – but the Archbishop of Dublin did not want to lend his name even to this object, and it was necessary to substitute the Bishop of Meath. You see with what difficulties we have to contend. There is a real conspiracy to render Protestant or unbelieving the education of the Catholic youth, and what is deplorable is that Catholic Bishops are among those who promote the views of our enemies. They are encouraging atheistic schools, and are themselves opposing an institution truly Catholic. Well *militia est vita hominum* ['the life of men is a warfare', a quotation from the *Book of Job*, 7:1].

9. Paul Cullen, letter on Education to the Chief Secretary

9.1. *Introduction.* Cullen was one of the most formidable churchmen in Irish history. He quickly came to dominate the Irish Catholic Church. His views on education made him an important political figure. He resolutely opposed non-denominational education at all levels. He played a critical role in getting the Synod of Thurles to condemn the Queen's Colleges. The following extract is from a comprehensive submission on Irish education sent to Edward Cardwell, Chief Secretary for Ireland on 18 March 1860, by Cullen and his fellow bishops. It expresses the strong views Cullen had on a variety of questions. This extract shows his considerable skill in argument: he uses past statements by senior British politicians to convince the Chief Secretary of the importance of providing for denominational education only. SOURCE: Paul Cullen et al., *A letter to the Right Hon. E. Cardwell, M.P., Chief Secretary for Ireland, on National Education* (Dublin, 1860), 3–5.

> **9.2.** ... Several most eminent British statesmen have expressed their views on this subject [education] with great force and authority. We make some few extracts from their speeches, not with a view of proving what is admitted, or that any doubt can be entertained as to their sentiments, but in order to show what they understood by religious education. We shall see whether they pretend that all secular knowledge, history, moral philosophy, the sciences, as far as they enter into an elementary course, should be taught independently of religion; and whether they would be satisfied with a system of exempting children from religious control whilst attending to the lessons of secular knowledge ...
>
> **9.3.** Lord Sandon [Dudley Ryder, 2nd Earl Harrowby], in 1847, referring to a speech of Lord John Russell, said that he 'was glad to hear the admission that religion was an essential part of everything worthy of the name of education ... The State admitted that education, in order to be effectual, must be religious ... He thought that religion ought to be interwoven with every part of their education: he meant that the man who taught should be a religious man, and that in his moral teaching he should always keep in view the principles of religion'.
>
> **9.4.** Lord Morpeth [George Howard, 7th Earl of Carlisle], now Lord Lieutenant of Ireland, explaining the reason why separate grants were to be made in England to the schools of each religious society, says: 'We might have taken a *uniform* scheme, in which we might have prescribed the same course to all alike, without adverting to the existing methods, and without adopting any special method of religious teaching; but I believe in my conscience that such a plan would not have met with the consent of either Parliament or of the people' ...

9.5. Lord John Russell, refuting the project of Mr [John Arthur] Roebuck to separate religion from education, said: 'I do not think that the future minister, contemplated by Mr. Roebuck, is likely to have a very long tenure of power, if "vote for education without religion" should be placed on his banner, and that schools entirely secular should be established by the State'.

9.6. Sir Robert Peel, said: 'I am for religious as opposed to a secular education. I do not think that a secular education would be acceptable to the people of this country. I believe, as the noble Lord [John Russell] has said, that such an education is only half an education, but with the most important half neglected'.

9.7. From these passages, it clearly results that those distinguished statesmen understood by religious education a system of general instruction have religion for its basis, having religion interwoven with it, and imparted by a master who should instruct by word and example. This is what those statesmen understood by religious education, and not a system excluding the teaching of religion, or restricting it to one hour, prohibiting during the remainder of the day any reference to it and its practices. In accordance with such opinions, a denominational or separate system, blending religion with every sort of instruction, has been sanctioned in England.

10. Paul Cullen, discourse on education to the Dublin clergy

10.1. *Introduction.* Cullen was insistent that the Catholic hierarchy should have control over schools, universities, and their curricula. Here we see why. In this extract, he outlines the historical context he created to sustain his views – a characteristic Catholic view of Irish history which sees it as the history of the sufferings of the Catholic Church. He places his own struggle against secular education within this construct; in effect, he embeds it in a long perspective of Catholic ills from the Tudors to the present. This is ideology, not history. His attack on Trinity College Dublin was to find resounding echoes among some of his twentieth-century successors. He gave this address at a meeting of the secular and regular clergy of Dublin, 18 December 1867. SOURCE: Patrick Francis Moran (ed.), *The pastoral letters and other writings of Cardinal Cullen* (3 vols, Dublin, 1882), ii, 123–43 (extract).

10.2. You are all aware of the events which brought on our present difficulties and struggles. In the sixteenth century, Henry VIII and his daughter Elizabeth, having assumed the headship of the Church, and wishing to imbue their subjects with their own doctrines, and to make them imitators of their own unholy works, determined to introduce a new system of instruction for the rising generations, and to despoil the Church of the authority given to her by Christ, to instruct all nations, to teach the truths of Revelation, and to prevent the spread of error.

10.3. With this view, notwithstanding the protestations, petitions, and complaints of the people, all monasteries, convents, colleges, and other places of education were seized on, and their properties confiscated, thus leaving our Catholic ancestors without means of bringing up their children in the true faith. To perpetuate this state of affairs, a most cruel code of penal laws was enacted against Catholic schools and schoolmasters at home, and against parents sending their children to foreign countries to be instructed in their own creed. Things remained in this deplorable condition for a long period, during which the boasted promoters of reformation and enlightenment left nothing undone to reduce the country to the lowest state of ignorance and degradation. If a spark of knowledge was preserved, that blessing is due to Rome, France, Spain, and Belgium, which opened the halls of their colleges and universities to the exile from Erin suffering for his faith, and to the courage of Irish youths, who, in their thirst for learning, did not hesitate to seek it beyond the seas, though they knew that on their return home they would be exposed to the operation of the most cruel laws for having done so.

10.4. Whilst all Catholic education was banished by confiscation and penal enactments from our shores, everything possible was done to encourage Protestantism, and to provide means for propagating its doctrines. Parochial schools, Erasmus Smith's schools, royal colleges, charter schools, and other institutions were gradually established, at the public expense, or from confiscated property, for the purpose of rooting out Catholicity, and establishing the church of Henry VIII and Elizabeth I. To strengthen the operation of these minor establishments, and to bind them together, a great university was founded at the end of the sixteenth century, and gradually enriched with State endowments, or with property confiscated from Catholics. To say nothing of other sources of income, this university, destined by its founder, Elizabeth, to be the bulwark of Protestantism and the bane of Catholicity in Ireland, possesses at present 199,000 acres of land, and has under its control thirty-one rich benefices of the Establishment.

10.5. In later times, those purely Protestant establishments have been supplanted by other schools, and principally by the Queen's Colleges, established on principles which exclude all Catholic teaching, and so favourable to indifferentism and infidelity, that Christ's Vicar on earth has declared them dangerous to faith and morals, and the faithful people of Ireland have always looked on them as a gigantic scheme of godless education.

11. Pope Pius IX, *Optime noscitis*, encyclical letter to the bishops on the Catholic University (1854)

11.1. *Introduction.* Pope Pius IX impatiently commands the Irish bishops to found a Catholic University in Ireland. They are to stop dithering and get on with the business.

They are to create a truly Catholic university. It is to be a moral institution whose professors are to be models of virtuous Catholic life. He approves their choice of John Henry Newman (1801–90) as Rector of the proposed University. The hand of Paul Cullen marks this letter of his friend and patron, Pius IX. SOURCE: Anne Freemantle, *The Papal Encyclicals in their historical context – the teachings of the Popes from Peter to John XXIII* (New York, 1963).

To the Venerable Brothers, the Archbishops and Bishops of Ireland.

Venerable Brothers, Greetings and Apostolic Benediction.

11.2. You know very well how great our joy and consolation was when we first learned that in your devotion, you willingly followed our advice and that of the Holy See. In the Synod of Thurles, held in 1850, you decided, among other things, to establish a Catholic University as soon as possible. There the youth of your Illustrious Nation could be shaped in piety and every virtue and educated in letters and in the more difficult disciplines free from any danger to their faith. You also remember clearly how we approved both the Acts of that Synod and the establishment of this University in our Apostolic Letter published on 23 March 1852. Then in our Encyclical Letter of 25 March 1852, which we sent to you, we gave thanks regarding this plan for the advancement of religion and knowledge. We also gave well-deserved praise to those faithful people who had already contributed substantial aid in support of that Catholic University in Ireland.

11.3. As we greatly desired to see this Catholic Lyceum or University founded quickly in Ireland, we recommended in our Apostolic Letter to Paul [Cullen], who was then Archbishop of Armagh, that the office of Apostolic Delegate be prolonged. By this office he could see to it that the decrees of the Synod of Thurles were diligently observed and especially that the establishment of the Catholic University which that Synod approved and which we confirmed was brought quickly to the desired result. Therefore, when that venerable brother was transferred to govern the archiepiscopal church of Dublin, it seemed appropriate to us that he should continue in the office of Apostolic Delegate in the same manner as we set forth in our Apostolic Letter of 3 May 1852. We thought for certain, that you would put your hand to the task without delay and that you would apply all of your understanding and enthusiasm toward the speedy founding of this University. We trust that great benefits will flow from it to the faithful.

11.4. Thus, it was with great annoyance that we learned that this Catholic University, which we and all good people desire, has not yet been founded, although you already have all the necessary materials to build it. Therefore, we write this letter to you and implore you to put aside all hesitation and to direct all your thoughts and attention with redoubled efforts toward its construction. With the goal of accomplishing this pious and salutary work more quickly, we command all of you to hold a meeting within a period of three months after you receive this letter with Paul, the Archbishop of Dublin. We name him as Apostolic Delegate; he will preside over this meeting. You will meet there and convene according to the rule of the sacred canons. After your plans have been discussed again without public celebration and you are all of one mind, may you arrange everything which pertains to the quick building and opening of the University.

11.5. It will be your Episcopal concern in this meeting to adopt appropriate plans so that this University may live up to the sanctity and dignity of the Catholic name with which it is adorned. Therefore, see to it that divine religion is considered the soul of the entire institution of learning. For that purpose encourage the fear of God and His Worship so that the sacred trust of faith may be preserved and all studies may proceed, joined in a close bond with religion. Thus may the shimmering rays of Catholic doctrine illuminate all kinds of intellectual pursuits. Decorous language should be firmly maintained so that whatever is Catholic, whatever proceeds from this See of Saint Peter, the safe harbour of the whole Catholic communion (St Jerome, *Epistle*, 16) and the mother and teacher (Council of Trent, Session 7 on Baptism, canon 3) of all churches, may be welcomed and believed. May whatever is against it be rejected, so that every error and profane novelty may be repelled and eliminated. The professors of this University should show themselves to be models of good works in doctrine, in purity, and in seriousness. Their primary concern should be shaping the minds of the youth to piety, decency, and every virtue; instructing them in the finest matters; and educating them carefully in letters and studies according to the teachings of the Catholic Church, which is the pillar and chief support of truth.

11.6. As we know that you have already chosen our beloved son, Father John Henry Newman, to govern that University, we want to approve your choice that this priest, blessed with such wonderful gifts of mind and soul and endowed with piety, sound doctrine, and zeal for the Catholic religion, assume the care and governance of this University and preside over it as Rector.

11.7. ... Therefore do not neglect in that same meeting to make plans by which you, fulfilling your ministry, may preserve the purity of our holy faith in those areas, promote worship, and encourage the proper education and sanctity of the clergy. May these plans enable you to educate the faithful entrusted to you in the commandments of holy religion, to strengthen them through the gifts of heavenly graces, to keep them away from poisoned pastures, and to guide them to good ones. Lead back to the one fold of Christ the unfortunates who stray from it. Destroy the snares, the deceptions, and the errors of our enemies and break their force.

11.8. Because you are aware of what bountiful fruits holy Missions bring to the Christian people with the help of heavenly grace, you should not neglect to form a company of priests, both secular and regular. This will ensure that you have a ready supply of energetic and industrious workers who, adorned with every virtue and handling the word of truth rightly, can exercise the salutary ministry of the Holy Missions beneficially in your dioceses.

11.9. Now, we must stress again with great fervour that you should commit all your efforts and authority to seeing that everyone devoutly obeys the Decrees of the Synod of Thurles which we approved and confirmed. They should zealously accomplish all that was ratified in those Decrees. In order to more easily accomplish this, promulgate the Decrees of the Synod of Thurles more solemnly. Command their observance in both Provincial and Diocesan Synods which, as you know, you should convene according to the rules of the Council of Trent …

Given in Rome at St Peter's on the 20th day of March in the year 1854, the eighth year of Our Pontificate.

12. 'Excesses and their direful effects'

12.1. *Introduction.* Daniel Murray, Archbishop of Dublin, died on 26 February 1852. Generally thought kind and mild-mannered, he was not afraid to speak his mind, even to Rome. His biographer, the Revd William Meagher, delivered an oration at his funeral where he acknowledged Murray's role in bringing about the practical improvement of the city's Catholics. Here he colourfully describes the loose morals of Dublin several decades earlier. SOURCE: Revd William Meagher, *Notices on the life of the Most Revd. Daniel Murray* (Dublin, 1853), 11–12.

12.2. The morals of the people of Dublin, Catholics among the rest, were hideously corrupted. The riches daily scattered through her streets in handfuls to purchase the luxuries of an opulent and profuse and dissolute aristocracy; the easy and plentiful earnings of flourishing manufacture, and of extensive and successful commerce, were seized every hour, through a series of years, for indulgence of vilest libertinism, and wildest extravagance. Vices, too gross to be more than alluded to, stalked through the streets shamelessly – the drunkard raved without obstruction, and the blasphemer shouted his impiety, and the gambler squandered in nights of dissipation what his days of toil had accumulated. And, strange to say, and suggestive of many a sad and solemn reflection, there was in our city as large an amount of physical wretchedness, particularly among the lower ranks, as now – as much squalid poverty – as much shivering nakedness – as much famine-stricken emaciation – as many ruined families – as many houseless orphans! Vice did more to fill the town with the agonies of human suffering than famine, and plague, and abject poverty have wrought in these latter days of woe. Flatter not yourselves, My Brethren, that these excesses and their direful effects were confined to sectarians [non-Catholics]; they were as rife, if not more so, amongst ourselves. Nor, unless by some standing social and religious miracle, could it be otherwise. Amid opportunities so numerous – examples so seductive – temptations so violent – with but a handful of clergy and a dozen small, mean and incommodious chapels to second the proverbial faith and innate pious tendencies of the people, what wonder that the multitude was hurried away in this torrent of iniquity? And the mortifying truth is, that in Dublin, at the period alluded to, amid many Catholics there were but few practical Christians; very few whose lives supplied that substantial and only unerring proof of profitable attachment to the faith – the constant and regular frequentation of the holy sacraments. As the climax of her griefs religion had to weep for the first time, perhaps, in this land, over the faltering fidelity and submission of many a son, led astray by the frenzy of recent revolution, and the false liberality of the day, and the desolating philosophism of France.

13. 'Avaritia' – the challenge of clerical reform

13.1. *Introduction.* The income of Catholic priests came mostly from dues paid by the laity at Christmas and Easter, in money and in kind. These were supplemented by payments for baptisms, marriages, funerals, dispensations, and masses. Sir Robert Peel introduced the Charitable Bequests Act (1844) to win over moderate Catholics. It enabled Catholics to leave money and property by will to the Catholic Church. It was intended to make parish priests less dependent on their flocks. Some clergy became very wealthy and clerical greed was one of the biggest problems facing the bishops – the problem of rapacious clergy and resistance by parishioners was long-standing. In the summer of 1831, the bishops of the Dublin province established a uniform pay-scale for clerical dues. The Synod of Thurles tried to ensure that any clerical wealth went to the Church, not the relatives of deceased priests. Title to church property was to be vested in trustees, among them the bishop. Clergy were not to own more than 15 acres, although many continued to do so in their relatives' names. The statutes of the Synod of Thurles, repeated and extended at the Synod of Maynooth (1875), ordered the clergy to set a good example to the laity. Cullen, as Apostolic Delegate was to preside at the National Synod in Maynooth.

13.2. In Document I, Fr James Maher (1793–1874) writes in 1842 to his nephew and godson Paul Cullen, then Rector of the Irish College in Rome. He names several recently deceased priests who had left very large bequests. He is surprised at the amounts and thinks this could damage the standing of the clergy among the poor. In another letter to Cullen (Document II) in 1843 he states that, while the condition of the people seems to be getting worse, the demands of the priests are increasing. Much time is given over each Sunday to outstanding dues and he fears that the people are taking things into their own hands. In Document III, Thomas Chisholm Anstey (1816–73), lawyer and politician,

writes from London on 17 November 1843 to Giovanni Brunelli, Secretary of the
Congregation of Propaganda Fide. Born in London, Anstey, a convert to Roman
Catholicism, was educated at University College, London. A champion of Roman
Catholic political interests and a keen supporter of Daniel O'Connell, he was well
informed on Irish affairs. He informs Brunelli about the high incomes of priests in some
parts of Connacht; the demands of the priests' relatives to profit from their wealth; and
the pressure on the laity, even the very poor, for dues and payments.

I

SOURCE: Maher to Cullen, 2 January 1842. Paul Cullen Papers, Archives of the Irish
College, Rome; printed in Emmet Larkin, 'Economic growth, capital investment, and
the Roman Catholic Church in nineteenth-century Ireland', *American Historical Review*,
72/3 (1967), 852–84: 861.

> **13.3.** Father Kearney's clerical savings (about £10,000, some say £12,000 [approx.
> €860,000–€1 million at 2009 values]) although bequeathed to charitable pur-
> poses have given little edification: how did [he] scrape together and hoard up,
> everyone asks, such an enormous sum? Legacy duty (it is now 10 per cent when
> property is bequeathed to those who are not next of kin) will be £1,000. What a
> waste! It could have been avoided by a transfer of the property to trustees ….
> Besides Kearney's £10,000 the Church has had another windfall in the death of
> the Revd. Nicholas Sharman of Kilkenny. He left £3,000 (approx. €260,000) to
> charitable purposes, the poor of his parish, and £500 to a sister. He had had some
> private property, and nobody therefore censures the bequest to his sister …
> Another rich priest (Tracy) died in Ossory a year or two since, intestate, leaving
> a large sum, several thousands, to be scrambled for by his next of kin. You have
> heard already of the £1,500 which the late Parish Priest of Allen (Dunne) died
> possessed of, and of the £1,000 which the niece of Father O'Rourke of Celbridge
> relieved him of. I had nearly forgotten old Prendergast's £6,000 (approx.
> €520,000). What do you think of this merchandize in the Church? All the cases
> I have mentioned, are of recent occurrence, and within a very circumscribed
> [narrow] circle. The economy of these money savers in the midst of a poor
> people has damaged the character of the clergy exceedingly.

II

SOURCE: Maher to Cullen, 21 February 1843. Paul Cullen Papers, Archives of the Irish
College, Rome; printed in Emmet Larkin, 'Economic growth, capital investment, and
the Roman Catholic Church in nineteenth-century Ireland', *American Historical Review*,
72/3 (1967), 852–84: 859.

> **13.4.** … In travelling through the Country I have observed with pain that the rel-
> ative position of the people and Clergy has been greatly changed. The people

have become very much poorer. And the Clergy have adopted a more expensive style of living. The best Catholic house in each Parish and the best style of living appears to be the Priest's. Time was when both parties were more upon an equality. The demands of the Priests on the People have greatly multiplied and the laity are beginning to complain. Dues, dues, is the perpetual cry, the constant Sunday's theme of some. The Altar is occupied for an hour every Sunday for the transactions of the Priests and oats and turf, and all the arrears of Baptisms and unctions. What a desecration! ... The people of some parts of Connaught, have combined to resist the payment of dues to the Priest, unless according to a scale which they themselves devised. This is a bad sign of the times. The movement however at present is nearly hushed, but I fear it will again break out.

III

SOURCE: Rome, *Scritture riferite nei congressi, Irlanda*, 28, folios 121–45; printed in Emmet Larkin, 'The devotional revolution in Ireland, 1850–75', *American Historical Review*, 77/3 (1972), 625–52: 634.

13.5 ... it is well known in every part of Ireland with which he is acquainted, and to the best of his belief also in other parts thereof, that however well disposed a parish priest or curate may be to relieve his parishioners or some of them from grievous and oppressive payments of the kinds specified [tithes, church dues, etc.], the relatives (often very numerous) of such ecclesiastics are certain to obstruct the concession by clamorous complaints ... against his unkindness to his own flesh and blood who, by his ill-timed liberality, he is defrauding of their hopes of succession to his property after his death and of occasional contributions out of the same during his lifetime; and to which succession and contributions they, in the popular opinion as well as in their own, have a kind of equitable claim, founded upon the consent, which his family is supposed to have given in the first instance, to his being withdrawn from field labour and domestic service in order to go to the seminary; and, that the fear of such complaints, remonstrances and appeals to popular opinion hath the effect of making the priests to be watchful and austere in the exact and undeviating levy of their aforesaid dues, is apparent from the greatness of their incomes; that is to say in Connaught, which is the cheapest [poorest] part of Ireland, and where money is twice as valuable as it is in London, there are very few parish priests, if any, whose incomes are less than 200 sterling (approx. €19,000 at 2009 values) per annum although not one farthing of such incomes is appropriated [given over] ... to any other purpose than the mere support of the priest. But in most parishes the income is very much higher and ranging to £500 (approx. €47,000) and upwards per annum; ... it is a vulgar and proverbial saying throughout Ireland that the best or richest matches are to be had with the kindred of priests and that their farms are certain to be well stocked and furnished.

14. The 'devotional revolution'

14.1. *Introduction.* The transformation of religious practice during Cullen's ministry is called the 'devotional revolution' by the historian Emmet Larkin. The statutes of Synod of Thurles instructed the Catholic clergy to administer the sacraments of confession and communion more frequently and only in church, if possible. Missions were held every few years in nearly every parish in the country in the 1850s. Given by skilled teams of priests drawn from religious orders, these encouraged confessions, deepened devotion, and taught the masses Christian doctrine. Cullen wrote in 1852 that he wished to 'enrol a large missionary body before next summer to wipe out the proselytizers everywhere'. Pious devotional exercises were introduced – the rosary, Forty Hours' Adoration, *via crucis* ('way of the cross' or 'stations of the cross'), perpetual adoration, novenas, benediction, vespers, devotion to the Sacred Heart and to the Immaculate Conception, tridua, jubilees, pilgrimages, processions, and retreats. Religious societies, sodalities, and confraternities were organised. These were voluntary associations of the faithful, guided by spiritual directors, for the promotion of special works of Christian charity or piety. Among these were the Society of St Vincent de Paul as well as temperance and altar societies, and sodalities devoted to the Virgin Mary. There was also a more widespread use of devotional objects – rosary beads, medals, missals, prayer books, catechisms, and holy pictures. According to Larkin, this was 'the period when the whole world of the senses was explored in these devotional exercises, and especially in the Mass, through music, singing, candles, vestments, and incense'. Cullen stated that he favoured going 'beyond strict practice for the sake of letting the bishops and clergy see the full solemnities of the Church'.

14.2. In Document I Cullen writes to Kirby in 1852 describing the excitement surrounding the jubilee celebrations in Dublin and the pious emotions of the laity. He is already planning more jubilees and he makes enquiries of Kirby about establishing additional sodalities and the rules governing them. Cullen wrote to Kirby again in 1853 (Document II) complaining that Archbishop Slattery of Cashel has done little to impose the statutes of the Synod of Thurles but other dioceses were slowly falling into line and the administration of the sacraments was being confined to churches as far as possible.

I

SOURCE: Cullen to Kirby, 20 December 1852. Kirby Papers, Archives of the Irish College, Rome; printed in Emmet Larkin, 'The devotional revolution in Ireland, 1850–75', *American Historical Review*, 77/3 (1972), 625–52: 646.

14.3 The Jubilee has succeeded beyond all hope. All the churches are crowded with people trying to go to confession. Were the priests ten times as many as they are they could not hear them all … I have done nothing lately but to cure invalid marriages and remedy similar impediments. We must beg of the Pope to give a

Jubilee of one month next May. It will put down all heresies and set things right … The priests are greatly fatigued with the Jubilee; otherwise I would apply at present to have it prolonged. Some of the people here are anxious I should establish in schools and convents the 'Child of Mary' such as they have in Waterford convent. Will you get me the faculties to do this, and to establish every other sodality? I would require to know what the indulgences are and what the rules.

II

SOURCE: Cullen to Kirby, 28 January 1853. Kirby Papers, Archives of the Irish College, Rome; printed in Emmet Larkin, 'The devotional revolution in Ireland, 1850–75', *American Historical Review*, 77/3 (1972), 625–52: 647.

14.4 In the diocese of Cashel there is a parish called Doon, where I have heard there are seven or eight hundred apostates … The Archbishop [Slattery] of Cashel does not want any noise made about it. Father Dowley, Superior of the Vincentians, recently offered to give a mission but so far the offer has not been acknowledged … The poor Archbishop is very timid, and believes that he is always on the verge of death, even though he is in good health … He is about the only bishop that has done nothing about what was prescribed in the Synod of Thurles … Baptisms and confessions remain as they formerly were, and they also celebrate marriages in private houses. In almost all the other dioceses something at least has been done … In this diocese of Dublin all marriages and baptisms are celebrated in the churches. In the city and in the towns all the confessions are heard in the churches. In all the mountainous places where there are no churches nearby, if the distance is not too great, I told the priest to find every means of transporting the people to those distant churches, but if that were not possible to hear confessions in private houses. …

JOHN PAUL MCCARTHY AND TOMÁS O'RIORDAN

CHAPTER II

Key concepts

1. Dowry

1. This was generally called 'fortune' in Ireland; *spré* in Irish. It is money or other property brought by a bride to her husband at marriage. It was an important matter in nineteenth-century Ireland, socially and economically.

1.2. There were new trends in marriage rates after the Famine. In 1845, the average male age at marriage was 25, the average female age 21. However, by 1914 the typical male married at 33 and the female at 28. In 1851 only 12 per cent of women between the ages 25 and 54 did not marry but in 1911 this had increased to 26 per cent. Parents now left their farms to one son, and the others had the choice of marrying a female who inherited a farm (and this meant a financial settlement, by which the in-coming husband, in Irish *cliamhain isteach*, brought the equivalent of a dowry to his bride), moving to the city or town, taking up a profession, emigrating, or joining a religious order. Heirs tended to postpone marriage until parents died and were generally unwilling to make dowryless marriages that would worsen their financial position or lower their status. It became increasingly difficult to marry outside one's own social class. Before the Famine it was quite usual for well-off farmers to bring in matchmakers to ensure that their children married well; but after the Famine most families did this. The dowry became a chief consideration when choosing a partner and farmers' children preferred not to marry rather than marry beneath them.

1.3. The dowry was often paid directly to the groom or to his father, sometimes to the groom's siblings. It did not guarantee the material welfare of the bride (as in many societies) and it might be disposed of by her husband's family as it pleased, for example, to provide a dowry for her sister-in-law.

1.4. Though some brides married without dowries, payment could be substantial for others. If a girl married into a large farm, a matching dowry was expected. At one time the average dowry payment was £3 an acre (approx. €280 at 2009 values). The need for such large sums helped parents to control their children's choice of marriage partner. Not surprisingly, dowries were often the cause of disputes, particularly because they were sometimes paid by instalments or full payment was delayed. The law limited women's property rights. Until the Married Women's Property Acts (1882–93) a married woman had no rights to property independent of her husband, whether acquired by gift, inheritance, or by her own earnings, and this included her dowry. The Court of Chancery enabled divorced women to apply for an unreturned dowry but this had no practical application for most people.

1.5. Emigration was a common escape from the dowry system. For example, most Irish female emigrants to Australia tended to marry: only 10 per cent of women who died in 1891 were unmarried; and they married at an earlier age than in Ireland, 24 or 25. Better marriage opportunities for Irish women, whose choices were restricted at home by the dowry system and who had a chance to better their social position through paid employment, was a strong 'pull factor' in female migration.

1.6. In the farming class, no land and no dowry usually meant no marriage and no prospects, and this was so until the mid-twentieth century. Most families dealt with this pragmatically, if harshly. One son inherited the farm; and a daughter or two might get a dowry. Very often, the rest had to fend for themselves: remain at home unmarried, leave, or emigrate. Even a girl entering a convent needed a dowry. In a land where industrialisation was very limited outside the north-east, there were few opportunities at home. The better-off farmers and others with some funds could and did send children into the religious life and this fitted well with Archbishop Cullen's plans for the Catholic Church.

1.7. BIBLIOGRAPHY: K.H. Connell, *Irish peasant society: four historical essays* (Oxford, 1968). J.M. Goldstrom & L.A. Clarkson (ed.), *Irish population economy and society: essays in honour of the late K.H. Connell* (Oxford, 1981). Conrad M. Arensberg & Solon T. Kimball, *Family and community in Ireland*, intro. by Anne Byrne, Ricca Edmondson & Tony Varley (3rd ed., Ennis, 2001) [first published 1940]. Richard Breen, 'Dowry payments and the Irish case', *Comparative Studies in Society and History*, 26 (1984), 280–96.

DONNCHADH Ó CORRÁIN AND TOMÁS O'RIORDAN

2. Economic depression

2.1. It was long believed that the backwardness of the Irish economy in the first half of the nineteenth century was a result of the abolition of protective tariffs in the decades after the Union. Under the terms of the Union, Ireland and Britain were to be a single free-trade area. It was agreed that some Irish industries needed time to adjust. Accordingly, it was arranged that there should be a 10 per cent duty on some eighteen products entering Ireland until 1821. These included leather, glass, and furniture. Woollen and cotton goods got even more favourable terms. In 1820, these duties were reviewed and the government first suggested that the 10 per cent rate should remain until 1825, then be phased out, and finally abolished in 1840. However, the free traders in the government had all duties abolished in 1824. Unprotected Irish industries then faced large-scale English competition.

2.2. In the decades before the Famine Irish cottage industries decayed. From the 1820s there was widespread distress and unemployment in much of the country as industries based on small-scale handicraft gradually gave way to cheaper imported mass-produced goods. One must take into account Ireland's 'economic situation' in the age of industrial revolution. Ireland's problems were, in many ways, like those in some parts of Britain and throughout much of Western Europe as the industrial revolution had its effects; regions previously prosperous began to decay and new centres of industry, wealth, and population arose. This dramatic change in the balance of economic activity depended on the location of sources of energy and raw materials. Ireland had little coal and no iron. Consequently, in the age of steam, it was handicapped from the start in any competition with the rest of the United Kingdom. Raw materials could be imported but this raised costs. Ports close to Britain enjoyed more favourable conditions. English factory production, particularly of textiles, became increasingly mechanised. The combination of increased output and reduced unit costs allowed English manufacturers to meet and beat any manufacturers sharing the same market.

2.3. Britain's increasing dominance of the Irish market owed much to quicker and cheaper transport. From the 1820s, packet steamers plying between the two countries greatly lowered transport time and costs. However, deeper penetration of the Irish market had to await the coming of the railways. This change in transport and costs was gradual and so, too, was the penetration of the Irish market by English goods. Difficulty of access gave some industries a temporary respite in their local markets. However, the railways finally made Britain and Ireland a single integrated market economy.

2.4. During the eighteenth century, Ulster, with its regional capital Belfast, had become the main centre of linen production. Apart from its natural resources – a good harbour, fast-flowing streams, a plentiful supply of flax – the region had a ready supply of able entrepreneurs and a distinctive rural economy in which agricultural cultivation was attuned to the work habits of the domestic linen workers. In the 1770s cotton was introduced. It centred on the north-east where many of the techniques already learnt in the production and sale of linen could be applied to cotton. Capital was available, and in 1810 there were over 20,000 employed in cotton spinning alone. The cotton era in the north-east was short-lived though. Protected by tariffs and based almost entirely on the home market, the industry faced a succession of crises in the early 1820s. It never recovered. The agricultural price slump after Waterloo (1815) led to a great fall off in consumer demand for cotton goods on the home market. Then, in the early 1820s, the abolition of protective tariffs left the industry open to competition from Lancashire.

2.5. Fortunately, the collapse of the cotton industry coincided with the recovery of linen. However, an abundant supply of cheap labour seriously held back the mechanisation of the linen industry. When the new wet-spinning process, invented in the 1820s, made it possible to spin fine linen yarn by machine, the manufacturers of the north-east invested in the new machines. Soon the industry was confined to Belfast and its surrounding areas. As late as 1817, as much as one-fifth of the total value of Irish linen production came from outside Ulster – Louth, Meath, Longford, Sligo, Mayo, and parts of Munster. By the mid-century, these pockets of linen production had almost disappeared.

2.6. The state of the Irish economy turned on the efficient use of the country's greatest natural resource, the land. The massive increase in population was a condition and a consequence of the expansion of agricultural output. By 1841 the population was more than eight million. The expansion of tillage required many labourers. Besides, increased yields in cereals were best achieved by crop rotation which meant extended cultivation of potatoes and root crops, and these were also labour intensive. Accelerated growth caused intense competition for land. This led to inflated rents and a rapid reduction in the rewards for labour. This explains why the profits of higher output did not reach the labourer, the cottier, or many smaller farmers.

2.7. Because agriculture was the basis of the Irish economy, the slump in food prices after Waterloo (1815) seriously altered the prospects for Irish agriculture. The slump was general, but prices dropped more for tillage than for grassland products. This was despite the efforts of the government which passed the Corn Laws to ensure a minimum price for Irish and British corn growers by protecting them from foreign competition. Immediately, it became very difficult for many farmers to keep up the payment of high rents. A small number of landlords lowered rents to meet the changed circumstances, but this was not general. As rents became harder to pay, some farmers found themselves falling heavily into arrears. Leases were renewed with difficulty and tenancies-at-will became increasingly widespread.

2.8. The rising economic hardship led to rising rural disorder. Land hunger and the struggle to survive drove the cottiers and labourers into the secret societies such as the Rockites, Whitefeet, and Terryalts. Threatening notices, cattle maiming, hay burning, ploughing up grassland, and personal assault were some of the means used by cottiers, labourers, and subsistence tenants to prevent evictions and to discourage tenants from taking holdings from which others had been evicted. These means were also used to keep down rents, to deter the tithe proctor, and above all to ensure that landlords and farmers did not convert conacre tillage lots into grass for bullocks. Rural disorder was checked by coercion: the government passed Insurrection and Whiteboy Acts to curtail secret societies. These agrarian disorders were symptoms of the serious difficulties that faced the agricultural economy before the Famine. Production continued to rise, but so did poverty because the profits of increased output were unequally shared – the rich got richer, the poor got poorer.

2.9. The role that the money supply played in the post-war economic recession is more difficult to measure. During the Napoleonic wars there was serious inflation in Britain and Ireland. With the return of peace the government pursued a 'sound money' policy and there followed a period of severe deflation during which the Irish pound was gradually devalued. The Bank of Ireland kept tight control on note issue and a shortage of credit contributed to the collapse of several banks and industries. The gold standard resumed in 1821 and the exchange rate remained steady until the merging of the Irish and English currencies in 1826.

2.10. The 1830s proved to be difficult – minor potato failures brought famine and there was chronic unemployment in town and country because of surplus labour and industrial decline. Population growth slowed and emigration rose. The performance of the pre-Famine economy was conditioned by population pressure, natural resources, social structures, the transformation of the market by price movements, and revolutionary changes in the means of production and distribution of consumer goods.

2.11. At the same time State intervention remained significant especially in currency and customs reforms and the removal of tariffs and bounties. It is clear that the Irish social system (or certain aspects of it) was the crucial obstacle to Irish economic health. It was argued that there was a shortage of capital due to the outflow of rents to absentee landowners, and investors were reluctant to sink capital in an unstable society. However, there was no shortage of capital in pre-Famine Ireland: the extent of Irish investment in Government stock and joint-stock banks later proves this. Irish investors, unwilling for the most part to put their money at risk, were tempted by greater security and higher profits to invest in Britain. It is unlikely that the chronic poverty, economic imbalance, and social disorder of the pre-Famine decades would have been solved simply by land reform and a better deal for the tenant farmer. Any real reform plan would have involved a fundamental redistribution of resources – a gigantic piece of social and economic engineering – and no Government was willing to undertake that.

2.12. BIBLIOGRAPHY: K.H. Connell, *The population of Ireland, 1750–1845* (Oxford, 1950). K.H. Connell, *Irish peasant society: four historical essays* (Oxford, 1967). L.M. Cullen, *An economic history of Ireland since 1660* (London, 1972). J.M. Goldstrom & L.A. Clarkson (eds), *Irish population economy and society: essays in honour of the late K.H. Connell* (Oxford, 1981). Joel Mokyr, *Why Ireland starved: a quantitative and analytical history of the Irish economy, 1800–1850* (London, 1983). Cormac Ó Gráda, *Ireland before and after the Famine: explorations in economic history, 1800–1925* (Manchester, 1988; 2nd ed., 1993). W.E. Vaughan (ed), *A new history of Ireland: Ireland under the Union, 1801–70* (Oxford, 1988). Andy Bielenberg, *Cork's industrial revolution* (Cork, 1991). Cormac Ó Gráda, *Ireland: a new economic history, 1780–1939* (Oxford, 1994).

MARGARET FITZPATRICK (WITH A CONTRIBUTION FROM TOMÁS O'RIORDAN)

3. Evangelicalism

3.1. The term 'Evangelicalism' is wide-ranging in that it covers very diverse Protestant groups. It comes from the Greek word *evangelion*, meaning 'the good news, the gospel'. During the Reformation, Martin Luther adopted the term. The name is still generally used for the Lutheran Church in Germany and Switzerland to distinguish it from Calvinist churches. In the English-speaking world, however, it refers to religious movements and denominations that sprang from a series of revivals that swept the Anglo-American world in the eighteenth and early nineteenth centuries.

3.2. The most important characteristics of Evangelicalism are justification by faith in Christ and his atonement for humanity's sins; the belief that the Bible, taken literally, is the only source of religious authority; conversion; deep personal piety; and the New Birth. Evangelicalism's origins in Ireland stretch back to Protestant religious societies in Dublin and elsewhere in the first half of the eighteenth century. The relatively lethargic and negligent Church of Ireland gave it an opening. It was only with the arrival of English evangelists, such as John Wesley (1703–91), who made 21 trips to Ireland, and George Whitefield (1714–70) – both of whom really belonged to the Methodist movement – that its missionary zeal first became evident.

3.3. Other missionaries have been active earlier, but the Evangelicals launched a sustained mission in the 1820s and later to convert Irish Catholics. This met with more success than is generally admitted, but its effect was not long lasting. The First Evangelical Revival was fired by the zeal of John Wesley (the founder of Methodism). Wesley thought Ireland the most spiritually benighted place he had ever been; he heartily disliked Calvinistic Presbyterianism; and he deplored Irish Catholicism. By the time of his death, there was a large Methodist community in Ireland (over 15,000) and Irish Methodism later spread to North America. Irish Evangelicalism also spread globally in the form of a non-denominational movement which began at Powerscourt in 1821, known simply as 'The Brethren'.

3.4. In Dublin, the impact of the Second Evangelical Revival was obvious in the second half of the nineteenth century. Inside and outside the principal Protestant denominations, thousands felt a renewed faith in Christ. The mail-boat arriving at Kingstown (now Dun Laoghaire) was the scene of spontaneous worship and Christian tears as passengers and crew felt the power of the Holy Spirit. In Abbey Street, thousands flocked to prayer meetings at the Metropolitan Hall. Hundreds gathered at York Street to hear the preaching of Henry Grattan Guinness. The city's architecture already reflected the revival: a huge auditorium seating 2,800 (now the Davenport Hotel) was built solely for the preaching of Joseph Denham Smith. In Cork, 2,000 people attended united prayer meetings, despite the opposition of the Church of Ireland bishop. The Revival spread to Carlow, Kerry, Sligo, Mayo and Limerick (where Smith preached to large meetings). In the North, it is said that 100,000 new members were added to the churches.

3.5. Throughout the nineteenth century, open-air preaching often provoked clashes with Catholic protesters. It also prompted an active concern for wider social welfare. Sunday schools, Bible classes, and young men's associations aimed to instruct the young. Many charitable and missionary societies were established to meet the social needs of the poor in Ireland. Hundreds of Irish men and women joined Evangelical missions to pagans worldwide.

3.6. In the nineteenth century its greatest gains were confined to the North where conversionism produced a great religious drama in the form of the Ulster Revival of 1859, characterised by frequent and lengthy churches services, ecstatic manifestations of spiritual feeling and lay leadership. Evangelical religion undoubtedly played a part in stiffening the anti-Catholicism of a significant number of Irish Protestants and has contributed to the distinctive religious and political colour of Northern Ireland in the twentieth century. The religious peak of Evangelicalism in Ireland is probably past, but new forms of enthusiastic popular Protestantism, from Pentecostalism to charismatic renewal, continue in Ulster.

3.7. BIBLIOGRAPHY: Charles Henry Crookshank, *History of Methodism in Ireland* (4 vols, Belfast & London, 1885–1960). Desmond Bowen, *Souperism: myth or reality* (Cork, 1970). Desmond Bowen, *The Protestant crusade in Ireland, 1800–70: a study of Protestant-Catholic relations between the Act of Union and Disestablishment* (Dublin, 1978). Keith Robbins, *Protestant Evangelicalism: Britain, Ireland, German and America, c.1750–c.1950* (Oxford, 1990). Samuel J. Rogal, *John Wesley in Ireland, 1747–1789* (Lampeter, 1993). Desmond Bowen, *History and the shaping of Irish Protestantism* (New York, 1995). John A. Vickers (ed.), *A dictionary of Irish Methodism in Britain and Ireland* (Peterborough, 2000).

MARGARET FITZPATRICK

4. Famine

4.1. Famine is an extreme shortage or a failure in food supplies over a prolonged period in a whole society, or in a large part of it. There were severe food shortages Ireland in the eighteenth and early nineteenth centuries – for example in 1728–9, 1740–41 (*bliain an áir* 'the year of the slaughter', when up to one-third of the rural population died of starvation and disease), 1756–7, 1800, 1807, 1816–7, 1821–2, 1830–4, 1836, and 1839 – but it was also common elsewhere in Europe. The last European famine was that of Finland and northern Sweden in 1866–8 when about 15 per cent of the entire population died. The Irish famine of 1816, when the potato crop failed, was the worst since 1740 and severe typhus followed. Approximately 50,000 died between 1817 and 1819 and between 1816 and 1842 there were at least 14 partial failures of the potato crop, the staple of peasant diet. Famine conditions returned to the West in 1878–81 and again in the 1890s.

4.2. An estimated million to a million-and-a-half people died in the Great Famine of 1845–9. By April 1847, up to 2,500 people per week were dying from starvation, and famine-related diseases. British intellectuals viewed the Famine as mainly the result of Irish fecklessness and the British government's chief famine administrator, Charles Edward Trevelyan, saw the Famine as God's judgement, however painful, on an irresponsible society.

4.3. The western seaboard was often worst affected in these crises because of its poverty, high population, and poor land. On each occasion, the government tried to cope with distress. It shipped oats, corn, and biscuit to the affected areas, and made funds available for harbour and fishery development and other public works. New roads were built.

Government inspectors were appointed to oversee fever hospitals, and money was spent on infirmaries. Food shortages and famine conditions also generated violent agrarian unrest in parts of the country and the government introduced harsh coercion measures to suppress any local discontent.

4.4. The political culture of the time encouraged philanthropy, and charitable organisations were founded in Britain to help the Irish poor, whose miserable plight was described by writers and travellers such as Walter Scott (1771–1832), Gustave de Beaumont (1802–66), Johann Georg Kohl (1808–78, a German geographer and traveller, writing in 1843) and Alexis de Tocqueville (1805–59, a French traveller and political analyst, writing of his visit to Ireland in 1835). Indeed, much of the relief work in 1845–9 fell to private initiative. Above all, Irish landlords were exhorted to do their duty by the poor. Some did, and spent substantial sums of money to help distressed areas. Many did not. However, it is certain that British government relief efforts during the Great Famine were inadequate and often callously indifferent.

4.5. BIBLIOGRAPHY: Dudley Edwards & T. Desmond Williams (eds), *The Great Famine* (Dublin, 1957; repr. with an introduction and bibliography by Cormac Ó Gráda, Dublin, 1994). Cecil Woodham-Smith, *The Great Hunger: Ireland 1845–49* (London, 1962). Mary E. Daly, *The Famine in Ireland* (Dundalk, 1986). Cormac Ó Gráda, *Studies in economic and social history: the Great Irish Famine* (Basingstoke, 1989). Austin Bourke, *'The visitation of God'? The potato and the Great Irish Famine*, ed. Jacqueline Hill & Cormac Ó Gráda (Dublin, 1993). Helen Litton, *The Irish Famine: an illustrated history* (Dublin, 1994; 2nd ed. Dublin, 2003). Donal A. Kerr, *'A nation of beggars'? Priests, people and politics in Famine Ireland, 1846–1852* (Oxford, 1994). Noel Kissane, *The Irish Famine: a documentary history* (Dublin, 1995). Cathal Póirtéir (ed.), *The Great Irish Famine* (Cork, 1995). John Killen, *The Famine decade: contemporary accounts, 1841–51* (Belfast, 1995). Peter Gray, *The Irish Famine* (London, 1995). David Dickson, *Arctic Ireland* (Belfast, 1997) [the extraordinary story of the great frost and famine of 1740–1]. Cormac Ó Gráda (ed.), *Famine 150* (Dublin, 1997). Christine Kinealy, *A death-dealing Famine: the Great Hunger in Ireland* (London & Chicago, 1997). Cormac Ó Gráda, *Black '47 and beyond: the great Irish Famine in history, economy, and memory* (Princeton, NJ, 1998). Peter Gray, *Famine, land and politics: British government and Irish society, 1843–1850* (Dublin, 1999). Carla King (ed.), *Famine, land and culture in Ireland: a documentary history* (Dublin, 2000). L. A. Clarkson & E. Margaret Crawford, *Feast and famine: a history of food and nutrition in Ireland, 1500–1920* (Oxford, 2001). James S. Donnelly, *The great Irish potato Famine* (Stroud, 2001). Christine Kinealy, *The Great Irish Famine: impact, ideology, and rebellion* (Basingstoke, 2002). Margaret M. Mulrooney (ed.), *Fleeing the Famine: North America and Irish refugees, 1845–1851* (New York, 2003). Robert F. Haines, *Charles Trevelyan and the Great Irish Famine* (Dublin, 2004). L.A. Clarkson & E. Margaret Crawford (ed.), *Famine and disease in Ireland* (5 vols, London, 2005).

TOMÁS O'RIORDAN

5. *Laissez-faire*

5.1. This term, borrowed from French (also *laisser-faire*), means 'Let (people) do (as they think best)'. This phrase expresses the 'principle that government should not interfere with the actions of individuals especially in industrial affairs and in trade' (*Oxford English Dictionary*). Much of the government's attitude to the Irish situation was determined by this fashionable philosophy of 'political economy' rather that by the facts. Ministers invoked the principles of *laissez-faire*, but in fact they did intervene, and often crudely. In the government's view, Ireland was an over-populated country where sub-division of land and dependence on the potato left peasant and landlord alike with too much idle time. Property owners should undertake the responsibilities of property. The lack of economic progress was seen as proof of fecklessness. Consequently, the solution to the Irish problem was to end the system of 'easy existence' by diversifying economic activity, stopping sub-division, reducing the role of the potato, and bringing men of energy and capital into the country.

5.2. In a period of crisis, such as the Famine, prejudice and fear were easily translated into policies. Ireland was caricatured for its poverty and seen as a possible threat to the economic prosperity of the United Kingdom as a whole. Britain was at this stage on the verge of industrial and imperial ascendancy and its leaders may have felt that it could be hampered by its closeness, geographically and politically, to an impoverished, over-populated, potato-fed, and priest-ridden Ireland.

5.3. Inquiries into the condition of Ireland in the nineteenth century focussed mostly on its poverty, its system of landholding, the size of its population and the backwardness of its agriculture, especially the continuing dependence on the potato. The debates that followed were shaped by the writings of some leading economists. One of the most influential doctrines was 'political economy'; Adam Smith was its principal proponent; and he set out his principles in his influential book, *An inquiry into the nature and causes of the wealth of nations.* He believed that the wealth of a nation could be increased if the market was free from constraints and government intervention was kept to a minimum. He applied the same principle to the relationship between the government and the individual and he used it to justify individualism and self-help. Adam Smith's ideas were complex, but they were often reduced to the simple slogan, *laissez-faire*, meaning no government interference.

5.4. Smith's ideological heirs included Thomas Malthus, Edmund Burke, David Ricardo, Nassau Senior, Harriet Martineau and Jeremy Bentham. These writers developed their individual and frequently contradictory interpretation of 'political economy'. Bentham summed up his principles: '*Laissez-faire*, in short, should be the general practice: every departure, unless required by some great good, is certain evil'. Government ministers from William Pitt to Lord John Russell were inspired by this philosophy. Edmund Burke in a memorandum to Pitt on the duty of government not to intervene during a period of scarcity assured the Prime Minister that even God was on their side.

5.5. Paradoxically 'political economy' existed in a period of increasing government action. Government intervention was frequent, piecemeal, and measured. In the case of the 1834 English Poor Law the government intervened to reduce costs. When it suited government, *laissez-faire* could be doctrine; when it did not, as in the case of the Corn Laws and the Navigation Acts, it was ignored. One of its main attractions was that 'ministers could take whatever suited them from political economy and reject whatever did not'. During the Famine, political economy was invoked to justify non-interference in the grain trade, following the disastrous blight of 1846–7. It had the strong support of political economists in the Whig Cabinet including Sir Charles Wood and the Colonial Secretary, Earl Grey. At the height of the distress, the writings of Adam Smith and Edmund Burke were sent to relief officers in Ireland, and they were encouraged to read them in their spare time.

5.6. During the decades before the Famine, much attention was focussed on Ireland's poverty and its fast-growing population. The problems of the country were being reduced to the fashionable Malthusian equation of a fast-growing population and heavy dependence on a single resource – the potato – that made vice and misery inevitable. Not even the most pessimistic observers thought a major famine was imminent and some were optimistic about the prospects of the country.

5.7. Official observers in Britain, many influenced by Thomas Malthus's ideas, were pessimistic about Ireland. The Census returns and other government inquiries confirmed that the country was suffering the many evils of heavy dependence on one crop, extensive poverty, and a fast-growing population. It was perhaps convenient and pragmatic to see Ireland, in Malthusian terms, as a society in crisis. To see Ireland as an economy trapped in a spiral of poverty, and social disaster as inevitable, was convenient: it made the government and its officials appear blameless.

5.8. BIBLIOGRAPHY: T.R. Malthus, *Occasional papers of T.R. Malthus on Ireland, population and political economy* (New York, 1963). J.M. Goldstrom & L.A. Clarkson (eds), *Irish population economy and society: essays in honour of the late K.H. Connell* (Oxford, 1981). Joel Mokyr, *Why Ireland starved: a quantitative and analytical history of the Irish economy, 1800–1850* (London, 1983). Cormac Ó Gráda, *Ireland: a new economic history, 1780–1939* (Oxford, 1994).

DONNCHADH Ó CORRÁIN AND TOMÁS O'RIORDAN

6. Landlordism

6.1. Landlords were owners or lease-holders of property who rented some or all their land to others. Some landlords were landowners; others had virtual ownership of land, that is, they held it on perpetuity leases or for terms of several hundred years.

6.2. Landlords of the nineteenth century and before have a bad image in the Irish popular mind. This reflects many things: nationalist writings, Land League propaganda, bitter memories of evictions, the landlords' colonial origins, and their predatory rents. By 1703, most Irish landlords were of English or Scots origin, and had got their property during the plantations and land confiscations of the sixteenth and seventeenth centuries, at the expense of the Gaelic Irish and the Old English aristocracy. Previously, land had been the basis of complex social and family ties that linked landowners, their kindred, their dependants, and their better-off tenants. They shared a cultural, religious, and lineage identity – but one that involved plenty of conflict and predatory rents. The lot of the labourers and the landless poor was miserable: the change of land ownership mattered nothing to them.

6.3. In contrast, the new landlords were generally linked to their tenants only by economic ties, and in most parts of Ireland, they were separated from them by language (English), religion (Anglican), origin (English and Scots), and culture (English). The descendants of the Gaelic and Old English upper class had not forgotten or forgiven their dispossession. The deep insecurity of the new landholders receded only after 1745.

6.4. By 1703, only 14 per cent of land remained in Catholic ownership and this figure was reduced further during the eighteenth century by the penal laws: Catholic landowners, for example MacGillycuddy of the Reeks, changed religion to keep their lands.

6.5. In the eighteenth century, absentee landlords (many of whom lived in England) were seen as a problem. They were denounced as feckless parasites who took their money and did nothing for their estates or tenants. They were (people said) a drain on Irish capital. Thomas Prior's *List of the absentees of Ireland and the yearly value of their estates and income spent abroad,* compiled in 1729, went into six editions before 1783. Arthur Young, writing in 1779, estimated that about £732,000 (approx €89 million at 2009 values) poured out of Ireland every year to landlords he condemned as 'lazy, trifling and negligent'. None of these early estimates is reliable. The first accurate survey, that of 1870, showed that 97 per cent of all Irish land was managed in the interests of landlords who lived off the rents, but a little short of half of them were resident. In the years before the Famine between one-third and a half of all landlords were absentees.

6.6. The 1870 figures reveal that about 49 per cent of landlords were usually absent, but that 36 per cent merely lived away from their estates, elsewhere in Ireland. As a result, landlords employed the often-detested land agents and sub-agents. These managed the estates, set the rents, and if necessary moved in the bailiffs and the police to evict tenants. Ireland's landlords differed greatly in wealth and attitudes and their numbers changed over time. As elsewhere in *ancien régime* Europe, landlords were a small elite that derived enormous economic, social, and political authority from their virtual monopoly of landownership.

6.7. The resident property owner, living in the Big House (many of which were built in the eighteenth century at great cost), was often the main source of employment in the area; the Big House employed servants and estate workers, its needs gave work to the local artisans, and the landlord commonly owned the local grain mill. Around their country houses revolved a social whirl of parties, heavy drinking, hunting, shooting and fishing; picnics for the ladies, croquet for the gentlemen. In general, the careers of the young men were predictable – public schools (that is, the private schools of the rich) in England, then university (Trinity, Oxford, or Cambridge) or a commission in the army, the better livings in the Church of Ireland or the higher offices in the government administration.

6.8. Their numbers rose from about 5,000 families in the 1780s when they owned over 95 per cent of all productive land and could be accurately described as a Protestant or Anglo-Irish ascendancy, to around 9,000 to 10,000 by the mid-nineteenth century. Their number reflected the overall performance of the agricultural economy. Head rents rose from about £5 million (approx. €600 million at 2009 values) in the 1780s to about £9 million (approx. €710 million) in 1800, and more slowly to £12 million (approx. €1 billion) in the early 1840s. By 1870 they were around £10 million (approx. €800 million). Behind these figures were great variations in the size and value of individual landlords' estates. The government returns of 1876 list 5,000 owners of between 100 and 1000 acres; 3,400 owners of between 1000 and 10,000; and 300 as owing over than 10,000 acres.

6.9. Although individual proprietors such as Lord Farnham in Co. Cavan or John Foster in Co. Louth were active advocates of farm improvement, very little of the landlords' wealth was reinvested in agriculture. More money seems to have been spent on maintaining a social 'presence' or on status-enhancing projects such as the construction (or re-construction) of large country houses and their associated parklands or laying out estate towns and villages.

6.10. Irish landlords were divided politically: between Whigs and Tories in the eighteenth century, and between various shades of Conservative, Liberal, Home Rule, and Unionist opinion in the nineteenth. They were at their most powerful during Grattan's parliament (1782–1801) when they controlled government and saw themselves as the (Protestant) Irish nation. By surrendering their political independence in the Act of Union, they consigned themselves to an increasingly marginalised role in the imperial British Parliament. Here, the challenge to the landlord's interests – driven by the need to solve Ireland's perennial land problems – led to the passing of successive Land Acts between 1870 and 1909. These Acts took most of the landlord's lands from them and established in their place deeply conservative peasant proprietors. They soon lost their authority and were quickly marginalised as a class when control of the political and economic life passed to others.

6.11. BIBLIOGRAPHY: J.E. Pomfret, *The struggle for land in Ireland, 1880–1923* (Princeton, NJ, 1930). Barbara L. Solow, *The land question and the Irish economy* (Cambridge, MA, 1971). W.A. Maguire, *The Downshire estates in Ireland, 1801–1845: the management of Irish* *landed estates in the early 19th century* (Oxford, 1972). Mark Bence-Jones, *Burke's Guide to country houses*, i: *Ireland* (London, 1978); revised as *A guide to Irish country houses* (London, 1988). Mark Bence-Jones, *Twilight of the Ascendancy* (London, 1987). Jacqueline Genet, *The Big House in Ireland* (Dingle, 1991). W.E. Vaughan, *Landlords and tenants in Ireland, 1848–1904* (2nd ed., Dublin, 1994). W.E. Vaughan, *Landlords and tenants in mid-Victorian Ireland* (Oxford, 1994). Andrés Eiríksson & Cormac Ó Gráda, *Irish landlords and the Great Famine* (Dublin, 1996). Valerie Pakenham, *The Big House in Ireland* (London, 2000). Gerard J. Lyne, *The Lansdowne estate in Kerry under the agency of William Steuart Trench, 1849–72* (Dublin, 2001). W.H. Crawford, *The management of a major Ulster estate in the late eighteenth century: the eighth earl of Abercorn and his Irish agents* (Dublin, 2001). T.C. Barnard, *A new anatomy of Ireland: the Irish Protestants, 1649–1770* (New Haven, 2003). Terence Dooley, *The Big Houses and landed estates in Ireland: a research guide* (Dublin, 2007).

DONNCHADH Ó CORRÁIN AND TOMÁS O'RIORDAN

7. Nationality, nation, nationalism

7.1. Nation, nationality and nationalism are linked concepts that have been among the most important forces in the political, social, and economic life of Western society for many centuries. As a group, they are as central as kingship, state, church, and class.

7.2. Scholars are not agreed about what a nation is or when nations came into being. There are two main views: the short one and the long. The short one is that the nation is modern and came into being some time during the eighteenth or nineteenth centuries (Hobsbawm, Gellner, Kedourie). Scholars do not agree when, or from where it emerged: the Enlightenment, American Revolution, French Revolution, Romanticism. According to the long view, the nation has its roots (in many cases) in the Middle Ages or earlier, in literacy in the vernacular, and in religions, especially the Bible (Hastings, Anthony Smith). It begins with an ethnicity, a large group of people with a shared identity, based on culture and spoken language. Some ethnicities become nations. A nation is more self-conscious than an ethnicity: it normally has a written literature in its own language, a self-conscious identity, claims to autonomy and to a specific territory (like Biblical Israel). Part of these claims are real, part imaginary.

7.3. The Irish learned classes were literate in Irish and in Latin in the early Middle Ages. They had begun to produce literature in their own language as early as the sixth century, the first in Western Europe. From the seventh century to the twelfth (when it reached its most elaborate form, in *An Leabhar Gabhála* 'the Book of the Taking of Ireland'), the Irish elite created a national identity, in the form of a striking myth of origin, founded on the Bible, that established the position of the Irish amongst the peoples of the world and traced the Irish ruling classes to a single source. They expressly state that they are a nation, as the Greeks, the Goths, the Gauls and others are or were nations. There were kings of Ireland in the eleventh and twelfth centuries and a myth of an immemorial kingship of Ireland was created. This was accompanied by a remarkable flowering of Christian culture and an extensive literature in medieval Irish. The claim to nationhood (drawing on this myth of origin) is eloquently expressed in the Remonstrance of Domhnall Ó Néill (who claimed to be king of Ireland) and of the Irish kings to Pope John XXII about 1317. This idea of nationhood and the same myth of origin again became important in the seventeenth century, when the Gaelic Irish and Old English in Ireland, both under attack, were trying to create a Catholic nation under a Stuart monarchy. They failed.

7.4. In the eighteenth century Ireland was dominated by the 'Protestant nation', namely, the narrow Protestant ruling class (little different from other European ruling classes) that owned most of the land and had a monopoly of political power and the professions. The government in London was determined to keep Ireland in a subordinate position, subject to the legislative authority of the British parliament. The position of the Protestant nation was early expressed by the learned William Molyneaux in his *The case of Ireland's being bound by Acts of Parliament in England stated* (1698): Ireland and England were sister kingdoms, subject to the same monarch, but Ireland was not subject to the British parliament. Jonathan Swift put the case more trenchantly in his *Drapier's letters* (1724): 'by the laws of God, of nature, of nations, and of your own country, you are and ought to be as free a people as your brethren in England'. With the American revolution in 1775, the constitutional demand became more insistent and finally the 'Patriots', Henry Grattan and his followers, won legislative independence in 1782, that is, that the Irish parliament alone had the right to legislate for Ireland. This lasted just eighteen years: it was swept away by the Act of Union in 1800. Some historians see this movement as 'colonial nationalism'.

7.5. In Ireland's case, nation and nationality are old, but nationalism, in the fullest sense, namely, that the nation should be an independent sovereign state and that all its members should struggle to achieve its independence and serve it, is an ideology of the nineteenth and twentieth centuries, as it is elsewhere in Europe. Nationalism draws on all kinds of sources – myth, legend, religion, history, art, culture, language, literature – to create a cult of the nation. Irish nationalists drew on the achievements of the early medieval Irish church, the golden age, the notion that Ireland was a holy island, the early origin myths, and the history of its medieval kings. Besides, Irish nationalism was self-consciously the heir of the colonial nationalism of the eighteenth century and celebrated Grattan and his 'Patriots'.

7.6. Political and cultural nationalism flowed in many streams in nineteenth-century Ireland and was understood in many different ways. Two main traditions can be discerned, though many held a position somewhere between. The one expressed itself through constitutional means, parliament, and peaceful agitation. Here belong O'Connell's Repeal campaign (it is doubtful whether O'Connell himself was truly a nationalist), and the Home Rule movement of Butt and Parnell (both of whom wanted much more than self-government for Ireland). The other was revolutionary, often secret and oath-bound, and sought an independent Ireland, usually a republican one, by military force. The IRB (or Fenians) best represent this tradition. They drew some inspiration from revolutionary France, but little by way of a social or political programme. Forms of government and political theories were, in their eyes, things to be worked out after independence. The support of the people ebbed and flowed, and very many, often the great majority, were indifferent. Most of the landlord class was committed to the Union with Britain, as were many Protestants in the north-east, and saw Ireland's best future as an integral part of the United Kingdom.

7.7. Thomas Davis and *The Nation* created a new Irish national identity in English, and this identity was elaborated in the balladry of the nineteenth century. Popular nationalist poets such as Thomas Moore, added to the repertoire, as did nationalist song-writers such as T.D. Sullivan, R.D. Joyce, Charles Kickham and others. Each political movement, each failed revolution, and each commemoration produced its crop of nationalist songs. The political attitudes of the ordinary people who sang them were at best ambiguous, often mawkishly sentimental.

7.8. The Gaelic League (*Connradh na Gaeilge*), founded by Eoin MacNeill (together with Douglas Hyde and others) brought a new and powerful element to nationalism: the preservation and revival of Irish as a living language and a conscious cultivation of the Gaelic past in all its cultural aspects. It was non-sectarian and non-political (until 1915 at least), but it had broadly nationalist objectives. It deepened and enriched the English-language nationalist rhetoric of Davis and those who followed him. It inspired a literary revival that could claim Yeats, Synge, and Lady Gregory amongst its leaders. It also inspired a literary revival in Irish and nearly every major figure in Irish writing belonged to it – Peadar Ó Laoghaire, Patrick Pearse, Pádraig Ó Conaire, Pádraig Ó Duinnín and others. Most of the leading Irish-language scholars of the early twentieth century began as members of the Gaelic League, notably Osborn Bergin and T.F. O'Rahilly. The Gaelic League was swept into the political ferment of the early twentieth century. Advanced physical-force nationalists joined it and many of those who took part in the Rising in Easter 1916 were members of the Gaelic League and drew inspiration from its cultural nationalist programme.

7.9. The destructiveness of Irish nationalism became more evident in the twentieth century. In 1913 armed Unionists (the Ulster Volunteer Force) confronted armed nationalists (the Irish Volunteers) in an uneasy stand-off – a portent of things to come. In 1916 the IRB core within the Irish Volunteers organised a Rising in Dublin. It failed. It was put down with unnecessary and unthinking brutality by the British authorities and many of its leaders were executed. This in turn led to odious guerrilla warfare and counter-insurgency in a large part of Ireland, 1919–21, ending in a truce and an Anglo-Irish Treaty. The terms of the Treaty were accepted by a parliamentary majority but did not meet the aspirations of more extreme Republicans (or satisfy the ambitions of their leaders). This led to a ruinous Civil War that ended in 1923 and caused bitterness and disillusion that lasted for more than a generation. Two separate states in Ireland, the Irish Free State and Northern Ireland, came into existence in 1920–1 under the government of Ireland Act (1920). Those who imagined themselves to be true nationalists and true Republicans remained hostile to both, and saw both as a betrayal of the Irish nation.

7.10. BIBLIOGRAPHY: Elie Kedourie, *Nationalism* (London, 1960). Ernest Gellner, *Nations and nationalism* (Oxford, 1983). Anthony D. Smith, *The ethnic origins of nations* (Oxford, 1986). E.J. Hobsbawm, *Nations and nationalism since 1780* (Cambridge, 1990). Liah Greenfeld, *Nationalism: five roads to modernity* (Cambridge, MA, 1992). Adrian Hastings, *The construction of nationhood: ethnicity, religion and nationalism* (Cambridge, 1997). Nicholas Mansergh, *Nationalism and independence: selected Irish papers*, ed. Diana Mansergh (Cork, 1997). Patrick J. Geary, *The myths of nations: the medieval origins of Europe* (Princeton, NJ, 2002). Anthony D. Smith, *Chosen peoples: sacred sources of national identity* (Oxford, 2003). Donnchadh Ó Corráin, 'Nationality and kingship in pre-Norman Ireland', in T.W. Moody (ed.), *Nationality and the pursuit of national independence* (Belfast, 1978) 1–35. R. Dudley Edwards, 'The contribution of Young Ireland to the development of the national idea', in Séamus Pender (ed.), *Féilscríbhinn Torna* (Cork, 1947), 115–33. E. Strauss, *Irish nationalism and British democracy* (London, 1951). Michael Hurst, *Parnell and Irish nationalism* (London, 1968). Robert Kee, *The green flag: a history of Irish nationalism* (London, 1972). R.V. Comerford, *Charles J. Kickham: a study in Irish nationalism and literature* (Portmarnock, 1979). Tom Garvin, *The evolution of Irish nationalist politics* (Dublin, 1981). J. Hutchison, *The dynamics of cultural nationalism: the Gaelic revival and the creation of the Irish nation state* (London, 1987). Tom Garvin, *Nationalist revolutionaries in Ireland, 1858–1928* (Oxford, 1987). Thomas E. Hachey & Lawrence J. McCaffrey, *Perspectives on Irish nationalism* (Lexington, KY, 1989). Paul Bew, *Ideology and the Irish question: Ulster Unionism and Irish nationalism, 1912–1916* (Oxford, 1994). Peter Collins (ed.), *Nationalism and Unionism: conflict in Ireland, 1885–1921* (Belfast, 1994). George Boyce, *Nationalism in Ireland* (London, 1995). Alvin Jackson, *Ireland 1798–1998: politics and war* (Oxford, 1999). Senia Pašeta, *Before the revolution: nationalism, social change and Ireland's Catholic elite, 1879–1922* (Cork, 1999). Mark Suzman, *Ethnic nationalism and state power: the rise of Irish nationalism, Afrikaner nationalism and Zionism* (Basingstoke, 1999). Alvin Jackson, *Home Rule: an Irish history, 1800–2000* (Oxford, 2004). Jonathan Githens-Mazer, *Myths and mysteries of the Easter rising: cultural and political nationalism in Ireland* (Dublin, 2006). Richard English, *Irish freedom* (London, 2007).

DONNCHADH Ó CORRÁIN

8. Physical force

8.1. The doctrine of 'physical force' is the belief that Ireland's political independence could only be achieved by military force. In the words of a later revolutionary, Patrick

Pearse, in 1914: 'nationhood is achieved' only 'by armed men'. This doctrine was well-rooted in the Republicanism of the IRB since its foundation in 1858: armed rebellion was the path to freedom and 'England's difficulty was Ireland's opportunity'. It drew its inspiration from the rebellion of 1798 and the rebellion of Robert Emmet.

8.2. The issue of 'physical' as against 'moral' force became crucial in the conflict, within the Repeal Association, between the pacifist constitutionalists led by Daniel O'Connell, and the increasingly impatient nationalists, who became Young Ireland and who turned, spectacularly unsuccessfully, to military force. O'Connell's Repeal movement, like all his campaigns, was based on the law, on the persuasive power of moral force, the self-evident rightness of the cause, and the mass support of the people. Ireland's freedom, he declared, was not worth one drop of blood. The parliamentary Home Rule movement inherited this tradition of moral force. The Irish politician and diplomat, Thomas Wyse (1791–1862), when reflecting on the successful campaign for Catholic Emancipation in 1829, highlighted the importance of 'moral force' in achieving it.

8.3. Differences between the Young Irelanders and O'Connell became pronounced in 1844 and 1845 as the British government began a programme of 'killing Repeal with kindness' through a series of conciliatory measures. The most controversial of these was the Queen's Colleges Act that placed restrictions on the teaching of religion and theology in the three colleges it established at Belfast, Cork, and Galway. Thomas Davis and O'Connell clashed bitterly over the measure at a famous meeting of the Repeal Association on 26 May 1845. O'Connell and most of the Catholic bishops condemned the measure for creating 'godless' institutions, while Young Ireland saw it as promoting a more pluralistic nationality. The death of Davis in 1845, and of O'Connell in 1847, allowed more militant voices to be heard. The failed attempt at revolution in 1848 and the rhetoric of its leaders, especially William Smith O'Brien and John Mitchell, inspired later proponents of physical force, notably the IRB.

8.4. The IRB doctrine of physical force remained that of the IRA, in its various manifestations and various guises, throughout the twentieth century.

8.5. BIBLIOGRAPHY: John O'Leary, *Recollections of Fenians and Fenianism* (2 vols, London, 1896). Desmond Ryan, *The phoenix flame: a study of Fenianism and John Devoy* (London, 1937). Maurice Harmon (ed.), *Fenians and Fenianism: centenary essays* (Dublin, 1968). Robert Kee, *The green flag: a history of Irish nationalism* (London, 1972). R.V. Comerford, *Charles J. Kickham: a study in Irish nationalism and literature* (Portmarnock, 1979). Seán Cronin, *Irish nationalism: a history of its roots and ideology* (Dublin, 1980). R.V. Comerford, *The Fenians in context: Irish politics and society, 1848–82* (Dublin, 1985). John Newsinger, *Fenianism in mid-Victorian Britain* (London, 1994). Owen McGee, *The IRB: the Irish Republican Brotherhood, from the Land League to Sinn Féin* (Dublin, 2005). M.J Kelly, *The Fenian ideal and Irish nationalism, 1882–1916* (Woodbridge, 2006).

MARGARET FITZPATRICK

9. Sectarianism

9.1. Sectarianism is defined as 'a complex of attitudes, beliefs, behaviours, and structures in which religion is a significant component and which (1) infringes civil or religious rights or (2) influences or causes conflict'. Sectarianism in Ireland gains 'its peculiar virulence because it involves not only religion, but religion combined with a tangle of other factors … culture, politics, economics and national identity' (*Sectarianism: a discussion document* (Belfast, 1993)). The roots of Irish sectarianism go back to the Reformation: religion became a defining element of communal identity. The three largest faiths – Roman Catholic, Church of Ireland and Presbyterian – clashed over which was the true church and who would be denied salvation. Later the labels 'Catholics' and 'Protestant' became more fully identified with conflicting national affiliations. The historian Brian Walker argues that the rise in literacy, the resolution of the land question, the growth of Belfast, and the strengthening of religious identities in the later nineteenth century furthered the development of Unionism and nationalism and that 'a more sensitive and effective government reaction to the situation in Ireland in the early 1870s could have undermined home rule and nationalist demands'.

9.2. Rural conflicts had been common since the late eighteenth century and Orangemen and Ribbonmen often clashed in Ulster in the 1820s. Such hostilities were fiercest in counties Londonderry, Tyrone, Down, Armagh, Cavan and Monaghan. They often took the form of riots at fairs or on the Twelfth of July and the destruction of property.

9.3. Demographic shifts brought sectarianism to Belfast where it was to have lasting impact on culture, politics, and religion. The city was largely free of sectarian strife in the eighteenth century as Catholics formed only a small proportion of the town's population. However, in the period 1834–71, Catholics were a significant minority, about one third. Migrants (of all denominations) from the countryside brought with them their sectarian fears and hatreds. The city's population increased from 20,000 in 1800, to 121,000 by 1851, and more than 390,000 by 1900. In September 1845, the *Vindicator* claimed that there were as many as 1,000 Ribbon society members in Belfast. A Catholic barrister writing to Dublin Castle in the 1830s stated that 'as in Antrim, it is extremely odd that the system [Ribbonism] prevails to a greater extent in Belfast than in any other town in the kingdom'. Tensions between the religious communities in the city frequently spilled over into violent conflict.

9.4. The 12 July 1813 witnessed one of the first riots of the century between Catholics and Protestants in North Street, Belfast. Orangemen returning from Lisburn were ambushed by Catholics wielding brick bats. Some of the armed Orangemen fired shots at the Catholic crowd – two were killed and four were seriously injured. Contemporary newspapers and State of the Country papers reveal that such clashes were all too frequent. The aggressive 'Second Reformation', and the attempted conversion of Catholics by Protestant missionaries increased tensions in the 1820s. Sectarian clashes continued into the 1830s and grew increasingly more violent.

9.5. The election of 1832, like most subsequent elections in Belfast, was acrimonious. The results revealed that the two Whig candidates, Dr Robert J. Tennent and William Sharman Crawford had been defeated by their Tory rivals, Lord Arthur Chichester and James E. Tennent. Most Whig votes had come from Catholics. Around noon a mob of Tory supporters 'armed with bludgeons' attacked the mainly Catholic Hercules Street (now Royal Avenue). After two hours of fierce fighting, they were driven back by the butchers' boys of Hercules Street. The *Northern Whig* described how bands in front of the Tory committee rooms played tunes like 'The Protestant Boys' and 'The Boyne Water.' The Tories then decided to chair their newly elected members in triumph through the streets. When they reached Hercules Street they were met by Catholics armed with knives and blunderbusses. The police arrived on the scene and opened fire. Four were killed – two elderly men and two teenage boys.

9.6. There was another 'very serious affray' in the city on Christmas day in 1833. People had gathered on Points Field to shoot wildfowl, and a riot began. Four or five Catholics were chased by a large mob into York Street. Later that day severe rioting broke out around Millfield and Peter's Hill. That night a young man was killed 'by the blow of a bludgeon' in a lane off Waring Street. More disturbances followed a Whig victory in 1835: Catholic and Protestant houses were attacked by roaming mobs and a cavalry charge restored order.

9.7. Almost every year there were riots on the Twelfth of July and these increased in ferocity as Belfast grew to be a great industrial city. Disturbances led to the suppression of the Orange Order and the Twelfth of July celebrations in the 1830s and 1840s. In 1845 the ban was lifted. On 12 July 1849 the Orange Lodges of Ballyward District (under police and military protection) had visited Tollymore Park, Co. Down, to honour the 4th Earl of Roden who was the Grand Master of Ireland. The Lodges turned homewards in procession through Bryansford. When Ribbonmen barred the road through the defile at the western end of what is now the Forest Park, the famous 'Battle of Dolly's Brae' was fought. This resulted in the deaths of at least five Catholics. Consequently, Orange marches were banned under the Party Processions Act (1850).

9.8. Riots that began as a reaction to street preaching reached a climax on 18 July 1857, a Saturday, when the mills stopped work at two o'clock. Stones prised from streets, and walls were heaped along the roads. The police were almost completely overcome by the rioters. After several hours of destruction, the constabulary moved in with loaded rifles. The sound of gunfire continued throughout the night and resumed the following day. On 1 August a Catholic mill-girl was shot dead by a bullet from Sandy Row and on 6 August Catholics formed a gun-club at a meeting in Smithfield. Further disturbances followed on 6 September when the Revd Hugh 'Roaring' Hanna, minister of Berry Street Presbyterian Church, addressed Protestants in front of Duncrue Salt Works. It took several charges of Hussars to clear the streets of rioters.

9.9. On Monday, 8 August 1864, Catholics, who had attended a ceremony to lay the foundation stone for a monument to Daniel O'Connell in Dublin, returned by rail to Belfast's Victoria Street station at 9 p.m. The train was greeted at Boyne Bridge by a burning effigy of O'Connell. There were almost continuous sectarian clashes for the rest of the month. Many mills were forced to close. As ferocious rioting broke out afresh the government sent from Dublin a train of 27 wagons carrying two field guns and reinforcements, raising the total engaged in restoring order in Belfast to 1,300 soldiers and 1,000 armed constabulary. But the disturbances continued.

9.10. On Tuesday 16 August, people from Sandy Row attacked the Dublin train. Subinspector John Caulfield, sword in hand, led the constabulary into Durham Street where he was met by a volley of bullets and paving stones. He drew his men up on Boyne Bridge and ordered them to fire. Meanwhile, the shipwrights marched into the town centre, plundered gun shops and hardware stores in High Street and returned to attack St Peter's Pro-Cathedral in the Falls. At Millfield they met the 84th Regiment under the command of Lieutenant Clayton. Even though there were now in Belfast six troops of the 4th Hussars, half a battery of artillery, the 89th Regiment of infantry, 1,000 Irish Constabulary, 150 town police, and 300 special constables, the fighting persisted. The hospitals were filled with the wounded and by 18 August, eleven had been killed.

9.11. Urban migration from the late eighteenth century meant that Derry became a predominantly Catholic city. In April 1869 there was sectarian rioting in city during the visit of Prince Arthur, Duke of Connacht and Strathearn. Two Apprentice Boys died of injuries sustained during the violence. The government's Londonderry Riot Inquiry of that year found that 'the character of the demonstrations (by the Apprentice Boys) has certainly undergone a change, and, among the Catholic lower classes at least, they are now regarded with the most hostile feelings'. Further riots followed in 1870. Due to their perceived lack of impartiality, the Borough police in both Belfast and Derry were disbanded and replaced by the Royal Irish Constabulary (RIC).

9.12. Belfast was not alone in being periodically convulsed by sectarian rioting: riots were on a large scale simply because of the city's great size. However, it was unique in the British Isles in having two very large indigenous but distinct groups violently hostile to each other. Commissions of Inquiry blamed provocative Protestant celebrations and many pointed to the Orange Order as a main cause of sectarianism. The Order, which had been poorly represented in Belfast at the beginning of the century, had 35 lodges there by 1851. Street preaching and the great Protestant revival of 1859, when 35,000 attended a monster meeting in the Botanic Gardens, also helped to emphasise religious divisions. As a result, Catholics joined Ribbon societies and Fenian circles which were usually more sectarian in character than their parent bodies in the south. Sectarianism was largely uninfluenced by levels of unemployment or economic factors. The great riots of 1864 came, for example, when Belfast was in the middle of the great linen boom of 1862–7.

9.13. BIBLIOGRAPHY: Raymond Crotty, *The Irish land question and sectarian violence* (Ilford, 1981). Jacqueline R. Hill, 'Artisans, sectarianism and politics in Dublin, 1829–48', in *Saothar: Journal of the Irish Labour History Society*, 7 (1981), 12–37. Brian Walker, 'Party organisation in Ulster, 1865–92: registration agents and their activities', in P. Roebuck (ed.) *Plantation to partition: essays in Ulster history in honour of J.L. McCracken* (Belfast, 1981). Ronnie Munck, 'Class conflict and sectarianism in Belfast: from it origins to the 1930s', in *Contemporary Crises*, 9 (1985), 149–67. Charles Dillon, 'The Ulster Canal and sectarian strife', in *Dúiche Néill*, 1:3 (1988), 95–98. Anthony D. Buckley, 'The spirit of Irish sectarianism', in *Canadian Journal of Irish Studies*, 15:2 (1989), 23–29. Joseph Liechty, *Roots of sectarianism in Ireland: chronology and reflections* (Belfast, 1993). Inter Church Centre, Belfast, *Sectarianism: a discussion document – the report of the working party on sectarianism* (Belfast, 1993). A.C. Hepburn, *A past apart: studies in the history of Catholic Belfast, 1850–1950* (Belfast, 1996). Joseph Liechty, 'Sectarianism and the churches: the legacy and the challenge', in Denis Carroll (ed.), *Religion in Ireland: past present and future* (Blackrock, 1999), 86–95. Sean Farrell, *Rituals and riots: sectarian violence and political culture in Ulster, 1784–1866* (Lexington, KY, 2000). Richard McMahon, '"The madness of party": sectarian homicide in Ireland, 1801–1850', in *Crime, Histoire et Sociétés*, 11:1 (2007), 83–112.

TOMÁS O'RIORDAN

10. The Union

10.1. Since the grant of Ireland to Henry II in 1155/6 by Pope Adrian IV and Henry's visit to Ireland in 1171/2, Ireland was a lordship attached to the English Crown, a jurisdiction separate from that of England. It remained so until 1541. Throughout the Middle Ages, Ireland had its own parliament, though its powers were limited, especially by Poynings' Law (1494) which required that all legislation proposed by the Irish Parliament should first be submitted to the King and his English Council, and the Irish Parliament might only be summoned if they approved of it. In 1541 the Act of 33 Henry VIII declared the King of England to be King of Ireland. This made Ireland a sister kingdom of England, sharing the same monarch. Constitutionally, this was the position of Ireland until the passing of the Act of Union in 1800.

10.2. The idea of a legislative union of Great Britain and Ireland had been considered many times in the eighteenth century. In 1707 England and Scotland were united by Act of Parliament. In 1709, the Irish House of Lords presented an address to the Lord Lieutenant expressing the hope that Irish Union with Britain would follow the Scottish one. This was rejected in England. When the idea of Union was suggested on the English side after the 1750s it was fiercely resisted in Ireland. The grant of legislative independence to the Irish Parliament in 1782 gave the impression that the idea had been dropped. However, the situation was changed by the war with France and still further by the 1798 Rebellion. A French expedition landed at Killala on 22 August 1798, and this showed that Ireland could be used as a base for an attack on Britain. Had there been peace at home and abroad, and no threat of a French attack, it is very unlikely that the Irish Parliament would have voted itself out of existence.

10.3. The British Prime Minister, Pitt, decided on union of the two kingdoms and in 1798 the Viceroy, Lord Cornwallis, was charged with the task of getting it through. Pitt's plan was that union and Catholic Emancipation should go together. The government's main argument was security: the Union was essential to preserve the Protestant ascendancy. Public feeling ran strongly against the Union and there were impassioned debates in the Irish Parliament. But these were concerns of the Irish Establishment, mostly the nobility, the gentry and office holders. Cornwallis said truly: 'The mass of the people of Ireland do not care one farthing about the Union'. It mattered very little to them whether the laws (which in any case they saw as unjust) were made in Dublin or London.

10.4. Pitt believed that it was crucial that the Union be carried by a large majority and that it should have public support, Catholic as well as Protestant. He sought the endorsement of the Catholic hierarchy who were led by the Archbishop of Dublin, John Thomas Troy. The hierarchy (who hated revolution as much as did the Protestant landlords) and the Catholic middle classes were willing to accept the Union if Catholic Emancipation followed. Lord Cornwallis and Viscount Castlereagh, the Chief Secretary, were authorised to assure them that indeed Emancipation would follow the Union, but the government would not allow Catholic Emancipation by the Irish Parliament. The only Catholic opposition came from Daniel O'Connell and a group of Catholic barristers.

10.5. The government was determined on Union and Castlereagh set ably to work, using every possible means to create a majority for it in the Irish Parliament. Peerages, jobs, and pensions were liberally promised. In Ireland, members of Parliament were returned by boroughs which were mostly corrupt and by counties where results were almost always determined by the landlords. Castlereagh did a deal with the borough owners: the going rate was £15,000 (approx. €1.2 million at 2009 values) per seat, paid equally to those who supported and opposed the Union. In all, over £1,250,000 (approx. €99 million) was spent in buying the boroughs. In the case of the counties, Castlereagh set out to win every possible vote by promises, threats, and bribes. Support for the Union was made a pre-condition for any government office or favour. As Castlereagh put it, his job was 'to buy out, and secure to the Crown forever, the fee simple of Irish corruption'.

10.6. Parliament met in January 1800 and its debates were lengthy and very heated. However, the Unionist majority cobbled together by Castlereagh could not be shaken and the government remained determined. The opposition's campaign came to nothing. As J.C. Beckett stated: 'The barristers, the Orangemen, the country gentry, protested and threatened. But what could they do? The national spirit of 1782 was dead; the revolutionaries of 1798 were either cowed, or indifferent to the fate of the ascendancy parliament; and the country was full of British troops'.

10.7. On 28 March 1800 the terms of the Union were agreed by both houses of the Irish Parliament. An identical Bill was laid before the British and Irish Parliaments. The British Act of Union became law on 2 July 1800; the royal assent was given to Irish Act of Union on 1 August 1800; and the Irish Parliament met for the last time on 2 August. The Act of Union came into force on 1 January 1801.

10.8. The terms of the Union were set out in eight articles: the first four dealt with political matters, the fifth with the church, the sixth with trade, the seventh with finance, and the eighth with law. The political articles created the 'United Kingdom of Great Britain and Ireland'. The Parliament of the United Kingdom was to have Irish representatives: 4 lords spiritual and 28 lords temporal, elected by the peers of Ireland, were to sit in the House of Lords; there were to be 100 Irish members of the House of Commons, 2 for each county, 2 for Dublin and Cork, and one for 31 towns and boroughs; and not more than 20 Irish MPs might hold gainful office under the Crown in Ireland at any one time. By the fifth article, the Church of Ireland and the Church of England were united. The sixth article established free trade between Ireland and Britain but duties on certain goods, notably textiles, were to remain for twenty years. The seventh article provided that the financial systems of the two countries should remain separate, though it was envisaged that under certain circumstances they should be united. Ireland was to contribute two-seventeenths to the expenditure of the United Kingdom. The eighth article provided that all laws and the jurisdiction of all courts at the time of the passing of the Act of Union should continue as they were before.

10.9. Under the Union Ireland had an administration separate from that of the United Kingdom, directed by a Lord Lieutenant and Chief Secretary, and real integration of the two countries did not take place. The power to make laws had moved from Dublin to London, but the same Protestant ascendancy remained in control of central and local government in Ireland. Those who had so eloquently opposed the Union soon took office in the Dublin government. As J.C. Beckett says, 'Within two decades, the Irish Protestants, as a body, had become ardent supporters of the Union, which they regarded as their only protection against the Roman Catholic majority. They were convinced that this support, self-interested as it was, gave them a special claim on government favour; and they tended to judge every government's Irish policy by its effect on their own position and influence'.

10.10. The Roman Catholics, whose leaders had supported the Union, turned against it, especially when the promise of Catholic Emancipation was not kept. The Act of Union was the context of all subsequent political activity in the nineteenth century, and in the early twentieth. In the words of Oliver MacDonagh, '… the Act of Union possessed for many the solemnity of fundamental law, far beyond the pretensions of ordinary legislation. With the finality of a vast constitutional rearrangement, it fenced in the range of the politically possible in the nineteenth century'.

10.11. Nationalists of all colours saw the Act of Union as illegal; moderates sought the restoration of the Irish Parliament, radicals sought an independent Irish Republic.

10.12. BIBLIOGRAPHY: Sir Jonah Barrington, *Historic memoirs of Ireland: comprising secret records of the national convention, the rebellion, and the Union with delineations of the principal characters* (2 vols, London, 1835). Sir Jonah Barrington, *The rise and fall of the Irish nation* (Dublin, 1833). J.C. Beckett, *The making of modern Ireland, 1603–1923* (London, 1966), 268–91. G.C. Bolton, *The passing of the Irish Act of Union: a study in parliamentary politics* (London, 1966). Oliver MacDonagh, *Ireland* (Englewood Cliffs, NJ, 1968), 1–21. Patrick Buckland, *Irish Unionism, 1885–1923: a documentary history* (Belfast, 1973). Oliver MacDonagh, 'Ireland and the Union, 1801–70', in W.E. Vaughan (ed.), *A new history of Ireland*, v: *Ireland under the Union, i: 1801–1870* (Oxford, 1989), 46–65. George Boyce & Alan O'Day (ed.), *Defenders of the Union: a survey of British and Irish Unionism since 1801* (London & New York, 2001). Peter Collins (ed.), *Nationalism and Unionism: conflict in Ireland, 1885–1921* (Belfast, 1994). Michael Brown, Patrick M. Geoghegan & James Kelly (eds), *Irish Act of Union, 1800: bicentennial essays* (Dublin, 2001). Patrick M. Geoghegan, *Lord Castlereagh* (Life and Times Series, No. 16) (Dundalk, 2002).

DONNCHADH Ó CORRÁIN AND TOMÁS O'RIORDAN

11. Ultramontanism

11.1. This is the tendency in the Roman Catholic Church to centralise power and authority in the hands of the Pope and the Papal Curia and to limit the role of national kings, governments, and diocesan bishops. Ultramontane means 'beyond the mountain' (that is, the Alps) and was applied to those who looked to Rome for decisions, took their lead from the Papacy, and supported papal policy, often without question. The First Vatican Council in 1870 was, in many ways, its defining moment. The opposite tendency is called Gallicanism (the term was originally especially applied to France, Latin *Gallia*) which minimised the authority of the Papacy over the national kings and governments, the national churches, the local bishops, and the practices of local churches.

11.2. It was believed that such central authority could help protect the Church against oppressive civil laws and unorthodox theologies. In the eighteenth century, Ultramontanism became a definite and conservative point of view, opposed to Gallicanism, to liberalism in theology, and to the French Revolution and the ideas proposed by it. In France, the Gallicans were discredited by their association with revolutionary ideas.

11.3. In the early nineteenth century, the Popes were careful not to push Ultramontanism too far, fearing a backlash from national governments and local hierarchies. They were willing to make concessions to national governments. When, for example, as a security measure to accompany a grant of Catholic Emancipation in 1808–14, it was proposed that the Crown should have the power to veto any Roman Catholic episcopal appointment if it thought the candidate politically unreliable, the Papacy was quite willing to make this concession. It was rejected by the majority of the Irish bishops, and even more forcefully by the organised Catholic laity.

11.4. Pope Pius IX (1846–78) took an extreme position on the powers of the Papacy. He extended papal authority in his *Syllabus of errors* (1864). It set out papal teaching in regard to the Church and its rights, civil society and the Church, and it asserted the temporal power of the Pope. It condemned rationalism, socialism, communism, and liberalism, and forbade Catholics to hold such beliefs or ideologies. Much of this teaching was embodied in the decisions of the First Vatican Council (1870). The Council also enacted the dogma of Papal Infallibility, namely, that in making solemn pronouncements on faith and morals the Pope could not err. In future, there was no room for Gallicanism. This was a triumph for Ultramontanists: the *Syllabus of errors* and the decisions of the First Vatican Council were their programme in the later nineteenth century.

11.5. Ultramontanism in Ireland is associated with the Rome-educated Paul Cullen (1803–78), Archbishop of Armagh, later Archbishop of Dublin (made a cardinal in June 1866). His object was to re-organise the Irish Catholic Church and bring it into total conformity with Rome in organisation, liturgy, cult and devotions. In this large project, he was successful and ever since his time the Irish Roman Catholic Church has been the most tamely ultramontane of the western churches.

11.6. BIBLIOGRAPHY: Jeffrey von Arx (ed.), *Varieties of Ultramontanism* (Washington, DC, 1998). Desmond Bowen, *Paul Cardinal Cullen and the shaping of modern Irish Catholicism* (Dublin, 1983).

DONNCHADH Ó CORRÁIN

CHAPTER 12

Key personalities

1. Mary Aikenhead (1787–1858)

1.1. Catholic nun and founder of the Irish Sisters of Charity. Mary Aikenhead was born 19 January 1787 in Cork city. Her mother, also called Mary, was a member of the wealthy Catholic merchant family, the Stackpooles, and her father, David Aikenhead, was a medical doctor and pharmacist. Her father was first-generation Irish with a Scottish military background. He was largely sympathetic to Irish Catholics because of their poverty, and the discriminatory property laws then in force. Mary was baptised a Protestant at Shandon Church in Cork city. As a young child, she was sent to the countryside to recover from ill-health. There, she lived for six years with a devout Catholic family, the O'Rourkes, who often brought her to church with them. Upon her return to Cork city, she often attended mass. Her maternal grandmother and a widowed aunt also introduced her to the Ursuline and Presentation nuns in the city. These early religious experiences had an important influence on her.

1.2. Aikenhead attended a city school. She was determined to continue practising the Catholic faith, but in secret because of her father's opposition. With the help of a housemaid, she attended mass every morning before breakfast. In 1801, when she was aged 14, her father's health declined. He converted to Catholicism on his deathbed. At the age of 16, she also converted publicly to the Catholic faith. When she finished school, she decided to dedicate herself to helping the poor in Cork. Through the connections of her good friend Anna Maria O'Brien (1785–1871), Aikenhead went to Dublin and was introduced to a circle of Catholic women engaged in helping the city's poor. As well as charitable work, she developed an interest in the religious life. After the death of her mother, Archbishop Murray of Dublin asked her to set up a congregation of Sisters of Charity and arranged the necessary authorisation from the Vatican.

1.3. To prepare for this, she entered the Bar Convent of the Institute of the Blessed Virgin in York, England, in June 1812. There she trained with other young Irish novices for three years. She took Sister Mary Augustine as her name in religion. She returned to Dublin in September 1815 and pronounced her vows to the archbishop. She opened her first convent in North William Street, Dublin and was appointed Superior-General of the new Congregation of the Irish Sisters of Charity, an uncloistered order. As well as the vows of poverty, chastity and obedience, which all religious took, the Sisters of Charity also took an oath of service to the poor. Under her guidance, the new order was devoted to helping prisoners, the poor, and the sick. She worked hard to build up the order and with voluntary assistance, established hospitals and schools throughout

Ireland. In 1816 she got papal recognition of her work but the Order's constitution had to wait until 1833 to get papal approval. Though very short of funds, Aikenhead opened a second convent in Stanhope Street in 1819, where she personally instructed the novices. The authorities at Kilmainham Gaol invited the Sisters of Charity to undertake prison visits: Aikenhead herself visited female prisoners who had been sentenced to death.

1.4. In spite of ill-health, she established ten new convents. The Sisters of Charity quickly gained a reputation for their great work amongst Ireland's poorest. They provided schools, hospitals, and refuges for women. They set up several convents in Dublin, as well as Peacock Lane, Cork (1826); Lady Lane, Waterford (1842); Clarinbridge, Galway (1844), and Clonmel, Co. Tipperary (1845). During the terrible cholera epidemic of 1832, the Sisters of Charity worked tirelessly to tend its victims.

1.5. Appalled by conditions in the poorest areas and especially the city slums, Aikenhead appealed for donations to start a hospital for the most needy. She bought the town house of Lord Meath in St Stephen's Green, Dublin, for £3,000, and opened it as St Vincent's Hospital in January 1834 – the first Catholic hospital in Ireland since the Reformation and the first to be run by nuns. At the start the hospital had no equipment and few qualified staff. Aikenhead sent sisters to Paris for training. Once established, it provided its own training courses. The rigorous standards of its training and the dedication of its staff quickly gained it a high reputation.

1.6. As the Order grew, Aikenhead's health deteriorated and she spent most of the last thirty years of her life in a wheelchair or on a couch, crippled with spinal problems, oedema, and eventually paralysis. But ill-health did not dampen her spirit and energy. She continued to play a very active role in organising the convents and raising money. New institutions were established abroad, including Australia. In 1838, the Archbishop of Sydney, Dr John Polding, asked her to send five sisters to Australia, which at that time had few institutions. The sisters set up Sydney's famous St Vincent's Hospital in 1857. In 1845 Aikenhead founded Our Lady's Hospice for the Dying at Harold's Cross, Dublin, and she herself died there in the summer of 1858. Her coffin was carried to the graveyard in Donnybrook by the workingmen of Dublin.

Her congregation has since spread to England, Scotland, the USA, Venezuela, Zambia and Nigeria. It administers large schools, orphanages, and hospitals. In 1921, Pope Benedict XV agreed to her beatification, the step before canonisation to sainthood. In 1958, the Irish government issued a stamp to commemorate her life's work.

1.7. BIOGRAPHY AND STUDIES: Maria Nethercott, *The story of Mary Aikenhead, foundress of the Irish Sisters of Charity* (New York, 1897). Anon., *The life and work of Mary Aikenhead, foundress of the Congregation of Irish Sisters of Charity, 1787–1858* (London, 1924). Margery Bailey Butler, *A candle was lit: life of Mother Mary Aikenhead* (Dublin &

London, 1953). Margaret M. Donovan, *Apostolate of love: Mary Aikenhead, 1787–1858* (Melbourne, 1979). Donal Blake, *Servant of the poor: Mary Aikenhead* (Dublin, 2002).

MARGARET FITZPATRICK AND TOMÁS O'RIORDAN

2. William Carleton (1794–1889)

2.1. A novelist, William Carleton was born 4 March 1794, in Prillisk, near Clogher, Co. Tyrone. His parents were small farmers and he was the youngest of fourteen children. They spoke Irish and English and had an interest in local history, story-telling, singing, and folklore. He was educated in hedge schools and later at a classical school run by the Revd Dr Keenan. This seems to have beeen a preparation for the priesthood but he abandoned this course and spent a good deal of his time idling. He left home and travelled around the county, taking temporary jobs as a teacher. When his family was evicted in 1813 he had joined the Ribbonmen, a secret agrarian society. He soon abandoned that, and remained a supporter of the Union throughout his life. He worked as private tutor to the children of a comfortable Co. Louth farmer. After reading La Sage's romantic *Gil Blas*, Carleton was fired with an enthusiasm to travel and see the world. He did not get far. He failed to get a teaching post at Clongowes Wood College, went to Dublin, and converted to Protestantism. It seems that this had little to do with religion: he wanted respectability and security in life. He held a few more temporary jobs as a teacher and then became a clerk in the Church of Ireland Sunday School Society. He later applied to join the army, addressing his application to the colonel in Latin. Around 1822 he married Jane Anderson, the daughter of a Protestant schoolmaster.

2.2. Through the Association for Discountenancing Vice, Carleton got teaching posts in Mullingar and Carlow. He soon returned to Dublin. He had been writing short stories and essays since his secondary school days. He drew on his knowledge of Irish life to write sketches for the *Christian Examiner*, an evangelical and anti-Catholic paper published by the Revd Caesar Otway, who encouraged him to write. Here his first article was entitled 'A Pilgrimage to Saint Patrick's Purgatory', based on his own youthful pilgrimage to Lough Derg. This was the start of a long and successful career as a novelist. Carleton's *Traits and stories of the Irish peasantry* (1830–3) won him a great reputation. He became friendly with the poet and scholar Samuel Ferguson and became well known in Dublin's literary world. He was an important contributor to the *Dublin University Magazine*, an important cultural journal, launched in 1833 by Isaac Butt, Caesar Otway, Ferguson and others. In 1837–8 it published his novel *Fardorougha, the miser* as a serial. This is a tale of the Irish passion for land.

2.3. Carleton offered to help Robert Peel to prevent Emancipation and to prove that O'Connell, the Catholic Association, and the priests were involved in agrarian crime. He denounced the Irishman, that 'creature of agitation', as 'a poor, skulking dupe' who was at once 'insolent and arrogant'. However, in 1843 he decided to write for *The Nation* and for the *Irish Tribune*, papers dedicated to the cause of Irish independence. He became acquainted with Thomas Davis, Charles Gavan Duffy and others in their circle. He knew most of the men who led the disastrous Young Ireland rising of 1848 and regarded them as 'insane politicians'. He never supported Young Ireland's nationalism. Carleton's concept of nationality was broad and avoided the traditional associations of race and creed. He cherished what was unique or valuable in Irish life, and records with wonderful fidelity the English speech of the country people of his day.

2.4. His *Traits and stories of the Irish peasantry* is based on his knowledge of the character and folklore of the people he grew up with or met on his travels. It gives an accurate and vivid description of life in rural Ireland in the early nineteenth century and offers a special insight into the experiences and minds of the people he knew best – small farmers, labourers, and craftsmen. It was an instant success, often reprinted. Pleased with the great response to his first major work, he published *Tales of Ireland* in 1834. Many of Carleton's novels – for example, *Valentine McClutchy* (1845), *Willy Reilly and his Dear Colleen Bawn* (1855), and *Redmond Count O'Hanlon, the Irish rapparee* (1862) – deal with pressing social and political issues of the day. His most famous novel, *The black prophet: a tale of Irish Famine* (1847), set during the Great Famine, describes the moral and social ills of Irish society and the horrors of famine. It is a powerfully emotive and provocative account that quickly became a bestseller. Other stories were prompted by the land problem and secret societies – themes and events that dominated people's minds.

2.5. Although Carleton was prolific and successful, he was eternally of money because of family expenses and his heavy drinking. Friends and admirers, including other prominent writers such as Maria Edgeworth, petitioned the government to give him some financial help, something that was common for public figures at this time. He was granted a civil list pension of £200 (approx. €15,000 at 2009 values). This was seen as a Whig ploy to keep him from writing in advanced revolutionary nationalist newspapers. This did not solve his money problems and copyright disputes and disagreements with his publisher did not help. Financial insecurity affected the quality of his writing. He accepted too many commissions and his writing suffered as he struggled to complete them quickly. Despite his great popularity in London (several publishers sought his work), he still had debts of several hundred pounds. His attempt to raise funds by public readings was hindered by his failing health, and the British Prime Minister Benjamin Disraeli refused to increase his pension. Nevertheless, Carleton continued to write until his death in Rathmines, Dublin, on 30 January 1869.

2.6. Modern literary critics describe his post-Famine work as mediocre in quality and often sentimental and moralising, except for his unfinished *Autobiography*. Nevertheless, his works are important sources for life and attitudes in nineteenth-century Ireland.

2.7. AUTOBIOGRAPHY, BIOGRAPHY AND STUDIES: William Carleton, *The autobiography of William Carleton* (London, 1968). D.J. O'Donoghue, *The life of William Carleton,* *being his autobiography and letters, and an account of his life and writings* (2 vols, London, 1896; repr. New York & London, 1979). Benedict Kiely, *Poor scholar: a study of the works and days of William Carleton* (London, 1947). Thomas Flanagan, *The Irish novelists, 1800–1850* (New York, 1959) 255–330. André Boué, *William Carleton: romancier Irlandais, 1794–1869* (Paris, 1978). Robert Lee Wolff, *William Carleton: Irish peasant novelist* (New York, 1981). Eileen A. Sullivan, *William Carleton* (Boston, 1983). Barbara Hayley, *Carleton's Traits and stories and the 19th century Anglo-Irish tradition*, Irish Literary Studies 12 (Gerrards Cross, 1983).

MARGARET FITZPATRICK

3. Paul Cullen (1803–78)

3.1. Paul Cullen was born on 29 April 1803, near Prospect, Co. Kildare, the third son in a family of fifteen children (eight boys and seven girls). He belonged to a prosperous farming family with clerical connections, and was educated initially at the Irish Quaker school in nearby Ballitore, founded in 1726 by Abraham Shackleton. In 1816, at the age of 14, he went to study for the priesthood at Carlow College. In 1820, he was offered a place at Maynooth College by Dr James Doyle, Bishop of Kildare and Leighlin (1819–34), to prepare for the priesthood. Doyle had been impressed by his abilities when he was a professor at Carlow College. Cullen's father was against his attending Maynooth because students had to swear an oath of allegiance to the King of England. Instead, at the urging of his uncle, James Maher, he was sent to the Urban College of Propaganda Fide in Rome. Aged 17 when he arrived in Rome, he was 47, a Roman by culture, and Archbishop of Armagh, when he left it. Rome had shaped his life.

3.2. In his first year, Cullen was recognised as a promising student, especially in languages (Latin, Hebrew and Italian), and was granted a free place in the college. He was an excellent student, a prize-winner with all the qualities of a good seminarian. In 1826, he took first prize in dogmatic and moral theology, Hebrew, and Greek. The prizes were presented by Pope Leo XII. He took his doctorate in theology in 1828, and defended it in the presence of the Pope. He was ordained in 1829 by Cardinal Pietro Caprano. His bishop, James Doyle, wanted him back in Ireland to teach in Carlow College, but the Roman authorities held on to him. Cullen was appointed Professor of Greek, Hebrew and Scripture in his old college. In 1832, he was made Rector of the Irish College in Rome by Pope Gregory XVI, a position he held until 1849.

3.3. Cullen was appointed the official agent in Rome of the Irish bishops. This had two important results. First, the position carried a salary of £100 per annum, a comfortable income. Second, as the bishops' agent (something he was very good at), he got to know about all Irish church business done at Rome, he became well known to the papal officials, and made powerful friends in the Curia. He was on the inside track. He was a close friend of the great scholar August Theiner, an expert consultant to the Curia, whose

Vetera monumenta (Rome, 1864) contains the Popes' correspondence about Ireland, 1216–1547.

3.4. The Irish College in Rome expanded under Cullen's careful rule. Student numbers doubled – from 20 in 1832 to over 40 in 1835. As Rector, he became a close friend of two popes, Gregory XVI and Pius IX. He used his position and contacts to protect the interests of the Irish church, and to counter British influence at the Vatican. Pope Gregory XVI, anxious to keep Cullen in Rome, presented him with the convent and beautiful church of St Agatha of the Goths on the Quirinal to house the expanding Irish community.

3.5. At home, the bishops were bitterly divided over education. Most accepted the national school system, established in 1832. Although the government controlled it, the Catholic Church was able to influence how the schools were run, and some bishops were satisfied with that. By 1838, John MacHale, Archbishop of Tuam, had persuaded himself that the British government was going to use the schools to undermine the faith of Irish Catholic children. But Daniel Murray, Archbishop of Dublin, was a member of the Board that governed the educational system. MacHale accused Murray of being a 'castle bishop' and a betrayer of his Church. A bitter public quarrel between the bishops went on for the next three years, and both sides made appeals to Rome. The Vatican consulted Cullen who advised that the schools were no danger to faith. In 1841, Propaganda gave its astute decision: let each bishop deal with the matter in his own diocese as he thought fit.

3.6. The quarrel between Murray and MacHale broke out again when the government decided to establish three non-denominational Queen's Colleges to give university education to Catholics and Presbyterians. Cullen and most of the bishops were unwisely and intemperately opposed to this plan, and in 1848 Pope Pius IX categorically condemned the Queen's Colleges as a danger to the faith.

3.7. Soon Rome was swept into revolution; the Pope fled in disguise, and a Roman Republic was proclaimed. In the crisis, Cullen made himself very useful. He took over as Rector of the Urban College which he skilfully protected. He was still Rector of the Irish College and he gave asylum there to several clerics and cardinals wanted by the republican regime. The Pope's gratitude knew no bounds. The Archbishop of Armagh, William Crolly, died in April 1849. The bishops were so bitterly divided that the Pope decided to appoint Crolly's successor himself. He selected his good friend Cullen in December 1849. He was consecrated as Archbishop of Armagh in February 1850 and sent to Ireland as Apostolic Delegate [papal representative to a country with no diplomatic relations with Rome] to reform the church and put an end to the in-fighting of the bishops. Cullen was an unconditional and life-long supporter of Pius IX. When Pius IX called on Catholics in early 1860 to help him defend his temporal power against France and Piedmont-Sardinia, Cullen launched a national appeal and collected the vast sum of

£80,000 (approx. €6.4 million). He also recruited an Irish Brigade, commanded by the handsome and ineffectual Major Myles O'Reilly, to defend the Papal States against Garibaldi in 1859. His reward: he was made cardinal in 1866 by Pius IX.

3.8. Within three months of his return to Ireland, Cullen undertook his first major task, the Synod of Thurles (1850), the first national synod held in Ireland for centuries. Its purpose was to restore ecclesiastical discipline and bring reform and unity to the divided Irish church. In May he was translated to Dublin. Now he was much concerned with education. He tried to counter the interdenominational education provided by the Queen's Colleges by establishing the Catholic University in 1854. He invited John Henry Newman, a distinguished Oxford convert from Anglicanism, to be the University's first Rector. Cullen's ambition – one shared by Newman – was that the Catholic University would become Europe's leading English-speaking Catholic University, and that it would attract students from the English-speaking world, including the United States. In this he was to be disappointed. The government yielded to Cullen's demand for denominational liberty in education, and set up the Powis Commission of Inquiry in 1869. This commission eventually adopted many of Cullen's proposals. One was the denominational training of teachers. In 1875, St Patrick's Training College, Drumcondra, was founded.

3.9. Cullen was also a strict disciplinarian and worked incessantly to improve the morale, the education, and the lives of the clergy. He was suspicious about Maynooth's independence (such as it was) and he got it firmly under the control of the bishops. In 1859, he founded the diocesan seminary, Holy Cross College at Clonliffe. He established the *Irish Ecclesiastical Record* in 1864, an official journal for the clergy to communicate papal encyclicals, decisions, and instructions to priests and religious, and to inform them on history, literature, and the Catholic position on current intellectual problems. This was part of his efforts to bring the Catholic Church in Ireland into line with Roman practice.

3.10. By 1860, Cullen had reduced MacHale's once formidable power base among the bishops to three or four in a body of thirty and he had become the dominant figure in the Irish church. He cared nothing for the criticisms of politicians, of any persuasion. He was against priests in politics and, heedless of his own unpopularity, he opposed all political movements that did not, in his view, serve the Catholic Church and Ireland. Though he had helped Frederick Lucas to win the Co. Meath seat in 1852, Cullen opposed the Independent Irish Party. He had a Roman cleric's hatred of secret societies. He condemned Young Ireland (he denounced Gavan Duffy as 'an Irish Mazzini'), the Fenians ('a compound of folly and wickedness'; he had them proscribed by Pius IX in 1870), and the Independent Irish Party as 'sowers of dissension, and a source of ruin to the Irish cause'. In 1861 he forbade the use of the Pro-Cathedral, Dublin, for the lying-in-state of Terence Bellew McManus, the Young Irelander. His petition to the Viceroy did, however, save General Thomas F. Burke, the Fenian leader, from hanging. He disapproved of the Home Rule movement and its leader, the Protestant Isaac Butt. His aim was to get redress by constitutional means for what he saw as the wrongs of previous centuries. He tried to channel nationalism away from the Fenians and to his own ends by establishing the National Association in 1864: its policies were denominational education, land reform, and the disestablishment of the Church of Ireland. It failed.

3.11. He played a leading part in the deeply reactionary First Vatican Council (1870). His definition of papal infallibility was adopted with minor modifications. He presided over the National Synod of Maynooth in 1875.

3.12. Cullen is the principal maker of the kind of modern Irish Catholicism that lasted from his day until the end of the twentieth century – pietistic, puritan, and priest-ridden, apart from a certain nationalist rebelliousness from time to time. He is responsible for 'the devotional revolution', including the introduction of the Italianate *Quarant' ore* or 'Forty Hours Adoration', 'Benediction' and other devotions; and a corresponding rejection of any traditional devotion to local saints, patterns, holy wells and the like, as superstitious and uncouth. Most new churches were dedicated to saints of the universal church, not Irish saints. Clerical numbers doubled. As one would expect, attendance at Sunday Mass rose dramatically, to over 90 per cent by the 1880s; and it remained at that high level for nearly a century. Parishes were subjected to 'missions', parish retreats by Redemptorists, Passionists, and other religious orders who, like fundamentalist Protestant preachers, harangued the people more on the fires of hell than the joys of heaven. The laity were organised into sodalities and confraternities to encourage religious devotions. There were nuns and teaching brothers who ran schools in most towns, and if their stated purpose was to teach the poor, in fact they formed the middle classes and made piety as much the mark of the bourgeoisie as manners.

3.13. Cullen's loyalty and commitment to the Holy See was profound. As Emmet Larkin states: 'he was first and foremost a Roman. His allegiance to Rome, in the person of the pope and his authority, temporal and spiritual, was uncompromising. How Rome stood … on any question was Cullen's point of departure'. And so far as he could make it, the Irish church was to be a Roman church in every aspect.

Cullen died suddenly at Eccles Street, Dublin on 24 October 1878. His funeral was a great public event. He was buried, according to his wishes, below the high altar in Holy Cross College, Clonliffe.

3.14. BIOGRAPHY, DOCUMENTS AND STUDIES: Patrick F. Moran (ed.), *The pastoral letters and other writings of Cardinal Cullen, Archbishop of Dublin* (Dublin, 1882). Peadar Mac Suibhne, *Paul Cullen and his contemporaries: with their letters from 1820–1902* (5 vols, Naas, 1961–77). E.R. Norman, *The Catholic Church and Ireland in the age of rebellion, 1859–1873* (London, 1965). E.D. Steele, 'Cardinal Cullen and Irish nationality', *Irish Historical Studies* 19 (1974–5), 239–60. Emmet Larkin, *The making of the Roman Catholic Church in Ireland, 1850–1860* (Chapel Hill, NC, 1980). Desmond Bowen, *Paul Cardinal Cullen and the shaping of modern Irish Catholicism* (Dublin, 1983). Emmet Larkin, *The consolidation of the Roman Catholic Church in Ireland, 1860–78* (Dublin, 1987). Colin

Barr, *Paul Cullen, John Henry Newman, and the Catholic University of Ireland, 1845–1865* (Notre Dame, IN, 2004).

DONNCHADH Ó CORRÁIN

4. William Dargan (1799–1867)

4.1. Engineer, railway contractor, and entrepreneur, William Dargan was born 28 February 1799, in Co. Carlow, the son of a small tenant farmer. From an early age he displayed a talent for mathematics. He was educated in England and served an apprenticeship in a surveyor's office. He was involved with George Stephenson's pioneering 'Rocket' project. Dargan was recommended by his local MP, Henry Brooke Parnell (who later became Secretary of State for War in the British cabinet), to the Scottish-born contractor Thomas Telford (1757–1834). Dargan's first job, though in Britain, was closely connected to Ireland. He helped Telford design and build the Holyhead Road (1820), which gave a better service to Dublin by allowing ships to dock in Holyhead Harbour rather than at Parkgate near Chester, a port subject to contrary winds. Dargan's intelligence and work so impressed Telford that when the new mail coach road was to be built from Dublin to Howth harbour, he entrusted the work to Dargan. On the successful completion of this road, the Treasury granted Dargan a gratuity of £300 (approx. €24,000 at 2009 values) in addition to his salary.

4.2. With his increased capital Dargan began his career as a contractor. He was awarded the contract for the embankment on the river Shannon, near Limerick. His first railway project in Ireland was the Dublin to Kingstown (Dún Laoghaire) line. Construction began in 1831. This was the first passenger railway line in Ireland and only the third in the United Kingdom. It was opened on 17 December 1838. Dargan was a far-sighted businessman and was involved in the construction of part of the Ulster railway line, the Dalkey line, the Thurles-Cork section of the main line from Dublin, the Mullingar-Galway section of the Midland Railway, the Belfast and Ballymena Railway, the first sections of the Belfast and Co. Down system, part of the main Dublin-Belfast line between Dundalk and Portadown, and the line from Newry to Warrenpoint. The Ulster Railway opened in August 1839, and the Great Southern and Western Railway in 1843–50. By 1853 he had constructed over 600 miles of railway, valued at £2 million (approx. €166 million), and he had contracts for a further 200 miles.

4.3. Dargan was also responsible for the construction of the Ulster Canal (1841), an ambitious project, connecting Lough Erne and Belfast. Built at a cost of £231,000 (approx. €19 million), he leased it for £400 a year. Dargan was involved in the improvements of the Belfast docks and was employed in the initial construction of what became the Harland and Wolff shipbuilding yards. The area first named Dargan's Island later became known as Queen's Island.

4.4. During this time successful railways made a great deal of money, because there was no real competition except from canals. He paid the highest wages and had a vast amount of credit at his disposal. It is estimated that he had paid out £4 million (approx. €350 million at 2009 values) in wages during the Famine years. Dargan's wealth increased substantially, but his subsequent business ventures outside of engineering projects did not prosper.

4.5. By the year 1849 Dargan began to consider how best he could use his fortune in the national interest. He made a generous donation towards the building of the National Gallery of Ireland and a statue in his memory still stands in front of the Gallery. Another major project was the introduction of flax into the south of Ireland. Flax was a crop grown in northern Ireland and was very profitable. He established mills in the Dublin area, and bought a large farm near Kildinan, some ten miles from Cork, on which he experimented in flax cultivation. He offered to supply all the local farmers with flax seed at his own expense, and to buy their crops from them at the current Belfast price. Unfortunately, very few farmers accepted his offer because many feared that flax would exhaust the soil; as a result, this expensive experiment failed miserably.

4.6. To draw attention to railways and their benefits to industry, Dargan organised and sponsored the Dublin Industrial Exhibition, which took place at the Royal Dublin Society, Ballsbridge, in 1853. Queen Victoria opened the exhibition. He provided the organisers with nearly £100,000 (approx. €8.3 million), a fifth of which he lost. His important contribution to engineering and the development of the railways was remarked upon by Queen Victoria. She later visited him at his house, Mount Anville, Dundrum, Dublin, on 29 August 1853, to offer him a baronetcy. He declined it.

4.7. His next project was the establishment of a great thread factory at Chapelizod, near Dublin, where he purchased and expanded large mill premises. This undertaking was another financial disaster. After several more financial misadventures, Dargan returned to railways. He became chairman of the Dublin, Wicklow and Wexford Railway, in which he invested nearly all his fortune. In connection with this line he spent large sums on the improvement of Bray, Co. Wicklow. He built the Turkish baths at the cost of £8,000 (approx. €700,000) and provided first-class hotel accommodation in the town. This expense, though large, would not have damaged him financially had the railway proved as successful as he had hoped. However, the depression in railway property, which had begun at this time, so lowered the value of all his investments that for a time they were of little value.

4.8. Dargan had always maintained full control of his affairs – he did not believe in employing managers – and when he fell from his horse in 1866 and was badly injured there was no one to take control of his many business interests. His affairs became disordered and his health and spirits were undermined as a result. He had to sell his splendid mansion in Dundrum but he kept his town house at 2 Fitzwilliam Square, Dublin.

He died here at the age of 68 on 7 February 1867. His widow was awarded a pension of £100 (approx. €8,000) a year on 18 June 1870. He is buried in Glasnevin cemetery where his tomb, like his statue at the National Gallery, carries the single word DARGAN.

4.9. BIOGRAPHY AND STUDIES: F.C. Wallace-Healy, *William Dargan, originator of the first Dublin Exhibition: a memoir* (Dublin, 1882). John Marshall, *A biographical dictionary of railway engineers* (Newton Abbot, 1978). Kevin O'Connor, *Ironing the land: the coming of the railway to Ireland* (Dublin, 1999). Fergus Mulligan, 'William Dargan: a business life' (PhD Thesis, Trinity College Dublin, 2002).

MARGARET FITZPATRICK (WITH A CONTRIBUTION BY TOMÁS O'RIORDAN)

5. Thomas Davis (1814–45)

5.1. Poet, journalist, and cultural nationalist, Thomas Davis was born on 24 October 1814, in Mallow, Co. Cork. He was the son of a British army surgeon, who died before he was born, and an Irish Protestant mother, Mary Atkins. In 1818, the family moved to Dublin where he was enrolled at Mr Mongan's School on Lower Mount Street. He proved to be a difficult pupil. In 1831 he entered Trinity College, Dublin where he studied history, law, political philosophy and works on travel. There he met people who remembered Wolfe Tone and Robert Emmet, both of whom had been Trinity College students and both of whom promoted the idea of a 'free and independent Ireland'. Davis found that his time spent at Trinity helped to broaden his mind. He graduated in 1836 and decided that he would travel to London and the Continent. In 1838 he returned to Trinity to complete his law studies and became Auditor of the College Historical Society. He was called to the Bar in 1837, but never practised. His eldest brother, John Nicholas Atkins Davis, a doctor, was also a famous genealogist, known by the nickname 'pedigree Davis'.

5.2. Davis first expressed his ideas of Irish nationality to the Dublin Historical Society in 1839 and subsequently in the *Citizen* (later the *Dublin Monthly Magazine*) and *Dublin Morning Register*. As Auditor of the Historical Society in 1840, he urged his audience to devote themselves to Ireland and the search for a national self-identity and used the famous phrase 'Gentlemen, you have a country'. He pleaded for serious Irish historical studies as a means of developing nationality, but above all he argued for Ireland's independence. During this time Daniel O'Connell was holding monster Repeal meetings all over the country in an attempt to persuade the British government to give Ireland back its parliament. Shortly after graduating from Trinity College, Davis joined O'Connell's Loyal National Repeal Association, thus beginning his political career. Davis had great respect for O'Connell the 'Liberator' but the two did not always agree.

5.3. In 1842–5, Davis assumed the leadership of those who left the Repeal movement to form a new political group known as the 'Young Ireland'. Like O'Connell the Young Irelanders demanded repeal of the Union. However, Davis challenged O'Connell's opposition to non-denominational education arguing that mixed education was essential for unity. Davis was disillusioned with constitutional methods and believed that Irish independence should be achieved even at the cost of bloodshed. He was more interested in promoting a vision of the future where a united Irish society would be governed by a proud and self-confident nationalism.

5.4. In 1840, Davis, along with John Blake Dillon and Charles Gavan Duffy, sub-edited the *Dublin Morning Register*. On 15 October 1842, he co-founded, again with Dillon and Duffy, *The Nation*, a weekly newspaper. Davis was its editor. In his editorials and poetry, he publicised his ideas on self-government in countless articles on Irish history and culture – antiquity, poetry, art, music, scenery, ethnology, and language. His first poem, 'My Grave' appeared in the third issue, signed 'A True Celt'. His nationalist verse gave the paper its distinctive character, introducing stirring and popular works to awaken a spirit of Irish nationalism. *The Nation* was a great success. It was read by more than a quarter of a million people, and its circulation was greater than that of any Dublin journal.

5.5. In the three years that Davis worked on the paper he wrote over 80 songs and ballads, as well as many articles and essays. In the first year alone, he wrote about 210 essays and editorials. He was paid nearly £500 (approx. €44,000 at 2009 values) per year for his work. Soon people started sending in their own poems and articles – at least twenty poems a week were coming in at the beginning of 1843. In that year a collection was made of the best works from the paper and printed under the title *The spirit of the nation*. In July 1843, it was selling at the rate of one hundred copies a day.

5.6. Davis was convinced that it was vital to reverse the anglicisation of Irish culture and he argued for the revival of the Irish language, declaring that 'a people without a language is only half a nation'. He tried to foster a nationality of the spirit by uniting the Irish of all religious traditions. His passionate spirited rhetoric had mass appeal, and his polished journalism inspired contemporaries with a vision of an Ireland free to pursue its own destiny. Davis was personally loyal to Daniel O'Connell, but was disappointed by his movement away from Repeal in 1844–5 and his alliance with the Whigs. Davis strongly supported the Colleges (Ireland) Act of 1845 but O'Connell was deeply opposed to the 'godless' Queen's Colleges and harshly criticised Davis.

5.7. Davis died of scarlet fever at just 31 years of age in his mother's house at 67 Baggot Street, Dublin, on 16 September 1845. Thousands attended his funeral, including representatives from the Corporation of Dublin, Young Ireland, the Eighty-Two Club, the Committee of the Repeal Association, and the antiquaries and scholars of the Royal Irish Academy. His fiancée, Annie Hutton, died prematurely in the summer of 1853, aged just 28.

5.8. Despite his youth and untimely death, Davis played a vital part in the birth of a strong cultural nationalism and has been celebrated as one of Ireland's greatest patriots. His prose and verse kindled enthusiasm and inspired his contemporaries with a vision of a free Ireland. His best known poems include 'A Nation Once Again', 'The West's Asleep', 'Lament for the Death of Owen Roe O'Neill', 'Fontenoy', 'Clare's Dragoons', 'Tom's Grave' and 'My Land'. T.W. Rolleston edited his prose works in 1890. His friend Charles Gavan Duffy wrote *A life of Davis* (1896) and a lengthy introduction to Davis's *The patriot parliament of 1689* (1893). Davis was named by Patrick Pearse, Arthur Griffith and John O'Leary as 'their master'. Griffith described him as 'the prophet I followed throughout my life, the man whose words and teachings I tried to translate into practice in politics'.

5.9. WRITINGS, BIOGRAPHY AND STUDIES: T.W. Rolleston (ed.), *The prose writings of Thomas Davis* (London, 1890) [online at http://www.ucc.ie/celt]. Arthur Griffith (ed.), *Thomas Davis: the thinker & teacher: the essence of his writings in prose and poetry* (Dublin, 1914). D.J. O'Donoghue (ed.), *Essays, literary and historical ... by Thomas Davis* (Dundalk, 1914). Charles Gavan Duffy, *Thomas Davis: the memoirs of an Irish patriot, 1840–46* (London, 1892). J.M. Hone, *Thomas Davis* (London & Dublin, 1934). M.J. McManus (ed.), *Thomas Davis and Young Ireland* (Dublin, 1945). J.L. Ahern, *Thomas Davis and his circle* (Waterford, 1945). T.W. Moody, *Thomas Davis, 1814–45* (Dublin, 1945). T.W. Moody, 'Thomas Davis and the Irish nation', *Hermathena*, 103 (1966), 5–31. Eileen Sullivan, *Thomas Davis* (Lewisburg, PA, 1978). John Neylon Moloney, *A soul came into Ireland: Thomas Davis 1814–1845, a biography* (Dublin, 1995). Sean Ryder, 'Speaking of '98: Young Ireland and republican memory', *Éire-Ireland*, 34 (1999), 51–69. Patrick Maume, 'Young Ireland, Arthur Griffith, and republican ideology: the question of continuity', *Éire-Ireland*, 34 (1999), 155–74. Gerry Kearns, 'Time and some citizenship: nationalism and Thomas Davis', *Bullán: an Irish Studies Review*, 5:2 (2001), 23–54. Helen Mulvey, *Thomas Davis and Ireland: a biographical study* (Washington, DC, 2003).

MARGARET FITZPATRICK

6. Charles Kickham (1828–82)

6.1. Author and Fenian leader, Charles J. Kickham was born on 9 May 1828, at Mullinahone in Co. Tipperary. A cousin of John O'Mahony, Kickham was the eldest of eight children of a prosperous shopkeeper. He was educated at Mullinahone, Co. Tipperary. It was hoped that he would practise medicine but an accident with gunpowder at the age of 13 permanently damaged his eyesight and hearing. His father was involved in anti-tithe meetings during the 1830s. The first popular movement to attract his attention was the temperance crusade launched by Fr Theobald Mathew in 1838. Kickham was influenced by the romantic ideological nationalism of Thomas Davis and the Young Irelanders. He was a also a supporter of the Repeal Association. He wrote pieces in *The Nation*, *The Celt*, *The Shamrock* and *The Irishman*. He founded a branch of the Young Ireland Confederate Club in Mullinahone in 1848 and was forced into hiding after the hapless rising at Ballingarry, Co. Tipperary.

6.2. In 1850, he worked for Tenant Right League but lost faith in political agitation after its failure in 1855. Kickham's politics became more radical and he joined the secret nationalist organisation, the Irish Republican Brotherhood (IRB) or the Fenians, in 1860. He was a committed separatist. He had a deep sense of veneration for America as a model of independent democratic nationhood and travelled there as an IRB delegate. He rose quickly up the ranks of the movement and was appointed by the Fenian leader, James Stephens, to sit on the Supreme Executive with Thomas Clarke Luby and John O'Leary. He contributed political articles to James Stephens' nationalist paper and IRB organ, the *Irish People*, which he later edited. This gave him the opportunity to develop his talents as a controversialist and propagandist. He dealt with many topics in its pages but his treatment of clerical attacks on Fenianism earned him lasting fame.

6.3. He was on the editorial staff of the *Irish People* and later became joint editor. On 15 September 1865, the Dublin Police, directed by the Castle, took possession of the *Irish People* headquarters at 12 Parliament Street and seized the entire contents of the office. The few members of the staff still on the premises were arrested and others were picked up on the street or in their homes. *Irish People* documents revealed Kickham's role in the Fenian conspiracy. On 11 November 1865, he was arrested with James Stephens. Nearly blind and almost completely deaf, Kickham was charged for writing 'treasonous' articles and for committing high treason. He was tried before Judge William Keogh and sentenced to fourteen years penal servitude. He was sent to Mountjoy Jail. On 10 February 1865, he was transferred to Pentonville Prison near London. During this time his health deteriorated because of the poor prison diet. On 14 May 1866, he was transferred to Portland Prison and later to the invalid prison at Woking in Surrey, where he served the remainder of his term. He was released in 1869, his health severely impaired, and he returned to Mullinahone, Co. Tipperary. Kickham was now the leading Fenian at liberty in Ireland. Following the annulment of the return of Jeremiah O'Donovan Rossa as MP for Tipperary, Kickham stood and polled 1,664 votes – defeated by just four votes.

6.4. In spite of his ill-health he moved to Dublin and resumed his career in the IRB. He became a member of the Supreme Council in 1872 and was its chairman until his death. He believed that the IRB should concentrate solely on winning complete independence for Ireland. If it became involved with any other issue (such as land reform), it would become corrupt and lose sight of its real objective. For Kickham, an Irish Republic could be won only by a rebellion led by the IRB and the opportune time to rebel was when Britain was engaged in a major war: 'England's difficulty is Ireland's opportunity'. Unfortunately for Kickham, Britain avoided any foreign entanglements in the early 1870s. He opposed with limited success the involvement of Fenians in the Home Rule Movement, in the New Departure, and in the Land War. However, he did not condone the agrarian outrages. He regarded the Land League's 'No Rent Manifesto' as 'criminal and cowardly'. In his opinion the Land League 'was bringing communism upon the country'. He was absolutely convinced that parliamentary politics was a 'harmful waste of time'.

6.5. Kickham was a prominent ballad writer and author of several books. His first novel *Sally Cavanagh* was written while he was in Woking prison. His sentimental, deeply nostalgic and farcical *Knocknagow, or, The Homes of Tipperary* (1879) was a huge and instant success and made him one of the most popular novelists of the nineteenth century. He published a volume of collected poems and stories in 1870. He is also well remembered for his songs, 'Rory of the Hill', 'The Irish Peasant Girl', and the ballad 'Patrick Sheehan'. Kickham often found himself in financial difficulty and a national collection was made to assist him in 1878. In his later years he did much of his writing from his bed. In 1880, he was knocked down and run over by a jaunting car in College Green and sustained a broken leg. On 19 August 1882, he suffered a stroke. Kickham died three days later at the age of 54, in Blackrock, Co. Dublin. His funeral was followed to Kingsbridge Station (now Heuston Station) by nearly ten thousand mourners. In contrast, he was buried in Mullinahone without any local clergy. The funeral oration was given by John Daly, the Limerick Fenian.

6.6. WRITINGS, BIOGRAPHY AND STUDIES: James Maher (ed.), *The valley near Slievenamon: a Kickham anthology* (Kilkenny, 1942). James Maher (ed.), *Sing a song of Kickham: songs of Charles J. Kickham* (Dublin, 1965). Richard J. Kelly, *Charles Joseph Kickham: patriot and poet* (Dublin, 1914). James J. Healy, *Life and times of Charles J. Kickham* (Dublin, 1915). William Murphy, *Charles J. Kickham: patriot, novelist and poet*, intro by Thomas Wall (Blackrock, 1976). R.V. Comerford, *Charles J. Kickham: a study in Irish nationalism and literature* (Portmarnock, 1979).

MARGARET FITZPATRICK

7. Asenath Nicholson (1792–1855)

7.1. Missionary, philanthropist and traveller, she was born Asenath Hatch in the village of Chelsea, eastern Vermont, in the United States on 24 February 1792. She was the daughter of early American settlers, Michael and Martha Hatch. Her religious affiliation is unknown but she was said to be a member of the Protestant Congregational Church. This church emphasised the importance of the Bible, freedom of the individual, and autonomy for local churches. Nicholson worked as a teacher in Chelsea during the summer months.

7.2. In the early 1830s, she moved to New York and opened a small school. There, she met and married Norman Nicholson (1790–1841), a merchant who was also interested in charity and reform. Together, they opened a temperance boarding house which provided cheap accommodation for poor working people and immigrants. It served a moral purpose also: encouraging personal reform and improvement. The Nicholsons were influenced by the ideas of Sylvester Graham (1784–1851), a prominent Presbyterian minister, a temperance crusader, and an advocate of vegetarianism. Graham also advocated abstinence and discipline in diet, cleanliness, and regular exercise as a means to a good moral life. The Nicholsons were liberals in politics, although described by some contemporaries as radicals because they condemned slavery and criticised colonialism. They operated several boarding houses in the city.

7.3. When visiting the slums near to her boarding houses, she was deeply moved by the plight of the immigrant poor, particularly the Irish in the Five Points area of New York. Nicholson was fascinated by the cheerfulness and patience of the Irish immigrants and decided after the death of her husband in 1841 to visit Ireland to study the people in their own environment. She arrived in 1844 and she travelled around the country for six months investigating the conditions in rural Ireland. She avoided cities and the society of the well-off. Her mission was to bring the Bible to the Irish poor. With a grant of Bibles from the Hibernian Society in Dublin, she distributed them to those who could read and arranged Bible readings for those who could not. She was critical of what she considered the idleness and indulgence of many upper- and middle-class Dublin women. She admired the women of the Belfast Ladies Association for the Relief of the Irish Destitution. She spent over a year travelling throughout the country, mostly on foot, often covering as much as 20 miles (32 km) in a day. During this time she wrote *Ireland's welcome to the stranger; or, An excursion through Ireland in 1844 and 1845* (published in 1847), which records her travels. She also warned of the dangers of unemployment in the Irish countryside. She was described by some as very eccentric, but her concern for the Irish and their wretchedness was sincere and heartfelt.

7.4. In 1846, Nicholson returned to Ireland. In January 1847, during the worst winter of the Famine, she began her one-woman relief operation in Dublin: a soup kitchen in Cook Street and the relief of the poor in the lanes of the Liberties. In July 1847, she left Dublin for the poorest regions of the West, from Ballina to Erris. She distributed food and clothing, visited the poor, the sick, and the starving and did her best to draw public attention in England and America to their wretched condition. She stayed here until the spring of 1848 and described her experiences in *Annals of the Famine* (1851) and *Lights and shades of Ireland* (1850). She emphasises the breadth and depth of her investigation, entering people's homes, in city and countryside: 'walking and riding, within and without, in castle and cabin, in bog and in glen, by land and by water, in church and chapel, with rector, curate and priest'. She concentrated on describing the nature of human suffering. She drew on the Bible, on hymns, and on literary allusions to describe the suffering of the Irish poor. She believed that the Famine's devastation was 'not a divine judgement, but the failure of man to use God's gifts responsibly'.

7.5. Nicholson criticised the Established Church for failing in its stewardship of its relief resources but above all she had contempt for the inadequate government schemes to relieve distress. She condemned the waste of grain in the making of alcohol. She distinguished between relief officials, whom she dismissed as bureaucratic, hierarchical and self-serving, and local volunteer workers, including clergy of all denominations and some resident landlords, whom she praised as compassionate and selfless. She reported that many government officials or 'hirelings' were guilty of crimes ranging from the unnecessary delay in distributing relief to embezzlement of government funds. She argued that provision of employment would be better than relief. She praised the establishment of industrial schools. She called for radicals such as the English abolitionist George Thompson to come and see the degraded conditions of people fed on a programme of government relief. She advised English MPs to call upon American assistance for Irish relief.

7.6. In her writings, Nicholson draws analogies between the position of American slaves and the Irish lower classes: 'never had I seen slaves so degraded. These poor creatures are in as virtual bondage to their landlords and superiors as is possible for the mind and body to be'. She stressed that her greatest object in writing *Lights and shades of Ireland* was to show the effects of the Famine on all classes, rather than to detail scenes of death by starvation.

7.7. In 1850, she travelled as an American delegate to the Universal Peace Conference in Frankfurt. She advocated radical reform, expressing her sympathy for the leaders of Young Irelanders, William Smith O'Brien and John Mitchell who, she believed, were driven into the rebellion of 1848 by their philanthropic love of country and deep sense of justice. She had little time for Daniel O'Connell's Repeal campaign because she believed that Ireland's need of employment and land reform were more pressing than Repeal.

7.8. She was, in principle, supportive of Protestant missionary colonies. However, she wanted conversions to come from conviction, not hunger. She exposed the Achill Mission for its lack of Christian charity. She admired the Famine work and the crusade for temperance of Fr Theobald Mathew of Cork.

7.9. Nicholson decided to leave Ireland in 1848 when she believed the worst of the Famine was over. She spent time in England and later on the Continent before returning to America in early 1852. Little is known about her life after that. She died of typhoid fever in New Jersey on 15 May 1855.

7.10. WRITINGS, BIOGRAPHY AND STUDIES: Asenath Nicholson, *Ireland's welcome to the stranger; or, An excursion through Ireland in 1844 and 1845* (London, 1847; repr. & ed. by Maureen Murphy, Dublin, 2002). Asenath Nicholson, *Annals of the Famine in Ireland in 1847, 1848 and 1849* (New York, 1851; repr. & ed. by Maureen Murphy, Dublin, 1988). Helen E. Hatton, *The largest amount of good: Quaker relief in Ireland, 1654–1921* (Kingston, ON, 1993). Chris Morash & Richard Hayes (eds), *Fearful realities: new perspectives on the Famine* (Dublin, 1996). Maureen Murphy, 'Asenath Nicholson and the Famine in Ireland', in Maryann Valiulis & Mary O'Dowd (eds), *Women in Irish history* (Dublin, 1997), 108–24. Melosina Lenox-Conyngham (ed.), *Diaries of Ireland: an anthology, 1590–1987* (Dublin, 1998).

MARGARET FITZPATRICK AND TOMÁS O'RIORDAN

8. Daniel O'Connell (1775–1847)

8.1. The 'Liberator', lawyer, and politician, Daniel O'Connell was born on 6 August 1775, in Carhan near Cahirciveen, Co. Kerry. The O'Connells were a wealthy landed family. O'Connell spent much of his early life with his uncle, Maurice, at Derrynane House near Waterville, Co. Kerry. He was educated at a small boarding school near Cork and later he attended Saint-Omer Irish College (1791–2) and Douai (1792–3), two of the best Catholic schools in France. There he witnessed the turmoil of the French Revolution which left him with a lifelong horror of violence for political ends. In 1794 O'Connell enrolled in Lincoln's Inn, London, and two years later transferred to the King's Inns, Dublin, to study law. While in London, O'Connell read the writings of the *philosophes* Voltaire and Rousseau, and the works of Godwin, Smith, and Bentham. These moulded his political and economic thinking, and made him a life-long democrat and radical.

8.2. O'Connell was called to the Irish Bar in 1798. He gained a reputation for his radical political views. He supported the liberal policies of the United Irishmen but the 1798 rebellion and the ensuing slaughter filled him with revulsion. His first political act was his public opposition to the Act of Union. From 1805, he championed the movement for Catholic Emancipation, which aimed at repealing the laws that limited the voting rights and educational opportunities of Catholics. He strongly opposed the proposed government Veto on the appointment of Catholic bishops. In 1811, he was elected chairman of the Catholic Committee. He mocked the 'beggarly Corporation' of Dublin and was challenged to a duel in 1815 by a member, John Norcot d'Esterre. O'Connell fatally wounded him but was extremely remorseful. D'Esterre's wife refused O'Connell's offer of a pension, but he later arranged an annuity for her daughter.

8.3. O'Connell set up many organisations to raise money for the cause of Emancipation, including the Catholic Association in 1823. This Association also campaigned for the repeal of the Act of Union, the end of the Irish tithe system, universal suffrage, and a secret ballot for parliamentary elections. He wholly rejected the use of violence in the pursuit of political objectives.

8.4. In 1828, he was elected to represent Co. Clare. However, because he was Catholic, he was not allowed take his seat. The British government, fearing a civil war or at least serious disorder in Ireland because of intense opposition to the existing anti-Catholic legislation, passed the Roman Catholic Relief Act (1829) which granted Catholic Emancipation. This enabled O'Connell to be elected as representative for Co. Kerry in 1830.

8.5. As 'Liberator' O'Connell was now Ireland's peerless political leader. He became a major figure in the House of Commons. He gave up his lucrative law practice to devote all his time to politics. On a wide range of issues he was a reformer and defender of liberty. He was active in the campaigns for parliamentary, legal, and prison reform, electoral reform and the secret ballot, free trade, the abolition of slavery, and Jewish eman-cipation. Towards the end of 1829, he declared to Sir Isaac Lyon Goldsmid, the leader of the Jews in England: 'You will find in me the constant and active friend to every meas-ure which tends to give the Jews an equality of civil rights with all other the King's sub-jects, a perfect unconditional equality'.

Speaking in the House of Commons in 1830, he said that 'by conceding the claims of the Jews, we should prove ourselves still more Christian by doing as we would be done by, and carrying into effect the principle of perfect freedom of conscience'.

8.6. He was a passionate opponent of racism and slavery. For him, slavery made the American Declaration of Independence a lie before God and he would never visit the United States because it was a slave-holding country. However, his overarching political objective was the Repeal of the Act of Union and the restoration of the Irish Parliament.

8.7. O'Connell and 39 of the Irish MPs returned in the general election of 1832 formed a pressure group in the House of Commons and O'Connell was able to make demands on the government. In 1835 he and his fellow Catholic MPs agreed to support Lord Melbourne and his Whig government in return for significant Irish reforms. Although the Whigs passed a Tithe Rentcharge Act (1838) and the Irish Municipal Reform Act (1840), O'Connell thought these inadequate. He was also totally opposed to the passing of the Irish Poor Law Act and when the Whigs refused to change it, he withdrew his sup-port for the government. In 1841, O'Connell represented Dublin City in parliament and also became the first Catholic Lord Mayor of Dublin since the seventeenth century.

8.8. The National Association of Ireland, commonly called the Repeal Association, was launched on 15 April 1840. O'Connell's chief lieutenant was his favourite son, John O'Connell (1810–58). The Association included many Young Irelanders who, unlike him, believed that independence could be won only by use of force. Publicity was gained in papers like *The Nation* and *The Pilot*. O'Connell announced that 1843 would be the 'Year of Repeal' and he began organising what *The Times* (London) called 'monster meetings' throughout the country. The first was at of Trim, Co. Meath which attracted a crowd of over 100,000. It was estimated that three-quarters of a million, assembled on the Hill of Tara to hear the 'Liberator' speak. Although O'Connell ensured that the huge crowds were orderly and peaceful, the government became concerned that there might be trouble. Sir Robert Peel, the British Prime Minister, decided to go on the offensive. He outlawed the subsequent proposed monster meeting, which was to be held at Clontarf on 8 October 1843. Although O'Connell called off the rally, he was arrested and charged with conspir-acy, and sentenced to a year's imprisonment and a fine of £2,000 (approx. €185,000 at 2009 values). He was also ordered to give securities of £5,000 (approx. €470,000) for seven years' good behaviour. Before entering Richmond Prison on 30 May 1844, O'Connell went to the House of Commons and made a brief speech to uproarious cheers from the opposition. His living conditions in prison were comfortable: he occupied a suite of rooms in the governor's house and his visitors could come and go as they pleased.

8.9. Three months later, on appeal, the House of Lords reversed the decision, and O'Connell left prison a hero in the fight for freedom of speech. His health had deteriorated while in prison and he was suffering from cardio-vascular disease. On his release, O'Connell continued his Repeal activities although a clear turning point had been reached. In 1845, he was unable to persuade Parliament to take more decisive steps in dealing with the Irish Famine. He provided what assistance he could on his own estates. In his last speech in the House of Commons on 8 February 1847, he predicted that unless more aid was forthcoming from the British government for Ireland 'one quarter of her population will perish'.

8.10. O'Connell came under attack from leading members of the Young Ireland movement who deemed his tactics ineffective. Weakened physically by overwork, disappointed by the failure of Repeal, worried over the disagreements with the Young Irelanders, and suffering increasingly from ill-health, O'Connell decided to go on a pilgrimage to Rome. When he reached Paris he was greeted by a large crowd of radicals who regarded him as the 'most successful champion of liberty and democracy in Europe'. He did not complete his journey to Rome: he died in Genoa on 15 May 1847. As he had requested, O'Connell's heart was buried in the Irish College in Rome (in a monument arranged by Charles Bianconi) and his body was interred in Glasnevin cemetery on 5 August 1847. Sackville Street, Dublin's main thoroughfare, was renamed O'Connell Street, and at the southern end near the Liffey the great statue of the Liberator by J.H. Foley was erected.

8.11. WRITINGS, BIOGRAPHY AND STUDIES: John O'Connell, *The Life and speeches of Daniel O'Connell* (2 vols, Dublin, 1846). T.C. Luby, *The life, opinions, conversations and eloquence of Daniel O'Connell* (New York, 1872). Michael MacDonagh, *The life of Daniel O'Connell* (London, 1903). Maurice R. O'Connell (ed.), *The correspondence of Daniel O'Connell* (8 vols, Dublin, 1972–80). Domhnall Ó Súilleabháin, *Beatha Dhomhnaill Uí Chonaill* (Dublin, 1936). Seán Ó Faoláin, *King of the beggars: a life of Daniel O'Connell* (London, 1938); Denis Gwynn, *Daniel O'Connell* (Oxford, 1947). Michael Tierney (ed.), *Daniel O'Connell: nine centenary essays* (Dublin, 1949). Angus MacIntyre, *The Liberator: Daniel O'Connell and the Irish party* (London, 1965). K.B. Nowlan, *The politics of Repeal: a study in the relations between Great Britain and Ireland, 1841–50* (London & Toronto, 1965). National Library of Ireland, *Daniel O'Connell: historical documents* (Dublin, 1978) [documents in facsimile with commentary]. D. MacCartney (ed.), *The world of Daniel O'Connell* (Dublin, 1980). K.B. Nowlan & Maurice R. O'Connell (eds), *Daniel O'Connell: portrait of a radical* (Belfast & New York, 1984). C.C. Trench, *The great Dan: a biography of Daniel O'Connell* (London, 1984). Oliver MacDonagh, *The hereditary bondsman: Daniel O'Connell, 1775–1829* (London, 1988). Oliver MacDonagh, *The emancipist: Daniel O'Connell, 1830–47* (London, 1989). Maurice R. O'Connell (ed), *Daniel O'Connell: political pioneer* (Dublin, 1991). Patrick M. Geoghegan, *King Dan: the rise of Daniel O'Connell, 1775–1829* (Dublin, 2008).

DONNCHADH Ó CORRÁIN AND TOMÁS O'RIORDAN

9. James Stephens (1824–1901)

9.1. Railway engineer, republican nationalist, and founder of the Fenians, James Stephens was born at Blackmill Street, Kilkenny, the son of John Stephens, an auctioneer's clerk. Educated at St Kieran's College, the young Stephens trained as an engineer. He worked on the Limerick and north Waterford railway line in 1843. A supporter of Young Ireland and the Irish Confederation, he served as *aide-de-camp* to William Smith O'Brien in the 1848 rising at Ballingarry, Co. Tipperary. Wounded in the skirmish, he escaped to Paris and was officially thought to have been killed. He was a 'participant observer' in the Paris Commune and the end of the Second Republic in France. In Paris, Stephens met the Young Irelanders, John O'Mahony and Michael Doheny. He was deeply influenced by the French radicals and the underground figures whom he met. He earned his living by teaching English. In 1856, he returned to Ireland disguised as a beggar. His purpose was to establish a new secret revolutionary society that would achieve Irish independence from Britain rule by military force.

9.2. A man of tremendous energy, he travelled some 3,000 miles around the country over the next two years, planning a secret physical-force movement that would be more durable than Young Ireland. This period earned him the title *An Seabhac Siubhlach* ('The Wandering Hawk'). He earned a living, for a time, teaching French to children of the constitutionalist John Blake Dillon.

9.3. In 1857, Stephens was contacted by an Emmet Monument Association emissary, Owen Considine (USA) who greatly encouraged him to establish a new revolutionary society. Stephens sent Joseph Denieffe to New York to seek money for the new movement. Just $400 (approx. €8,500) was raised and it was used to found the new organisation on St Patrick's Day 1858. At first it was called the Irish Revolutionary Brotherhood and became known later as the Irish Republican Brotherhood (IRB). It was a secret and oath-bound society. Stephens structured it on military principles. He was 'head centre'. It made its chief appeal to artisans and shop assistants rather than country people. The strong opposition of the Catholic Church doubtless kept many potential members from joining. The IRB recruited members through Jeremiah O'Donovan Rossa, John Devoy, William Roantree and Patrick 'Pagan' O'Leary. During this time John O'Mahony founded an American auxiliary known as the 'American Brotherhood'. The term 'Fenian' came to be applied generally to both organisations.

9.4. In 1858, Stephens went to America to raise funds for the IRB. When he returned to Ireland in 1859, the authorities knew well who he was and what he was doing, and he was forced to return to America. He seized nominal headship of the sister movement in the USA in early 1859. From 1861 to 1866, Stephens's influence was at its height. The IRB flourished in Ireland, Britain and the USA. He returned to Ireland in 1861, and he established the weekly propagandist newspaper, the *Irish People* (1863), which carried extensive national and international news. Charles Kickham, Thomas Clarke Luby and John

O'Leary later edited this paper. In November 1863, Stephens married Jane Hopper (1843–98), daughter of John and Rosanna Hopper, small-scale merchants and rentiers of Kingstown (Dún Laoghaire).

9.5. In 1864, his relations with O'Mahony and the American wing broke down. He made no secret of his low opinion of the American Fenians. The Americans and many Irish members were annoyed by Stephens's dictatorial attitude. He constantly complained that the Americans were not supplying him with promised arms and money, and he greatly exaggerated the numbers at his own disposal. In 1865, Stephens suspended a planned rising. During the same year, government officials raided IRB headquarters in Dublin, the newspaper office of the *Irish People*. Most of the leaders were arrested and were convicted of treason and felony and sentenced to penal servitude. Stephens, having avoided immediate arrest, was picked up with Kickham, convicted of conspiracy and imprisoned in Richmond Gaol, Dublin. However, with Devoy's help, he escaped and fled to Paris and then to New York. The government suppressed the *Irish People*.

9.6. By 1866, the Fenian movement was seriously divided. Stephens's attempts to bring the factions together were unsuccessful. By October, he had failed either to heal the breach or raise badly needed funds. Stephens promised that 1866 would be the year of decision, a year when, with American help, he would personally lead a rising in Ireland. The Americans now pressed for action but in December he again tried to persuade them to postpone the rising. Stephens was denounced at the Fenian Convention. Colonel Thomas Kelly replaced him as 'Head Centre'. Kelly was sent to Ireland in January 1867 with a group of Irish-Americans to plan the ill-fated rising of 1867.

9.7. Stephens's reputation and influence suffered irreparable damage. The leaders of the rising of March 1867, and of the IRB after 1867, repudiated him. The American Fenians denounced him as a 'rogue, impostor, and traitor'. Stephens went to France where he worked as a journalist and an English teacher. He spent time in New York from 1871 to 1874 and returned again in 1879 in an attempt to re-establish himself with Irish revolutionaries there. In 1885, he was expelled by the French authorities, who feared possible involvement with the Dynamiters. This was a group within the Fenians, known as the 'Triangle', who organised a concerted dynamiting campaign against Britain, 1881–5. He spent the period 1885–7 in Belgium before again returning to Paris. Through the intervention of Charles Stewart Parnell and friends in Ireland, Stephens was permitted to return to Ireland in 1891. He spent the remainder of his life in seclusion in Blackrock, Co. Dublin, avoiding politics. His only brief appearance was at the centenary celebrations of the United Irishmen in 1898, which had been organised by the Supreme Council of the IRB. Stephens died at Blackrock, Co. Dublin, on 29 April 1901.

9.8. BIOGRAPHY AND STUDIES: John O'Leary, *Recollections of Fenians and Fenianism* (2 vols, London, 1896; repr. with intro. by Marcus Bourke, Shannon, 1969). Desmond Ryan, *The phoenix flame: a study of Fenianism and John Devoy* (London, 1937). James

Maher, *Chief of the Comeragh: a John O'Mahony anthology* (Mullinahone, 1957). Desmond Ryan, *The Fenian chief: a biography of James Stephens*, with an introductory memoir by Patrick Lynch (Dublin, 1967). Maurice Harmon (ed.), *Fenians and Fenianism: centenary essays* (Dublin, 1968). T.W. Moody (ed.), *The Fenian movement* (Cork, 1968). Leon Ó Broin, *Revolutionary underground: the story of the Irish Revolutionary Brotherhood, 1858–1924* (Dublin, 1976). Oliver P. Rafferty, *The church, the state and the Fenian threat, 1861–75* (Basingstoke, 1999).

MARGARET FITZPATRICK

10. Charles Edward Trevelyan (1807–86)

10.1. A British civil servant, Charles Edward Trevelyan was born 2 April 1807, in Taunton, Somerset, England. His father George (1764–1827) was an Anglican archdeacon. He was educated at Taunton Grammar School, Charterhouse, and East India College, Haileybury. In 1826, he joined the East India Company's Bengal civil service.

10.2. In 1827, he was appointed assistant to Sir Charles Metcalfe, the Commissioner at Delhi. He devoted himself to improving the conditions of the Indian population and tackling corrupt British administration. He also donated some of his own money for public works in Delhi. He carried out inquiries that led to the abolition of transit duties which had long hindered the internal trade of India. In 1831, he was removed to Calcutta, and became the Deputy Secretary to the government in the political department. Trevelyan was especially anxious to give Indians a European education. In 1835, largely owing to his persistence, the government decided to educate the Indians in European literature and science. He published an account of this in *On the education of the people of India*.

10.3. In 1838, he returned to England and in 1840 he became Assistant Secretary to the Treasury in London and held that office until 1859. This position put him in charge of the administration of government relief to the victims of the Irish Famine. In the middle of that crisis Trevelyan published his views on the matter. He saw the Famine as a 'mechanism for reducing surplus population'.

10.4. But it was more: 'The judgement of God sent the calamity to teach the Irish a lesson; that calamity must not be too much mitigated … The real evil with which we have to contend is not the physical evil of the Famine, but the moral evil of the selfish, perverse and turbulent character of the people'.

Such racist and sectarian views of the Irish were common enough within the English governing classes and were more crudely expressed by others. For the most part, Trevelyan's views reflected the prevailing Whig economic and social opinion and that of the Prime Minister, Lord John Russell, who held office from 1846 until 1852.

10.5. Trevelyan was unbending. He firmly believed in *laissez faire* (essentially; in this case that the importing of food should be left to the food merchants), he thought that the government should not intervene, and warned of the danger that people might get into the habit of depending on the state. From March 1846, he controlled the public works through the disbursement of public funds. Under Trevelyan, relief by public works in 1846–7 was too little too late, but also it was slow, inefficient and sometimes corrupt. He defended the export of grain from famine-stricken Ireland on the grounds that the government should not interfere with free trade. When his own administrators described this export of food as 'a most serious evil', Trevelyan refused even to consider banning it. When rioting broke out in protest against at the export of corn, he sent 2,000 troops, well provisioned with beef, pork and biscuits, 'to be directed on particular ports at short notice'.

10.6. He was against railway construction as a form of relief and successfully opposed Russell's scheme for the distribution of some £50,000 (approx. €4.25 million) worth of seed to tenant farmers. The failure of government relief schemes finally became clear to Trevelyan and early in 1847 soup kitchens were organised under a high-level government commission. They worked poorly.

10.7. In the autumn of 1847, Trevelyan ended government-sponsored aid to the distressed Poor Law districts although there was an outbreak of cholera. He declared that the Famine was over, and that from now on Irish landlords were to be responsible for financing relief works. He gained a well-deserved reputation as a cold-hearted and uncompassionate administrator. On 27 April 1848, he was given a knighthood for his services to Ireland. *The Irish crisis,* published in 1848, contains his unsympathetic views on the Famine and its victims.

10.8. After the Famine in Ireland, he continued to play an important role in government in Britain and its colonies. In 1853 he headed an inquiry on how to improve the civil service. His work transformed it. Higher educational standards and competitive admission examinations made the civil service better qualified and more efficient. Regarded as the father of the modern civil service, he was portrayed as Sir Gregory Hardlines in Anthony Trollope's novel *The three clerks* (1858).

10.9. In 1858, after the uprising known as the Indian Mutiny, Trevelyan returned to India as Governor of Madras where his reforms were important, especially police reform. He returned again to India as Finance Minister from 1862 to 1865. His time in office was marked by important administrative reforms and by extensive measures for the development of the resources of India by means of public works. He was made a baronet in 1874. On his return to England in 1865 he directed his energy to the organisation of the army. Later he got involved in a variety of social problems, notably charities and pauperism. He died at 67 Eaton Square, London, 19 June 1886.

10.10. BIOGRAPHY, WRITINGS AND STUDIES: Sir Charles Trevelyan, *The Irish crisis, being a narrative of the measures for the relief of the distress caused by the Great Irish Famine of 1846–7* (London, 1880), repr. from the *Edinburgh Review,* 175 (January, 1848). Thomas

P. O'Neill, 'The organisation and administration of relief, 1845–52', in R.D. Edwards & T.D. Williams (eds), *The Great Famine* (Dublin, 1956), 209–60; repr. with intro. by Cormac Ó Gráda (Dublin, 1994). Cecil Woodham-Smith, *The Great Hunger: Ireland, 1845–9* (London, 1962). Mary Daly, *The Famine in Ireland* (Dundalk, 1986). J.M. Hernon, 'A Victorian Cromwell: Sir Charles Trevelyan, the Famine and the age of improvement', *Éire-Ireland*, 22 (1987), 15–29. Cormac Ó Gráda, *The Great Irish Famine* (London, 1989). Christine Kinealy, *This Great Calamity: the Great Irish Famine, 1845–52* (Dublin, 1994). Noel Kissane, *The Irish Famine: a documentary history* (Dublin, 1995), 45–59. Cathal Póirtéir (ed.), *The Great Irish Famine* (Dublin, 1995). Christine Kinealy, *A death-dealing Famine: the great hunger in Ireland* (Chicago & London, 1997). Cormac Ó Gráda, *Black '47 and beyond: the Great Irish Famine in history, economy, and memory* (Princeton, NJ, 1998). Christine Kinealy, *The Great Irish Famine: impact, ideology, and rebellion* (Basingstoke, 2002). Robin Haines, *Charles Trevelyan and the Great Irish Famine* (Dublin, 2004).

DONNCHADH Ó CORRÁIN AND TOMÁS O'RIORDAN

Index